A LITTLE GREEK READER

A Little Greek Reader

JAMES MORWOOD

STEPHEN ANDERSON

OXFORD
UNIVERSITY PRESS

Oxford University Press is a department of the University of Oxford. It furthers the University's objective of excellence in research, scholarship, and education by publishing worldwide.

Oxford New York

Auckland Cape Town Dar es Salaam Hong Kong Karachi
Kuala Lumpur Madrid Melbourne Mexico City Nairobi
New Delhi Shanghai Taipei Toronto

With offices in

Argentina Austria Brazil Chile Czech Republic France Greece
Guatemala Hungary Italy Japan Poland Portugal Singapore
South Korea Switzerland Thailand Turkey Ukraine Vietnam

Published in the United States of America by
Oxford University Press
198 Madison Avenue, New York, NY 10016
http://www.oup.com

Library of Congress Cataloging-in-Publication Data

A little Greek Reader / James Morwood, Stephen Anderson.
pages cm
ISBN 978-0-19-931172-9
1. Greek literature.   2. Greek language—Grammar.   3. Greek language—
Readers.   I. Morwood, James.   II. Anderson, Stephen, 1954–
PA3416.A5Z3 2015
488.6′421—dc23

2014010926

Printing number: 9 8 7 6 5 4 3 2 1

Printed in the United States of America
on acid-free paper

Contents

Introduction   xv

1. **THE INDICATIVE TENSES OF THE VERB**   1
   1.1   Vitruvius 9, *Preface* 10   1
   1.2   Herodotus, *Histories* 7.228.2   1
   1.3   Appian, *Civil War* 2.91   2
   1.4   Pindar, *Pythian* 8.20   2
   1.5   Euripides, *Medea* 364   2
   1.6   Demosthenes, *De Corona* 191   2
   1.7   Thucydides, *Histories* 2.70.1   3
   1.8   Sophocles, *Philoctetes* 1066–71   3
   1.9   Euripides, *Electra* 967–70   4
   1.10   Plato, *Crito* 43a–b   5

2. **BASIC USE OF CASES**   7
   2.1   Nominative   7
      (I)   Thucydides, *Histories* 1.89.1   7
      (II) Aeschylus, *Choephoroe* 1–2   8
   2.2   Genitive   8
      (I)   Plato, *Charmides* 153a   8
      (II) Plato, *Phaedo* 118a   9

2.3   Dative   9
   (I)   Homer, *Odyssey* 6.246   9
   (II) Thucydides, *Histories* 1.86.3   9
2.4   Accusative   10
2.5   Vocative   10
2.6   Euripides, *Supplices* 399–405   10
2.7   *St. Luke's Gospel* 2.8–12   11
2.8   Homer, *Iliad* 1.357–64   12
2.9   Lysias 1.22–24   13
2.10 Euripides, *Alcestis* 185–96   14

3.   ADJECTIVES   15
3.1   Plato, *Ion* 533e–34b   15
3.2   Plato, *Symposium* 221c   16
3.3   Graffito from Mount Hymettus   16
3.4   Herodotus, *Histories* 1.1   17
3.5   Euripides, *Medea* 49–55   18
3.6   Homer, *Iliad* 6.414–16, 421–30   18

4.   TIME, PLACE AND SPACE   20
4.1   Plato, *Apology* 17d   20
4.2   Sophocles, *Philoctetes* 1337–42   21
4.3   Xenophon, *Hellenica* 1.1.14–16   21
4.4   Homer, *Odyssey* 2.171–76   22
4.5   Plato, *Laws* 642d–e   23
4.6   Thucydides, *Histories* 1.94.1–2   24
4.7   Euripides, *Iphigenia in Tauris* 767–76   24
4.8   Homer, *Iliad* 1.17–21   25
4.9   Xenophon, *Hellenica* 6.4.19–20   26
4.10 Xenophon, *Anabasis* 1.4.11   27

5.   PERSONAL PRONOUNS AND αὐτός   28
5.1   Plato, *Gorgias* 474b   28
5.2   Xenophon, *Anabasis* 1.6.7   28
5.3   Plato, *Apology* 38d–39a   29

5.4	Euripides, *Medea* 271–76	29
5.5	Thucydides, *Histories* 2.61.2	30
5.6	Thucydides, *Histories* 4.78.4	30
5.7	Antiphon, *On the murder of Herodes* 50	31
5.8	Lysias 1.12–13	31
5.9	Thucydides, *Histories* 4.14.1	32

6. INDEFINITE AND DEMONSTRATIVE PRONOUNS — 33

6.1	Xenophon, *Anabasis* 3.1.4	34
6.2	Euripides, *Alcestis* 136–40	35
6.3	Xenophon, *Hellenica* 5.1.13	35
6.4	Homer, *Iliad* 10.382–89	36
6.5	*St. Mark's Gospel* 14. 22–26	36
6.6	Sophocles, *Oedipus Tyrannus* 1047–57	37
6.7	Xenophon, *Cyropaedia* 7. 3.2	38
6.8	Euripides, *Orestes* 1140–48	39
6.9	Demosthenes, *De Corona* 304–305	40
6.10	Herodotus, *Histories* 2.100	41

7. PARTICIPLES 1 — 43

7.1	Thucydides, *Histories* 3.112.2	43
7.2	Xenophon, *Memorabilia* 4.4.4	43
7.3	Demosthenes, *De Corona* 124	44
7.4	Homer, *Iliad* 22.131–38	44
7.5	Thucydides, *Histories* 6.59.4	45
7.6	Xenophon, *Anabasis* 2.3.21	45
7.7	Thucydides, *Histories* 8.68.1	46
7.8	Thucydides, *Histories* 4.39.3	46
7.9	Thucydides 2.59.2	47
7.10	Euripides, Fragment 461	47

8. RELATIVE CLAUSES — 48

8.1	Menander, *Sententiae* 560, 583	48
8.2	Xenophon, *Cyropaedia* 3.3.44	49

8.3	Sophocles, *Oedipus at Colonus* 49–53	49
8.4	Thucydides, *Histories* 1.95.5–6	50
8.5	Euripides, *Iphigenia in Tauris* 1289–95	51
8.6	Lysias 12.16–17	52
8.7	Homer, *Iliad* 1.35–42	53
8.8	Andocides, *De Mysteriis* 61–62	53
8.9	Euripides, *Heraclidae* 945–52	55
8.10	Thucydides, *Histories* 1.128.5–7	55

9. PARTICLES   57

9.1	Plato, *Apology* 26c	57
9.2	Homer, *Iliad* 1.505–10	58
9.3	Euripides, *Hippolytus* 1243–48	58
9.4	Euripides, *Electra* 228–31	59
9.5	Sophocles, *Ajax* 1355–59	59
9.6	Aristophanes, *Lysistrata* 908–14	60
9.7	Herodotus, *Histories* 2.49.1	61
9.8	Plato, *Lysis* 219c	61
9.9	Demosthenes, *On the Chersonese* 42	62
9.10	Homer, *Iliad* 4.401–5	63

10. INDIRECT STATEMENT ~ Review for Friday   64

10.1	(I)	Demosthenes, *De Corona* 169	65
	(II)	Plato, *Apology* 21c	65
	(III)	Demosthenes *Olynthiac* 1.15	66
10.2		Xenophon, *Anabasis* 4.8.4	66
10.3		Euripides, *Medea* 1293–1300	66
10.4		Xenophon, *Hellenica* 4.2.1	67
10.5		Lysias 23.5–7	68
10.6		Homer, *Iliad* 13.361–73	69
10.7		Thucydides, *Histories* 2.3.1–3	71
10.8		Euripides, *Medea* 446–58	72
10.9		Plato, *Republic* 2.359d–60a	72
10.10		Plato, *Republic* 2.360a–c	74

11. DIRECT AND INDIRECT QUESTIONS   75

   11.1   Sophocles, *Oedipus at Colonus* 1–4   75

   11.2   Sophocles, *Antigone* 1211–12   76

   11.3   Sophocles, *Oedipus at Colonus* 881–89   76

   11.4   Plato, *Protagoras* 310d   77

   11.5   Thucydides, *Histories* 1.5.1–2   77

   11.6   Plato, *Apology* 21a–b   79

   11.7   Herodotus, *Histories* 1.31   80

   11.8   Xenophon, *Memorabilia* 1.2.45   80

12. COMMANDS, PROHIBITIONS, WISHES   82

   12.1   Two Extracts from Homer's *Odyssey*   83

       (I)   *Odyssey* 1.1–2   83

       (II) *Odyssey* 1.169–72   83

   12.2   Thucydides, *Histories* 1.86.5   83

   12.3   Two Extracts from Tragedy   84

       (I)   Aeschylus, *Persae* 402–5   84

       (II) Euripides, *Iphigenia at Aulis* 495–99   84

   12.4   *St. Luke's Gospel* 18.18–25   85

   12.5   Euripides, *Phoenissae* 1442–53   86

   12.6   Aristophanes, *Acharnians* 280–99   87

   12.7   Thucydides, *Histories* 2.12.2–3   88

   12.8   Xenophon, *Hellenica* 4.1.37–39   89

   12.9   Euripides, *Electra* 1060–73   90

   12.10 Homer, *Iliad* 3.424–36   91

13. PURPOSE CLAUSES   92

   13.1   Homer, *Iliad* 2.381   92

   13.2   Xenophon, *Anabasis* 1.4.18   92

   13.3   Lysias 1.4   93

   13.4   Xenophon, *Memorabilia* 4.4.16   93

   13.5   Homer, *Iliad* 1.522–27   94

   13.6   Xenophon, *Cyropaedia* 1.2.3   94

   13.7   Xenophon, *Anabasis* 1.1.3   95

13.8   Thucydides, *Histories* 1.29.1   96

13.9   Demosthenes, *Olynthiac* 1.2   96

13.10   Demosthenes, *Olynthiac* 2.11   97

13.11   Sophocles, *Electra* 378–84   97

14. RESULT CLAUSES   99

14.1   Euripides, *Hecuba* 730   99

14.2   Lysias 12.4   99

14.3   Plato, *Symposium* 215e–16a   100

14.4   Sophocles, *Antigone* 449–55   101

14.5   *St. John's Gospel* 3.16   102

14.6   Xenophon, *Anabasis* 7.4.2–4   102

14.7   Thucydides, *Histories* 3.49.1–3   103

14.8   Euripides, *Phoenissae* 361–64   104

14.9   Xenophon, *Anabasis* 2.2.17–18   104

14.10   Lysias 3.6–8   105

15. CONDITIONALS 1   107

15.1   Homer, *Iliad* 1.564   107

15.2   Plato, *Phaedrus* 228a   107

15.3   Demosthenes, *On the Liberty of the
        Rhodians* 23   108

15.4   Xenophon, *Anabasis* 2.5.41   108

15.5   Thucydides, *Histories* 3.54.3–4   108

15.6   Xenophon, *Cyropaedia* 3.2.13   109

15.7   Plato, *Republic* 5.473c–e   110

15.8   Aristophanes, *Frogs* 584–88   111

15.9   Euripides, *Phoenissae* 1615–21   111

15.10   Lysias 7.41   112

16. CONDITIONALS 2   113

16.1   Xenophon, *Cyropaedia* 1.2.16   113

16.2   Lysias 2.78–80   114

16.3   Euripides, *Helen* 68–77   115

16.4   Plato, *Apology* 32d   116
16.5   Homer, *Iliad* 5. 674–82   117
16.6   Thucydides, *Histories* 8.96.3–4   118
16.7   Aeschylus, *Agamemnon* 34–39   118
16.8   Homer, *Iliad* 2.483–92   119
16.9   Herodotus, *Histories* 2.173.2–4   120

17. PARTICIPLES 2   122
17.1   Homer, *Iliad* 12.392–93   122
17.2   Xenophon, *Anabasis* 3.3.1   122
17.3   Herodotus 1.30.1   123
17.4   Xenophon, *Anabasis* 1.2.22   123
17.5   Euripides, *Hecuba* 303–5   123
17.6   Plato, *Protagoras* 358d   124
17.7   Plato, *Alcibiades* 1.115a–b   124
17.8   Homer, *Iliad* 24.477–84   125
17.9   Herodotus 4.136.1–2   126
17.10 Plato, *Euthydemus* 272d–e   127

**18. VERBS OF FEARING, PRECAUTION
AND PREVENTING**   129
18.1   (I)   Euripides, *Medea* 37   129
       (II)   Xenophon, *Anabasis* 1.10.9   129
       (III) Aristophanes, *Clouds* 492–93   130
       (IV)   Thucydides, *Histories* 3.53.2   130
       (V)   Thucydides, *Histories* 1.136.1   130
18.2   Euripides, *Medea* 282–89   131
18.3   Xenophon, *Anabasis* 1.7.6   132
18.4   Homer, *Odyssey* 5.299–307   132
18.5   *St. Matthew's Gospel* 1.19–22   133
18.6   (I)   Isocrates 2.37   134
       (II)   Sophocles, *Trachiniae* 1129   134
       (III) Demosthenes, *De Falsa Legatione* 92   134
18.7   Xenophon, *Anabasis* 1.3.11   135

18.8 (I)   Herodotus, *Histories* 2.20.2   136
      (II)   Sophocles, *Antigone* 441–43   136
      (III) Plato, *Hippias Minor* 369d   136
18.9   Thucydides, *Histories* 3.1   137
18.10 Euripides, *Phoenissae* 1172–86   137

19. INDEFINITE SENTENCES   139
19.1   Xenophon, *Cyropaedia* 1.1.2   139
19.2   Homer, *Iliad* 9.312–13   140
19.3   Lysias 12.41   140
19.4   Sophocles, *Antigone* 574–81   140
19.5   Xenophon, *Cyropaedia* 5.3.55   141
19.6   Thucydides, *Histories* 2.34.3–5   141
19.7   Demosthenes, *De Corona* 235   142
19.8   Thucydides, *Histories* 1.99.3   143
19.9   Homer, *Iliad* 1.163–71   144
19.10 Xenophon, *Agesilaos* 7.3   144

20. TEMPORAL CLAUSES   146
20.1 (I)   Demosthenes, *Olynthiac* 1.20   146
      (II)   Xenophon, *Anabasis* 1.6.5   147
      (III) Sophocles, *Antigone* 91   147
20.2   Thucydides, *Histories* 2.21.1–2   147
20.3   Euripides, *Hecuba* 10–27   148
20.4   Arrian, *Anabasis* 5.18.6   149
20.5   Xenophon, *Anabasis* 7.2.31   151
20.6 (I)   I *Corinthians* 11.26   152
      (II)   Homer, *Odyssey* 5.55–58   152
      (III) Isocrates 1.24   152
      (IV)   Thucydides, *Histories* 2.93.1   153
20.7   Aeschylus, *Persae* 421–28   153
20.8   Xenophon, *Anabasis* 5.7.3–5   154
20.9   Euripides, *Medea* 1021–39   155

21. IMPERSONAL VERBS AND VERBAL

ADJECTIVES   157

21.1   Xenophon, *Anabasis* 3.2.15   157

21.2   Plato, *Crito* 44c   157

21.3   Xenophon, *Cyropaedia* 7.2.28   158

21.4   Andocides 4.17   158

21.5   Euripides, *Medea* 238–43   159

21.6   Demosthenes, *Philippic* 3.70   160

22. ADDITIONAL PROSE PASSAGES   162

22.1   Herodotus, *Histories* 1.8   162

22.2   Herodotus, *Histories* 2.68   163

22.3   Thucydides, *Histories* 6.57   165

22.4   Thucydides, *Histories* 8.1   167

22.5   Xenophon, *Hellenica*, 4.2.10–12   168

22.6   Xenophon, *Memorabilia* 2.1.21–22   169

22.7   Plato, *Apology*, 22a–c   171

22.8   Plato, *Phaedo* 117e–18a   172

22.9   Lucian, *Vera Historia* 2, 35–36   173

22.10 *The Acts of the Apostles* 9.1–12   174

23. ADDITIONAL VERSE PASSAGES   177

23.1   Homer, *Iliad* 6, 466–84   177

23.2   Homer, *Odyssey* 22.1–21   178

23.3   Sophocles, *Ajax* 541–59   180

23.4   Euripides, *Hippolytus* 1–22   181

23.5   Sophocles, *Antigone*, 781–800   182

23.6   Euripides, *Medea* 1251–70   184

23.7   Aristophanes, *Frogs*, 1198–1221   185

23.8   Aristophanes, *Clouds* 1–18   187

23.9   Theocritus 11.17–37   189

23.10 Callimachus, *Epigrammata* 2   190

APPENDICES   193

   The Greek Writers   193

   Dialect   200

   Two Important Greek Meters   205

   Some Literary Terms   210

   Map: Greece and the Aegean   218

VOCABULARY   221

ABOUT THE AUTHORS   294

Introduction

This book is planned as a companion volume to *A Little Latin Reader* by Mary English and Georgia Irby. Like them, we have provided an extensive selection of readings from original prose and verse to illustrate the use made by the ancient authors themselves of the various grammatical features that students are expected to learn and absorb.

There are, however, some respects in which our book differs from its Latin counterpart:

1 We provide at the beginning of each chapter a bare-bones account of the grammatical principle in question.
2 The notes following each passage do not usually deal with matters of vocabulary, but confine themselves to elucidations of meaning and explanations of interesting or difficult features of Greek grammar, style and culture.
3 There is a complete vocabulary list of unglossed words at the end of the book.
4 Our notes do not appear as a continuous passage, divided only by semicolons, but rather as separate entries with line numbers.

We would like to stress that this book is not conceived as providing a freestanding course in itself. Rather it is intended to serve as a supplementary volume, offering brief original reading matter to illustrate key features of Greek grammar and syntax. We hope that it will offer valuable resources for the review of grammar through reading, either throughout or at the end of an intermediate course in the second year of college and university study. At the same time, we believe that the content of the passages is often of considerable intrinsic interest and that the range of authors we have chosen will go some way toward offering a panorama of classical Greek literature.

The passages in each chapter vary in length and difficulty and cover a wide range of Greek authors. Teachers and instructors will be free to pick and choose as they please: only rarely, we expect, will a class tackle every passage in every chapter.

For the purposes of reading the passages aloud, although we have not marked in the chapters the length of vowels which could be either long or short, we have included macra in the vocabulary. The introduction to the vocabulary explains our procedure.

There are five appendices at the end. The first deals with Homeric grammar, Herodotean forms and New Testament Greek. It should be noted that forms and usages explained in these sections will not be commented on in the notes at the end of each passage. A list of important literary terms comes next, and then a section on two important meters, the Homeric hexameter and the iambic trimeter. Some short biographical notes on the authors of all our passages follow, and finally, just before the vocabulary, we print a map of Greece and the Aegean.

We have incurred many debts in the production of this book, and in particular would like to thank Charles Cavaliere and Claudia Dukeshire at OUP New York: their help and encouragement have sustained us through the various stages of the book's production. We should like also to express our gratitude to the outside readers commissioned by OUP NY who assessed the initial proposal and manuscript: Elizabeth A. Fisher, George Washington University;

Richard Rader, University of California, Santa Barbara; and Blaise Nagy, College of the Holy Cross; as well as several reviewers who wish to remain anonymous. Thanks too are due to John Penney, who gave valuable advice on metrical matters; to John Falconer, who provided the initial design for our cover and offered constant support throughout the project; to Richard Ashdowne, who did sterling work in keying in the extensive vocabulary list; and to Frederique Jouhandin and Joanna Lees of OUP Oxford, who kindly arranged for the production of pre-publication copies, so that we could trial the book's content at the 2013 JACT Greek Summer School held at Bryanston School, Dorset, UK. Finally we are grateful to the Summer School's authorities for giving us permission to do this, and to the members of Groups 35 (Lavinia Abell, Harry Blake, Huw Braithwaite, Gavin Jackson, Lydia Kanari-Naish, Helena Khullar Sofia Tavener, and Ravi Willder) and 45 (Simon Aitken, Alec Badenoch, Naomi Bradshaw, Grace Cleary, Xavier Greenwood, Theo Heren, Joanna Langley, Louis Prosser, Luisa Riberi and Lucy Valsamidis): their willing involvement, their eagle eyes, and their many perceptive comments have made this a better book.

James Morwood
WADHAM COLLEGE, OXFORD

Stephen Anderson
WINCHESTER COLLEGE

August 2014

CHAPTER 1

The Indicative Tenses of the Verb

There are six main active indicative tenses in Greek: the present, future, imperfect, aorist, perfect and pluperfect. There is also a future perfect tense ("will have"), but this is not common and is not included below. There are complete sets of active and passive tenses; in the middle, the tenses of the indicative are the same as those of the passive in the present and imperfect, perfect and pluperfect tenses, but there are separate future and aorist tenses.

1.1   Vitruvius 9, *Preface* 10: Archimedes' exclamation on discovering the principle of the displacement of water.

εὕρηκα!

1.2   Herodotus, *Histories* 7.228.2: an epitaph by Simonides for the force of 300 Spartans (Lacedaemonians) who died bravely fighting the invading Persians at Thermopylae in 480 BC.

Ὦ ξεῖν', ἀγγέλλειν Λακεδαιμονίοις ὅτι τῇδε
κείμεθα, τοῖς κείνων ῥήμασι πειθόμενοι.

Notes: 1. **ξεῖν'**: the Ionic form of ξέν'.
ἀγγέλλειν: the infinitive is used as an imperative.
2. **ῥήμασι**: ῥῆμα = saying, precept.

1.3   Appian, *Civil War* 2.91: Julius Caesar's famous quip after his lightning victory over Pharnaces, king of the Bosporus.

ἔγω δὲ ἦλθον, εἶδον, ἐνίκησα.

What is the Latin for this? *Veni, vidi, vici*

1.4   Pindar, *Pythian* 8.20: Pindar, the great poet who celebrated Greek athletic achievements, warns against reliance on force; it can lead to the downfall of the man who depends on it.

βία δὲ καὶ μεγάλαυχον ἔσφαλεν ἐν χρόνῳ.

Notes: 1. **μεγάλαυχον**: "(the) very boastful (man)."
ἔσφαλεν: (from σφάλλω, a Doric form of the aorist), a gnomic aorist conveying a general truth, e.g., "Curiosity killed the cat" or "Too many cooks spoil the broth." Translate as a present tense.

1.5   Euripides, *Medea* 364: Medea complains about the bad treatment that she is receiving from every quarter.

Μήδεια

κακῶς πέπρακται πανταχῇ· τίς ἀντερεῖ;

Notes: 1. **ἀντερεῖ**: future of ἀντιλέγω.

1.6   Demosthenes, *De Corona* 191: the great Athenian orator attacks his political enemy Aeschines for having remained silent at the meetings of the assembly while he himself had come forward to give good advice.

σοῦ δ᾿ ἀφώνου κατ᾿ ἐκείνους τοὺς χρόνους ἐν ταῖς
ἐκκλησίαις καθημένου, ἐγὼ παριὼν ἔλεγον. ἐπειδὴ δ᾿
οὐ τότε, ἀλλὰ νῦν δεῖξον. εἰπὲ τίς ἢ λόγος, ὅντιν᾿ ἐχρῆν
εὐπορεῖν, ἢ καιρὸς συμφέρων ὑπ᾿ ἐμοῦ παρελείφθη τῇ
πόλει;

5

Notes: 1. **ἀφώνου**: "without saying anything."
2–3. **ἐπειδὴ δ᾿ οὐ τότε**: "since (you did) not (point it out [lit. show]) then."
4–5. **εἰπὲ τίς ἢ λόγος ... ἢ καιρός**: "tell me either what counsel [lit. word] ... or (what) opportunity."

ὄντιν᾽ ἐχρῆν εὐπορεῖν: "which I ought to have provided" (lit. "which it was necessary [for me] to provide").
3–4. τῇ πόλει: dative of advantage.

1.7 Thucydides, *Histories* 2.70.1: starvation reduces the people of Potidaea to cannibalism as they are being besieged by the Athenians, and they enter into talks about an agreement with the enemy generals.

> τοῦ δ᾽ αὐτοῦ χειμῶνος οἱ Ποτειδεᾶται ἐπειδὴ οὐκέτι
> ἐδύναντο πολιορκούμενοι ἀντέχειν, ἀλλ᾽ αἵ τε ἐς τὴν
> Ἀττικὴν ἐσβολαὶ Πελοποννησίων οὐδὲν μᾶλλον
> ἀπανίστασαν τοὺς Ἀθηναίους ὅ τε σῖτος ἐπελελοίπει, καὶ
> ἄλλα τε πολλὰ ἐπεγεγένητο αὐτόθι ἤδη βρώσεως πέρι   5
> ἀναγκαίας καί τινες καὶ ἀλλήλων ἐγέγευντο, οὕτω δὴ
> λόγους προσφέρουσι περὶ ξυμβάσεως τοῖς στρατηγοῖς
> τῶν Ἀθηναίων τοῖς ἐπὶ σφίσι τεταγμένοις, Ξενοφῶντί
> τε τῷ Εὐριπίδου καὶ Ἑστιοδώρῳ τῷ Ἀριστοκλείδου καὶ
> Φανομάχῳ τῷ Καλλιμάχου.   10

Notes: 1. ἐπειδή—: the clauses following ἐπειδή continue until ἐγέγευντο in line **6**.
3–4. οὐδὲν μᾶλλον ἀπανίστασαν τοὺς Ἀθηναίους: "had been no more successful in making the Athenians withdraw their troops" (lit. "had not at all more made the Athenians leave"). The hope had been that the Peloponnesian attacks on Attica, the Athenians' home territory, would cause the latter to call their troops back from Potidaea (in northeast Greece).
5–6. βρώσεως πέρι ἀναγκαίας: "because of starvation" (lit. "because of needed food").
8. τοῖς ἐπὶ σφίσι τεταγμένοις: "who were in charge of the operations against them" (lit. "the ones assigned against them").

1.8 Sophocles, *Philoctetes* 1066–71: two Greek leaders, Odysseus and Neoptolemus, have sailed to the island where the crippled Philoctetes has been abandoned with the bow that, it now transpires, is vital for the Greeks to possess if they are to take the city of Troy. They succeed in tricking him into giving up the bow. Odysseus wants to sail away with it and leave Philoctetes behind but Neoptolemus is more sympathetic to him.

Φιλοκτήτης   Ὀδυσσεύς

Φιλ. ὦ σπέρμ᾽ Ἀχιλλέως, οὐδὲ σοῦ φωνῆς ἔτι
γενήσομαι προσφθεγκτός, ἀλλ᾽ οὕτως ἄπει;

Ὀδ. (to *Neoptolemus*)
χώρει σύ· μὴ πρόσλευσσε, γενναῖός περ ὤν,
ἡμῶν ὅπως μὴ τὴν τύχην διαφθερεῖς.

Φιλ. ἦ καὶ πρὸς ὑμῶν ὧδ᾽ ἔρημος, ὦ ξένοι,   5
λειφθήσομαι δὴ κοὐκ ἐποικτερεῖτέ με;

Notes: 1. **ὦ σπέρμ᾽ Ἀχιλλέως:** = "o seed (i.e., son) of Achilles," i.e.,
Neoptolemus.
οὐδέ: introduces two questions only the first of which is negative =
"'shall I not become ... but will you ... ?'" Philoctetes feels he is being
abandoned by Neoptolemus, who has promised to take him home.
1–2. **σοῦ φωνῆς προσφθεγκτός:** = "addressed by your voice."
3. **μὴ πρόσλευσσε**: i.e., at Philoctetes. Odysseus fears that if
Neoptolemus stays and looks at Philoctetes, his heart will melt.
περ: = καίπερ.
4. **ὅπως μή**: translate at the start of the line: "so that you don't"
(purpose clause).
5. **ἦ**: introduces a question; see p. **75**.
πρός + gen.: = by.
ὑμῶν: i.e., Neoptolemus and his crew.
6. **κοὐκ:** = καὶ οὐκ (crasis).

1.9   Euripides, *Electra* 967–70: Electra and her brother, Orestes,
are about to murder their mother, Clytemnestra, in revenge for her
killing of her husband and their father, Agamemnon. They have
now seen her, and Orestes is having doubts about whether he can go
through with the matricide.

Ὀρέστης   Ἠλέκτρα

Ὀρ. τί δῆτα δρῶμεν; μητέρ᾽ ἦ φονεύσομεν;

Ἠλ. μῶν σ᾽ οἶκτος εἷλε, μητρὸς ὡς εἶδες δέμας;

Ὀρ. φεῦ· πῶς γὰρ κτάνω νιν, ἥ μ᾽ ἔθρεψε κἄτεκεν;

Ἠλ. ὥσπερ πατέρα σὸν ἥδε κἀμὸν ὤλεσεν.

Notes: 1. **δρῶμεν**: deliberative subjunctive: "are we to do?"
ἦ: introduces a question; see p. **75**.

2. **μῶν**: here, as often, introducing a question expecting the answer no.
3. **κἄτεκεν**: καὶ ἔτεκεν (crasis); ἔτεκεν is from τίκτω.

1.10 Plato, *Crito* 43a–b: Socrates has been condemned to death and is in prison. Crito has gone to visit him and has been admitted by the guard to his cell, where he found him sleeping.

Σωκράτης Κρίτων

Σω. θαυμάζω ὅπως ἠθέλησέ σοι ὁ τοῦ δεσμωτηρίου
φύλαξ ὑπακοῦσαι.

Κρ. συνήθης ἤδη μοί ἐστιν, ὦ Σώκρατες, διὰ τὸ πολλάκις
δεῦρο φοιτᾶν, καί τι καὶ εὐεργέτηται ὑπ' ἐμοῦ.

Σω. ἄρτι δὲ ἥκεις ἢ πάλαι;   5

Κρ. ἐπιεικῶς πάλαι.

Σω. εἶτα πῶς οὐκ εὐθὺς ἐπήγειράς με, ἀλλὰ σιγῇ
παρακάθησαι;

Κρ. οὐ μὰ τὸν Δία, ὦ Σώκρατες, οὐδ' ἂν αὐτὸς ἤθελον
ἐν τοσαύτῃ τε ἀγρυπνίᾳ καὶ λύπῃ εἶναι, ἀλλὰ καὶ σοῦ 10
πάλαι θαυμάζω αἰσθανόμενος ὡς ἡδέως καθεύδεις·
καὶ ἐπίτηδές σε οὐκ ἤγειρον ἵνα ὡς ἥδιστα διάγῃς.
καὶ πολλάκις μὲν δή σε καὶ πρότερον ἐν παντὶ τῷ βίῳ
ηὐδαιμόνισα τοῦ τρόπου, πολὺ δὲ μάλιστα ἐν τῇ νῦν
παρεστώσῃ συμφορᾷ, ὡς ῥᾳδίως αὐτὴν καὶ πρᾴως 15
φέρεις.

Notes: 3–4. **διὰ τὸ πολλάκις δεῦρο φοιτᾶν**: "on account of (my) frequently coming here," i.e., "because I come here so often."
4. **καί τι καί**: "and also in some way."
6. **ἐπιεικῶς πάλαι**: "a reasonably long time ago."
7. **πῶς**: i.e., "how come you didn't . . ."
9. **οὐ μὰ τὸν Δία, ὦ Σώκρατες, οὐδ' ἂν αὐτὸς ἤθελον**: "No, by Zeus, Socrates, nor would I myself wish. . . ."
11. **πάλαι θαυμάζω**: the present tense is regularly used with πάλαι to convey the meaning "I have been doing something for a long time and still am now." θαυμάζω can take a genitive of the person wondered at.
12. **ἵνα ὡς ἥδιστα διάγῃς**: "so that you can pass (the time) as pleasantly as possible."

13–14. **ἐν παντὶ τῷ βίῳ ηὐδαιμόνισα τοῦ τρόπου**: "throughout your life
[lit. in your whole life] I have counted you fortunate in your tempera-
ment." Crito, like Socrates, is an old man.

14–15. **ἐν τῇ νῦν παρεστώσῃ συμφορᾷ**: = "in the bad situation in which
you now are."

15. **ὡς**: "(I count you fortunate in) how...."

CHAPTER 2

Basic Use of Cases

Nominative: subject of a finite verb and complement of verbs such as *to be* and *to become*.

Genitive: possession, the whole of which a part is specified (partitive), and after many prepositions, especially those expressing motion away from.

Dative: indirect object, possession (with the verb *to be*), and after prepositions denoting place where.

Accusative: direct object of a verb, accusative of respect, and after many prepositions, especially those expressing motion toward.

Vocative: person spoken to, with or without the interjection ὦ.

In each of the first five sections an individual case is highlighted. The remaining five extracts exhibit a variety of uses of all the cases.

2.1 Nominative

(I) Thucydides, *Histories* 1.89.1: Thucydides introduces his account of the growth of Athenian power between the Persian and Peloponnesian Wars.

οἱ γὰρ Ἀθηναῖοι τρόπῳ τοιῷδε ἦλθον ἐπὶ τὰ πράγματα ἐν οἷς ηὐξήθησαν.

Notes: 1. **τὰ πράγματα**: "the circumstances/situation."
2. **ηὐξήθησαν**: "they grew to power" (lit. "they were increased").

7

(II) Aeschylus, *Choephoroe* 1–2: Orestes, returning to Argos to avenge his father's murder, asks Hermes for divine assistance.

Ὀρέστης

Ἑρμῆ χθόνιε, πατρῷ᾽ ἐποπτεύων κράτη,
σωτὴρ γενοῦ μοι ξύμμαχός τ᾽ αἰτουμένῳ.

Notes: 1. **Ἑρμῆ χθόνιε**: "Hermes of the Underworld"; the god is invoked by Orestes as the protector of his dead father's powers.
πατρῷ᾽: = πατρῷα; the short alpha has been elided before a following vowel.
2. **σωτὴρ … ξύμμαχός**: both nominatives are complements of the imperative γενοῦ.
μοι … αἰτουμένῳ: "at my request" (lit. "to me requesting [it]").

2.2   Genitive

(I) Plato, *Charmides* 153a: Socrates arrives back in Athens after serving in the army at Potidaea. He heads for Taureas' wrestling school.

ἥκομεν τῇ προτεραίᾳ ἑσπέρας ἐκ Ποτειδαίας ἀπὸ τοῦ
στρατοπέδου, οἷον δὲ διὰ χρόνου ἀφιγμένος ἀσμένως ᾖα
ἐπὶ τὰς συνήθεις διατριβάς. καὶ δὴ καὶ εἰς τὴν Ταυρέου
παλαίστραν τὴν καταντικρὺ τοῦ τῆς Βασίλης ἱεροῦ
εἰσῆλθον, καὶ αὐτόθι κατέλαβον πάνυ πολλούς, τοὺς μὲν   5
καὶ ἀγνῶτας ἐμοί, τοὺς δὲ πλείστους γνωρίμους.

Notes: 1. **ἥκομεν**: imperfect (1st plural) of ἥκω = "we had come."
τῇ προτεραίᾳ ἑσπέρας: "on the previous day in the evening": dative of "time when" and genitive of "time within which" (see Chapter 4) in the same expression.
ἐκ Ποτειδαίας: Potidaea was a Corinthian colony in Chalcidice. It was part of the Athenian Empire, but revolted from Athens in 432 BC, being retaken in 430 after a siege. It is to this campaign that Socrates here refers.
2. **οἷον … ἀφιγμένος**: οἷον + participle = "since," i.e., "since I had arrived"; διὰ χρόνου: "after some time."
3. **συνήθεις διατριβάς**: "customary haunts."
καὶ δὴ καί: "and indeed."
Ταυρέου: Taureas is the name of some professional trainer.

4. **καταντικρὺ … ἱεροῦ**: "opposite the Queen's temple": there was a shrine of Basile, or the Queen, of whom we know nothing else, somewhere south of the Acropolis in Athens.

(II) Plato, *Phaedo* 118a: Phaedo's conclusion of his account to Echecrates of the death of Socrates.

ἥδε ἡ τελευτή, ὦ Ἐχέκρατες, τοῦ ἑταίρου ἡμῖν ἐγένετο,
ἀνδρός, ὡς ἡμεῖς φαῖμεν ἄν, τῶν τότε ὧν ἐπειράθημεν
ἀρίστου καὶ ἄλλως φρονιμωτάτου καὶ δικαιοτάτου.

Notes: 1. **ὦ Ἐχέκρατες**: the setting of Plato's dialogue is the house of Echecrates at Phlius, a city in the northern Peloponnese, not far from Nemea. Echecrates has asked Phaedo to tell him about Socrates' final hours.
2. **φαῖμεν ἄν**: "we would say," a potential optative.
2–3. **τῶν τότε … ἀρίστου**: "best of those then of whom we had had experience." τῶν τότε is a partitive genitive, ὧν genitive after πειράομαι.

2.3 Dative

(I) Homer, *Odyssey* 6.246: Nausicaa instructs her handmaidens to give the shipwrecked Odysseus, still unknown to them, food and drink.

ἀλλὰ δότ᾽, ἀμφίπολοι, ξείνῳ βρῶσίν τε πόσιν τε.

Notes: 1. **ξείνῳ**: = ξένῳ.

(II) Thucydides, *Histories* 1.86.3: the ephor* Sthenelaidas, just before the outbreak of the Peloponnesian War, contrasts Sparta's resources with those of other states.

ἄλλοις μὲν γὰρ χρήματά ἐστι πολλὰ καὶ νῆες καὶ ἵπποι,
ἡμῖν δὲ ξύμμαχοι ἀγαθοί.

Notes: 1. **ἄλλοις**: possessive dative with ἐστί, as also ἡμῖν later in the sentence.
2. **ξύμμαχοι**: = σύμμαχοι.

---

* Ephors were senior members of the Spartan Assembly. Five were elected annually, with particular responsibility to exercise control over the conduct of the two kings.

2.4   Accusative

Thucydides, *Histories* 7.29.4: some Thracian mercenaries show their bloodthirsty nature in the Boeotian town of Mycalessus (413 BC).

> ἐσπεσόντες δὲ οἱ Θρᾷκες ἐς τὴν Μυκαλησσὸν τάς τε
> οἰκίας καὶ τὰ ἱερὰ ἐπόρθουν καὶ τοὺς ἀνθρώπους ἐφόνευον
> φειδόμενοι οὔτε πρεσβυτέρας οὔτε νεωτέρας ἡλικίας,
> ἀλλὰ πάντας ἑξῆς, ὅτῳ ἐντύχοιεν, καὶ παῖδας καὶ γυναῖκας
> κτείνοντες, καὶ προσέτι καὶ ὑποζύγια καὶ ὅσα ἄλλα ἔμψυχα   5
> ἴδοιεν.

Notes: 3. **φειδόμενοι . . . ἡλικίας**: "sparing neither old nor young," (lit. "sparing neither older nor younger age").
4. **ὅτῳ ἐντύχοιεν**: ὅτῳ is an abbreviated form of ᾧτινι (dative of ὅστις) = "whoever they met."
5–6. **ὅσα ἄλλα ἔμψυχα ἴδοιεν**: "any other living thing they saw."

2.5   Vocative

(I) Xenophon, *Symposium* 1.15: Philip the comedian, having fallen silent and lain down at a dinner party where no one was laughing at his jokes, is questioned by Callias and admits that he is in pain.

> καὶ ὁ Καλλίας, τί τοῦτ᾽, ἔφη, ὦ Φίλιππε; ἀλλ᾽ ἦ ὀδύνη
> σε εἴληφε; καὶ ὃς ἀναστενάξας εἶπε· ναὶ μὰ Δί᾽, ἔφη, ὦ
> Καλλία, μεγάλη γε.

Notes: 1. **ἀλλ᾽ ἦ**: "can it be that," a common formula for introducing questions of surprise.
2. **εἴληφε**: perfect active (3rd singular) of λαμβάνω.
καὶ ὅς: "and he," like ὁ δέ.
ναὶ μὰ Δί᾽: "yes, by Zeus." Oaths introduced by νή or ναὶ μά are affirmative, those introduced by μά alone or οὐ μά negative.
3. **μεγάλη**: Philip's great pain, as a continuation of the passage makes clear, is his sadness at his own perception that laughter seems no longer to have a role in human affairs.

2.6   Euripides, *Supplices* 399–405: a Theban herald is rebuked by Theseus for his assumptions about the government of the city of Athens.

Κῆρυξ   Θησεύς

Κη. τίς γῆς τύραννος; πρὸς τίν' ἀγγεῖλαί με χρὴ
λόγους Κρέοντος, ὃς κρατεῖ Κάδμου χθονὸς
Ἐτεοκλέους θανόντος ἀμφ' ἑπταστόμους
πύλας ἀδελφῇ χειρὶ Πολυνείκους ὕπο;

Θη. πρῶτον μὲν ἤρξω τοῦ λόγου ψευδῶς, ξένε,   5
ζητῶν τύραννον ἐνθάδ'· οὐ γὰρ ἄρχεται
ἑνὸς πρὸς ἀνδρός, ἀλλ' ἐλευθέρα πόλις.

Notes: 2. **Κρέοντος**: Creon, Oedipus' brother-in-law, is now king of
Thebes.
Κάδμου χθονός: = Thebes.
3–4. **Ἐτεοκλέους . . . Πολυνείκους ὕπο**: the herald refers to the single
combat of Oedipus' two sons in the conflict of the Seven against Thebes.
Both brothers died, each mortally wounded by the other, though
here the herald mentions only Polynices' slaughter of Eteocles (see
Chapter 12, no. 5); ἀμφ' ἑπταστόμους πύλας: "at the seven-mouthed
gates," a slightly tautologous expression since the mouths are the gates
themselves; ἀδελφῇ χειρὶ Πολυνείκους ὕπο: "at the hands of his brother
Polynices" (lit. "by a brother's hand, by Polynices"); note the anastrophe
in ὕπο, i.e., the throwing back of the accent to the first syllable,
something that occurs when a dissyllabic preposition follows its noun.
5. **ἤρξω**: aorist middle (2nd singular) of ἄρχω. Notice that ἄρχεσθαι
is used in two consecutive lines with different meanings. Here it is
middle meaning "to begin," while in the next line it is passive and
means "to be ruled."
7. **ἑνὸς πρὸς ἀνδρός**: = ἑνὸς ὑπ' ἀνδρός.
ἀλλ' ἐλευθέρα πόλις: understand ἐστί.

2.7 *St. Luke's Gospel* 2. 8–12: the angels tell the shepherds of the
birth of Christ.

καὶ ποιμένες ἦσαν ἐν τῇ χώρᾳ τῇ αὐτῇ ἀγραυλοῦντες
καὶ φυλάσσοντες φυλακὰς τῆς νυκτὸς ἐπὶ τὴν ποίμνην
αὐτῶν. καὶ ἰδοὺ ἄγγελος Κυρίου ἐπέστη αὐτοῖς καὶ δόξα
Κυρίου περιέλαμψεν αὐτούς, καὶ ἐφοβήθησαν φόβον
μέγαν. καὶ εἶπεν αὐτοῖς ὁ ἄγγελος· Μὴ φοβεῖσθε· ἰδοὺ   5
γὰρ εὐαγγελίζομαι ὑμῖν χαρὰν μεγάλην ἥτις ἔσται παντὶ

τῷ λαῷ, ὅτι ἐτέχθη ὑμῖν σήμερον σωτὴρ ὅς ἐστιν Χριστὸς
Κύριος ἐν πόλει Δαυΐδ. καὶ τοῦτο ὑμῖν τὸ σημεῖον,
εὑρήσετε βρέφος ἐσπαργανωμένον, κείμενον ἐν φάτνῃ.

Notes: 1. **ἀγραυλοῦντες**: present participle of ἀγραυλέω = "I stay in
the fields."

2. **φυλάσσοντες φυλακάς**: "keeping watch," a cognate accusative, i.e.,
when the noun in the accusative derives from the same root as the verb.

3. **ἐπέστη**: "came up to," intransitive aorist (2nd singular) of ἐφίστημι.

3–4. **δόξα Κυρίου**: "the glory of the Lord."

4–5. **ἐφοβήθησαν φόβον μέγαν**: another cognate accusative, lit. "they
feared a great fear."

6. **εὐαγγελίζομαι**: "I bring good news (of)," cf. the English "evangelize."

7. **ἐτέχθη**: aorist passive (3rd singular) of τίκτω.

8. **ἐν πόλει Δαυΐδ**: i.e., in Bethlehem, the traditional birthplace of King
David, where Joseph had to go for the census, because "he was of the
house and lineage of David."

καὶ . . . σημεῖον: understand ἔσται.

9. **ἐσπαργανωμένον**: perfect participle passive of σπαργανόω ("I wrap
in swaddling clothes").

2.8   Homer, *Iliad* 1.357–64: Thetis responds to the tearful appeal of
her son, Achilles.

ὣς φάτο δάκρυ χέων, τοῦ δ' ἔκλυε πότνια μήτηρ
ἡμένη ἐν βένθεσσιν ἁλὸς παρὰ πατρὶ γέροντι·
καρπαλίμως δ' ἀνέδυ πολιῆς ἁλὸς ἠΰτ' ὀμίχλη,
καί ῥα πάροιθ' αὐτοῖο καθέζετο δάκρυ χέοντος,
χειρί τέ μιν κατέρεξεν ἔπος τ' ἔφατ' ἔκ τ' ὀνόμαζε·   5
τέκνον, τί κλαίεις; τί δέ σε φρένας ἵκετο πένθος;
ἐξαύδα, μὴ κεῦθε νόῳ, ἵνα εἴδομεν ἄμφω.

Notes: 1. **ὣς φάτο**: Achilles is the subject; φάτο: Homeric imperfect/
strong aorist (3rd singular) of φημί, indistinguishable in meaning from
ἔφη; cf. ἔφατ' in line 5.

4. **καθέζετο**: the normal imperfect of καθέζομαι in prose is ἐκαθεζόμην,
but in all poetry, not just Homer, καθεζόμην as here.

5. **μιν**: = αὐτόν.

6. **σε φρένας**: a double accusative of motion toward, "to your heart."

7. **εἴδομεν**: Homeric subjunctive (first plural) of οἶδα.

2.9 Lysias 1.22–24: Euphiletus, on trial for the murder of his wife's lover, Eratosthenes, tells the court how he came to discover his victim *in flagrante delicto* with his wife.

> Σώστρατος ἦν μοι ἐπιτήδειος καὶ φίλος. τούτῳ ἡλίου
> δεδυκότος ἰόντι ἐξ ἀγροῦ ἀπήντησα· εἰδὼς δ' ἐγὼ ὅτι
> τηνικαῦτα ἀφιγμένος οὐδένα καταλήψοιτο οἴκοι τῶν
> ἐπιτηδείων, ἐκέλευον συνδειπνεῖν· καὶ ἐλθόντες οἴκαδε
> ὡς ἐμέ, ἀναβάντες εἰς τὸ ὑπερῷον ἐδειπνοῦμεν. ἐπειδὴ   5
> δὲ καλῶς αὐτῷ εἶχεν, ἐκεῖνος μὲν ἀπιὼν ᾤχετο, ἐγὼ δ'
> ἐκάθευδον. ὁ δ' Ἐρατοσθένης, ὦ ἄνδρες, εἰσέρχεται, καὶ
> ἡ θεράπαινα ἐπεγείρασά με εὐθὺς φράζει ὅτι ἔνδον ἐστί.
> κἀγὼ εἰπὼν ἐκείνῃ ἐπιμελεῖσθαι τῆς θύρας, καταβὰς
> σιωπῇ ἐξέρχομαι, καὶ ἀφικνοῦμαι ὡς τὸν καὶ τόν, καὶ   10
> τοὺς μὲν ἔνδον κατέλαβον, τοὺς δὲ οὐδ' ἐπιδημοῦντας
> ηὗρον. παραλαβὼν δ' ὡς οἷόν τε ἦν πλείστους ἐκ τῶν
> παρόντων ἐβάδιζον. καὶ δᾷδας λαβόντες ἐκ τοῦ ἐγγύτατα
> καπηλείου εἰσερχόμεθα, ἀνεῳγμένης τῆς θύρας καὶ ὑπὸ
> τῆς ἀνθρώπου παρεσκευασμένης. ὤσαντες δὲ τὴν   15
> θύραν τοῦ δωματίου οἱ μὲν πρῶτοι εἰσιόντες ἔτι εἴδομεν
> αὐτὸν κατακείμενον παρὰ τῇ γυναικί, οἱ δ' ὕστερον ἐν τῇ
> κλίνῃ γυμνὸν ἑστηκότα.

Notes: 1. **ἐπιτήδειος καὶ φίλος**: "a close and dear friend."
2. **ἐξ ἀγροῦ**: "from the country," i.e., from outside the city. Euphiletus was a farmer and would have had to go out of the city daily to work on his land.
4–5. **οἴκαδε ὡς ἐμέ**: "home to my place."
6. **καλῶς αὐτῷ εἶχεν**: "he had had his fill" (lit. "it was well with him"), ἔχειν, as regularly with an adverb, meaning "to be."
ἀπιὼν ᾤχετο: "took his leave and departed."
7. **εἰσέρχεται**: the large number of historic presents from this point on, some five of them, help present a vivid picture at this crucial point in Euphiletus' account.
9. **κἀγὼ εἰπὼν ἐκείνῃ**: = καὶ ἐγὼ (crasis) εἰπὼν ἐκείνῃ ("and I, telling her"). εἰπών is here followed by an indirect command.
10. **τὸν καὶ τόν**: "this one and that one."
11. **οὐδ' ἐπιδημοῦντας**: "not even (= οὐδ') in town."

12. **ὡς οἷόν τε ἦν πλείστους**: the fully written out form of the regular ὡς + superlative (= ὡς πλείστους) = "as many as possible."
14–15. **οὐδ᾽ ἐπιδημοῦντας**: "not even (= οὐδ᾽) in town."
ὑπὸ τῆς ἀνθρώπου: "by the girl." Note this feminine use of ἄνθρωπος.

2.10   Euripides, *Alcestis* 185–96: a maidservant tells of the sad scene in Admetus' palace as his wife, Alcestis, soon to die on his behalf, says farewell to her children and the members of her household.

Θεράπαινα

ἐπεὶ δὲ πολλῶν δακρύων εἶχεν κόρον,
στείχει προνωπὴς ἐκπεσοῦσα δεμνίων,
καὶ πολλὰ θαλάμων ἐξιοῦσ᾽ ἐπεστράφη
κἄρριψεν αὑτὴν αὖθις ἐς κοίτην πάλιν.
παῖδες δὲ πέπλων μητρὸς ἐξηρτημένοι   5
ἔκλαιον· ἡ δὲ λαμβάνουσ᾽ ἐς ἀγκάλας
ἠσπάζετ᾽ ἄλλοτ᾽ ἄλλον ὡς θανουμένη.
πάντες δ᾽ ἔκλαιον οἰκέται κατὰ στέγας
δέσποιναν οἰκτίροντες, ἡ δὲ δεξιὰν
προύτειν᾽ ἑκάστῳ, κοὔτις ἦν οὕτω κακὸς   10
ὃν οὐ προσεῖπε καὶ προσερρήθη πάλιν.
τοιαῦτ᾽ ἐν οἴκοις ἐστὶν Ἀδμήτου κακά.

Notes: 1. **εἶχεν**: the subject is Alcestis, who has been crying in her bedroom.
2. **στείχει προνωπής**: historic present = "she went stumbling forward."
3. **πολλά**: used adverbially = πολλάκις.
4. **κἄρριψεν**: crasis for καὶ ἔρριψεν.
αὖθις ἐς κοίτην πάλιν: "back again onto the bed."
5. **ἐξηρτημένοι**: perfect participle passive of ἐξαρτάω = "hanging from" (lit. "having been hung from").
7. **ἄλλοτ᾽ ἄλλον**: "one after another" (lit. "another one at another time").
ὡς θανουμένη: "since she was going to die."
10. **κοὔτις**: crasis for καὶ οὔτις.
11. **ὃν . . . πάλιν**: "that she did not speak to him and was spoken to in return." Euripides uses a relative clause where we might expect a result clause; προσεῖπον and προσερρήθην are used in Attic as the aorist active and aorist passive repectively of προσαγορεύω.

CHAPTER 3

Adjectives

Adjectives agree with their nouns in gender, number and case; they are positioned in much the same way as in English. If their noun has an article, the adjective usually comes between the article and the noun (the attributive position). This can be varied, especially if the adjective is a long word or there is more than one adjective, or an adjectival phrase is used, by repeating the article after the noun and following it with the adjective(s) or adjectival phrase. Note that οὗτος, ἐκεῖνος and ὅδε always come outside the article and noun, either before or after them: they are generally used with the definite article.

3.1   Plato, *Ion* 533e–34b: Socrates explains that poets create their work not through thought and skill but through inspiration.

> πάντες γὰρ οἵ τε τῶν ἐπῶν ποιηταὶ οἱ ἀγαθοὶ οὐκ ἐκ
> τέχνης ἀλλ᾽ ἔνθεοι ὄντες καὶ κατεχόμενοι πάντα ταῦτα
> τὰ καλὰ λέγουσι ποιήματα, καὶ οἱ μελοποιοὶ οἱ ἀγαθοὶ
> ὡσαύτως, ὥσπερ οἱ κορυβαντιῶντες οὐκ ἔμφρονες ὄντες
> ὀρχοῦνται, οὕτω καὶ οἱ μελοποιοὶ οὐκ ἔμφρονες ὄντες   5
> τὰ καλὰ μέλη ταῦτα ποιοῦσιν, ἀλλ᾽ ἐπειδὰν ἐμβῶσιν
> εἰς τὴν ἁρμονίαν καὶ εἰς τὸν ῥυθμόν, βακχεύουσι καὶ
> κατεχόμενοι, ὥσπερ αἱ βάκχαι ἀρύονται ἐκ τῶν ποταμῶν
> μέλι καὶ γάλα κατεχόμεναι, ἔμφρονες δὲ οὖσαι οὔ, καὶ τῶν

μελοποιῶν ἡ ψυχὴ τοῦτο ἐργάζεται, ὅπερ αὐτοὶ λέγουσι.   10
λέγουσι γὰρ δήπουθεν πρὸς ἡμᾶς οἱ ποιηταὶ ὅτι ἀπὸ
κρηνῶν μελιρρύτων ἐκ Μουσῶν κήπων τινῶν καὶ ναπῶν
δρεπόμενοι τὰ μέλη ἡμῖν φέρουσιν ὥσπερ αἱ μέλιτται, καὶ
αὐτοὶ οὕτω πετόμενοι· καὶ ἀληθῆ λέγουσι.

Notes: 1. **τῶν ἐπῶν**: "of epic poetry."
2. **κατεχόμενοι**: "possessed."
4. **οἱ κορυβαντιῶντες**: the Corybantes were priests of the goddess Cybele and worshipped her with wild music and frenzied dancing.
6. **ποιοῦσιν**: i.e., "write."
6–7. **ἐπειδὰν ἐμβῶσιν εἰς τὴν ἁρμονίαν καὶ εἰς τὸν ῥυθμόν**: "whenever they start singing harmoniously and rhythmically" (lit. "whenever they enter upon harmony and rhythm").
8. **αἱ βάκχαι**: the bacchantes, the ecstatic worshippers of Bacchus, god of wine and the liberated spirit.
ἀρύονται: "draw" (of liquids).
10. **ὅπερ**: "just as" (lit. "the very thing that").
11. **δήπουθεν**: "I think."
11–12. **ἀπὸ κρηνῶν μελιρρύτων ἐκ Μουσῶν κήπων τινῶν καὶ ναπῶν**: "from honey-dropping springs in certain gardens and glades of the Muses."

3.2   Plato, *Symposium* 221c: Alcibiades, in his praise of Socrates, explains that he is quite unlike anybody else.

πολλὰ μὲν οὖν ἄν τις καὶ ἄλλα ἔχοι Σωκράτη ἐπαινέσαι καὶ
θαυμάσια· ἀλλὰ τῶν μὲν ἄλλων ἐπιτηδευμάτων τάχ᾽ ἄν
τις καὶ περὶ ἄλλου τοιαῦτα εἴποι, τὸ δὲ μηδενὶ ἀνθρώπων
ὅμοιον εἶναι, μήτε τῶν παλαιῶν μήτε τῶν νῦν ὄντων, τοῦτο
ἄξιον παντὸς θαύματος.   5

Notes: 1. **ἄν τις … ἔχοι … Σωκράτη ἐπαινέσαι**: "one could find [lit. have] … to praise (in) Socrates."
3–4. **τὸ … εἶναι**: "the fact that he is." μή is the regular negative with the infinitive (except in indirect statement), hence its compounds here. τοῦτο picks this up: "*this* fact."

3.3   In this graffito cut into a rock on Mount Hymettus near Athens, the writer declares his passion.

Adjectives 17

ΔΕΙΝΙΑΣ ΚΑΛΟΣ

3.4 Herodotus, *Histories* 1.1: the historian explains his aims in writing his history and says that the experts believe that the Phoenicians launched the conflict between the Greeks and the barbarians.

Ἡροδότου Ἁλικαρνησσέος ἱστορίης ἀπόδεξις ἥδε, ὡς μήτε
τὰ γενόμενα ἐξ ἀνθρώπων τῷ χρόνῳ ἐξίτηλα γένηται,
μήτε ἔργα μεγάλα τε καὶ θωμαστά, τὰ μὲν Ἕλλησι τὰ δὲ
βαρβάροισι ἀποδεχθέντα, ἀκλεᾶ γένηται, τά τε ἄλλα καὶ
δι' ἣν αἰτίην ἐπολέμησαν ἀλλήλοισι.   5

Περσέων μέν νυν οἱ λόγιοι Φοίνικας αἰτίους φασὶ
γενέσθαι τῆς διαφορῆς. τούτους γὰρ ἀπὸ τῆς Ἐρυθρῆς
καλεομένης θαλάσσης ἀπικομένους ἐπὶ τήνδε τὴν
θάλασσαν, καὶ οἰκήσαντας τοῦτον τὸν χῶρον τὸν καὶ
νῦν οἰκέουσι, αὐτίκα ναυτιλίῃσι μακρῇσι ἐπιθέσθαι,   10
ἀπαγινέοντας δὲ φορτία Αἰγύπτιά τε καὶ Ἀσσύρια τῇ τε
ἄλλῃ ἐσαπικνέεσθαι καὶ δὴ καὶ ἐς Ἄργος.

Notes: 1. **Ἁλικαρνησσέος**: Herodotus came from Halicarnassus (now Bodrum on the Aegean coast of Turkey). This word meaning Halicarnassian is in the genitive;
ἱστορίης ἀπόδεξις ἥδε: lit. "this (is) the display of the enquiry."
ὡς: "so that" (a purpose clause).
2. **ἐξίτηλα**: "forgotten."
3–4. **τὰ μὲν Ἕλλησι τὰ δὲ βαρβάροισι ἀποδεχθέντα**: "some produced [lit. displayed] by Greeks, others by barbarians."
4–5. **τά τε ἄλλα καὶ δι' ἣν αἰτίην**: lit. "both the other things and because of what reason . . ." i.e., "in particular the reason that. . . ."
6. **Περσέων . . . οἱ λόγιοι**: "the learned men of the Persians."
φασί: the accusative and infinitive construction after this verb continues through the next sentence.
7–8. **τῆς Ἐρυθρῆς καλεομένης θαλάσσης**: "what is called the Red Sea"; in fact Herodotus is here referring to the Persian Gulf.
9. **τόν**: Ionic relative pronoun = Attic ὅν.
10. **ναυτιλίῃσι μακρῇσι ἐπιθέσθαι**: "began to make long trading voyages."
11. **ἀπαγινέοντας . . . φορτία Αἰγύπτιά τε καὶ Ἀσσύρια**: "transporting Egyptian and Assyrian goods."
12. **τῇ τε ἄλλῃ**: "both elsewhere." Argos is part of Greece.

3.5 Euripides, *Medea* 49–55: in answer to the Tutor's questions, the Nurse explains to her fellow slave that she is standing alone lamenting outside the house because of her sympathy with her mistress, Medea, who has been abandoned by her husband, Jason.

Παιδαγωγός   Τροφός

Πα. παλαιὸν οἴκων κτῆμα δεσποίνης ἐμῆς,
τί πρὸς πύλαισι τήνδ᾽ ἄγουσ᾽ ἐρημίαν
ἕστηκας, αὐτὴ θρεομένη σαυτῇ κακά;
πῶς σοῦ μόνη Μήδεια λείπεσθαι θέλει;

Τρ. τέκνων ὀπαδὲ πρέσβυ τῶν Ἰάσονος,   5
χρηστοῖσι δούλοις ξυμφορὰ τὰ δεσποτῶν
κακῶς πίτνοντα, καὶ φρενῶν ἀνθάπτεται.

Notes: 1. **οἴκων**: poetic plural: it simply means "house," though the plural suggests that it is a grand one.
2. **τήνδ᾽ ἄγουσ᾽ ἐρημίαν**: "being alone like this," lit. "conducting this loneliness."
3. **θρεομένη**: "crying aloud."
4. **σοῦ μόνη**: "alone without you."
6. **ξυμφορά**: "(are/is) a disaster": ξυμφορά is a noun.
7. **κακῶς πίτνοντα**: "when they turn out badly."

3.6 Homer, *Iliad* 6.414–16, 421–30: Andromache explains to her husband, Hector, that all of her family (who had lived in Thēbē) have died or been killed by Achilles and thus he is everything to her.

ἤτοι γὰρ πατέρ᾽ ἁμὸν ἀπέκτανε δῖος Ἀχιλλεύς,
ἐκ δὲ πόλιν πέρσεν Κιλίκων εὖ ναιετάουσαν
Θήβην ὑψίπυλον...
οἳ δέ μοι ἑπτὰ κασίγνητοι ἔσαν ἐν μεγάροισιν
οἳ μὲν πάντες ἰῷ κίον ἤματι Ἄϊδος εἴσω·   5
πάντας γὰρ κατέπεφνε ποδάρκης δῖος Ἀχιλλεὺς
βουσὶν ἐπ᾽ εἰλιπόδεσσι καὶ ἀργεννῆς ὀίεσσι.
μητέρα δ᾽, ἣ βασίλευεν ὑπὸ Πλάκῳ ὑληέσσῃ,
τὴν ἐπεὶ ἂρ δεῦρ᾽ ἤγαγ᾽ ἅμ᾽ ἄλλοισι κτεάτεσσιν,
ἂψ ὅ γε τὴν ἀπέλυσε λαβὼν ἀπερείσι᾽ ἄποινα,   10

πατρὸς δ᾽ ἐν μεγάροισι βάλ᾽ Ἄρτεμις ἰοχέαιρα.

Ἕκτορ ἀτὰρ σύ μοί ἐσσι πατὴρ καὶ πότνια μήτηρ

ἠδὲ κασίγνητος, σὺ δέ μοι θαλερὸς παρακοίτης.

Notes: 1. **ἤτοι**: "truly."

ἀμόν: = Attic ἐμόν.

2. **ἐκ … πέρσεν**: "he sacked" (tmesis).

Κιλίκων: "of the Cilicians."

εὖ ναιετάουσαν: "well-situated."

4. **ἔσαν**: = Attic ἦσαν.

5. **ἰῷ**: dat. of ἰός = one.

Ἄϊδος εἴσω: "to (the house) of Hades."

6. **κατέπεφνε**: "killed."

7. **βουσὶν ἐπ᾽ εἰλιπόδεσσι καὶ ἀργεννῇς ὀίεσσι**: "in charge of the cattle with their rolling gait and the bright white sheep."

8. **μητέρα**: the object of βάλ᾽ four lines later.

ὑπὸ Πλάκῳ ὑληέσσῃ: "beneath well-wooded Mount Plakos." Plakos was a spur of Mount Ida, south of Troy.

9. **κτεάτεσσιν**: "possessions" (dative plural).

10. **ἀπερείσι᾽ ἄποινα**: "a limitless ransom."

11. **Ἄρτεμις ἰοχέαιρα**: "Artemis, shooter of arrows," is regularly the goddess responsible for the sudden death of women.

12. **ἐσσι**: "you are."

CHAPTER 4

Time, Place and Space

TIME

Time *how long*: accusative
Time *within which*: genitive
Time *when*: dative

4.1 Plato, *Apology* 17d: Socrates, on trial in Athens at the age of seventy, points out that he is entirely unfamiliar with the language of the courts.

> ἔχει γὰρ οὑτωσί. νῦν ἐγὼ πρῶτον ἐπὶ δικαστήριον
> ἀναβέβηκα, ἔτη γεγονὼς ἑβδομήκοντα· ἀτεχνῶς οὖν
> ξένως ἔχω τῆς ἐνθάδε λέξεως.

Notes: 1. **ἔχει γὰρ οὑτωσί**: "for the fact of the matter is this"; ἔχειν when used with an adverb regularly means "to be"; the iota attached to οὕτως (the deictic iota) strengthens the demonstrative force of the word.
1–2. **ἐπὶ δικαστήριον ἀναβέβηκα**: "I have appeared in court"; ἀναβαίνω ("I go up") is the correct technical term here because both accused and accuser spoke from a platform that they had to mount.
2. **ἔτη γεγονὼς ἑβδομήκοντα**: "at the age of seventy" (lit. "born for seventy years"), an accusative of time how long.
3. **ξένως ἔχω**: "I am a stranger to" (+ genitive); cf. on ἔχει γὰρ οὑτωσί above.
τῆς ἐνθάδε λέξεως: "the style of speech here," i.e., in court.

4.2 Sophocles, *Philoctetes* 1337–42: Neoptolemus explains to Philoctetes, suffering from a snake bite in the foot, how he knows that his wound will be cured and that Troy is soon to fall.

Νεοπτόλεμος

ἀνὴρ γὰρ ἡμῖν ἐστιν ἐκ Τροίας ἁλούς,
Ἕλενος ἀριστόμαντις, ὃς λέγει σαφῶς
ὡς δεῖ γενέσθαι ταῦτα· καὶ πρὸς τοῖσδ᾽ ἔτι
ὡς ἔστ᾽ ἀνάγκη τοῦ παρεστῶτος θέρους
Τροίαν ἁλῶναι πᾶσαν· ἢ δίδωσ᾽ ἑκὼν   5
κτείνειν ἑαυτόν, ἢν τάδε ψευσθῇ λέγων.

Notes: 1. **ἁλούς**: aorist participle of ἁλίσκομαι ("I am captured"). ἁλῶναι later in the passage is aorist infinitive of the same verb.
2. **ἀριστόμαντις**: "the best of prophets."
3. **ταῦτα**: refers to the cure of Philoctetes' foot by the sons of Asclepius at Troy.
καὶ πρὸς τοῖσδ᾽ ἔτι: understand λέγει; πρός + dative = "in addition to."
4. **τοῦ παρεστῶτος θέρους**: "in the course of the present summer." παρεστῶτος is the neuter genitive singular of παρεστώς ("being present"), intransitive perfect participle active of παρίστημι.
5. **ἤ**: "alternatively," i.e., if he is wrong.
5–6. **δίδωσ᾽ … κτείνειν ἑαυτόν**: "he gives himself for slaughter" (lit. "he gives himself over [to us] to slaughter"); κτείνειν: an infinitive of purpose.

4.3 Xenophon, *Hellenica* 1.1.14–16: Alcibiades addresses his forces before putting out to sea for Cyzicus, where a Spartan fleet under Mindarus and Persian land forces under Pharnabazus awaits him.

ταύτην μὲν οὖν τὴν ἡμέραν αὐτοῦ ἔμειναν, τῇ δὲ ὑστεραίᾳ
Ἀλκιβιάδης ἐκκλησίαν ποιήσας παρεκελεύετο αὐτοῖς
ὅτι ἀνάγκη εἴη καὶ ναυμαχεῖν καὶ πεζομαχεῖν καὶ
τειχομαχεῖν· Οὐ γὰρ ἔστιν, ἔφη, χρήματα ἡμῖν, τοῖς δὲ
πολεμίοις ἄφθονα παρὰ βασιλέως. τῇ δὲ προτεραίᾳ, ἐπειδὴ   5
ὡρμίσαντο, τὰ πλοῖα πάντα καὶ τὰ μικρὰ συνήθροισε παρ᾽
ἑαυτόν, ὅπως μηδεὶς ἐξαγγείλαι τοῖς πολεμίοις τὸ πλῆθος
τῶν νεῶν, ἐπεκήρυξέ τε, ὃς ἂν ἁλίσκηται εἰς τὸ πέραν

διαπλέων, θάνατον τὴν ζημίαν. μετὰ δὲ τὴν ἐκκλησίαν
παρασκευασάμενος ὡς ἐπὶ ναυμαχίαν ἀνηγάγετο ἐπὶ τὴν   10
Κύζικον ὕοντος πολλῷ.

Notes: 1. **αὐτοῦ**: adverbial usage = "just there."
5. **βασιλέως**: the noun βασιλεύς without an article regularly refers to
the king of Persia.
6. **ὡρμίσαντο**: as regularly in a temporal (or relative) clause, this aorist
should be translated as a pluperfect, as also here the two subsequent
aorists in the main clause, συνήθροισε and ἐπεκήρυξε.
καὶ τὰ μικρά: "even the small ones."
7. **ἐξαγγείλαι**: aorist optative active (3rd singular) of ἐξαγγέλλω.
8. **εἰς τὸ πέραν**: "over to the other side."
9. **θάνατον τὴν ζημίαν**: understand ἐκείνῳ ἔσεσθαι.
10–11. **τὴν Κύζικον**: Cyzicus was a a colony, possibly of Corinthian
origin, on the Arctonessus peninsula in the southern Propontis.
11. **ὕοντος πολλῷ**: "in heavy rain." Note here the one-word genitive
absolute from ὕει ("it rains") rather than the accusative absolute that
one might expect with an impersonal verb, perhaps because the subject
in this case was thought of as being Ζεύς (the weather god) or θεός.

4.4   Homer, *Odyssey* 2.171–76: the aged seer Halitherses declares
that his former prophecy about the return of Odysseus is now being
brought to pass.

καὶ γὰρ κείνῳ φημὶ τελευτηθῆναι ἅπαντα,
ὥς οἱ ἐμυθεόμην, ὅτε Ἴλιον εἰσανέβαινον
Ἀργεῖοι, μετὰ δέ σφιν ἔβη πολύμητις Ὀδυσσεύς.
φῆν κακὰ πολλὰ παθόντ', ὀλέσαντ' ἄπο πάντας ἑταίρους,
ἄγνωστον πάντεσσιν ἐεικοστῷ ἐνιαυτῷ   5
οἴκαδ' ἐλεύσεσθαι· τὰ δὲ δὴ νῦν πάντα τελεῖται.

Notes: 1. **καὶ γάρ**: "for in fact."
κείνῳ: "for him," i.e., Odysseus. κεῖνος is a variant form of ἐκεῖνος.
2. **ἐμυθεόμην**: as often in Homer, there is no contraction.
Ἴλιον: the accusative is used here without a preposition to indicate
motion toward (see below).
3. **σφιν**: = αὐτοῖς.
4. **φῆν**: = ἔφην. In the indirect statement that follows understand
αὐτόν.
ὀλέσαντ' ἄπο: = ἀπολέσαντα.
5. **ἐεικοστῷ**: = εἰκοστῷ.

6. **ἐλεύσεσθαι**: from ἐλεύσομαι, used as future of ἔρχομαι.
τά: "these things," the article, as always in Homer, being essentially a demonstrative.

4.5 Plato, *Laws* 642d–e: Clinias of Crete reminds an Athenian stranger of a prophecy made by his kinsman Epimenides.

> τῇδε γὰρ ἴσως ἀκήκοας ὡς Ἐπιμενίδης γέγονεν, ἀνὴρ
> θεῖος, ὃς ἦν ἡμῖν οἰκεῖος, ἐλθὼν δὲ πρὸ τῶν Περσικῶν
> δέκα ἔτεσιν πρότερον παρ᾽ ὑμᾶς κατὰ τὴν τοῦ θεοῦ
> μαντείαν, θυσίας τε ἐθύσατό τινας ἃς ὁ θεὸς ἀνεῖλεν, καὶ
> δὴ καὶ φοβουμένων τὸν Περσικὸν Ἀθηναίων στόλον,   5
> εἶπεν ὅτι δέκα μὲν ἐτῶν οὐχ ἥξουσιν, ὅταν δὲ ἔλθωσιν,
> ἀπαλλαγήσονται πράξαντες οὐδὲν ὧν ἤλπιζον, παθόντες
> τε ἢ δράσαντες πλείω κακά.

Notes: 1. **τῇδε**: to be taken with γέγονεν = "was born here," i.e., in Crete, where the conversation is taking place.
Ἐπιμενίδης: a holy man of Crete who is variously thought to have been active around 600 or, as here, 500 BC.
2. **ἐλθὼν δέ**: the ὡς clause continues right to the end.
2–3. **πρὸ ... πρότερον**: "some ten years before the Persian War," i.e., the First Persian War (lit. "before the Persian War, ten years previously").
3. **παρ᾽ ὑμᾶς**: "to you," i.e., to Athens.
4. **ἀνεῖλεν**: ἀναιρέω is regularly used of the instructions or orders of an oracle.
6. **δέκα ... ἐτῶν**: "within ten years," a genitive of time within which.
7. **ἀπαλλαγήσονται**: future passive (3rd plural) of ἀπαλλάσσω; ἀπαλλάσσομαι commonly means "I depart."
οὐδὲν ὧν: = οὐδὲν ἐκείνων ἅ (relative attraction).
8. **ἢ δράσαντες**: "than they had done" (lit. "than having done").

PLACE

Place is usually indicated by prepositions in Greek.

> Prepositions + accusative indicate motion *toward*, e.g.,
> πρός, εἰς, ἐπί, παρά
> Prepositions + genitive indicate motion *away from*, e.g., ἀπό,
> ἐκ, παρά
> Prepositions + dative indicate place *where*, e.g., ἐν, πρός,
> παρά

Note also: 1. The suffix -δε or -σε indicating motion *toward*, e.g.,
Ἀθήναζε, οἴκαδε
2. The suffix -θεν indicating motion *away from*, e.g., Ἀθήνηθεν, οἴκοθεν
3. The *locative* case indicating place *where*, e.g., Ἀθήνησι(ν), οἴκοι
4. Many adverbs, e.g., ἐκεῖ, οὐδαμοῦ, πανταχοῦ, which themselves may
have the suffixes -δε and -θεν, e.g., ἐκεῖσε, ἐκεῖθεν

4.6   Thucydides, *Histories* 1.94.1–2: some exploits of Pausanias the
Spartan just after the Second Persian War (478 BC).

Παυσανίας δὲ ὁ Κλεομβρότου ἐκ Λακεδαίμονος
στρατηγὸς τῶν Ἑλλήνων ἐξεπέμφθη μετὰ εἴκοσι νεῶν ἀπὸ
Πελοποννήσου· ξυνέπλεον δὲ καὶ Ἀθηναῖοι τριάκοντα
ναυσὶ καὶ τῶν ἄλλων ξυμμάχων πλῆθος. καὶ ἐστράτευσαν
ἐς Κύπρον καὶ αὐτῆς τὰ πολλὰ κατεστρέψαντο, καὶ   5
ὕστερον ἐς Βυζάντιον Μήδων ἐχόντων, καὶ
ἐξεπολιόρκησαν ἐν τῇδε τῇ ἡγεμονίᾳ.

Notes: 2–3. **ἀπὸ Πελοποννήσου**: to be taken closely with εἴκοσι νεῶν =
"twenty ships from the Peloponnese."
5. **αὐτῆς τὰ πολλὰ κατεστρέψαντο**: "subdued most of it."
6. **Μήδων ἐχόντων**: a genitive absolute = "which was under Median
control" (lit. "the Medes holding it").
7. **ἐν τῇδε τῇ ἡγεμονίᾳ**: "during this period of office," i.e., of Pausanias.

4.7   Euripides, *Iphigenia in Tauris* 767–76: unaware of their true
identities, Iphigenia, now a priestess in the land of the Taurians,
repeats to Orestes and Pylades the contents of a letter she wishes
them to deliver to Orestes in Argos.

Πυλάδης   Ἰφιγένεια

Πυ.   σήμαινε δ᾽ ᾧ χρὴ τάσδ᾽ ἐπιστολὰς φέρειν
προς Ἄργος ὅ τι τε χρὴ κλύοντα σοῦ λέγειν.

Ἰφ.   ἄγγελλ᾽ Ὀρέστῃ, παιδὶ τῷ Ἀγαμέμνονος·
Ἡ 'ν Αὐλίδι σφαγεῖσ᾽ ἐπιστέλλει τάδε
ζῶσ᾽ Ἰφιγένεια, τοῖς ἐκεῖ δ᾽ οὐ ζῶσ᾽ ἔτι.   5

Ὀρ.   ποῦ δ᾽ ἔστ᾽ ἐκείνη; κατθανοῦσ᾽ ἥκει πάλιν;

'Ιφ.   ἥδ' ἣν ὁρᾷς σύ· μὴ λόγων ἔκπλησσέ με.
      Κόμισαί μ' ἐς Ἄργος, ὦ σύναιμε, πρὶν θανεῖν,
      ἐκ βαρβάρου γῆς καὶ μετάστησον θεᾶς
      σφαγίων, ἐφ' οἷσι ξενοφόνους τιμὰς ἔχω.   10

Notes: 2. **πρὸς Ἄργος**: although really an expression of "motion toward," good English requires this phrase to be translated as "at Argos."

2. **ὅ τι ... λέγειν**: understand με with χρή (lit. "what I must say hearing it from you").

4. **Ἡ 'ν Αὐλίδι σφαγεῖσ'**: "who was sacrificed at Aulis." Agamemnon had to sacrifice his daughter Iphigenia at Aulis, so that the fleet could set sail for Troy; in fact, a deer was substituted for her, and she was whisked away to the land of the Taurians. 'ν: = ἐν (by prodelision).

5. **ἐκεῖ**: = ἐν Ἄργει.

7. **μὴ ... με**: "don't interrupt me" (lit. "don't drive me away from my words").

8. **Κόμισαί**: aorist imperative middle (2nd singular) of κομίζω.

9. **ἐκ βαρβάρου γῆς**: βάρβαρος is a two-termination adjective.
μετάστησον: weak (i.e., transitive) aorist imperative (2nd singular) of μεθίστημι ("remove [me]").

9–10. **θεᾶς σφαγίων**: "from the goddess's sacrifices," i.e., "from sacrifices *to* the goddess."

10. **ἐφ' οἷσι ... ἔχω**: "at which I have a stranger-slaying sacred office." Iphigenia's specific job as a priestess is to assist in the sacrifice of any Greek who comes to the Taurian land.

4.8   Homer, *Iliad* 1.17–21: Chryses, priest of Apollo, asks the Greeks to release his daughter Chryseis.

      Ἀτρεῖδαί τε καὶ ἄλλοι ἐϋκνήμιδες Ἀχαιοί,
      ὑμῖν μὲν θεοὶ δοῖεν Ὀλύμπια δώματ' ἔχοντες
      ἐκπέρσαι Πριάμοιο πόλιν, εὖ δ' οἴκαδ' ἱκέσθαι·
      παῖδα δ' ἐμοὶ λύσαιτε φίλην, τὰ δ' ἄποινα δέχεσθαι,
      ἁζόμενοι Διὸς υἱὸν ἑκηβόλον Ἀπόλλωνα.   5

Notes: 1. **Ἀτρεῖδαι ... ἄλλοι ἐϋκνήμιδες Ἀχαιοί**: vocatives.

2. **δοῖεν**: the optative here expresses a wish.

4. **λύσαιτε**: the optative here, formally a wish, in reality expresses a polite imperative = "please release."
δέχεσθαι: infinitive used for imperative.

4.9 Xenophon, *Hellenica* 6.4.19–20: after the Battle of Leuctra (371 BC) the Thebans appeal in vain to the Athenians for help against the Spartans.

Οἱ δὲ Θηβαῖοι εὐθὺς μὲν μετὰ τὴν μάχην ἔπεμψαν εἰς
Ἀθήνας ἄγγελον ἐστεφανωμένον, καὶ ἅμα μὲν τῆς νίκης
τὸ μέγεθος ἔφραζον, ἅμα δὲ βοηθεῖν ἐκέλευον, λέγοντες
ὡς νῦν ἐξείη Λακεδαιμονίους πάντων ὧν ἐπεποιήκεσαν
αὐτοὺς τιμωρήσασθαι. τῶν δὲ Ἀθηναίων ἡ βουλὴ   5
ἐτύγχανεν ἐν ἀκροπόλει καθημένη. ἐπεὶ δ᾽ ἤκουσαν τὸ
γεγενημένον, ὅτι μὲν σφόδρα ἠνιάθησαν πᾶσι δῆλον
ἐγένετο· οὔτε γὰρ ἐπὶ ξένια τὸν κήρυκα ἐκάλεσαν, περί τε
τῆς βοηθείας οὐδὲν ἀπεκρίναντο. καὶ Ἀθήνηθεν μὲν οὕτως
ἀπῆλθεν ὁ κῆρυξ.   10

Notes: 2. **ἐστεφανωμένον**: perfect participle passive of στεφανόω
("I garland") = "wearing a garland," because he was, at least partially,
announcing a victory.

4–5. **Λακεδαιμονίους ... τιμωρήσασθαι**: "to take vengeance on the
Spartans." An accusative after τιμωρέω or τιμωρέομαι invariably
indicates the people who suffer, so that the verb means "I take
vengeance upon"; a dative indicates those who are helped, the verb
then meaning "I avenge"; πάντων ὧν ἐπεποιήκεσαν αὐτούς: "for all the
things they had done to them." πάντων ὧν = πάντων ἅ, a case of relative
attraction, so that ποιέω here effectively takes two accusatives, as also
in the phrases ἀγαθὰ ποιέω ("I do good to") and κακά ποιέω ("I do
harm to").

6. **ἐτύγχανεν ... καθημένη**: "happened to be seated." Note this
common usage of τυγχάνω with a participle.

6–7. **τὸ γεγενημένον**: "what had happened." This participial
expression takes the place of an indirect question.

SPACE

Extent of space is expressed by the accusative.

A genitive of measurement is usually used with the accusatives
of respect τὸ μῆκος, τὸ εὖρος, τὸ ὕψος and τὸ βάθος to express
length, breadth, height and depth.

4.10   Xenophon, *Anabasis* 1.4.11: on his march inland Cyrus reaches the city of Thapsacus and at last tells his Greek mercenaries that they are marching against the king of Persia.

ἐντεῦθεν ἐξελαύνει σταθμοὺς τρεῖς παρασάγγας
πεντεκαίδεκα ἐπὶ τὸν Εὐφράτην ποταμόν, ὄντα τὸ εὖρος
τεττάρων σταδίων· καὶ πόλις αὐτόθι ᾠκεῖτο μεγάλη
καὶ εὐδαίμων Θάψακος ὄνομα. ἐνταῦθα ἔμεινεν ἡμέρας
πέντε. καὶ Κῦρος μεταπεμψάμενος τοὺς στρατηγοὺς τῶν   5
Ἑλλήνων ἔλεγεν ὅτι ἡ ὁδὸς ἔσοιτο πρὸς βασιλέα μέγαν
εἰς Βαβυλῶνα· καὶ κελεύει αὐτοὺς λέγειν ταῦτα τοῖς
στρατιώταις καὶ ἀναπείθειν ἕπεσθαι.

Notes: 1. **σταθμοὺς τρεῖς**: "three days' march."

1–2. **παρασάγγας πεντεκαίδεκα**: "fifteen parasangs." The parasang was a Persian measure of distance, roughly 6 kilometers, or a little over 3.5 miles.

2–3. **τὸ εὖρος τεττάρων σταδίων**: "four stades wide." A stade (στάδιον, pl. στάδια or στάδιοι) was a Greek measure of distance, approximately 180 meters, or 560 feet.

4. **ὄνομα**: an accusative of respect doing just the same job as the dative ὀνόματι would have done = "by name."

5. **Κῦρος**: i.e., Cyrus the Younger, son of Darius II.

6. **βασιλέα μέγαν**: "the great king" is Cyrus' elder brother Artaxerxes II, whose throne he wishes to usurp.

CHAPTER 5

Personal Pronouns and αὐτός

I. PERSONAL PRONOUNS

We here show usages of the Greek words for "I" (ἐγώ), "you" (sing.), (σύ), "we" (ἡμεῖς), "you" (plur.) (ὑμεῖς). The enclitic forms of the singular pronouns, με, σου, σοι, σε, are used when the pronoun is unemphatic, while the longer forms ἐμοῦ, ἐμοί, ἐμέ and the accented σοῦ, σοί, σέ are used when the pronoun is emphatic.

5.1 Plato, *Gorgias* 474b: Socrates tells Polus that everybody agrees on one fundamental belief.

> ἐγὼ γὰρ δὴ οἶμαι καὶ ἐμὲ καὶ σὲ καὶ τοὺς ἄλλους ἀνθρώπους
> τὸ ἀδικεῖν τοῦ ἀδικεῖσθαι κάκιον ἡγεῖσθαι καὶ τὸ μὴ
> διδόναι δίκην τοῦ διδόναι.

Notes: 2–3. **τοῦ ἀδικεῖσθαι . . . τοῦ διδόναι**: genitives of comparison after the comparative adjective κάκιον.

5.2 Xenophon, *Anabasis* 1.6.7: Cyrus questions Orontas, pointing out that Orontas, after doing him injury, had realized that his own power was unimpressive and sought Cyrus' pardon.

> οὐκοῦν, ἔφη ὁ Κῦρος, ὁπότ᾽ αὖ ἔγνως τὴν σαυτοῦ δύναμιν,
> ἐλθὼν ἐπὶ τὸν τῆς Ἀρτέμιδος βωμὸν μεταμέλειν τέ σοι

ἔφησθα καὶ πείσας ἐμὲ πιστὰ πάλιν ἔδωκάς μοι καὶ ἔλαβες
παρ᾽ ἐμοῦ; καὶ ταῦθ᾽ ὡμολόγει Ὀρόντας.

Notes: 3. **πιστά**: "pledges."

5.3 Plato, *Apology* 38d–39a: Socrates has been condemned to
death by an Athenian jury. He says that this is because he would not
pander to their expectations of how a defendant ought to behave.
He is resolutely unwilling to do this.

ἀλλ᾽ ἀπορίᾳ μὲν ἑάλωκα, οὐ μέντοι λόγων, ἀλλὰ τόλμης
καὶ ἀναισχυντίας καὶ τοῦ μὴ ἐθέλειν λέγειν πρὸς ὑμᾶς
τοιαῦτα οἷ᾽ ἂν ὑμῖν μὲν ἥδιστα ἦν ἀκούειν—θρηνοῦντός
τέ μου καὶ ὀδυρομένου καὶ ἄλλα ποιοῦντος καὶ λέγοντος
πολλὰ καὶ ἀνάξια ἐμοῦ, ὡς ἐγώ φημι, οἷα δὴ καὶ εἴθισθε   5
ὑμεῖς τῶν ἄλλων ἀκούειν. ἀλλ᾽ οὔτε τότε ᾠήθην δεῖν ἕνεκα
τοῦ κινδύνου πρᾶξαι οὐδὲν ἀνελεύθερον, οὔτε νῦν μοι
μεταμέλει οὕτως ἀπολογησαμένῳ, ἀλλὰ πολὺ μᾶλλον
αἱροῦμαι ὧδε ἀπολογησάμενος τεθνάναι ἢ ἐκείνως ζῆν.
οὔτε γὰρ ἐν δίκῃ οὔτ᾽ ἐν πολέμῳ οὔτ᾽ ἐμὲ οὔτ᾽ ἄλλον   10
οὐδένα δεῖ τοῦτο μηχανᾶσθαι, ὅπως ἀποφεύξεται πᾶν
ποιῶν θάνατον.

Notes: 1. **ἑάλωκα**: (from ἁλίσκομαι) "I have been caught, caught out."
5. **εἴθισθε**: (from ἐθίζω) "you have become accustomed."
6. **ᾠήθην**: aorist of οἶμαι = I think.
9. **τεθνάναι**: perfect infinitive of θνήσκω = I die.
11–12. **ἀποφεύξεται . . . θάνατον**: "he will escape death."

5.4 Euripides, *Medea* 271–76: King Creon tells the barbarian
princess Medea that he is exiling her and her children from his
country.

Κρέων

σὲ τὴν σκυθρωπὸν καὶ πόσει θυμουμένην,
Μήδει᾽, ἀνεῖπον τῆσδε γῆς ἔξω περᾶν

φυγάδα, λαβοῦσαν δισσὰ σὺν σαυτῇ τέκνα,
καὶ μή τι μέλλειν· ὡς ἐγὼ βραβεὺς λόγου
τοῦδ᾽ εἰμί, κοὐκ ἄπειμι πρὸς δόμους πάλιν   5
πρὶν ἄν σε γαίας τερμόνων ἔξω βάλω.

Notes: 1. **σκυθρωπόν**: "grim-faced," "sullen."
2. **ἀνεῖπον**: "I order" (dramatic aorist).
3. **δισσὰ ... τέκνα**: "(your) two children."
4. **βραβεὺς λόγου τοῦδ᾽**: "enforcer of this order" (lit. "word").
5. **δόμους**: the poetic plural tells us that it is a grand house; it is in fact the royal palace.

II. αὐτός

This pronoun means self (himself, herself, itself) when it stands outside the article and the noun (before or after); it means "the same" when it comes after the article.

When it stands on its own in the nominative it means "self"; on its own in all other cases, it means "him, her, it".

5.5   Thucydides, *Histories* 2.61.2: the Athenians have turned on their leading statesman, Pericles, because of their sufferings in the Peloponnesian War. He defends himself on the grounds of his consistency.

καὶ ἐγὼ μὲν ὁ αὐτός εἰμι καὶ οὐκ ἐξίσταμαι· ὑμεῖς δὲ
μεταβάλλετε ...

Notes: 1. **ἐξίσταμαι**: "I change my position."

5.6   Thucydides, *Histories* 4.78.4: the Spartan Brasidas asks the Thessalians, who are friendly with Sparta's enemy Athens, to allow him to pass through their territory.

ἔλεγε δὲ καὶ αὐτὸς ὁ Βρασίδας τῇ Θεσσαλῶν γῇ καὶ αὐτοῖς
φίλος ὢν ἰέναι καὶ Ἀθηναίοις πολεμίοις οὖσι καὶ οὐκ
ἐκείνοις ὅπλα ἐπιφέρειν, Θεσσαλοῖς τε οὐκ εἰδέναι καὶ
Λακεδαιμονίοις ἔχθραν οὖσαν ὥστε τῇ ἀλλήλων γῇ μὴ
χρῆσθαι, νῦν τε ἀκόντων ἐκείνων οὐκ ἂν προελθεῖν (οὐδὲ   5
γὰρ ἂν δύνασθαι), οὐ μέντοι ἀξιοῦν γε εἴργεσθαι.

Notes: 1. **αὐτοῖς**: i.e., to the Thessalians.
2–3. **φίλος ὢν ἰέναι καὶ ... ὅπλα ἐπιφέρειν**: "that he was coming as a friend (to) ... and that he was bearing arms" (against—with dative).
3–5. **καὶ Λακεδαιμονίοις ἔχθραν οὖσαν ὥστε τῇ ἀλλήλων γῇ μὴ χρῆσθαι**: "that there was any ill feeling between the Thessalians and Lacedaemonians that prevented either of them from passing through the territory of the other."
4. **ὥστε**: + infinitive = with the result that (see result clauses, Chapter 14)
6. **οὐ μέντοι ἀξιοῦν γε εἴργεσθαι**: "but he did not think it right that he should be prevented" (still part of the indirect statement construction).

5.7 Antiphon, *On the murder of Herodes* 50: the person who sticks to his story even after being tortured is more to be trusted than the man who changes it.

> ποτέρῳ οὖν εἰκός ἐστι πιστεῦσαι, τῷ διὰ τέλους τὸν
> αὐτὸν ἀεὶ λόγον λέγοντι, ἢ τῷ τοτὲ μὲν φάσκοντι τοτὲ δ᾽
> οὔ; ἀλλὰ καὶ ἄνευ βασάνου τοιαύτης οἱ τοὺς αὐτοὺς αἰεὶ
> περὶ τῶν αὐτῶν λόγους λέγοντες πιστότεροί εἰσι τῶν
> διαφερομένων σφίσιν αὐτοῖς.   5

Notes: 1. **διὰ τέλους**: "throughout."
2. **τοτὲ μὲν φάσκοντι τοτὲ δ᾽**: "at one moment saying something, at another. . . ."
3. **καὶ ἄνευ βασάνου τοιαύτης**: "quite apart from the kind of torture employed." Under Athenian law slaves giving evidence in a law court were tortured. The idea was to make them more afraid of the state than of their master.
4–5. **τῶν διαφερομένων σφίσιν αὐτοῖς**: "people being inconsistent with themselves" (genitive of comparison).

5.8 Lysias 1.12–13: the speaker tells how his baby was wailing and he ordered his wife to go and breastfeed the child. Since, as the speaker will later discover, she had her boyfriend in the house, she extemporized a wheeze to lock him in a room.

> καὶ ἐγὼ τὴν γυναῖκα ἀπιέναι ἐκέλευον καὶ δοῦναι τῷ
> παιδίῳ τὸν τιτθόν, ἵνα παύσηται κλᾶον. ἡ δὲ τὸ μὲν

πρῶτον οὐκ ἤθελεν, ὡς ἂν ἀσμένη με ἑωρακυῖα ἥκοντα
διὰ χρόνου· ἐπειδὴ δὲ ἐγὼ ὠργιζόμην καὶ ἐκέλευον αὐτὴν
ἀπιέναι, 'ἵνα σύ γε' ἔφη 'πειρᾷς ἐνταῦθα τὴν παιδίσκην·   5
καὶ πρότερον δὲ μεθύων εἷλκες αὐτήν.' κἀγὼ μὲν ἐγέλων,
ἐκείνη δὲ ἀναστᾶσα καὶ ἀπιοῦσα προστίθησι τὴν θύραν,
προσποιουμένη παίζειν, καὶ τὴν κλεῖν ἐφέλκεται. κἀγὼ
τούτων οὐδὲν ἐνθυμούμενος οὐδ' ὑπονοῶν ἐκάθευδον
ἄσμενος, ἥκων ἐξ ἀγροῦ.   10

Notes: 3–4. **ὡς ἂν ἀσμένη με ἑωρακυῖα ἥκοντα διὰ χρόνου**: "as if she
was delighted that she had seen me after I had come (home) after a
(long) time."
5. **πειρᾷς ἐνταῦθα τὴν παιδίσκην**: "may make a pass here at the maid."
6. **εἷλκες**: "you tried to manhandle."
κἀγώ: crasis.
7. **προστίθησι**: i.e., "shuts."
8. **τὴν κλεῖν ἐφέλκεται**: "she pulls out the key."

5.9 Thucydides, *Histories* 4.14.1: the Athenians win a naval
victory.

οἱ δ' Ἀθηναῖοι γνόντες καθ' ἑκάτερον τὸν ἔσπλουν
ὥρμησαν ἐπ' αὐτούς, καὶ τὰς μὲν πλείους καὶ μετεώρους
ἤδη τῶν νεῶν καὶ ἀντιπρῴρους προσπεσόντες ἐς φυγὴν
κατέστησαν, καὶ ἐπιδιώκοντες ὡς διὰ βραχέος ἔτρωσαν
μὲν πολλάς, πέντε δὲ ἔλαβον, καὶ μίαν τούτων αὐτοῖς   5
ἀνδράσιν.

Notes: 1. **γνόντες**: aorist participle of γιγνώσκω; they realized that the
Spartans had not blocked the entrances to the bay.
καθ' ἑκάτερον τὸν ἔσπλουν: "through both entrances."
2–3. **τὰς ... πλείους καὶ μετεώρους ἤδη τῶν νεῶν καὶ ἀντιπρῴρους**:
"the majority of the ships (which were) out from the land [lit. on the
high sea] with their prows facing them."
4. **ὡς διὰ βραχέος**: "as (best they could) over the short distance."
ἔτρωσαν: "they crippled" (lit. "wounded").
5–6. **αὐτοῖς ἀνδράσιν**: "crew [lit. men] and all," an idiomatic use of
αὐτός.

CHAPTER 6

Indefinite and Demonstrative Pronouns

The **indefinite pronoun** τις has the same forms as the interrogative τίς; but, since it is an enclitic, it usually throws back its accent to the last syllable of the previous word. It cannot stand first in its word group.

τις may be used as a pronoun (*someone, something*), as an indefinite article/adjective (*a, a certain*, plural *some*), or to modify the meaning of adjectives, adverbs or numerals.

The following examples should be carefully studied:

ἀφίκετό τις	*someone arrived*
ἠκούσαμέν τι	*we heard something*
εἴδομέν τινας	*we saw some people*
στρατιώτης τις ἀφίκετο	*a (certain) soldier arrived*
στρατιώτας τινὰς εἴδομεν	*we saw some soldiers*
ἀνήρ τις φοβερός ἀφίκετο	*a (certain) frightening man arrived*
φοβερός τις ἀνὴρ ἀφίκετο	*a frightening sort of man arrived*
τριάκοντά τινας εἴδομεν	*we saw some thirty people*

The main **demonstrative pronouns** are οὗτος, ὅδε (both *this*) and ἐκεῖνος (*that*). οὗτος in all its forms can be emphasized by the addition of ῑ, the so-called deictic iota (οὑτοσί *this man here*), and ἐκεῖνος has an alternative form, κεῖνος, used mostly, but not exclusively, in poetry.

In prose all these pronouns are used with the definite article, and are placed in the predicative position, i.e., either before the article or after the noun (οὗτος ὁ στρατιώτης, ὅδε ὁ παῖς, ὁ ἀνὴρ ἐκεῖνος).

Of the two words that mean "this," as a very general principle οὗτος (with its adverb οὕτως) looks backward to something just mentioned, while ὅδε and its adverb ὧδε usually look forward. But there are many exceptions in both directions.

Other demonstrative pronouns are τοιόσδε (*of such a kind*) and τοσόσδε (*so great, so much,* plural *so many*), both pointing forward to what follows; and τοιοῦτος (*of such a kind*) and τοσοῦτος (*so great, so much,* plural *so many*), both pointing backward to what came before.

6.1 Xenophon, *Anabasis* 3.1.4: Xenophon begins his account of how he came to join Cyrus' expedition against his brother Artaxerxes.

ἦν δέ τις ἐν τῇ στρατιᾷ Ξενοφῶν Ἀθηναῖος, ὃς οὔτε
στρατηγὸς οὔτε λοχαγὸς οὔτε στρατιώτης ὢν
συνηκολούθει, ἀλλὰ Πρόξενος αὐτὸν μετεπέμψατο
οἴκοθεν ξένος ὢν ἀρχαῖος· ὑπισχνεῖτο δὲ αὐτῷ, εἰ ἔλθοι,
φίλον αὐτὸν Κύρῳ ποιήσειν, ὃν αὐτὸς ἔφη κρείττω ἑαυτῷ   5
νομίζειν τῆς πατρίδος.

Notes: 3. **συνηκολούθει, ἀλλὰ . . . μετεπέμψατο**: English translation will be most fluent if a colon rather than a comma is imagined after συνηκολούθει ("was accompanying [the expedition]"), ἀλλά is translated as "rather" and the aorist μετεπέμψατο translated as a pluperfect.
Πρόξενος: a native of Thebes and commander of the Boeotian contingent in Cyrus' army.
4. **ξένος**: "guest-friend"; ξενία was a formal tie of hospitality between cities, families or individual citizens and foreign states. Any friend from abroad was automatically a ξένος.
5–6. **ὃν αὐτὸς . . . πατρίδος**: lit. "whom he himself said he thought better for himself than his native land." Proxenus means that his prospects under Cyrus were better than any he might have had at home in Thebes.

6.2   Euripides, *Alcestis* 136–40: the chorus note the arrival on stage of a maid in floods of tears and wonder whether Alcestis is still alive or already dead.

Χορός

ἀλλ᾽ ἥδ᾽ ὀπαδῶν ἐκ δόμων τις ἔρχεται
δακρυρροοῦσα· τίνα τύχην ἀκούσομαι;
πενθεῖν μέν, εἴ τι δεσπόταισι τυγχάνει,
συγγνωστόν· εἰ δ᾽ ἔτ᾽ ἐστὶν ἔμψυχος γυνὴ
εἴτ᾽ οὖν ὄλωλεν εἰδέναι βουλοίμεθ᾽ ἄν.   5

Notes: 1. **ἥδ᾽ … ἔρχεται**: "here comes"; ὅδε is regularly used in drama to point to someone or something on stage, and especially, as here, to indicate the arrival of a new character.
ὀπαδῶν … τις: "one of the maidservants."
4. **συγγνωστόν**: understand ἐστίν ("it is excusable").
εἰ δ᾽: εἰ here introduces an indirect question.
5. **εἴτ᾽ οὖν**: "or if in fact"; οὖν in this combination calls special attention to the alternative to which it belongs.
βουλοίμεθ᾽ ἄν: potential optative ("we should like").

6.3   Xenophon, *Hellenica* 5.1.13: to the huge delight of his sailors, the popular commander, Teleutias, retakes charge of the Spartan navy (388 BC). He begins an honest but encouraging speech.

ἐκ δὲ τούτου οἱ Λακεδαιμόνιοι Τελευτίαν αὖ ἐκπέμπουσιν
ἐπὶ ταύτας τὰς ναῦς ναύαρχον. ὡς δὲ εἶδον αὐτὸν ἥκοντα οἱ
ναῦται, ὑπερήσθησαν. ὁ δ᾽ αὐτοὺς συγκαλέσας εἶπε τοιάδε·
Ὦ ἄνδρες στρατιῶται, ἐγὼ χρήματα μὲν οὐκ ἔχων ἥκω· ἐὰν
μέντοι θεὸς ἐθέλῃ καὶ ὑμεῖς συμπροθυμῆσθε, πειράσομαι   5
τὰ ἐπιτήδεια ὑμῖν ὡς πλεῖστα πορίζειν.

Notes: 1. **ἐκ … τούτου**: this expression, regularly translated as "after this" (cf. the more common μετὰ ταῦτα), has also a strong sense of "as a result of this," in this case the fact that Teleutias' predecessor, Eteonicus, had so forfeited his men's respect, by not paying them, that they refused to row at his command.
3. **εἶπε τοιάδε**: "spoke as follows" (lit. "said such things").
6. **τὰ ἐπιτήδεια … ὡς πλεῖστα**: "as many provisions as possible."

6.4   Homer, *Iliad* 10.382–89: the Trojan Dolon has been surprised on a night reconnaissance expedition by Odysseus and Diomedes. In terror for his life he has just offered to ransom himself from his own supply of gold, bronze and iron.

τὸν δ᾽ ἀπαμειβόμενος προσέφη πολύμητις Ὀδυσσεύς·
Θάρσει, μηδέ τί τοι θάνατος καταθύμιος ἔστω.
ἀλλ᾽ ἄγε μοι τόδε εἰπὲ καὶ ἀτρεκέως κατάλεξον·
πῇ δὴ οὕτως ἐπὶ νῆας ἀπὸ στρατοῦ ἔρχεαι οἶος
νύκτα δι᾽ ὀρφναίην, ὅτε θ᾽ εὕδουσι βροτοὶ ἄλλοι;   5
ἤ τινα συλήσων νεκύων κατατεθνηώτων;
ἦ σ᾽ Ἕκτωρ προέηκε διασκοπιᾶσθαι ἕκαστα
νῆας ἔπι γλαφυράς; ἦ σ᾽ αὐτὸν θυμὸς ἀνῆκε;

Notes: 2. **Θάρσει... ἔστω**: despite Odysseus' encouraging tone, Diomedes later brutally beheads Dolon with his sword; μηδέ τί: the τι (its accent in the text is thrown back from the enclitic τοι that follows) is adverbial ("in any way"); τοι = σοι.
4. **πῇ δή**: "just why?"
οὕτως: "like this."
ἔρχεαι: = ἔρχει, present tense (2nd singular) of ἔρχομαι.
6. **ἤ τινα... κατατεθνηώτων**: "is it to strip one of the corpses of the dead [lit. dead corpses]?" συλήσων is a future participle of purpose, and κατατεθνηώτων the Homeric perfect participle (genitive plural) of καταθνήσκω.
7. **προέηκε**: Homeric form of προῆκε.
διασκοπιᾶσθαι: "to spy out," an infinitive of purpose.
8. **ἦ... ἀνῆκε**: "or did your own heart prompt you" (lit. "or did your heart prompt you yourself"]?"

6.5   *St. Mark's Gospel* 14. 22–26: from St. Mark's account of the Last Supper.

καὶ ἐσθιόντων αὐτῶν λαβὼν ὁ Ἰησοῦς ἄρτον εὐλογήσας
ἔκλασε, καὶ ἔδωκεν αὐτοῖς, καὶ εἶπε· Λάβετε, φάγετε·
τοῦτό ἐστι τὸ σῶμά μου. καὶ λαβὼν τὸ ποτήριον
εὐχαριστήσας ἔδωκεν αὐτοῖς, καὶ ἔπιον ἐξ αὐτοῦ πάντες.
καὶ εἶπεν αὐτοῖς· Τοῦτό ἐστι τὸ αἷμά μου τῆς καινῆς   5
διαθήκης τὸ περὶ πολλῶν ἐκχυνόμενον. ἀμὴν λέγω ὑμῖν ὅτι

οὐκέτι οὐ μὴ πίω ἐκ τοῦ γεννήματος τῆς ἀμπέλου ἕως τῆς
ἡμέρας ἐκείνης ὅταν αὐτὸ πίνω καινὸν ἐν τῇ βασιλείᾳ τοῦ
Θεοῦ. καὶ ὑμνήσαντες ἐξῆλθον εἰς τὸ ὄρος τῶν ἐλαιῶν.

Notes: 5–6. **τῆς καινῆς διαθήκης**: "of the new covenant." The new covenant
is the new "deal" or arrangement between man and God, brought into
effect by the earthly life, death and resurrection of Jesus Christ.
6. **τὸ περὶ πολλῶν ἐκχυνόμενον**: "which is poured out for many";
ἐκχύνω is a later form of ἐκχέω ("I pour out").
ἀμήν: a Hebrew adverb meaning "verily, of a truth."
7. **οὐκέτι οὐ μὴ πίω**: οὐ μή with the aorist subjunctive denotes a strong
denial = "I will no longer drink of."
γεννήματος: the "product" or "fruit" of the vine, i.e., wine.
ἕως: used here as a preposition with the genitive meaning "until."
8. **βασιλείᾳ**: "kingdom," not to be confused with βασίλεια ("queen,
princess").
9. **τὸ ὄρος τῶν ἐλαιῶν**: "the Mount of Olives," a rocky ridge east of the
old city in Jerusalem, so called for the olive groves that once covered its
slopes.

6.6 Sophocles, *Oedipus Tyrannus* 1047–57: after hearing from
a Corinthian messenger that he was given to him in infancy by a
Theban herdsman, and is not in fact the son of Polybus of Corinth,
Oedipus attempts to discover the herdsman's identity. Jocasta has
now realized the awful truth about who Oedipus actually is.

Οἰδίπους   Χορός   Ἰοκάστη

Οἰ. ἔστιν τις ὑμῶν τῶν παρεστώτων πέλας,
      ὅστις κάτοιδε τὸν βοτῆρ᾽ ὃν ἐννέπει,
      εἴτ᾽ οὖν ἐπ᾽ ἀγρῶν εἴτε κἀνθάδ᾽ εἰσιδών;
      σημήναθ᾽, ὡς ὁ καιρὸς ηὑρῆσθαι τάδε.
Χο. οἶμαι μὲν οὐδέν᾽ ἄλλον ἢ τὸν ἐξ ἀγρῶν,   5
      ὃν κἀμάτευες πρόσθεν εἰσιδεῖν· ἀτὰρ
      ἥδ᾽ ἂν τάδ᾽ οὐχ ἥκιστ᾽ ἂν Ἰοκάστη λέγοι.
Οἰ. γύναι, νοεῖς ἐκεῖνον, ὅντιν᾽ ἀρτίως
      μολεῖν ἐφιέμεσθα; τόνδ᾽ οὗτος λέγει;
Ἰο. τί δ᾽ ὅντιν᾽ εἶπε; μηδὲν ἐντραπῇς· τὰ δὲ   10
      ῥηθέντα βούλου μηδὲ μεμνῆσθαι μάτην.

Notes: 1. **τῶν παρεστώτων πέλας**: "who are standing nearby."
παρεστώτων is genitive plural masculine of παρεστώς, alternative
intransitive perfect participle of παρίστημι (the other is παρεστηκώς).
3. **εἴτ᾽ οὖν**: "whether in fact," cf. on line 2 above.
κἀνθάδ᾽: = καὶ ἐνθάδε ("here also"), i.e., in town.
4. **ὡς ... τάδε**: "as it is time for these things to be discovered";
understand ἐστίν with ὁ καιρός, which is then followed by an
accusative and infinitive (lit. "time that these things be discovered");
the perfect infinitive ηὑρῆσθαι stresses the desired completion of the
action = "discovered once and for all."
5. **οὐδέν᾽ ἄλλον**: understand αὐτὸν εἶναι ("that he is none other").
6. **κἀμάτευες**: = καὶ ἐμάτευες ("you were also seeking").
7. **ἥδ᾽ ... Ἰοκάστη**: "Jocasta here"; the demonstrative, as often,
indicates the arrival on stage of a new character; οὐχ ἥκιστ᾽: "not least,"
i.e., "best."
9. **ἐφιέμεσθα**: = ἐφιέμεθα.
τόνδ᾽ οὗτος λέγει: "is it of him that this man is speaking?"
10. **τί δ᾽ ὄντιν᾽ εἶπε**: "why (*sc.* bother about) whom he meant?"
μηδὲν ἐντραπῇς: "pay no attention at all." μή with the aorist
subjunctive expresses a specific negative command.
10–11. **τὰ δὲ ... μάτην**: "as for what's been said, don't even think
about it—it'd be pointless" (lit. "as to the things said, don't wish
even—pointlessly—to remember them"). ῥηθέντα is the neuter
accusative plural of ἐρρήθην, regularly used as the aorist passive of
λέγω.

6.7   Xenophon, *Cyropaedia* 7. 3.2: Cyrus learns of the death of his
friend and ally Abradatas.

ὁ δὲ Κῦρος καλέσας τινὰς τῶν παρόντων ὑπηρετῶν,
Εἴπατέ μοι, ἔφη, ἑωράκέ τις ὑμῶν Ἀβραδάταν; θαυμάζω
γάρ, ἔφη, ὅτι πρόσθεν θαμίζων ἐφ᾽ ἡμᾶς νῦν οὐδαμοῦ
φαίνεται. τῶν οὖν ὑπηρετῶν τις ἀπεκρίνατο ὅτι Ὦ
δέσποτα, οὐ ζῇ, ἀλλ᾽ ἐν τῇ μάχῃ ἀπέθανεν ἐμβαλὼν τὸ   5
ἅρμα εἰς τοὺς Αἰγυπτίους· οἱ δ᾽ ἄλλοι πλὴν τῶν ἑταίρων
αὐτοῦ ἐξέκλιναν, ὥς φασιν, ἐπεὶ τὸ στῖφος εἶδον τὸ
τῶν Αἰγυπτίων. καὶ νῦν γε, ἔφη, λέγεται αὐτοῦ ἡ γυνὴ
ἀνελομένη τὸν νεκρὸν καὶ ἐνθεμένη εἰς τὴν ἁρμάμαξαν,
ἐν ᾗπερ αὐτὴ ὠχεῖτο, προσκεκομικέναι αὐτὸν ἐνθάδε ποι   10
πρὸς τὸν Πακτωλὸν ποταμόν.

Notes: 2. **Ἀβραδάταν**: a king, perhaps fictional, of Susa; initially an ally of the Assyrians against Cyrus the Great, but later one of his allies. His story, particularly his romance with his wife Pantheia, is related over the course of books 5–7 of the *Cyropaedia*.

3. **θαμίζων**: "coming frequently."

4–5. **ἀπεκρίνατο ὅτι Ὦ δέσποτα**: ὅτι serves simply to indicate the direct speech, a bit like quotation marks, and shouldn't be translated.

6–7. **τῶν ἑταίρων αὐτοῦ**: "his retinue," including, of course, Abradatas himself.

10–11. **ἐνθάδε ποι ... Πακτωλόν**: "to some place here by the River Pactolus." The Pactolus is a tributary of the Hermus in Lydia; its sands contained gold, in mythology because it was by washing in its stream that King Midas freed himself of his "golden touch."

6.8 Euripides, *Orestes* 1140–48: Pylades assures Orestes, now condemned to death along with his sister Electra, that killing Helen will be a good idea.

Πυλάδης

ὁ μητροφόντης δ᾿ οὐ καλῇ ταύτην κτανών,
ἀλλ᾿ ἀπολιπὼν τοῦτ᾿ ἐπὶ τὸ βέλτιον πεσῇ,
Ἑλένης λεγόμενος τῆς πολυκτόνου φονεύς.
οὐ δεῖ ποτ᾿, οὐ δεῖ, Μενέλεων μὲν εὐτυχεῖν,
τὸν σὸν δὲ πατέρα καὶ σὲ κἀδελφὴν θανεῖν,   5
μητέρα τε—ἐῶ τοῦτ᾿· οὐ γὰρ εὐπρεπὲς λέγειν—
δόμους δ᾿ ἔχειν σοὺς δι᾿ Ἀγαμέμνονος δόρυ
λαβόντα νύμφην· μὴ γὰρ οὖν ζῴην ἔτι,
ἢν μὴ 'π᾿ ἐκείνῃ φάσγανον σπασώμεθα.

Notes: 1. **ὁ μητροφόντης**: "the matricide," a reference to Orestes' earlier murder of his mother, Clytemnestra.

καλῇ: future middle (2nd singular) of καλέω with passive sense.

ταύτην: "her," i.e., Helen.

2. **ἀπολιπὼν τοῦτ᾿**: "leaving behind this [title]."

ἐπὶ τὸ βέλτιον πεσῇ: "you will come [lit. fall] to something better."

3. **Ἑλένης ... τῆς πολυκτόνου**: Helen is πολυκτόνος as she is regarded as responsible for the slaughter of all those who fell at Troy.

4. **οὐ δεῖ ποτ᾿, οὐ δεῖ**:, note the emphatic repetition. It can be captured in English by something like "it is never, never right."

5. **κἀδελφήν**: crasis for καὶ ἀδελφήν.

6. **μητέρα τε—ἐῶ τοῦτ'**: "and your mother—but I let that matter go." Pylades diplomatically says no more about Clytemnestra's murder: matricide is in a different category from all the rest.

7. **δόμους δ' ἔχειν σούς**: "and that *he* should have your house": Pylades reverts again, awkwardly, to Menelaus as subject of the infinitive ἔχειν. Once Orestes has been put to death, Menelaus will succeed to his property in Argos.

8. **νύμφην**: "his bride," i.e., Helen.

ζῴην: present optative (1st singular) of ζάω.

9. **ἤν**: = ἐάν.

6.9 Demosthenes, *De Corona* 304–305: Demosthenes makes clear to the Athenians that had there been just one man like him in each Greek state, Greece could have avoided her current misfortunes.

> εἰ δ' οἷος ἐγὼ παρ' ὑμῖν κατὰ τὴν ἐμαυτοῦ τάξιν, εἷς ἐν
> ἑκάστῃ τῶν Ἑλληνίδων πόλεων ἀνὴρ ἐγένετο, μᾶλλον
> δ' εἰ ἕν' ἄνδρα μόνον Θετταλία καὶ ἕν' ἄνδρ' Ἀρκαδία
> ταὐτὰ φρονοῦντ' ἔσχεν ἐμοί, οὐδένες οὔτε τῶν ἔξω Πυλῶν
> Ἑλλήνων οὔτε τῶν εἴσω τοῖς παροῦσι κακοῖς ἐκέχρηντ'   5
> ἄν, ἀλλὰ πάντες ἂν ὄντες ἐλεύθεροι καὶ αὐτόνομοι μετὰ
> πάσης ἀδείας ἀσφαλῶς ἐν εὐδαιμονίᾳ τὰς ἑαυτῶν ᾤκουν
> πατρίδας, τῶν τοσούτων καὶ τοιούτων ἀγαθῶν ὑμῖν καὶ
> τοῖς ἄλλοις Ἀθηναίοις ἔχοντες χάριν δι' ἐμέ.

Notes: 1–2. **εἰ δ' ... ἐγένετο**: after translating εἰ δ' ("but if"), go straight to εἷς ... ἐγένετο, returning then to οἷος ἐγὼ ... τάξιν ("such as I was in my own appointed role among you").

2–3. **μᾶλλον δ' εἰ**: "or rather if."

4. **ταὐτὰ φρονοῦντ' ... ἐμοί**: "with the same views as I have"; ταὐτά = τὰ αὐτά.

4–5. **τῶν ἔξω Πυλῶν Ἑλλήνων**: "of the Greeks beyond Thermopylae." What then will τῶν εἴσω be?

5–6. **ἐκέχρηντ' ἄν**: pluperfect (3rd plural) of χράομαι ("would have experienced"). The pluperfect, rather than the more normal aorist, in this unfulfilled past condition emphasizes that the evils are still continuing.

6. **ἀλλὰ πάντες ἄν**: ἄν is to be taken with ᾤκουν.

8. **τῶν τοσούτων καὶ τοιούτων ἀγαθῶν**: "for such manifold blessings" (lit. "for so many and such blessings").

9. **τοῖς ἄλλοις Ἀθηναίοις**: "the rest of the Athenians."

10. **ἔχοντες χάριν**: both χάριν ἔχω and χάριν οἶδα are regularly used to mean "I am grateful."

6.10   Herodotus, *Histories* 2.100: Nitocris, queen of Egypt, wreaks a terrible vengeance on the murderers of her brother.

> μετὰ δὲ τοῦτον κατέλεγον οἱ ἱρέες ἐκ βύβλου ἄλλων
> βασιλέων τριηκοσίων καὶ τριήκοντα οὐνόματα. ἐν
> τοσαύτῃσι δὲ γενεῇσι ἀνθρώπων ὀκτωκαίδεκα μὲν
> Αἰθίοπες ἦσαν, μία δὲ γυνὴ ἐπιχωρίη, οἱ δὲ ἄλλοι ἄνδρες
> Αἰγύπτιοι. τῇ δὲ γυναικὶ οὔνομα ἦν, ἥτις ἐβασίλευσε, τό   5
> περ τῇ Βαβυλωνίῃ, Νίτωκρις· τὴν ἔλεγον τιμωρέουσαν
> ἀδελφεῷ, τὸν Αἰγύπτιοι βασιλεύοντα σφέων ἀπέκτειναν,
> ἀποκτείναντες δὲ οὕτω ἐκείνῃ ἀπέδοσαν τὴν βασιληίην,
> τούτῳ τιμωρέουσαν πολλοὺς Αἰγυπτίων διαφθεῖραι
> δόλῳ. ποιησαμένην γάρ μιν οἴκημα περίμηκες ὑπόγαιον   10
> καινοῦν τῷ λόγῳ, νόῳ δὲ ἄλλα μηχανᾶσθαι· καλέσασαν δέ
> μιν Αἰγυπτίων τοὺς μάλιστα μεταιτίους τοῦ φόνου ᾔδεε
> πολλοὺς ἱστιᾶν, δαινυμένοισι δὲ ἐπεῖναι τὸν ποταμὸν δι᾽
> αὐλῶνος κρυπτοῦ μεγάλου. ταύτης μὲν πέρι τοσαῦτα
> ἔλεγον, πλὴν ὅτι αὐτήν μιν, ὡς τοῦτο ἐξέργαστο, ῥῖψαι ἐς   15
> οἴκημα σποδοῦ πλέον, ὅκως ἀτιμώρητος γένηται.

Notes: 1. **τοῦτον**: "him," i.e., King Min or Menes, the first king of Dynasty I and founder of Memphis, c. 3200 BC.

ἱρέες: = ἱερῆς

ἐκ βύβλου: "from a papyrus roll."

5–6. **τό περ τῇ Βαβυλωνίῃ**: "just as of [lit. "to"] the Babylonian (queen)." Herodotus tells (*Histories*, 1, 185) of a Babylonian queen with the same name.

6. **τήν**: connecting relative, subject of διαφθεῖραι.

7. **ἀδελφεῷ**: = ἀδελφῷ.

8. **οὕτω**: "then" (lit. "thus," i.e., by killing).

9. **τούτῳ τιμωρέουσαν**: picks up the previous τιμωρέουσαν ἀδελφεῷ after the two intervening clauses.

10. **ποιησαμένην γάρ μιν**: "for (they said that) having made … she"; the indirect speech continues right down to δι᾽ αὐλῶνος κρυπτοῦ μεγάλου.

τῷ λόγῳ, νόῳ δέ: "in word, but in fact" (lit. "in mind'"). Such a contrast is normally indicated by λόγῳ and ἔργῳ.

Αἰγυπτίων ... ᾔδεε: "those of the Egyptians who she knew were most responsible for the murder"; τούς: relative pronoun; ᾔδεε : = ᾔδει, past tense (third singular) of οἶδα.

πολλοὺς ἱστιᾶν: "held a great feast" (lit. "entertained many"); ἱστιάω = ἑστιάω.

ἐπεῖναι: Ionic aorist infinitive active of ἐφίημι ("I let in").

ταύτης ... πέρι: notice the anastrophe, the throwing back of the accent on a disyllabic preposition when it follows its noun.

τοσαῦτα: "no more than this" (lit. "[just] so much").

πλὴν ὅτι: "except that," a formula that does not affect the sentence's overall construction. μιν: = (here) ἑαυτήν.

ἐξέργαστο: probably middle in meaning ("when she had done this"), rather than passive ("when this had been done"). Note the pluperfect stressing the completion of the action. ἀτιμώρητος: "unpunished." Nitocris commits suicide so that no one can punish her for what she has done.

CHAPTER 7

Participles 1

1

Participles are verbal adjectives; i.e., they are formed from verbs and so describe an action, but they are adjectives and so in Greek regularly agree with a noun or pronoun, or with a noun or pronoun understood.

The future participle, often with ὡς, can express purpose (see Chapter 13).

7.1 Thucydides, *Histories* 3.112.2: the Athenian general Demosthenes moves off to attack the Ambraciots. The mountains referred to are in a region called Amphilochia.

> ὁ δὲ Δημοσθένης δειπνήσας ἐχώρει καὶ τὸ ἄλλο στράτευμα
> ἀπὸ ἑσπέρας εὐθύς, αὐτὸς μὲν τὸ ἥμισυ ἔχων ἐπὶ τῆς
> ἐσβολῆς, τὸ δ᾽ ἄλλο διὰ τῶν Ἀμφιλοχικῶν ὀρῶν.

Notes: 1. **καὶ τὸ ἄλλο στράτευμα**: "and the rest of the army (set out too)."
2. **ἀπὸ ἑσπέρας εὐθύς**: "immediately after nightfall" (lit. evening).
2–3. **ἐπὶ τῆς ἐσβολῆς**: "toward the pass."

7.2 Xenophon, *Memorabilia* 4.4.4: on trial for his life in a case brought against him by Meletus, Socrates did not stoop to degrading methods of avoiding the death penalty.

καὶ ὅτε τὴν ὑπὸ Μελήτου γραφὴν ἔφευγε . . . ἐκεῖνος
οὐδὲν ἠθέλησε τῶν εἰωθότων ἐν τῷ δικαστηρίῳ παρὰ
τοὺς νόμους ποιῆσαι, ἀλλὰ ῥᾳδίως ἂν ἀφεθεὶς ὑπὸ τῶν
δικαστῶν, εἰ καὶ μετρίως τι τούτων ἐποίησε, προείλετο
μᾶλλον τοῖς νόμοις ἐμμένων ἀποθανεῖν ἢ παρανομῶν ζῆν.　5

Notes: 1. **τὴν . . . γραφὴν ἔφευγε**: "he was put on trial" (lit. "he was
running away from the indictment").
2. **τῶν εἰωθότων**: "of the things usually done" (lit. "of the usual things").
3. **ῥᾳδίως ἂν ἀφεθείς**: "though he would easily have been acquitted":
ἀφεθείς is the aorist passive participle of ἀφίημι.
4. **προείλετο**: from προαιρέομαι.

7.3 Demosthenes, *De Corona* 124: Demosthenes has just said that
the law courts are not places for airing scurrilous gossip. He asks
Aeschines whether he is the enemy of the city or of Demosthenes
himself.

ταῦτα τοίνυν εἰδὼς Αἰσχίνης οὐδὲν ἧττον ἐμοῦ, πομπεύειν
ἀντὶ τοῦ κατηγορεῖν εἵλετο. οὐ μὴν οὐδ' ἐνταῦθ' ἔλαττον
ἔχων δίκαιός ἐστιν ἀπελθεῖν. ἤδη δ' ἐπὶ ταῦτα πορεύσομαι,
τοσοῦτον αὐτὸν ἐρωτήσας. πότερόν σέ τις, Αἰσχίνη, τῆς
πόλεως ἐχθρὸν ἢ ἐμὸν εἶναι φῇ;　5

Notes: 1. **πομπεύειν**: "to fling insults."
2. **εἵλετο**: from αἱρέομαι.
2–3. **οὐ μὴν οὐδ' ἐνταῦθ' ἔλαττον ἔχων δίκαιός ἐστιν ἀπελθεῖν**: "yet it
is not right that he should get off [lit. go away] here with any less himself."
3. **ἐπὶ ταῦτα**: i.e., to the invective to come.
4–5. **τις . . . φῇ**: lit. "someone says," i.e., "people say (that)."

7.4 Homer, *Iliad* 22.131–38: the Trojan leader Hector has resolved
to stand fast to meet Achilles, the son of Peleus, but as the Greek
warrior advances on him, he turns and runs.

ὣς ὅρμαινε μένων, ὃ δέ οἱ σχεδὸν ἦλθεν Ἀχιλλεὺς
ἶσος Ἐνυαλίῳ κορυθάϊκι πτολεμιστῇ
σείων Πηλιάδα μελίην κατὰ δεξιὸν ὦμον
δεινήν· ἀμφὶ δὲ χαλκὸς ἐλάμπετο εἴκελος αὐγῇ

ἢ πυρὸς αἰθομένου ἢ ἠελίου ἀνιόντος.   5

Ἕκτορα δ᾽, ὡς ἐνόησεν, ἕλε τρόμος· οὐδ᾽ ἄρ᾽ ἔτ᾽ ἔτλη

αὖθι μένειν, ὀπίσω δὲ πύλας λίπε, βῆ δὲ φοβηθείς·

Πηλεΐδης δ᾽ ἐπόρουσε ποσὶ κραιπνοῖσι πεποιθώς.

Notes: 1. **οἱ σχεδόν**: "near him."

2. **Ἐνναλίῳ κορυθάϊκι πτολεμιστῇ**: Enyalios (i.e., Ares, the god of war), the warrior with his waving crest.

3. **Πηλιάδα μελίην**: "his Pelian ash spear": the spear had been given to Achilles' father, Peleus, by the centaur Chiron, who lived on Mount Pelion.

κατά: here "over."

4. **ἀμφί**: "around (him)."

6. **ἕλε**: aorist of αἱρέω.

7. **φοβηθείς**: φοβέω = I put to flight.

8. **ἐπόρουσε**: "rushed after him."

ποσὶ κραιπνοῖσι πεποιθώς: "trusting in his swift feet."

7.5 Thucydides, *Histories* 6.59.4: the tyrant of Athens Hippias is driven out by the Spartans but takes refuge with Darius, king of Persia, and returns with the latter's forces to Marathon to try to reestablish his rule. Medes is another name for Persians.

τυραννεύσας δὲ ἔτη τρία Ἱππίας ἔτι Ἀθηναίων καὶ παυθεὶς

ἐν τῷ τετάρτῳ ὑπὸ Λακεδαιμονίων καὶ Ἀλκμεωνιδῶν τῶν

φευγόντων, ἐχώρει ὑπόσπονδος ἔς τε Σίγειον καὶ παρ᾽

Αἰαντίδην ἐς Λάμψακον, ἐκεῖθεν δὲ ὡς βασιλέα Δαρεῖον,

ὅθεν καὶ ὁρμώμενος ἐς Μαραθῶνα ὕστερον ἔτει εἰκοστῷ   5

ἤδη γέρων ὢν μετὰ Μήδων ἐστράτευσεν.

Notes: 1. **ἔτη τρία ... ἔτι**: "for three years more."

1–3. **παυθεὶς ... ὑπὸ Λακεδαιμονίων καὶ Ἀλκμεωνιδῶν τῶν φευγόντων**: "after being deposed [lit. having been stopped] by the Spartans and the Alcmaeonids in exile." The Alcmaeonids were a prominent aristocratic Athenian family.

3. **ἐχώρει ὑπόσπονδος**: "he retired under a treaty." For Sigeion and Lampsacus, see map. Aiantides was the tyrant of Lampsacus and Hippias' son-in-law.

7.6 Xenophon, *Anabasis* 2.3.21: the Greek Clearchus explains to the Persian king's ambassador that he and his fellow Greeks fought against him only because they were misled by the pretender to his throne.

πρὸς ταῦτα μεταστάντες οἱ Ἕλληνες ἐβουλεύοντο· καὶ
ἀπεκρίναντο, Κλέαρχος δ᾽ ἔλεγεν· ἡμεῖς οὔτε συνήλθομεν
ὡς βασιλεῖ πολεμήσοντες οὔτε ἐπορευόμεθα ἐπὶ βασιλέα,
ἀλλὰ πολλὰς προφάσεις Κῦρος ηὕρισκεν, ὡς καὶ σὺ εὖ
οἶσθα, ἵνα ὑμᾶς τε ἀπαρασκεύους λάβοι καὶ ἡμᾶς ἐνθάδε   5
ἀγάγοι.

Notes: 1. **πρὸς ταῦτα μεταστάντες**: "withdrawing in view of these things."
3. **ὡς ... πολεμήσοντες**: ὡς with the future participle expressing purpose.
5. **ἀπαρασκεύους**: "unprepared."
6. **ἀγάγοι**: aorist optative of ἄγω.

II

The definite article with the participle is often the equivalent of a relative clause.

7.7 Thucydides, *Histories* 8.68.1: the anti-democratic Peisander moves a resolution.

ἦν δὲ ὁ μὲν τὴν γνώμην ταύτην εἰπὼν Πείσανδρος, καὶ
τἆλλα ἐκ τοῦ προφανοῦς προθυμότατα ξυγκαταλύσας τὸν
δῆμον.

Notes: 1–2. **καὶ τἆλλα ἐκ τοῦ προφανοῦς**: "in other respects also to all appearances."
2. **ξυγκαταλύσας**: "having helped in overthrowing."
2–3. **τὸν δῆμον**: i.e., the democracy.

III

Note the frequent use of participles with such adverbs as ἅτε (ἅτε δή), οἷα or οἷον (*inasmuch as, seeing that*), ὡς (*on the grounds that*), καίπερ (*although*), and ὥσπερ (*as, as if*). Negative οὐ.

7.8 Thucydides, *Histories* 4.39.3: Cleon, a leading Athenian politician and general, fulfills his promise to end a campaign against the

Spartans, the leaders of the Peloponnesian forces, by capturing the
Spartans stranded on an island off Pylos within twenty days.

οἱ μὲν δὴ Ἀθηναῖοι καὶ οἱ Πελοποννήσιοι ἀνεχώρησαν τῷ
στρατῷ ἐκ τῆς Πύλου ἑκάτεροι ἐπ᾽ οἴκου, καὶ τοῦ Κλέωνος
καίπερ μανιώδης οὖσα ἡ ὑπόσχεσις ἀπέβη· ἐντὸς γὰρ
εἴκοσιν ἡμερῶν ἤγαγε τοὺς ἄνδρας, ὥσπερ ὑπέστη.

Notes: 2. ἐπ᾽ οἴκου: "to home."
3. ἀπέβη: i.e., "came to pass."
4. ὑπέστη: "he had promised."

7.9 Thucydides 2.59.2: the Athenians turn on Pericles on the
grounds that he had persuaded them to fight the Spartans.

καὶ τὸν μὲν Περικλέα ἐν αἰτίᾳ εἶχον ὡς πείσαντα σφᾶς
πολεμεῖν καὶ δι᾽ ἐκεῖνον ταῖς ξυμφοραῖς περιπεπτωκότες,
πρὸς δὲ τοὺς Λακεδαιμονίους ὥρμηντο ξυγχωρεῖν· καὶ
πρέσβεις τινὰς πέμψαντες ὡς αὐτοὺς ἄπρακτοι ἐγένοντο.
πανταχόθεν τε τῇ γνώμῃ ἄποροι καθεστηκότες ἐνέκειντο   5
τῷ Περικλεῖ.

Notes: 2. ταῖς ξυμφοραῖς περιπεπτωκότες: "having fallen amid
disasters."
3. ὥρμηντο: "they were eager."
4. ἄπρακτοι: "without achieving anything."
5. πανταχόθεν: "in every way."
ἄποροι καθεστηκότες: lit. "reduced to a state of helplessness."
ἐνέκειντο: "they attacked" (ἔγκειμαι + dat.)

IV

Participles are often used with the meaning of the protasis in conditional clauses. Negative μή.

7.10 Euripides, Fragment 461: happiness calls for hard work.

οὐκ ἂν δύναιο μὴ καμὼν εὐδαιμονεῖν.

Notes: 1. μὴ καμών: = εἰ μὴ κάμοις (from κάμνω).

CHAPTER 8

Relative Clauses

The most common relative pronoun is ὅς, ἥ, ὅ ("who, which, that"). In a relative clause it agrees with its antecedent in gender and number, but its case is determined by its function in its own clause.

Other relative pronouns are ὅσπερ, ἥπερ, ὅπερ (a more specific form of ὅς, ἥ, ὅ), ὅστις, ἥτις, ὅ τι (more general); οἷος, -α, -ον ("of the kind that"); and ὅσος, -η, -ον (sing. "as much as," pl. "as many as").

Two types of Relative Attraction should be noted: (1) of the antecedent into the relative clause, and (2), more commonly, of the relative pronoun into the case of its antecedent, especially when the relative would be accusative, and the antecedent is genitive or dative.

Relative clauses may also be introduced by relative adverbs, especially οὗ, ὅπου, ἔνθα, all meaning "where."

8.1 Menander, *Sententiae* 560, 583: self-love is normal, but divine love lethal.

(I) οὐκ ἔστιν οὐδείς, ὅστις οὐχ αὑτόν φιλεῖ.

(II) ὃν οἱ θεοὶ φιλοῦσιν, ἀποθνῄσκει νέος.

Notes: 1. **οὐκ ἔστιν οὐδείς**: the two negatives, in this order (simple followed by compound), reinforce each other ("there is no one").

αὐτόν: a regular contraction of ἑαυτόν, the reflexive pronoun.
2. **ὃν οἱ θεοὶ φιλοῦσιν**: the antecedent is here omitted ("[He] whom…").

8.2 Xenophon, *Cyropaedia* 3.3.44: an Assyrian king encourages his troops before battle.

> ἄνδρες Ἀσσύριοι, νῦν δεῖ ἄνδρας ἀγαθοὺς εἶναι· νῦν γὰρ
> ὑπὲρ ψυχῶν τῶν ὑμετέρων ἀγὼν καὶ ὑπὲρ γῆς ἐν ᾗ ἔφυτε
> καὶ περὶ οἴκων ἐν οἷς ἐτράφητε, καὶ ὑπὲρ γυναικῶν τε καὶ
> τέκνων καὶ περὶ πάντων ὧν πέπασθε ἀγαθῶν. νικήσαντες
> μὲν γὰρ ἁπάντων τούτων ὑμεῖς ὥσπερ πρόσθεν κύριοι   5
> ἔσεσθε· εἰ δ᾽ ἡττηθήσεσθε, εὖ ἴστε ὅτι παραδώσετε ταῦτα
> πάντα τοῖς πολεμίοις.

Notes: 1. **ἀγαθούς**: "brave" here, rather than the more general "good."
2. **ἀγών**: crasis for ὁ ἀγών.
ἔφυτε: "you were born," intransitive aorist (2nd plural) of φύω. This aorist, ἔφυν, like the perfect πέφυκα, regularly has a present meaning ("I am by nature"), but not here.
3. **ἐτράφητε**: aorist passive (2nd plural) of τρέφω ("I bring up/rear").
4. **πάντων ὧν πέπασθε ἀγαθῶν**: = πάντων τῶν ἀγαθῶν ἃ πεπᾶσθε ("all the blessings you possess"). There is attraction here both of the relative pronoun into the case of the antecedent, and of part of the antecedent into the relative clause. πεπᾶσθε: perfect (2nd person) of πάομαι ("I acquire").
6. **εἰ δ᾽ ἡττηθήσεσθε**: this use of εἰ with the future indicative, rather than ἐάν with the subjunctive, is particularly appropriate given the threatening nature of the main clause.

8.3 Sophocles, *Oedipus at Colonus* 49–53: Oedipus, wandering with his daughter Antigone, wants to know exactly where he is.

Οἰδίπους   Ξένος

Οἰ. πρός νυν θεῶν, ὦ ξεῖνε, μή μ᾽ ἀτιμάσῃς,
τοιόνδ᾽ ἀλήτην, ὧν σε προστρέπω φράσαι.
Ξε. σήμαινε, κοὐκ ἄτιμος ἔκ γ᾽ ἐμοῦ φανεῖ.
Οἰ. τίς ἔσθ᾽ ὁ χῶρος δῆτ᾽, ἐν ᾧ βεβήκαμεν;
Ξε. ὅσ᾽ οἶδα κἀγὼ πάντ᾽ ἐπιστήσει κλύων.   5

Notes: 1. **πρός νυν θεῶν**: "by the gods, then": note the inferential (and enclitic) particle νυν, to be distinguished from the adverb νῦν ("now," "at this time").

1–2. **μή μ᾽ ἀτιμάσῃς ... ὧν**: the relative is attracted into the case of the antecedent, itself here, as often, omitted = ἐκείνων ἅ ("don't deny me the honor of the things which"); τοιόνδ᾽ ἀλήτην: "such a wanderer as I am."

3. **κοὐκ**: = crasis for καὶ οὐκ.

ἔκ γ᾽ ἐμοῦ: "at least by me."

4. **τίς ... δῆτ᾽**: "what then."

5. **ὅσ᾽ οἶδα κἀγὼ πάντ᾽**: "all that I for my part [lit. I also] know"; κἀγώ: crasis for καὶ ἐγώ.

8.4 Thucydides, *Histories* 1.95.5–6: Pausanias the Spartan is acquitted of the major charges against him, but the Spartans lose overall command of the Greek forces (477 BC).

> ἐλθὼν δὲ ἐς Λακεδαίμονα τῶν μὲν ἰδίᾳ πρός τινα
> ἀδικημάτων ηὐθύνθη, τὰ δὲ μέγιστα ἀπολύεται μὴ ἀδικεῖν·
> κατηγορεῖτο δὲ αὐτοῦ οὐχ ἥκιστα μηδισμὸς καὶ ἐδόκει
> σαφέστατον εἶναι. καὶ ἐκεῖνον μὲν οὐκέτι ἐκπέμπουσιν
> ἄρχοντα, Δόρκιν δὲ καὶ ἄλλους τινὰς μετ᾽ αὐτοῦ στρατιὰν   5
> ἔχοντας οὐ πολλήν· οἷς οὐκέτι ἐφίεσαν οἱ ξύμμαχοι τὴν
> ἡγεμονίαν.

Notes: 1–2. **τῶν μὲν ... ἀδικημάτων**: "for his private wrongdoings against anyone." τῶν ἀδικημάτων is genitive after εὐθύνω ("I call to account").

2. **τὰ δὲ μέγιστα ... ἀδικεῖν**: "but was acquitted of the most serious injustices." τὰ ... μέγιστα is an internal accusative with ἀδικεῖν; ἀπολύεται: historic present; μὴ ἀδικεῖν: a redundant μή with the infinitive after a verb containing a negative idea (here ἀπολύω, where the sense is of "not condemning").

3. **κατηγορεῖτο ... αὐτοῦ**: "was laid to his charge."

μηδισμός: "Medism," the regular term used for pro-Persian sympathy or support.

3–4. **ἐδόκει σαφέστατον εἶναι**: note the impersonal usage = "it seemed to be a very clear case."

4. **ἐκπέμπουσιν**: historic present.

6. **οἷς**: the equivalent of ἀλλὰ τούτοις. A connecting relative, as here, has the force of a demonstrative pronoun ("this/that") with a connecting particle.

ἐφίεσαν: imperfect indicative active (2nd plural) of ἐφίημι ("I entrust").

8.5 Euripides, *Iphigenia in Tauris* 1289–95: a messenger, looking for the king, reports to the chorus the departure of Pylades and Orestes.

Ἄγγελος   Χορός

Αγ. βεβᾶσι φροῦδοι δίπτυχοι νεανίαι
Ἀγαμεμνονείας παιδὸς ἐκ βουλευμάτων
φεύγοντες ἐκ γῆς τῆσδε καὶ σεμνὸν βρέτας
λαβόντες ἐν κόλποισιν Ἑλλάδος νεώς.

Χο. ἄπιστον εἶπας μῦθον· ὃν δ᾽ ἰδεῖν θέλεις   5
ἄνακτα χώρας, φροῦδος ἐκ ναοῦ συθείς.

Αγ. ποῖ; δεῖ γὰρ αὐτὸν εἰδέναι τὰ δρώμενα.

Notes: 1. **βεβᾶσι φροῦδοι**: "have departed and gone,": the repetition adds emphasis to the young men's departure. βεβᾶσι is an Attic form of the 3rd person plural of the perfect of βαίνω = (βεβήκασι).
δίπτυχοι νεανίαι: "the two young men." δίπτυχος ("twofold") is used here in the plural to mean simply "two."
2. **Ἀγαμεμνονείας παιδός**: note the feminine adjective. "Agamemnon's daughter" is, of course, Iphigenia.
ἐκ βουλευμάτων: the preposition ἐκ here indicates means, i.e., "by the contrivances."
3. **σεμνὸν βρέτας**: in order to be released from attacks by the Furies, the result of having murdered his mother, Orestes was under instruction from Apollo to bring back to Greece a statue of Artemis housed in a temple in the land of the Taurians (modern Crimea).
4. **κόλποισιν**: κόλπος is used of any "fold" or "hollow," here, in an extended dative plural, of a ship's hold.
Ἑλλάδος νεώς: Ἑλλάς, here in the genitive, is used adjectivally to mean "Greek."
5–6. **ὃν δ᾽ ἰδεῖν θέλεις ἄνακτα χώρας**: the antecedent is here attracted into the relative clause = ἄναξ δὲ χώρας ὃν ἰδεῖν θέλεις.
6. **φροῦδος**: understand ἐστίν.
συθείς: aorist participle passive of σεύω = "in haste" (lit. "set in rapid motion").
7. **τὰ δρώμενα**: "what is happening," the participial phrase taking the place of an indirect question.

8.6   Lysias 12.16–17: Lysias tells of his escape after being arrested in Athens by the Thirty Tyrants, and of their execution of his brother Polemarchus.

ταῦτα διανοηθεὶς ἔφευγον, ἐκείνων ἐπὶ τῇ αὐλείῳ θύρᾳ
τὴν φυλακὴν ποιουμένων· τριῶν δὲ θυρῶν οὐσῶν, ἃς ἔδει
με διελθεῖν, ἅπασαι ἀνεῳγμέναι ἔτυχον. ἀφικόμενος δὲ
εἰς Ἀρχένεω τοῦ ναυκλήρου ἐκεῖνον πέμπω εἰς ἄστυ,
πευσόμενον περὶ τοῦ ἀδελφοῦ· ἥκων δὲ ἔλεγεν ὅτι   5
Ἐρατοσθένης αὐτὸν ἐν τῇ ὁδῷ λαβὼν εἰς τὸ δεσμωτήριον
ἀπαγάγοι. καὶ ἐγὼ τοιαῦτα πεπυσμένος τῆς ἐπιούσης
νυκτὸς διέπλευσα Μέγαράδε. Πολεμάρχῳ δὲ παρήγγειλαν
οἱ τριάκοντα τοὐπ᾽ ἐκείνων εἰθισμένον παράγγελμα,
πίνειν κώνειον, πρὶν τὴν αἰτίαν εἰπεῖν δι᾽ ἥντινα ἔμελλεν   10
ἀποθανεῖσθαι· οὕτω πολλοῦ ἐδέησε κριθῆναι καὶ
ἀπολογήσασθαι.

Notes: 1. **ἔφευγον**: an inceptive imperfect, i.e., "I began to flee/I took to flight."

1–2. **ἐκείνων . . . τὴν φυλακὴν ποιουμένων**: "while they kept guard." "They" are the representatives of the Thirty.

3. **ἀνεῳγμέναι ἔτυχον**: "happened to be open." The perfect participle here, in this normal construction with τυγχάνω, indicates a present continuous state that is the result of a past action.

4. **εἰς Ἀρχένεω**: = εἰς τὸν Ἀρχένεω οἶκον. Ἀρχένεω is genitive of Ἀρχένεως, a proper noun of the so-called Attic declension.

5. **πευσόμενον**: future participle of purpose.

6. **Ἐρατοσθένης**: one of the Thirty Tyrants who came to power in Athens in 404 BC. This passage is an extract from the speech Lysias made against Eratosthenes in court, accusing him of the murder of his brother.

7–8. **τῆς ἐπιούσης νυκτός**: a genitive of time within which = "in the course of the ensuing night."

8. **Μέγαράδε**: the suffix -δε indicates motion toward (see Chapter 4). For Megara, see map.

9. **τοὐπ᾽ ἐκείνων εἰθισμένον παράγγελμα**: "the customary instruction in their time." τοὐπ᾽ = τὸ ἐπί (by crasis); ἐπί is used with the genitive to mean "in the time of"; εἰθισμένον: perfect participle passive of ἐθίζω ("I accustom").

11. **οὕτω πολλοῦ ἐδέησε**: "so far was he from." This expression is regularly used, as here, with an infinitive.

8.7 Homer, *Iliad* 1.35–42: the priest Chryses prays to Apollo to punish the Greeks for the abduction of his daughter.

> πολλὰ δ' ἔπειτ' ἀπάνευθε κιὼν ἠρᾶθ' ὁ γεραιὸς
> Ἀπόλλωνι ἄνακτι, τὸν ἠΰκομος τέκε Λητώ·
> κλῦθί μευ ἀργυρότοξ', ὃς Χρύσην ἀμφιβέβηκας
> Κίλλάν τε ζαθέην Τενέδοιό τε ἶφι ἀνάσσεις,
> Σμινθεῦ εἴ ποτέ τοι χαρίεντ' ἐπὶ νηὸν ἔρεψα,   5
> ἢ εἰ δή ποτέ τοι κατὰ πίονα μηρί' ἔκηα
> ταύρων ἠδ' αἰγῶν, τόδε μοι κρήηνον ἐέλδωρ·
> τείσειαν Δαναοὶ ἐμὰ δάκρυα σοῖσι βέλεσσιν.

Notes: 1. **ἠρᾶθ'**: imperfect (3rd singular) of ἀράομαι ("I pray").
2. **τόν**: the relative pronoun in Homer regularly has the same form as the definite article, though not in the nominative masculine singular, which (cf. the following line) remains as in Attic.
3. **κλῦθί μευ**: "hear me." κλῦθι is a strong aorist imperative; μευ = μου.
3–4. **ὃς Χρύσην ... ἀνάσσεις**: Chryse and Cilla were towns near Troy, Tenedos a small island off its coast, famous as the retreat of the main Greek force when they pretended to depart, leaving behind the Wooden Horse. ἀμφιβέβηκας: "protect" (lit. "have encompassed, gone around"). ἶφι: "by might." The instrumental ending -φι is here used with the noun ἴς ("strength/force").
5. **Σμινθεῦ**: "Smintheus," i.e., mouse god (σμίνθος was an old word for "mouse"). This title of Apollo, found only here, seems to derive from a time when the god was worshipped in animal form. Since the Greeks regularly linked mice with epidemic disease, it is particularly appropriate here, given what is soon to happen, that Chryses should appeal to Apollo in this guise.
τοι: = σοι, as also in the following line.
ἐπὶ ... ἔρεψα: tmesis of the aorist indicative active (1st singular) of ἐπερέφω ("I roof over"); cf. κατὰ ... ἔκηα in the following line (from κατακαίω); νηόν: Ionic form of ναόν = Attic νεών ("temple").
7. **κρήηνον**: aorist imperative from κραιαίνω, a lengthened form of κραίνω ("I accomplish, fulfill").
8. **τείσειαν Δαναοί**: a wish, i.e., "may the Danaans (= Greeks) pay for." **σοῖσι βέλεσσιν**: "with your arrows." It is by shooting arrows at them that Apollo, the archer-god, will spread plague among the Greeks.

8.8 Andocides, *De Mysteriis* 61–62: Andocides, who has just explained in court how he stopped his companions from mutilating the Herms (see note on line 4) when the idea was first mooted, goes on to show that he wasn't involved either when it actually happened.

ὕστερον δ᾽ ἐγὼ μὲν ἐν Κυνοσάργει ἐπὶ πωλίον ὅ μοι ἦν
ἀναβὰς ἔπεσον καὶ τὴν κλεῖν συνετρίβην καὶ τὴν κεφαλὴν
κατεάγην, φερόμενός τε ἐπὶ κλίνης ἀπεκομίσθην οἴκαδε·
αἰσθόμενος δ᾽ Εὐφίλητος ὡς ἔχοιμι, λέγει πρὸς αὐτοὺς
ὅτι πέπεισμαι ταῦτα συμποιεῖν καὶ ὡμολόγηκα αὐτῷ   5
μεθέξειν τοῦ ἔργου καὶ περικόψειν τὸν Ἑρμῆν τὸν παρὰ
τὸ Φορβαντεῖον. ταῦτα δ᾽ ἔλεγεν ἐξαπατῶν ἐκείνους·
καὶ διὰ ταῦτα ὁ Ἑρμῆς ὃν ὁρᾶτε πάντες, ὁ παρὰ τὴν
πατρῴαν οἰκίαν τὴν ἡμετέραν, ὃν ἡ Αἰγῇς ἀνέθηκεν, οὐ
περιεκόπη μόνος τῶν Ἑρμῶν τῶν Ἀθήνησιν, ὡς ἐμοῦ τοῦτο   10
ποιήσοντος, ὡς ἔφη πρὸς αὐτοὺς Εὐφίλητος.

Notes: 1. **ἐν Κυνοσάργει**: Cynosarges, a place just east of Athens on the southern bank of the River Ilissos, had a shrine of Heracles and a gymnasium.

ὅ μοι ἦν: "which I had" (lit. "which there was to me"), an instance of the possessive dative.

2–3. **τὴν κλεῖν ... κατεάγην**: "broke my collarbone and fractured my skull." Both verbs are aorist passive (lit. "I was broken" and "I was fractured"), and both nouns are accusatives of respect (lit. "as to my collarbone" and "as to my head").

4. **Εὐφίλητος**: one of the ringleaders of the group of young men responsible for the mutilation of the Herms. Herms were quadrangular stone pillars showing an erect phallus and a bust of the god Hermes. They were regarded as protectors of cities and homes, and were particularly common in Athens, e.g., at crossroads, in sanctuaries and at private doorways. Their mutilation throughout the city on a single night shortly before the departure of the Sicilian Expedition in 415 BC was widely regarded as an omen of ill luck.

ὡς ἔχοιμι: "in what state I was." ἔχειν with an adverb regularly means "to be."

λέγει πρὸς αὐτούς: "said to them," i.e., "the other members of the group." λέγει is an historic present.

6. **τὸν Ἑρμῆν**: "the Herm," as also in the next sentence.

7. **τὸ Φορβαντεῖον**: "the shrine of Phorbas," charioteer of Theseus and a local Attic hero.

9. **ἡ Αἰγής**: "the Aegeid tribe," one of the ten established in Athens by the constitution of Cleisthenes in 508–507 BC.

10–11. **ὡς ἐμοῦ … Εὐφίλητος**: the alleged reason expressed by ὡς ἐμοῦ τοῦτο ποιήσοντος is further reinforced by the clause that follows ("since I was going to do this, as Euphiletus said to them").

8.9   Euripides, *Heraclidae* 945–52: Alcmena, mother of the now-dead Heracles, addresses Eurystheus, the king of Tiryns, now a captive, for whom her son carried out his famous labors.

Ἀλκμήνη

ἐκεῖνος εἶ σύ, βούλομαι γὰρ εἰδέναι,		
ὃς πολλὰ μὲν τὸν ὄνθ' ὅπου 'στὶ νῦν ἐμὸν		
παῖδ' ἀξιώσας, ὦ πανοῦργ', ἐφυβρίσαι		
ὕδρας λέοντάς τ' ἐξαπολλύναι λέγων		(950)
ἔπεμπες; ἄλλα δ' οἷ' ἐμηχανῶ κακὰ	5	(951)
σιγῶ· μακρὸς γὰρ μῦθος ἂν γένοιτό μοι.		(952)
τί γὰρ σὺ κεῖνον οὐκ ἔτλης καθυβρίσαι		(948)
ὃς καὶ παρ' Ἅιδην ζῶντά νιν κατήγαγες;		(949)

Notes: 2. **πολλά**: to be taken with ἐφυβρίσαι ("to heap many insults on").
τὸν ὄνθ' … νῦν: "who is where he is now," a euphemism for "who is now dead." ὅπου is a relative adverb.
4–5. **λέγων ἔπεμπες**: "sent [him] off with instructions."
5. **ἄλλα … οἷ' ἐμηχανῶ κακά**: "such other evils as you devised." κακά, part of the antecedent, is attracted into the relative clause.
6. **ἂν γένοιτό**: "it would be," a potential optative.
7. **τί … οὐκ ἔτλης καθυβρίσαι**: "for what insult did you not dare to inflict on him"; κεῖνον = ἐκεῖνον.
8. **νιν**: = αὐτόν.

8.10   Thucydides, *Histories* 1.128.5–7: Pausanias intrigues with the king of Persia, 478 BC.

Βυζάντιον γὰρ ἑλὼν τῇ προτέρᾳ παρουσίᾳ μετὰ τὴν ἐκ
Κύπρου ἀναχώρησιν (εἶχον δὲ Μῆδοι αὐτὸ καὶ βασιλέως
προσήκοντές τινες καὶ ξυγγενεῖς οἳ ἑάλωσαν ἐν αὐτῷ) τότε
τούτους οὓς ἔλαβεν ἀποπέμπει βασιλεῖ κρύφα τῶν ἄλλων

ξυμμάχων, τῷ δὲ λόγῳ ἀπέδρασαν αὐτόν. ἔπρασσε δὲ   5
ταῦτα μετὰ Γογγύλου τοῦ Ἐρετριῶς, ᾧπερ ἐπέτρεψε τό τε
Βυζάντιον καὶ τοὺς αἰχμαλώτους. ἔπεμψε δὲ καὶ ἐπιστολὴν
τὸν Γόγγυλον φέροντα αὐτῷ· ἐνεγέγραπτο δὲ τάδε ἐν
αὐτῇ, ὡς ὕστερον ἀνηυρέθη· Παυσανίας ὁ ἡγεμὼν τῆς
Σπάρτης τούσδε τέ σοι χαρίζεσθαι βουλόμενος ἀποπέμπει   10
δορὶ ἑλών, καὶ γνώμην ποιοῦμαι, εἰ καὶ σοὶ δοκεῖ, θυγατέρα
τε τὴν σὴν γῆμαι καί σοι Σπάρτην τε καὶ τὴν ἄλλην Ἑλλάδα
ὑποχείριον ποιῆσαι. δυνατὸς δὲ δοκῶ εἶναι ταῦτα πρᾶξαι
μετὰ σοῦ βουλευόμενος. εἰ οὖν τί σε τούτων ἀρέσκει, πέμπε
ἄνδρα πιστὸν ἐπὶ θάλασσαν δι᾽ οὗ τὸ λοιπὸν τοὺς λόγους   15
ποιησόμεθα.

Notes: 1. **τῇ προτέρᾳ παρουσίᾳ**: "when he was there before [lit. "on his previous presence"]." See 4.6.

3. **ἑάλωσαν**: aorist (third plural) of ἁλίσκομαι ("I am captured").

4. **ἀποπέμπει**: historic present.

5. **τῷ δὲ λόγῳ ἀπέδρασαν αὐτόν**: "saying that they had escaped from him" (lit. "but in word they ran away from him"); ἀπέδρασαν: aorist indicative active (3rd person) of ἀποδιδράσκω.

6. **τοῦ Ἐρετριῶς**: "the Eretrian." Eretria is a town on the island of Euboea: see map.

8. **ἐνεγέγραπτο**: pluperfect passive (3rd singular) of ἐγγράφω.

10–11. **τούσδε ... ἀποπέμπει δορὶ ἑλών**: "sends back these prisoners of war" (lit. "sends back these [people] having taken them by the spear"); ἑλών: aorist participle active of αἱρέω (from εἶλον).

11. **γνώμην ποιοῦμαι**: "I make a proposal." Note the abrupt change from third person to first.

12. **τὴν ἄλλην Ἑλλάδα**: "the rest of Greece."

14. **σε ... ἀρέσκει**: this verb normally takes the dative, not the accusative, as here.

15. **τὸ λοιπόν**: "in future," an adverbial accusative.

15–16. **τοὺς λόγους ποιησόμεθα**: "we shall communicate."

CHAPTER 9

Particles

Greek particles are short words (e.g., ἄρα, δή, δῆτα, πέρ) that never change and serve one of the following functions:

1. They can connect one utterance to a preceding one.
2. They can qualify a word, phrase, or clause ("even," "also," "anyway," etc.).
3. They can "color" a word, phrase, or clause, conveying what is often expressed in spoken English by volume and tone of voice ("he did that," "he did that!") and in written English by italics, exclamation points, quotation marks, etc.

In the following passages the particles are printed in bold. You should discuss the effect they are having in their context.

9.1 Plato, *Apology* 26c: Socrates asks his prosecutor whether he is accusing him of teaching that the wrong gods exist or of not believing in the gods at all.

> ἐγὼ γὰρ οὐ δύναμαι μαθεῖν πότερον λέγεις διδάσκειν με
> νομίζειν εἶναί τινας θεούς—καὶ αὐτὸς **ἄρα** νομίζω εἶναι
> θεοὺς καὶ οὐκ εἰμὶ τὸ παράπαν ἄθεος οὐδὲ ταύτῃ ἀδικῶ—
> οὐ **μέντοι** οὖσπερ **γε** ἡ πόλις ἀλλὰ ἑτέρους, καὶ τοῦτ᾽ ἔστιν
> ὅ μοι ἐγκαλεῖς, ὅτι ἑτέρους, ἢ παντάπασί με φὴς οὔτε   5
> αὐτὸν νομίζειν θεοὺς τούς τε ἄλλους ταῦτα διδάσκειν.

Notes: 1. **διδάσκειν με**: "that I teach (people) to. . . ."

2. **ἄρα**: probably correcting a false impression: "certainly."

3. **τὸ παράπαν**: "altogether," "completely."

4. **οὕσπερ γε ἡ πόλις**: "those precise gods that the city (believes in)."

5. **ὅτι ἑτέρους**: "that (I believe in) other (gods)."

παντάπασι: "quite simply": take with νομίζειν.

9.2   Homer, *Iliad* 1.505–10: Thetis begs Zeus to honor her son Achilles, whom Agamemnon has slighted by taking away his captive woman. She asks him to let the Trojans have supremacy over the Greeks (Achaeans) so that they realize what they have lost by Achilles' withdrawal from the fighting. Zeus, who dwells on Mount Olympus, is naturally "Olympian."

> τίμησόν μοι υἱὸν ὃς ὠκυμορώτατος ἄλλων
> ἔπλετ᾽· **ἀτάρ** μιν νῦν **γε** ἄναξ ἀνδρῶν Ἀγαμέμνων
> ἠτίμησεν· ἑλὼν **γὰρ** ἔχει γέρας αὐτὸς ἀπούρας.
> **ἀλλὰ** σύ **πέρ** μιν τῖσον, Ὀλύμπιε μητίετα Ζεῦ·
> τόφρα **δ**᾽ ἐπὶ Τρώεσσι τίθει κράτος ὄφρ᾽ ἂν Ἀχαιοὶ   5
> υἱὸν ἐμὸν τίσωσιν ὀφέλλωσίν **τέ** ἑ τιμῇ.

Notes: 1–2. **ὠκυμορώτατος ἄλλων ἔπλετ᾽**: "is the most short-fated (i.e., doomed to an early death) of all men" (lit. "of other men"). The superlative and the genitive of comparison combine the idea that he, the most short-fated man, is more short-fated than all the others.

3. **ἑλών**: aorist participle of αἱρέω.

ἀπούρας: from ἀπαυράω = I snatch away.

4. **τῖσον**: aorist imperative of τίνω.

μητίετα: counselor

5. **τόφρα . . . ὄφρ᾽**: "for as long as (it takes) until."

ἐπὶ . . . τίθει: imperative; tmesis, so take both words together as one.

6. **ὀφέλλωσίν . . . ἑ**: "pay him his debt."

9.3   Euripides, *Hippolytus* 1243–48: A messenger who was one of those present at the scene recounts how Hippolytus has been mortally damaged after being dragged along the ground entangled in the reins of his chariot. His attendants are slow to reach him. The fearsome bull that caused the disaster has disappeared.

Ἄγγελος

πολλοὶ **δὲ** βουληθέντες ὑστέρῳ ποδὶ
ἐλειπόμεσθα. **χὢ μὲν** ἐκ δεσμῶν λυθεὶς
τμητῶν ἱμάντων οὐ κάτοιδ᾽ ὅτῳ τρόπῳ
πίπτει, βραχὺν **δὴ** βίοτον ἐμπνέων ἔτι·
ἵπποι **δ᾽** ἔκρυφθεν καὶ τὸ δύστηνον τέρας
ταύρου λεπαίας οὐ κάτοιδ᾽ ὅποι χθονός.

5

Notes: 1. **βουληθέντες**: i.e., to come to Hippolytus' help.
ὑστέρῳ ποδί: "with lagging foot."
2. **ἐλειπόμεσθα**: note the insertion of σ here to help with the scansion.
This is common in the first person plural of the middle and passive.
χὢ: crasis of καὶ ὁ.
2–3. **ἐκ δεσμῶν … τμητῶν ἱμάντων**: lit. "from the bonds of the cut
leather straps," i.e., "from the reins of leather."
3. **οὐ κάτοιδ᾽ ὅτῳ τρόπῳ**: "somehow or other," lit. "I do not know in
what way."
5. **ἔκρυφθεν**: epic 3rd person plural of the aorist passive. The
monstrous bull is hidden as well as the horses.
6. **λεπαίας οὐ κάτοιδ᾽ ὅποι χθονός**: "I know not where in that rocky
land."

9.4 Euripides, *Electra* 228–31: Orestes, who has not yet revealed
his identity, tells his sister Electra that her brother is still alive.

Ὀρέστης   Ἠλέκτρα

Ὀρ. ἥκω φέρων σοι σοῦ κασιγνήτου λόγους.
Ἠλ. ὦ φίλτατ᾽, **ἆρα** ζῶντος ἢ τεθνηκότος;
Ὀρ. ζῇ· πρῶτα **γάρ** σοι τἀγάθ᾽ ἀγγέλλειν θέλω.
Ἠλ. εὐδαιμονοίης, μισθὸν ἡδίστων λόγων.

Notes: 2. **ζῶντος ἢ τεθνηκότος**: agreeing with σοῦ κασιγνήτου in the
previous line, i.e., "(are the words about your brother) living or dead?"
Thus: "is he alive or dead?"
4. **εὐδαιμονοίης**: the optative expresses a wish.
μισθὸν: in apposition to the wish, i.e. "(as) a reward (for)."

9.5 Sophocles, *Ajax* 1355–59: Odysseus and Agamemnon argue
about how to treat the corpse of Ajax, a once courageous fighter on

the Greek side who attempted to kill their leaders and has now committed suicide. Odysseus wishes to show respect toward his body.

Ὀδυσσεύς   Ἀγαμέμνων

Ὀδ. ὅδ᾽ ἐχθρὸς ἀνήρ, ἀλλὰ γενναῖός ποτ᾽ ἦν.

Ἀγ. τί ποτε ποήσεις; ἐχθρὸν ὧδ᾽ αἰδεῖ νέκυν;

Ὀδ. νικᾷ **γὰρ** ἀρετή με τῆς ἔχθρας πολύ.

Ἀγ. τοιοίδε **μέντοι** φῶτες ἔμπληκτοι βροτῶν.

Ὀδ. ἦ κάρτα πολλοὶ νῦν φίλοι καὖθις πικροί.   5

Notes: 1. **ὅδ᾽ ἀνήρ**: i.e. Ajax.

ὁ ἀνήρ = xxxx

2. **ποήσεις**: verse form of ποιήσεις.

3. **γάρ**: when γάρ comes as the second word in a line of stichomythia (a line-by-line exchange) it often carries the meaning of "yes, for" or "no, for" depending on the context.

ἀρετή: = ἡ ἀρετή.

τῆς ἔχθρας: genitive of comparison: i.e., "in comparison with."

4. **τοιοίδε . . . φῶτες ἔμπληκτοι βροτῶν**: lit. "such men are the unstable of mankind," i.e., men who can give up their enmity like Odysseus.

5. **ἦ κάρτα**: lit. "truly very much," i.e., "it is certainly true that . . ."

καὖθις: = καὶ αὖθις = "and in turn."

9.6 Aristophanes, *Lysistrata* 908–14: Cinesias starts by getting his baby child out of the way in his keenness to have sex with his wife Myrrhine. But she has sworn to go on a sex strike and invents excuses. She says that she cannot attend any religious function if they have intercourse. Cinesias answers that she can purify herself in the Clepsydra spring.

Κινησίας   Μυρρίνη

Κιν. μὰ Δί᾽ **ἀλλὰ** τοῦτό γ᾽ οἴκαδ᾽, ὦ Μανῆ, φέρε.
ἰδοὺ τὸ **μέν** σοι παιδίον **καὶ δὴ** ᾽κποδών,
σὺ **δ᾽** οὐ κατακλινεῖ; **Μυρ.** ποῦ **γὰρ** ἄν τις καί, τάλαν,
δράσειε τοῦθ᾽; **Κιν.** ὅπου; τὸ τοῦ Πανὸς καλόν.

Μυρ. καὶ πῶς ἔθ᾽ ἁγνὴ **δῆτ᾽** ἂν ἔλθοιμ᾽ ἐς πόλιν;   5

Κιν. κάλλιστα **δήπου** λουσαμένη τῇ Κλεψύδρᾳ.

Μυρ. ἔπειτ᾽ ὀμόσασα **δῆτ᾽** ἐπιορκήσω, τάλαν;

Notes: 1. **τοῦτο**: i.e., the baby.

2. **'κποδών**: = ἐκποδών

Μανῆ: Manes (here in the vocative) is a common name for a slave.

3. **γάρ**: see the note on γάρ in the passage above.

τάλαν: "my dear."

4. **τὸ τοῦ Πανός**: "the grotto of Pan," a cave-sanctuary with erotic associations under the north face of the Acropolis. Supply the verb "to be": "Pan's grotto is fine."

5. **ἔθ'**: = ἔτι.

δῆτ': "then," "in that case" (cf. line 7).

6. **δήπου**: "obviously," "of course."

9.7 Herodotus, *Histories* 2.49.1: Melampus, the son of Amytheon, introduced Dionysus and his phallic procession to the Greeks.

ἤδη **ὦν** δοκέει μοι Μελάμπους ὁ Ἀμυθέωνος τῆς θυσίης
ταύτης οὐκ εἶναι ἀδαὴς ἀλλ' ἔμπειρος. Ἕλλησι **γὰρ δὴ**
Μελάμπους ἐστὶ ὁ ἐξηγησάμενος τοῦ Διονύσου τό **τε**
οὔνομα **καὶ** τὴν θυσίην **καὶ** τὴν πομπὴν τοῦ φαλλοῦ·
ἀτρεκέως **μὲν** οὐ πάντα συλλαβὼν τὸν λόγον ἔφηνε, ἀλλ'   5
οἱ ἐπιγενόμενοι τούτῳ σοφισταὶ μεζόνως ἐξέφηναν· τὸν δ'
ὦν φαλλὸν τὸν τῷ Διονύσῳ πεμπόμενον Μελάμπους ἐστὶ
ὁ κατηγησάμενος, καὶ ἀπὸ τούτου μαθόντες ποιεῦσι τὰ
ποιεῦσι Ἕλληνες.

Notes: 1. **ἤδη**: here = "this being so."

2. **ἀδαής**: "ignorant."

4. **τὴν πομπὴν τοῦ φαλλοῦ**: "the procession of the phallus": a giant phallus was carried in a procession.

5. **ἀτρεκέως ... οὐ πάντα συλλαβὼν τὸν λόγον ἔφηνε**: "to speak precisely, he did not fully sum up the doctrine or communicate it in its entirety." More literally, "he did not reveal the doctrine having summed it all up."

6. **οἱ ἐπιγενόμενοι τούτῳ σοφισταί**: "the teachers who came after him."

7. **φαλλὸν τὸν τῷ Διονύσῳ πεμπόμενον**: "the phallic procession in honor of Dionysus."

8. **ὁ κατηγησάμενος**: "the man who introduced."

9.8 Plato, *Lysis* 219c: in this conversation (with Menexenus) Socrates argues that something friendly involves another friendly force.

ἡ ἰατρική, φαμέν, ἕνεκα τῆς ὑγιείας φίλον.

ναί.

οὐκοῦν καὶ ἡ ὑγίεια φίλον;

πάνυ γε.

εἰ ἄρα φίλον, ἕνεκά του.   5

ναί.

φίλου γέ τινος δή, εἴπερ ἀκολουθήσει τῇ πρόσθεν
ὁμολογίᾳ.

πάνυ γε.

οὐκοῦν καὶ ἐκεῖνο φίλον αὖ ἔσται ἕνεκα φίλου;   10

ναί.

Notes: 1. **ἡ ἰατρική**: "the doctor's (skill)." τέχνη is understood.
φίλον: "[is] something friendly."
3. **οὐκοῦν**: one should be sure to translate the part of οὐκοῦν with the
accent on but also try to translate the other syllable: "and so, isn't ... ?"
5. **ἕνεκά του**: "because of something." του is a variant form of τινός.
7–8. **ἀκολουθήσει τῇ πρόσθεν ὁμολογίᾳ**: "it will be in accordance
with what we agreed before."

9.9 Demosthenes, *On the Chersonese* 42: the orator says that the
Athenians are good at thwarting the ambitions of others, and so
Philip of Macedon is understandably wary of them.

ἐστὲ γὰρ ὑμεῖς οὐκ αὐτοὶ πλεονεκτῆσαι καὶ κατασχεῖν
ἀρχὴν εὖ πεφυκότες, ἀλλ᾽ ἕτερον λαβεῖν κωλῦσαι καὶ
ἔχοντ᾽ ἀφελέσθαι δεινοί, καὶ ὅλως ἐνοχλῆσαι τοῖς ἄρχειν
βουλομένοις καὶ πάντας ἀνθρώπους εἰς ἐλευθερίαν
ἐξελέσθαι ἕτοιμοι. οὔκουν βούλεται τοῖς ἑαυτοῦ καιροῖς   5
τὴν παρ᾽ ὑμῶν ἐλευθερίαν ἐφεδρεύειν, οὐδὲ πολλοῦ δεῖ, οὐ
κακῶς οὐδ᾽ ἀργῶς ταῦτα λογιζόμενος.

Notes: 2. **εὖ πεφυκότες**: "well adapted by nature to" + inf.
2–3. **ἀλλ᾽ ἕτερον λαβεῖν κωλῦσαι καὶ ἔχοντ᾽ ἀφελέσθαι δεινοί**:
"but you're terribly good (δεινοί) at stopping someone else taking
something and once he's got it taking it away from him."
3. **ὅλως ἐνοχλῆσαι**: "to give a great deal of annoyance to" + dat.
4–5. **πάντας ἀνθρώπους εἰς ἐλευθερίαν ἐξελέσθαι**: "to bring all men
to freedom."
5. **οὔκουν βούλεται**: "and so he (Philip) doesn't want": see note on
οὐκοῦν in the passage above, observing the different accent.

5–6. **τοῖς ἑαυτοῦ καιροῖς τὴν παρ’ ὑμῶν ἐλευθερίαν ἐφεδρεύειν**: "to have your tradition of liberty watching to seize every chance against himself."

6. **οὐδὲ πολλοῦ δεῖ**: "far from it!"

7. **κακῶς**: "wrongly."

9.10 Homer, *Iliad* 4.401–5: Agamemnon unjustly rebukes Diomedes on the battlefield. The latter says nothing in response but his second-in-command, Sthenelus, the son of the brutish Capaneus, is less self-controlled.

> ὣς φάτο, τὸν δ’ οὔ τι προσέφη κρατερὸς Διομήδης
> αἰδεσθεὶς βασιλῆος ἐνιπὴν αἰδοίοιο·
> τὸν δ’ υἱὸς Καπανῆος ἀμείψατο κυδαλίμοιο·
> ‘Ἀτρεΐδη μὴ ψεύδε’ ἐπιστάμενος σάφα εἰπεῖν·
> ἡμεῖς **τοι** πατέρων μέγ’ ἀμείνονες εὐχόμεθ’ εἶναι.’   5

Notes: 1. **ὣς φάτο**: "thus he spoke."
2. **αἰδεσθεὶς βασιλῆος ἐνιπὴν αἰδοίοιο**: "feeling respect at the reprimand (ἐνιπήν) of the revered king."
3. **κυδαλίμοιο**: "glorious" (in genitive).
4. **μὴ ψεύδε’ ἐπιστάμενος σάφα εἰπεῖν**: "don't tell lies since you know the truth well." The infinitive εἰπεῖν is used as an imperative.
5. **εὐχόμεθ’**: "we claim (to be)," "we boast (that we are)."

CHAPTER 10

Indirect Statement

An indirect statement occurs when what someone *says, thinks, sees, hears, knows*, etc., is reported by another. In English the subordinate clause is regularly introduced by *that*, though this is sometimes omitted. In Greek there are three different constructions for dealing with the indirect statement.

1 The ὅτι or ὡς construction is regularly used after verbs of *saying,* especially λέγω and its aorist εἶπον. It is not used after φημί or verbs of *thinking.* The verb in the indirect statement retains both mood and tense of the original direct speech, though in historic sequence the mood may be optative, the tense still remaining that of the original direct. The negative is regularly οὐ.

2 After φημί and verbs of *thinking* the verb in an indirect statement goes into the infinitive. The tense of the infinitive corresponds to that of the original words of the direct statement. If the subject of the indirect statement is different from that of the main verb, it will be in the accusative; if it is the same, it is usually not expressed but will be in the nominative if it is included. The negative is regularly οὐ. Note that *say that ... not* is οὐ φημί, and *think that ... not* is οὐκ οἴομαι or οὐ νομίζω. ἐλπίζω *I hope,* ὑπισχνέομαι *I promise,* ὄμνυμι

I swear, and ἀπειλέω *I threaten* are generally followed by a future infinitive. The negative after these verbs is μή.

3. Indirect statements after verbs of *knowing* and *perceiving,* and a few others, are regularly expressed with a participle rather than an infinitive. Just as with the infinitive construction, if the subject of the indirect statement is the same as that of the main verb, it is either omitted or is in the nominative; if different, it is in the accusative. The participle agrees with its subject in the normal way. The negative is οὐ. The ὅτι construction is also found after many of these verbs, particularly οἶδα and ἐπίσταμαι.

10.1

(I) Demosthenes, *De Corona* 169: worrying news arrives in Athens.

ἑσπέρα μὲν γὰρ ἦν, ἧκε δ' ἀγγέλλων τις ὡς τοὺς πρυτάνεις ὡς Ἐλάτεια κατείληπται.

Notes: 1. **ἧκε**: "had come," the imperfect of ἥκω.
τοὺς πρυτάνεις: "the *prytaneis.*" At Athens, after the constitutional reforms of Cleisthenes (508–507 BC), each of the ten tribes chose fifty men every year to serve on the Boule (Council). Each group of fifty, then, served as the Council's executive committee for one-tenth of the year, during which period they were known as *prytaneis,* or "presidents."
2. **Ἐλάτεια**: a city in Phocis, whose occupation by Philip of Macedon in 339 BC caused great panic in Athens.

(II) Plato, *Apology* 21c: Socrates, in the course of his quest to prove that he is not the wisest of all men, attempts to point out to a politician whom he has questioned that his wisdom is illusory.

κἄπειτα ἐπειρώμην αὐτῷ δεικνύναι ὅτι οἴοιτο μὲν εἶναι σοφός, εἴη δ' οὔ.

Notes: 1. **κἄπειτα**: crasis for καὶ ἔπειτα.
1–2. **δεικνύναι … δ' οὔ**: constructions (I) and (II) above are both illustrated in these few short words.

(III) Demosthenes *Olynthiac* 1.15: Demosthenes assures the Athenians that, if they're not careful, war will be on the way.

πρὸς θεῶν, τίς οὕτως εὐήθης ἐστὶν ὑμῶν ὅστις ἀγνοεῖ τὸν
ἐκεῖθεν πόλεμον δεῦρ᾽ ἥξοντα, ἂν ἀμελήσωμεν;

Notes: 1. **πρὸς θεῶν**: "by the gods," an oath.
1–2. **τὸν ἐκεῖθεν πόλεμον**: "the war there" (lit. "from there"), i.e., in Chalcidice, a promontory in northern Greece, from where the citizens of Olynthus are asking the Athenians for help against Philip of Macedon.
2. **δεῦρ᾽**: i.e., to Athens.
ἄν: = ἐάν. (see p. 107)

10.2   Xenophon, *Anabasis* 4.8.4: when Xenophon and his men face some hostile Macronians, one of his soldiers, a former slave, realizes he knows the language and acts as an interpreter.

ἔνθα δὴ προσέρχεται Ξενοφῶντι τῶν πελταστῶν ἀνὴρ
Ἀθήνησι φάσκων δεδουλευκέναι, λέγων ὅτι γιγνώσκοι
τὴν φωνὴν τῶν ἀνθρώπων. καὶ οἶμαι, ἔφη, ἐμὴν
ταύτην πατρίδα εἶναι· καὶ εἰ μή τι κωλύει, ἐθέλω αὐτοῖς
διαλεχθῆναι. ἀλλ᾽ οὐδὲν κωλύει, ἔφη, ἀλλὰ διαλέγου καὶ   5
μάθε πρῶτον τίνες εἰσίν. οἱ δ᾽ εἶπον ἐρωτήσαντος ὅτι
Μάκρωνες.

Notes: 1. **πελταστῶν**: peltasts were lightly armed troops, so called from their distinctive leather or wicker shield, the πέλτη.
3. **φωνήν**: "language" (lit. voice).
4. **εἰ μή τι κωλύει**: "if there is no objection" (lit. "if nothing prevents it").
6. **ἐρωτήσαντος**: understand αὐτοῦ, a one-word genitive absolute = "when he had asked the question."
6–7. **ὅτι Μάκρωνες**: understand εἰσίν/εἶεν.

10.3   Euripides, *Medea* 1293–1300: Jason, who has just lost his new bride and her father to Medea's witchcraft, asks the women of the chorus if she is still at home or has already departed in exile.

Ἰάσων

γυναῖκες, αἳ τῆσδ᾽ ἐγγὺς ἕστατε στέγης,
ἆρ᾽ ἐν δόμοισιν ἡ τὰ δείν᾽ εἰργασμένη

Μήδεια τοισίδ᾽ ἢ μεθέστηκεν φυγῇ;
δεῖ γάρ νιν ἤτοι γῆς γε κρυφθῆναι κάτω
ἢ πτηνὸν ἆραι σῶμ᾽ ἐς αἰθέρος βάθος,   5
εἰ μὴ τυράννων δώμασιν δώσει δίκην.
πέποιθ᾽ ἀποκτείνασα κοιράνους χθονὸς
ἀθῷος αὐτὴ τῶνδε φεύξεσθαι δόμων;

Notes: 1. **ἔστατε:** = ἐστήκατε.
3. **μεθέστηκεν:** "has she departed."
4. **νιν:** = αὐτήν.
ἤτοι: = ἤ τοι ("either in truth")
5. **ἐς αἰθέρος βάθος:** βάθος can refer to height as well as to depth = "to the heights of the sky."
6. **εἰ μή** … : "if she is not to. …"
τυράννων δώμασιν: "to the royal household."
7. **πέποιθ᾽:** = **πέποιθε** ("does she imagine"). Notice that πέποιθα (intransitive perfect of πείθω) means "I trust/am confident."

10.4 Xenophon, *Hellenica* 4.2.1: the Spartan king, Agesilaus, is recalled from service in Asia to deal with an emergency at home (394 BC).

Ἀγησίλαος μὲν δὴ ἐν τούτοις ἦν. οἱ δὲ Λακεδαιμόνιοι
ἐπεὶ σαφῶς ἤσθοντο τά τε χρήματα ἐληλυθότα εἰς τὴν
Ἑλλάδα καὶ τὰς μεγίστας πόλεις συνεστηκυίας ἐπὶ
πολέμῳ πρὸς ἑαυτούς, ἐν κινδύνῳ τε τὴν πόλιν ἐνόμισαν
καὶ στρατεύειν ἀναγκαῖον ἡγήσαντο εἶναι. καὶ αὐτοὶ μὲν   5
ταῦτα παρεσκευάζοντο, εὐθὺς δὲ καὶ ἐπὶ τὸν Ἀγησίλαον
πέμπουσιν Ἐπικυδίδαν. ὁ δ᾽ ἐπεὶ ἀφίκετο, τά τε ἄλλα
διηγεῖτο ὡς ἔχοι καὶ ὅτι ἡ πόλις ἐπιστέλλοι αὐτῷ βοηθεῖν
ὡς τάχιστα τῇ πατρίδι. ὁ δὲ Ἀγησίλαος ἐπεὶ ἤκουσε,
χαλεπῶς μὲν ἤνεγκεν, ἐνθυμούμενος καὶ οἵων τιμῶν καὶ   10
οἵων ἐλπίδων ἀποστεροῖτο, ὅμως δὲ συγκαλέσας τοὺς
συμμάχους ἐδήλωσε τὰ ὑπὸ τῆς πόλεως παραγγελλόμενα,
καὶ εἶπεν ὅτι ἀναγκαῖον εἴη βοηθεῖν τῇ πατρίδι· Ἐὰν
μέντοι ἐκεῖνα καλῶς γένηται, εὖ ἐπίστασθε, ἔφη, ὦ
ἄνδρες σύμμαχοι, ὅτι οὐ μὴ ἐπιλάθωμαι ὑμῶν, ἀλλὰ πάλιν   15

παρέσομαι πράξων ὧν ὑμεῖς δεῖσθε. ἀκούσαντες ταῦτα
πολλοὶ μὲν ἐδάκρυσαν, πάντες δ᾽ ἐψηφίσαντο βοηθεῖν
μετ᾽ Ἀγησιλάου τῇ Λακεδαίμονι.

Notes: 1. **ἐν τούτοις ἦν**: "was thus occupied" (lit. "was in these things"), i.e., with a campaign in Asia against the King of Persia.
2. **τά ... χρήματα**: i.e., money earlier sent from Persia and distributed to the leaders of various Greek states on the understanding that they would make war on Sparta—a ploy to ensure Agesilaus' recall.
ἐληλυθότα: participle (accusative neuter plural) from ἐλήλυθα, used as the perfect of ἔρχομαι.
3. **τὰς μεγίστας πόλεις συνεστηκυίας**: "that the greatest states had formed a coalition" (lit. "were standing together," from συνέστηκα, intransitive perfect of συνίστημι).
4. **ἐν κινδύνῳ ... ἐνόμισαν**: understand εἶναι.
7–8. **τά τε ἄλλα ... ὡς ἔχοι**: "both how everything else was." Note this regular use of ἔχειν with an adverb meaning "to be," and also that, in accordance with the common Greek idiom τὰ ἄλλα, really the subject of the indirect question, appears as object of the introductory verb; cf. the Biblical English "I know thee who thou art" (*St. Luke* 4.34).
10–11. **οἵων τιμῶν καὶ οἵων ἐλπίδων**: i.e., those involved in his planned subjugation of Persia to Greece.
11–12. **τοὺς συμμάχους**: Agesilaus' allies are other Greeks fighting with him in Asia.
15. **οὐ μὴ ἐπιλάθωμαι**: οὐ μή with the aorist subjunctive (or future indicative) expresses an emphatically negative statement ("I will certainly not forget you").
16. **ὧν ὑμεῖς δεῖσθε**: understand ἐκεῖνα before ὧν. Agesilaus refers again to his (and his allies') desires to overthrow Persia.

10.5 Lysias 23.5–7: the speaker, who is attempting to prove that Pancleon isn't a Plataean, seeks information from various natives of that city resident in Attica.

καὶ πρῶτον μὲν Εὐθύκριτον, ὃν πρεσβύτατόν τε
Πλαταιέων ἐγίγνωσκον καὶ μάλιστα ᾤμην εἰδέναι,
ἠρόμην εἴ τινα γιγνώσκοι Ἱππαρμοδώρου υἱὸν Παγκλέωνα
Πλαταιέα· ἔπειτα δέ, ἐπειδὴ ἐκεῖνος ἀπεκρίνατό μοι
ὅτι τὸν Ἱππαρμόδωρον μὲν γιγνώσκοι, υἱὸν δὲ ἐκείνῳ
οὐδένα οὔτε Παγκλέωνα οὔτε ἄλλον οὐδένα εἰδείη ὄντα,
ἠρώτων δὴ καὶ τῶν ἄλλων ὅσους ἤδη Πλαταιέας ὄντας.

most accurate

πάντες οὖν, ἀγνοοῦντες τὸ ὄνομα αὐτοῦ, ἀκριβέστατα ἂν
ἔφασάν με πυθέσθαι ἐλθόντα εἰς τὸν χλωρὸν τυρὸν τῇ ἕνῃ
καὶ νέᾳ· ταύτῃ γὰρ τῇ ἡμέρᾳ τοῦ μηνὸς ἑκάστου ἐκεῖσε   10
συλλέγεσθαι τοὺς Πλαταιέας. ἐλθὼν οὖν εἰς τὸν τυρὸν
ταύτῃ τῇ ἡμέρᾳ ἐπυνθανόμην αὐτῶν, εἴ τινα γιγνώσκοιεν
Παγκλέωνα πολίτην σφέτερον. καὶ οἱ μὲν ἄλλοι οὐκ
ἔφασαν γιγνώσκειν, εἷς δέ τις εἶπεν ὅτι τῶν μὲν πολιτῶν
οὐδενὶ εἰδείη τοῦτο ὂν τὸ ὄνομα, δοῦλον μέντοι ἔφη ἑαυτοῦ   15
ἀφεστῶτα εἶναι Παγκλέωνα, τήν τε ἡλικίαν λέγων τὴν
τούτου καὶ τὴν τέχνην ᾗ οὗτος χρῆται.

Notes: 1–2. **ὂν ... ἐγίγνωσκον**: understand ὄντα.

2. **μάλιστα**: with εἰδέναι ("was best informed").

5–6. **ὑὸν δὲ ἐκείνῳ οὐδένα ... εἰδείη ὄντα**: "but didn't know that he had any son."

7. **ἠρώτων δή**: "I went on to ask" (lit. "[then] indeed I began asking").

9. **ἐλθόντα**: the participle takes the place of a conditional clause ("if I were to go").

τὸν χλωρὸν τυρόν: lit. "the fresh cheese," i.e., the cheese market, as also τὸν τυρόν in the following sentence.

9–10. **τῇ ἕνῃ καὶ νέᾳ**: understand ἡμέρᾳ = "on the last day of the month." A new month was regarded as beginning on the evening of the last day of the old month. That day was therefore dubbed "the old (ἕνη) and the new (νέα)."

11. **συλλέγεσθαι τοὺς Πλαταιέας**: still accusative and infinitive after ἔφασαν.

15–16. **δοῦλον ... Παγκλέωνα**: "but that there was a runaway [ἀφεστῶτα, lit. "having revolted"] slave of his own (called) Pancleon."

17. **τούτου**: "of this man," i.e., the defendant.

τὴν τέχνην ᾗ οὗτος χρῆται: "the trade that the defendant practices," that of a fuller, as is clear elsewhere in the speech.

10.6 Homer, *Iliad* 13.361–73: Idomeneus kills Othryoneus of Cabesus, a suitor for the hand of Cassandra, Priam's daughter, fated always to prophesy the truth, but never to be believed.

ἔνθα μεσαιπόλιός περ ἐὼν Δαναοῖσι κελεύσας
Ἰδομενεὺς Τρώεσσι μετάλμενος ἐν φόβον ὦρσε.
πέφνε γὰρ Ὀθρυονῆα Καβησόθεν ἔνδον ἐόντα,
ὅς ῥα νέον πολέμοιο μετὰ κλέος εἰληλούθει,

ἤτεε δὲ Πριάμοιο θυγατρῶν εἶδος ἀρίστην   5
Κασσάνδρην ἀνάεδνον, ὑπέσχετο δὲ μέγα ἔργον,
ἐκ Τροίης ἀέκοντας ἀπωσέμεν υἷας Ἀχαιῶν.
τῷ δ᾽ ὁ γέρων Πρίαμος ὑπό τ᾽ ἔσχετο καὶ κατένευσε
δωσέμεναι· ὃ δὲ μάρναθ᾽ ὑποσχεσίῃσι πιθήσας.
Ἰδομενεὺς δ᾽ αὐτοῖο τιτύσκετο δουρὶ φαεινῷ,   10
καὶ βάλεν ὕψι βιβάντα τυχών· οὐδ᾽ ἤρκεσε θώρηξ
χάλκεος, ὃν φορέεσκε, μέσῃ δ᾽ ἐν γαστέρι πῆξε.
δούπησεν δὲ πεσών.

Notes: 1. **μεσαιπόλιός περ ἐὼν**: "though his hair was going gray."
μεσαιπόλιος is a poetic form of μεσοπόλιος, περ stands for καίπερ,
as regularly in Homer, and ἐών is the Homeric form of ὤν, present
participle of εἰμί (cf. ἐόντα in line 3).
Δαναοῖσι κελεύσας: "urging on the Danaans," i.e., the Greeks. Note
that κελεύω is here used with the dative.
2. **μετάλμενος**: aorist participle of μεθάλλομαι ("I leap among").
ἐν … ὦρσε: tmesis for ἐνῶρσε, aorist (third singular) of ἐνόρνυμι
("I arouse/stir up").
3. **πέφνε**: "he slew." The strong aorist ἔπεφνον, here without an augment,
is the most common of the very few parts of φένω that are found.
Καβησόθεν ἔνδον ἐόντα: this phrase should mean "in the house,
having come from Cabesus," an odd way to refer to someone who is
actually on the field of battle and about to be killed there. We have
here, it seems, an example of a misused formula. The important fact
about Othryoneus is that he has left Cabesus and is now in Troy; to
express this, the poet has casually used a formulaic phrase suggesting
that he is actually inside Priam's house, even though this is not the case
at this point in the narrative. Translate "a visitor from Cabesus." The
exact location of Cabesus, presumably somewhere close to Troy, is
unknown.
4. **νέον**: "recently."
πολέμοιο μετὰ κλέος: "drawn by news of the war."
εἰληλούθει: pluperfect (third singular) of ἔρχομαι.
5. **εἶδος ἀρίστην**: "most beautiful" (lit. "best in form").
7. **ἐκ Τροίης … υἷας Ἀχαιῶν**: the indirect statement after ὑπέσχετο,
with its future infinitive ἀπώσεμεν (from ἀπωθέω), explains the μέγα
ἔργον; ἀέκοντας = ἄκοντας.
8. **ὑπό … ἔσχετο**: tmesis for ὑπέσχετο.
9. **ὑποσχεσίῃσι**: Priam's, presumably.

πιθήσας: "trusting in," from πιθέω, a collateral form of πείθω.
11. βάλεν...τυχών: "hit him full on as he strode high" (lit. "struck him striding high, having hit the mark").
12. ὃν φορέεσκε: "which he customarily wore." φορέεσκε is the iterative imperfect (indicating regular occurrence) from φορέω.
πῆξε: the subject is the spear.

10.7 Thucydides, *Histories* 2.3.1–3: when their city is suddenly taken at night by some Thebans, the Plataeans at first come to terms with them, but then begin to mount resistance.

οἱ δὲ Πλαταιῆς ὡς ᾔσθοντο ἔνδον τε ὄντας τοὺς Θηβαίους
καὶ ἐξαπιναίως κατειλημμένην τὴν πόλιν, καταδείσαντες
καὶ νομίσαντες πολλῷ πλείους ἐσεληλυθέναι—οὐ γὰρ
ἑώρων ἐν τῇ νυκτί—πρὸς ξύμβασιν ἐχώρησαν καὶ τοὺς
λόγους δεξάμενοι ἡσύχαζον, ἄλλως τε καὶ ἐπειδὴ ἐς οὐδένα   5
οὐδὲν ἐνεωτέριζον. πράσσοντες δέ πως ταῦτα κατενόησαν
οὐ πολλοὺς τοὺς Θηβαίους ὄντας καὶ ἐνόμισαν ἐπιθέμενοι
ῥᾳδίως κρατήσειν· τῷ γὰρ πλήθει τῶν Πλαταιῶν οὐ
βουλομένῳ ἦν τῶν Ἀθηναίων ἀφίστασθαι. ἐδόκει οὖν
ἐπιχειρητέα εἶναι, καὶ ξυνελέγοντο διορύσσοντες τοὺς   10
κοινοὺς τοίχους παρ᾽ ἀλλήλους, ὅπως μὴ διὰ τῶν ὁδῶν
φανεροὶ ὦσιν ἰόντες, ἁμάξας τε ἄνευ τῶν ὑποζυγίων ἐς τὰς
ὁδοὺς καθίστασαν, ἵνα ἀντὶ τείχους ᾖ, καὶ τἆλλα ἐξήρτυον
ᾗ ἕκαστον ἐφαίνετο πρὸς τὰ παρόντα ξύμφορον ἔσεσθαι.

Notes: 3. πολλῷ πλείους: i.e., than had actually done so.
5. ἄλλως τε καὶ ἐπειδή: "especially since" (lit. "both otherwise and since").
5–6. ἐς οὐδένα οὐδὲν ἐνεωτέριζον: "they were offering no violence to anyone." The subject is the Thebans.
6. πράσσοντες δέ πως ταῦτα: "but while, in some way or other, they were engaged on this." πως (lit. somehow) indicates that unnecessary details are omitted from the account.
8–9. τῷ γὰρ πλήθει...ἦν: an idiomatic Thucydidean usage = "for the majority of the Plataeans did not want" (lit. "it was not to the majority [of the population] of Plataea wanting").
10. ἐπιχειρητέα εἶναι: "that an attempt should be made."
10–11. τοὺς κοινοὺς τοίχους: "the party walls."
11. παρ᾽ ἀλλήλους: with ξυνελέγοντο.

10.8 Euripides, *Medea* 446–58: Jason points out to Medea that her exile is the direct result of her foolish anger.

Ἰάσων

οὐ νῦν κατεῖδον πρῶτον ἀλλὰ πολλάκις
τραχεῖαν ὀργὴν ὡς ἀμήχανον κακόν.
σοὶ γὰρ παρὸν γῆν τήνδε καὶ δόμους ἔχειν
κούφως φερούσῃ κρεισσόνων βουλεύματα,
λόγων ματαίων οὕνεκ᾽ ἐκπεσῇ χθονός.   5
κἀμοὶ μὲν οὐδὲν πρᾶγμα· μὴ παύσῃ ποτὲ
λέγουσ᾽ Ἰάσον᾽ ὡς κάκιστός ἐστ᾽ ἀνήρ.
ἃ δ᾽ ἐς τυράννους ἐστί σοι λελεγμένα,
πᾶν κέρδος ἡγοῦ ζημιουμένη φυγῇ.
κἀγὼ μὲν αἰεὶ βασιλέων θυμουμένων   10
ὀργὰς ἀφῄρουν καί σ᾽ ἐβουλόμην μένειν·
σὺ δ᾽ οὐκ ἀνίεις μωρίας, λέγουσ᾽ ἀεὶ
κακῶς τυράννους· τοιγὰρ ἐκπεσῇ χθονός.

Notes: 2. **τραχεῖαν ὀργὴν ὡς ἀμήχανον κακόν**: understand ἐστί. The real subject of the indirect statement, τραχεῖαν ὀργὴν, appears as object of the introductory verb (cf. "Ἰάσον" in line 7).
3. **παρόν**: accusative absolute, as regularly with impersonal verbs—"it being possible."
5. **οὕνεκ᾽**: = ἕνεκα.
6. **κἀμοί**: crasis for καὶ ἐμοί.
οὐδὲν πρᾶγμα: understand ἐστί = "it is no big deal."
8. **ἃ δ᾽**: "but as for the things that."
τυράννους: "the royal family"; cf. line 13, and βασιλέων in line 10.
σοι: "by you," dative of agent with a perfect passive.
9. **πᾶν κέρδος ἡγοῦ**: understand εἶναι.
10. **κἀγώ**: crasis for καὶ ἐγώ.
11. **ἀφῄρουν**: "I tried to take away," a common meaning of the imperfect.
12. **ἀνίεις**: imperfect active (2nd singular) of ἀνίημι = "you wouldn't let go of."
12–13. **λέγουσ᾽ ... κακῶς**: "speaking ill of" or "bad-mouthing."
13. **ἐκπεσῇ χθονός**: a smug repetition of the same words as in line 5.

10.9 Plato, *Republic* 2.359d–60a: in an attempt to persuade Socrates that the just practice justice unwillingly and only because they lack the opportunity to be unjust, Glaucon begins the story of the ancestor of Gyges of Lydia and his magic ring.

εἶναι μὲν γὰρ αὐτὸν ποιμένα θητεύοντα παρὰ τῷ τότε
Λυδίας ἄρχοντι, ὄμβρου δὲ πολλοῦ γενομένου καὶ σεισμοῦ,
ῥαγῆναί τι τῆς γῆς καὶ γενέσθαι χάσμα κατὰ τὸν τόπον
ᾗ ἔνεμεν. ἰδόντα δὲ καὶ θαυμάσαντα καταβῆναι καὶ ἰδεῖν
ἄλλα τε δὴ ἃ μυθολογοῦσιν θαυμαστὰ καὶ ἵππον χαλκοῦν,   5
κοῖλον, θυρίδας ἔχοντα, καθ᾽ ἃς ἐγκύψαντα ἰδεῖν ἐνόντα
νεκρόν, ὡς φαίνεσθαι μείζω ἢ κατ᾽ ἄνθρωπον, τοῦτον
δὲ ἄλλο μὲν οὐδέν, περὶ δὲ τῇ χειρὶ χρυσοῦν δακτύλιον
ὄντα περιελόμενον ἐκβῆναι. συλλόγου δὲ γενομένου τοῖς
ποιμέσιν εἰωθότος, ἵν᾽ ἐξαγγέλλοιεν κατὰ μῆνα τῷ βασιλεῖ   10
τὰ περὶ τὰ ποίμνια, ἀφικέσθαι καὶ ἐκεῖνον ἔχοντα τὸν
δακτύλιον· καθήμενον οὖν μετὰ τῶν ἄλλων τυχεῖν τὴν
σφενδόνην τοῦ δακτυλίου περιαγαγόντα πρὸς ἑαυτὸν
εἰς τὸ εἴσω τῆς χειρός, τούτου δὲ γενομένου ἀφανῆ αὐτὸν
γενέσθαι τοῖς παρακαθημένοις, καὶ διαλέγεσθαι ὡς περὶ   15
οἰχομένου. καὶ τὸν θαυμάζειν τε καὶ πάλιν ἐπιψηλαφῶντα
τὸν δακτύλιον στρέψαι ἔξω τὴν σφενδόνην, καὶ στρέψαντα
φανερὸν γενέσθαι.

Notes: 1. **εἶναι μὲν γὰρ αὐτὸν ποιμένα**: the whole of Glaucon's story is in extended indirect speech, or *oratio obliqua*, as it is sometimes known. Right from the start, translation will be clearest if presented in direct speech (*oratio recta*) = "For he was a shepherd...."
5. **ἄλλα ... θαυμαστά**: θαυμαστά has been attracted into the relative clause, but is really part of the antecedent = "both other wonders indeed (δή) of mythology [lit. of which men tell myths]."
6. **καί**: "and in particular."
7. **καθ᾽ ἃς ἐγκύψαντα**: "stooping down and peeping in by which."
ὡς φαίνεσθαι: "as it seemed." The verb in this subordinate clause in indirect speech is attracted into the infinitive.
μείζω ἢ κατ᾽ ἄνθρωπον: "of larger than human proportions."
7–9. **τοῦτον δὲ ... περιελόμενον ἐκβῆναι**: τοῦτον still refers to the shepherd = "and he made his way out, having taken nothing else save a gold ring that was around its finger" (lit. hand).
9–10. **συλλόγου ... εἰωθότος**: "customary meeting."

10. **κατὰ μῆνα**: "each month."

12–13. **τὴν σφενδόνην τοῦ δακτυλίου**: "the collet of the ring," i.e., that part which broadens out like the cup of a sling.

15–16. **καὶ διαλέγεσθαι ὡς περὶ οἰχομένου**: understand αὐτούς with διαλέγεσθαι = "and they spoke of him as of one departed."

16. **τόν**: article as demonstrative, = "he."

ἐπιψηλαφῶντα: "fumbling with."

10.10   Plato, *Republic* 2.360a–c: Glaucon finishes the story and draws his conclusions.

> καὶ τοῦτο ἐννοήσαντα ἀποπειρᾶσθαι τοῦ δακτυλίου
> εἰ ταύτην ἔχοι τὴν δύναμιν, καὶ αὐτῷ οὕτω συμβαίνειν,
> στρέφοντι μὲν εἴσω τὴν σφενδόνην ἀδήλῳ γίγνεσθαι,
> ἔξω δὲ δήλῳ· αἰσθόμενον δὲ εὐθὺς διαπράξασθαι τῶν
> ἀγγέλων γενέσθαι τῶν παρὰ τὸν βασιλέα, ἐλθόντα δὲ καὶ   5
> τὴν γυναῖκα αὐτοῦ μοιχεύσαντα, μετ' ἐκείνης ἐπιθέμενον
> τῷ βασιλεῖ ἀποκτεῖναι καὶ τὴν ἀρχὴν οὕτω κατασχεῖν. εἰ
> οὖν δύο τοιούτω δακτυλίω γενοίσθην, καὶ τὸν μὲν ὁ δίκαιος
> περιθεῖτο, τὸν δὲ ὁ ἄδικος, οὐδεὶς ἂν γένοιτο, ὡς δόξειεν,
> οὕτως ἀδαμάντινος, ὃς ἂν μείνειεν ἐν τῇ δικαιοσύνῃ καὶ   10
> τολμήσειεν ἀπέχεσθαι τῶν ἀλλοτρίων καὶ μὴ ἅπτεσθαι,
> ἐξὸν αὐτῷ καὶ ἐκ τῆς ἀγορᾶς ἀδεῶς ὅτι βούλοιτο λαμβάνειν,
> καὶ εἰσιόντι εἰς τὰς οἰκίας συγγίγνεσθαι ὅτῳ βούλοιτο, καὶ
> ἀποκτεινύναι καὶ ἐκ δεσμῶν λύειν οὕστινας βούλοιτο, καὶ
> τἆλλα πράττειν ἐν τοῖς ἀνθρώποις ἰσόθεον ὄντα.   15

Notes: 2. **εἰ**: "to see whether."

4. **διαπράξασθαι**: "he brought it about that."

4–5. **τῶν ἀγγέλων**: i.e., "one of the messengers."

8. **δύο τοιούτω δακτυλίω γενοίσθην**: "there were to be two such rings"; note the dual forms.

10. **ὃς ... δικαιοσύνῃ**: "as to persevere in justice." The relative with the optative and ἄν here takes the place of ὥστε to express result.

12. **ἐξόν**: accusative absolute = "it being possible."

13. **συγγίγνεσθαι**: "to have sex with."

15. **τἆλλα**: crasis for τὰ ἄλλα.

ἰσόθεον ὄντα: "just as if he were a god" (lit. "being equal to a god").

CHAPTER 11

Direct and Indirect Questions

DIRECT QUESTIONS

Direct questions are introduced:

> *either* by a question word (e.g., who? what? where?) *or*
> by ἆρα or ἦ, suggesting no expected answer (an open
> question.)
> *either* by ἆρα οὐ, ἆρ᾽ οὐ *or* οὐκοῦν expecting the answer
> yes, *or* μή, ἆρα μή or μῶν expecting the answer no.
> πότερον . . . ἤ is used with double questions. (Do not trans-
> late πότερον in direct questions.)

Sometimes questions are not introduced by any words at all; the fact
that such sentences are questions is communicated in modern texts
by the use of a question mark (;) at the end.

11.1   Sophocles, *Oedipus at Colonus* 1–4: the blind and aged Oedipus asks his daughter Antigone to what city and among what men
they have come.

Οἰδίπους

τέκνον τυφλοῦ γέροντος Ἀντιγόνη, τίνας
χώρους ἀφίγμεθ᾽ ἢ τίνων ἀνδρῶν πόλιν;
τίς τὸν πλανήτην Οἰδίπουν καθ᾽ ἡμέραν
τὴν νῦν σπανιστοῖς δέξεται δωρήμασιν;

Notes: 3. **πλανήτην**: "wandering."
καθ᾽ ἡμέραν τὴν νῦν: "today."
4. **σπανιστοῖς … δωρήμασιν**: "with scanty gifts."

11.2 Sophocles, *Antigone* 1211–12: Creon fears that what he is about to discover may be terrible, but he tries to keep it an open question.

Κρέων

ὦ τάλας ἐγώ,

ἆρ᾽ εἰμὶ μάντις;

11.3 Sophocles, *Oedipus at Colonus* 881–89: Creon is about to commit the hubristic act of trying to seize Oedipus. The chorus are on Oedipus' side. The disturbance leads to the entry of Theseus, the king of the area, who has been sacrificing to the sea-god Poseidon.

Οἰδίπους Χορός Κρέων Θησεύς

Οἰ. ἀκούεθ᾽ οἷα φθέγγεται; **Χο.** τά γ᾽ οὐ τελεῖ.
ἴστω μέγας Ζεύς. **Κρ.** Ζεύς γ᾽ ἂν εἰδείη, σὺ δ᾽ οὔ.

Χο. ἆρ᾽ οὐχ ὕβρις τάδ᾽; **Κρ.** ὕβρις, ἀλλ᾽ ἀνεκτέα.

Χο. ἰὼ πᾶς λεώς, ἰὼ γᾶς πρόμοι,
μόλετε σὺν τάχει, μόλετ᾽, ἐπεὶ πέραν   5
περῶσ᾽ οἵδε δή.

Θη. (entering) τίς ποθ᾽ ἡ βοή; τί τοὔργον;

Notes: 1. **τά γ᾽ οὐ τελεῖ**: i.e., he won't carry out his threats.
2. **ἴστω**: third person imperative of οἶδα: "let (him) know." Zeus is the god of suppliants and Oedipus has supplicated the chorus.
Ζεύς γ᾽ ἂν εἰδείη, σὺ δ᾽ οὔ: "Zeus may know but you don't."
3. **ἀνεκτέα**: (nominative neuter plural) "(you) must put up with."
4. **γᾶς**: Doric form of γῆς.
5. **μόλετε σὺν τάχει**: "come quickly!"
5–6. **πέραν περῶσ᾽ οἵδε δή**: "these men (Creon's soldiers) are crossing our borders."
7. **τοὔργον**: = τὸ ἔργον.

11.4 Plato, *Protagoras* 310d: Hippocrates is so excited by the teacher Protagoras' arrival in Athens that he goes to see Socrates early in the morning to tell him about it. Socrates responds by indulging in some characteristic teasing.

'ἐπειδὴ δὲ τάχιστά με ἐκ τοῦ κόπου ὁ ὕπνος ἀνῆκεν, εὐθὺς
ἀναστὰς οὕτω δεῦρο ἐπορευόμην.' καὶ ἐγὼ γιγνώσκων
αὐτοῦ τὴν ἀνδρείαν καὶ τὴν πτοίησιν, 'τί οὖν σοι,' ἦν δ' ἐγώ,
'τοῦτο; μῶν τί σε ἀδικεῖ Πρωταγόρας;' καὶ ὃς γελάσας, 'νὴ
τοὺς θεούς,' ἔφη, 'ὦ Σώκρατες, ὅτι γε μόνος ἐστὶ σοφός,   5
ἐμὲ δὲ οὐ ποιεῖ.' 'ἀλλὰ ναὶ μὰ Δία,' ἔφην ἐγώ, 'ἂν αὐτῷ διδῷς
ἀργύριον καὶ πείθῃς ἐκεῖνον, ποιήσει καὶ σὲ σοφόν.'

Notes: 1. **ἐπειδὴ . . . τάχιστά με ἐκ τοῦ κόπου ὁ ὕπνος ἀνῆκεν**: "as soon as I had slept off my fatigue" (lit. "as soon as sleep had released me from fatigue").
2. **οὕτω**: "like this," "as you can see."
3. **τὴν ἀνδρείαν**: "(his) gallant spirit."
τὴν πτοίησιν: "the flutter (he was in)"
4–5. **ὃς γελάσας . . . ἔφη**: "he said with a laugh."
νὴ τοὺς θεούς: "by the gods." Hippocrates says that Protagoras *is* wronging him.
6. **ἐμὲ δὲ οὐ ποιεῖ**: "but he doesn't make me (wise)."
μὰ Δία: "by Zeus."
ἄν: = ἐάν: "if."

INDIRECT QUESTIONS

A verb in which the voice, ears, eyes or mind or one of the senses is used followed by a word that asks a question (who, when, what, etc.) is followed in Greek by an interrogative pronoun plus a verb in the indicative, though in historic sequence the optative may be used—with a less "vivid" force than the indicative. It is the more common form.

11.5 Thucydides, *Histories* 1.5.1–2: in olden times both the Greeks and the barbarians turned to piracy. The old poets make it clear that this was not viewed as shameful, and the tradition continues.

οἱ γὰρ Ἕλληνες τὸ πάλαι καὶ τῶν βαρβάρων οἵ τε ἐν τῇ
ἠπείρῳ παραθαλάσσιοι καὶ ὅσοι νήσους εἶχον, ἐπειδὴ
ἤρξαντο μᾶλλον περαιοῦσθαι ναυσὶν ἐπ᾽ ἀλλήλους,
ἐτράποντο πρὸς λῃστείαν, ἡγουμένων ἀνδρῶν οὐ τῶν
ἀδυνατωτάτων κέρδους τοῦ σφετέρου αὐτῶν ἕνεκα   5
καὶ τοῖς ἀσθενέσι τροφῆς, καὶ προσπίπτοντες πόλεσιν
ἀτειχίστοις καὶ κατὰ κώμας οἰκουμέναις ἥρπαζον καὶ
τὸν πλεῖστον τοῦ βίου ἐντεῦθεν ἐποιοῦντο, οὐκ ἔχοντός
πω αἰσχύνην τούτου τοῦ ἔργου, φέροντος δέ τι καὶ δόξης
μᾶλλον· δηλοῦσι δὲ τῶν τε ἠπειρωτῶν τινὲς ἔτι καὶ νῦν, οἷς   10
κόσμος καλῶς τοῦτο δρᾶν, καὶ οἱ παλαιοὶ τῶν ποιητῶν τὰς
πύστεις τῶν καταπλεόντων πανταχοῦ ὁμοίως ἐρωτῶντες
εἰ λῃσταί εἰσιν ...

Notes: 1. **τὸ πάλαι**: "in ancient times."

1–2. **οἵ ... ἐν τῇ ἠπείρῳ παραθαλάσσιοι**: "those occupying coastal regions on the mainland."

2. **ὅσοι**: "all those who."

3. **περαιοῦσθαι ναυσίν**: "to traffic with their ships."

4. **ἐτράποντο πρὸς λῃστείαν**: "they turned to piracy." ἐτράποντο is the aorist middle of τρέπω.

4–5. **ἡγουμένων ἀνδρῶν οὐ τῶν ἀδυνατωτάτων**: "led by the most powerful men," lit., "not the most powerless of men leading" (genitive absolute).

6. **τοῖς ἀσθενέσι τροφῆς**: "the provision of food for the weak."

6–7. **προσπίπτοντες πόλεσιν ἀτειχίστοις καὶ κατὰ κώμας οἰκουμέναις**: "falling on unwalled communities with the population scattered in villages."

8. **τὸν πλεῖστον τοῦ βίου ἐντεῦθεν**: "most of their livelihood from that."

8–9. **οὐκ ... πω**: "not yet."

τούτου τοῦ ἔργου: "this business," the subject of the two participles in the genitive absolute construction.

10–11. **οἷς κόσμος καλῶς τοῦτο δρᾶν**: lit. "for whom to do this well is an ornament," i.e., "who take successful piracy as a compliment."

11–12. **τὰς πύστεις τῶν καταπλεόντων πανταχοῦ ὁμοίως**: i.e., "the regular question (put to) all who arrive by sea," lit. "the questionings everywhere in a similar way of those who arrive by sea." Thucydides goes on to say that there is no criticism from the questioner if the answer is that they are pirates.

11.6   Plato, *Apology* 21a–b: Socrates explains to the jury that Apollo's oracle at Delphi had said in response to a friend of his called Chaerephon that nobody was wiser than he was.

ἐμός τε ἑταῖρος ἦν ἐκ νέου καὶ ὑμῶν τῷ πλήθει ἑταῖρός τε
καὶ συνέφυγε τὴν φυγὴν ταύτην καὶ μεθ' ὑμῶν κατῆλθε.
καὶ ἴστε δὴ οἷος ἦν Χαιρεφῶν, ὡς σφοδρὸς ἐφ' ὅτι
ὁρμήσειεν. καὶ δή ποτε καὶ εἰς Δελφοὺς ἐλθὼν ἐτόλμησε
τοῦτο μαντεύσασθαι—καί, ὅπερ λέγω, μὴ θορυβεῖτε, ὦ   5
ἄνδρες—ἤρετο γὰρ δὴ εἴ τις ἐμοῦ εἴη σοφώτερος. ἀνεῖλεν
οὖν ἡ Πυθία μηδένα σοφώτερον εἶναι. καὶ τούτων πέρι ὁ
ἀδελφὸς ὑμῖν αὐτοῦ οὑτοσὶ μαρτυρήσει, ἐπειδὴ ἐκεῖνος
τετελεύτηκεν. σκέψασθε δὴ ὧν ἕνεκα ταῦτα λέγω· μέλλω
γὰρ ὑμᾶς διδάξειν ὅθεν μοι ἡ διαβολὴ γέγονεν. ταῦτα γὰρ   10
ἐγὼ ἀκούσας ἐνεθυμούμην οὑτωσί· 'τί ποτε λέγει ὁ θεός,
καὶ τί ποτε αἰνίττεται; ἐγὼ γὰρ δὴ οὔτε μέγα οὔτε σμικρὸν
σύνοιδα ἐμαυτῷ σοφὸς ὤν· τί οὖν ποτε λέγει φάσκων ἐμὲ
σοφώτατον εἶναι; οὐ γὰρ δήπου ψεύδεταί γε· οὐ γὰρ θέμις
αὐτῷ.'   15

Notes: 1. **ἐκ νέου**: "from his youth."
ὑμῶν τῷ πλήθει ἑταῖρός: lit. "a companion to the greater number of you," i.e., "a partisan of democracy."
2. **συνέφυγε τὴν φυγὴν ταύτην καὶ μεθ' ὑμῶν κατῆλθε**: "he shared this [i.e., the recent] exile and came back with you": in 404 BC after the installation by the Spartans of a brutal puppet government, many democrats had fled from Athens. Democracy was reinstated—and the exiles returned—eight months later.
3–4. **ὡς σφοδρὸς ἐφ' ὅτι ὁρμήσειεν**: "impetuous (he was) on whatever (idea) he was keen on."
5. **τοῦτο μαντεύσασθαι**: "to put this question to the oracle." The oracle of Apollo, the god of prophecy, at Delphi gave responses to those who consulted it through an inspired priestess, the Pythia.
ὅπερ λέγω, μὴ θορυβεῖτε: "don't create an uproar at what I say."
5–6. **ὦ ἄνδρες**: i.e., the men on the jury trying Socrates.
6. **ἀνεῖλεν**: "responded."
7. **ἡ Πυθία**: i.e., Apollo's priestess, the Pythia.

8. **οὑτοσί**: the iota suffix gives the meaning "this here," i.e., "here in court."

11. **λέγει**: i.e., "mean."

12. **αἰνίττεται**: "is he hinting (getting) at."

οὔτε μέγα οὔτε σμικρὸν: "neither in a great or small way." He is *totally* sure that …

13. **σύνοιδα ἐμαυτῷ**: "I am conscious in myself."

14. **θέμις**: = "right": a god cannot lie.

11.7 Herodotus, *Histories* 1.31: to the massive irritation of Croesus, the king of Lydia, Solon has pronounced not him but an obscure Athenian called Tellos the happiest of men. Croesus, who had assumed that Solon would single out him, asks the latter whom he would put next. Solon chooses two equally obscure Argives called Cleobis and Biton.

> ὡς δὲ τὰ κατὰ τὸν Τέλλον προετρέψατο ὁ Σόλων τὸν
> Κροῖσον εἴπας πολλά τε καὶ ὀλβία, ἐπειρώτα τίνα δεύτερον
> μετ᾽ ἐκεῖνον ἴδοι, δοκέων πάγχυ δευτερεῖα γῶν οἴσεσθαι.
> ὁ δ᾽ εἶπε ʻΚλέοβίν τε καὶ Βίτωνα.ʼ

Notes: 1. **κατὰ**: "about."

προετρέψατο: Solon "led" Croesus "on" by saying (εἴπας)….

2. **ἐπειρώτα**: "he asked."

3. **ἴδοι**: "had seen."

δοκέων πάγχυ δευτερεῖα γῶν οἴσεσθαι: "fully believing that he would at least win second prize."

DELIBERATIVE QUESTIONS

In questions in which the speaker asks what he *is to* do or say the aorist subjunctive is used. Negative μή.

11.8 Xenophon, *Memorabilia* 1.2.45: when the minority imposes its will on the majority without persuasion, is that force? And what about when the majority imposes its will on the minority without persuasion?

> ὅσα δὲ οἱ ὀλίγοι τοὺς πολλοὺς μὴ πείσαντες, ἀλλὰ
> κρατοῦντες γράφουσι, πότερον βίαν φῶμεν ἢ μὴ φῶμεν

εἶναι; πάντα μοι δοκεῖ, φάναι τὸν Περικλέα, ὅσα τις μὴ
πείσας ἀναγκάζει τινὰ ποιεῖν, εἴτε γράφων εἴτε μή, βία
μᾶλλον ἢ νόμος εἶναι. καὶ ὅσα ἄρα τὸ πᾶν πλῆθος κρατοῦν   5
τῶν τὰ χρήματα ἐχόντων γράφει μὴ πείσαν, βία μᾶλλον ἢ
νόμος ἂν εἴη;

Notes: 1. **ὅσα**: "all the things that."
μὴ πείσαντες: the negative μή tells us that the participle is being used
conditionally: i.e., "if they do not persuade. . . ." (see p. 47).
2. **γράφουσι**: "decree."
φῶμεν: deliberative subjunctive of φημί: "are we to say . . ." The ὅσα
clause is dependent on this verb.
3–5. **πάντα μοι δοκεῖ . . . ὅσα . . . εἶναι**: "all the things that [lit. as many
as] . . . seem to me to be. . . ."
3. **φάναι τὸν Περικλέα**: someone is telling us that Pericles said this,
hence the accusative and infinitive (from φημί) construction; translate
"Pericles said."
5. **κρατοῦν**: neuter present participle + gen.: "dominating. . . ."

CHAPTER 12

Commands, Prohibitions, Wishes

Commands (2nd and 3rd person) are expressed by the imperative. The present imperative is used for general commands, the aorist for specific and more urgent instructions.

Prohibitions are expressed by μή with the present imperative (general), or μή with the aorist subjunctive (particular).

First person commands, known as exhortations, are expressed by the present or aorist subjunctive: present for general, aorist for particular. The negative is μή.

Both subjunctive and imperative can be preceded by ἄγε (ἄγετε), φέρε or ἴθι ("come"). Even when the verb that follows is plural, the singular form is regularly found.

Indirect Commands are expressed by the infinitive, just as in English; negative μή.

Wishes for the future: εἴθε or εἰ γάρ (both of which may be omitted) with the present or aorist optative; negative μή.

Wishes for present and past: εἴθε or εἰ γάρ (which may *not* be omitted) with the imperfect indicative (present) or aorist indicative (past); or ὤφελον (aorist of ὀφείλω) with present or aorist infinitive. ὤφελον may, but need not, be preceded by εἴθε, εἰ γάρ, or ὡς.

12.1   Two extracts from Homer's *Odyssey*

(I)   *Odyssey* 1.1–2: the poet asks for the Muse's inspiration as he embarks on the tale of Odysseus and his travels.

ἄνδρα μοι ἔννεπε, μοῦσα, πολύτροπον, ὃς μάλα πολλὰ
πλάγχθη, ἐπεὶ Τροίης ἱερὸν πτολίεθρον ἔπερσε·

Notes: 1. **ἔννεπε**: imperative of ἐννέπω, lengthened Homeric form of ἐνέπω ("I tell/relate").
2. **πλάγχθη**: unaugmented aorist (3rd singular) of πλάζομαι ("I wander").

(II)   *Odyssey* 1.169–72: Telemachus quizzes Athene, disguised as Mentes, on her identity and the details of her travel to Ithaca.

ἀλλ' ἄγε μοι τόδε εἰπὲ καὶ ἀτρεκέως κατάλεξον·
τίς πόθεν εἰς ἀνδρῶν; πόθι τοι πόλις ἠδὲ τοκῆες;
ὁπποίης τ' ἐπὶ νηὸς ἀφίκεο· πῶς δέ σε ναῦται
ἤγαγον εἰς Ἰθάκην; τίνες ἔμμεναι εὐχετόωντο;

Notes: 2. **τίς πόθεν εἰς ἀνδρῶν**: note that two questions are contained here in a single phrase; εἰς = εἶ, 2nd singular of the present of εἰμί.
πόθι: = ποῦ.
τοκῆες: = τοκῆς.
3. **ὁπποίης**: = ὁποίας, an indirect interrogative, as if κατάλεξον had immediately preceded; but still to be translated as a direct question.
ἀφίκεο: uncontracted form of ἀφίκου, 2nd singular of ἀφικόμην, aorist of ἀφικνέομαι.

12.2   Thucydides, *Histories* 1.86.5: the warmongering Sthenelaidas urges his fellow Spartans to go forth against the Athenians.

ψηφίζεσθε οὖν, ὦ Λακεδαιμόνιοι, ἀξίως τῆς Σπάρτης τὸν
πόλεμον, καὶ μήτε τοὺς Ἀθηναίους ἐᾶτε μείζους γίγνεσθαι
μήτε τοὺς ξυμμάχους καταπροδιδῶμεν, ἀλλὰ ξὺν τοῖς θεοῖς
ἐπίωμεν ἐπὶ τοὺς ἀδικοῦντας.

Notes: 1. **ἀξίως τῆς Σπάρτης**: "in a manner worthy of Sparta."
2. **μείζους γίγνεσθαι**: i.e., "to become more powerful."
3. **ξὺν τοῖς θεοῖς**: "with the help of the gods."

12.3   Two extracts from tragedy.

(I)   Aeschylus, *Persae* 402–5: the battle cry of the Greeks at
Salamis, as reported by a messenger to Queen Atossa, Xerxes'
mother.

Ἄγγελος

ὦ παῖδες Ἑλλήνων ἴτε,
ἐλευθεροῦτε πατρίδ᾽, ἐλευθεροῦτε δὲ
παῖδας, γυναῖκας, θεῶν τε πατρῴων ἕδη,
θήκας τε προγόνων· νῦν ὑπὲρ πάντων ἀγών.

Notes: 4. **νῦν ὑπὲρ πάντων ἀγών**: understand ἐστίν ("now is the
struggle for everything").

(II)   Euripides, *Iphigenia at Aulis* 495–99: faced with the reality
of Iphigenia's sacrifice, Menelaus suggests to Agamemnon that
they disband their forces; he renounces any role in dealing with
the oracles concerning his niece.

Μενέλαος

ἴτω στρατεία διαλυθεῖσ᾽ ἐξ Αὐλίδος,
σὺ δ᾽ ὄμμα παῦσαι δακρύοις τέγγων τὸ σόν,
ἀδελφέ, κἀμὲ παρακαλῶν ἐς δάκρυα.
εἰ δέ τι κόρης σῆς θεσφάτων μέτεστι σοί,
μὴ μοὶ μετέστω· σοὶ νέμω τοὐμὸν μέρος.   5

Notes: 1. **ἴτω**: imperative (third singular) of εἶμι (I shall go).
στρατεία: usually an "expedition" or "a campaign," but here, as only
rarely, meaning "army/expeditionary force."
2. **παῦσαι**: aorist imperative (2nd singular) of παύομαι ("I cease").
3. **κἀμέ**: crasis for καὶ ἐμέ; cf. τοὐμόν for τὸ ἐμόν two lines down.
4. **εἰ ... τι ... μέτεστι σοί**: "if you have any part in" (lit. "if there is any
share to you").
κόρης σῆς θεσφάτων: "the oracles concerning your daughter," an
objective genitive.
5. **μετέστω**: imperative (3rd singular) of μέτεστι.

12.4 *St. Luke's Gospel* 18.18–25: "it is easier for a camel to go through a needle's eye, than for a rich man to enter into the kingdom of God."

καὶ ἐπηρώτησέν τις αὐτὸν ἄρχων λέγων, Διδάσκαλε
ἀγαθέ, τί ποιήσας ζωὴν αἰώνιον κληρονομήσω; εἶπε δὲ
αὐτῷ ὁ Ἰησοῦς, Τί με λέγεις ἀγαθόν; οὐδεὶς ἀγαθὸς, εἰ
μὴ εἷς, ὁ θεός. τὰς ἐντολὰς οἶδας· Μὴ μοιχεύσῃς, Μὴ
φονεύσῃς, Μὴ κλέψῃς, Μὴ ψευδομαρτυρήσῃς, Τίμα   5
τὸν πατέρα σου καὶ τὴν μητέρα. ὁ δὲ εἶπεν, Ταῦτα πάντα
ἐφύλαξα ἐκ νεότητος. ἀκούσας δὲ ὁ Ἰησοῦς εἶπεν αὐτῷ,
Ἔτι ἕν σοι λείπει· πάντα ὅσα ἔχεις πώλησον καὶ διάδος
πτωχοῖς, καὶ ἕξεις θησαυρὸν ἐν τοῖς οὐρανοῖς, καὶ δεῦρο
ἀκολούθει μοι. ὁ δὲ ἀκούσας ταῦτα περίλυπος ἐγενήθη· ἦν   10
γὰρ πλούσιος σφόδρα. ἰδὼν δὲ αὐτὸν ὁ Ἰησοῦς εἶπεν Πῶς
δυσκόλως οἱ τὰ χρήματα ἔχοντες εἰς τὴν βασιλείαν τοῦ
θεοῦ εἰσπορεύονται· εὐκοπώτερον γάρ ἐστιν κάμηλον διὰ
τρήματος βελόνης εἰσελθεῖν ἢ πλούσιον εἰς τὴν βασιλείαν
τοῦ θεοῦ εἰσελθεῖν.   15

Notes: 1. **τις...ἄρχων**: "a certain ruler," i.e., a member of the Sanhedrin, the supreme court of ancient Israel.
2. **τί ποιήσας...κληρονομήσω**: lit. "having done what shall I inherit," i.e., "what shall I do to inherit."
3. **Τί με λέγεις ἀγαθόν;** : τί here, as regularly, = "why?"
4. **οἶδας**: = οἶσθα, 2nd singular of οἶδα.
4–6. **Μὴ μοιχεύσῃς...μητέρα**: numbers seven, six, eight, nine, and five of the Ten Commandments (as in *Exodus* 20).
8. **λείπει**: "is lacking."
9. **δεῦρο**: used with an imperative like ἄγε ("come/come on"); cf. ἄγε δεῦρο with an imperative in Homer and tragedy.
10. **ἐγενήθη**: aorist passive with same meaning as aorist middle ἐγένετο.
11–12. **Πῶς δυσκόλως**: "with what difficulty," an exclamation.
13–14. **εὐκοπώτερον γάρ ἐστιν κάμηλον...εἰσελθεῖν**: the actual construction here is accusative and infinitive, i.e., "it is easier that a camel enter in...." διὰ τρήματος βελόνης: a τρῆμα is a perforation or hole; in the case of a βελόνη (a needle), its eye.

12.5 Euripides, *Phoenissae* 1442–53: a messenger reports the last words of Polynices as he and his brother, Eteocles, lie dying after fatally wounding each other in single combat.

Ἄγγελος

ὁ δ᾽ ἦν ἔτ᾽ ἔμπνους, πρὸς κασιγνήτην δ᾽ ἰδὼν
γραῖάν τε μητέρ᾽ εἶπε Πολυνείκης τάδε·
Ἀπωλόμεσθα, μῆτερ· οἰκτίρω δὲ σὲ
καὶ τήνδ᾽ ἀδελφὴν καὶ κασίγνητον νεκρόν.
φίλος γὰρ ἐχθρὸς ἐγένετ᾽, ἀλλ᾽ ὅμως φίλος.   5
θάψον δέ μ᾽, ὦ τεκοῦσα, καὶ σύ, σύγγονε,
ἐν γῇ πατρῴᾳ, καὶ πόλιν θυμουμένην
παρηγορεῖτον, ὡς τοσόνδε γοῦν τύχω
χθονὸς πατρῴας, κεἰ δόμους ἀπώλεσα.
ξυνάρμοσον δὲ βλέφαρά μου τῇ σῇ χερί,   10
μῆτερ—τίθησι δ᾽ αὐτὸς ὀμμάτων ἔπι—
καὶ χαίρετ᾽· ἤδη γάρ με περιβάλλει σκότος.

Notes: 1. **ὁ δ᾽**: "but the other." The messenger who has just been describing Eteocles' final moments now speaks of his brother, Polynices. **κασιγνήτην**: i.e., Antigone.

2. **γραῖάν ... μητέρ᾽**: i.e., Jocasta, in this version of the story still alive at this stage.

3. **Ἀπωλόμεσθα**: = ἀπωλόμεθα. Polynices' inclusion of his dead brother (κασίγνητον νεκρόν) in what follows suggests that here he is referring only to himself = "I am undone/finished."

4. **τήνδ᾽ ἀδελφήν**: "my sister here," a common way of translating the demonstrative ὅδε.

5. **φίλος ... φίλος**: lit. "for dear [to me] he became my enemy, but [was] nonetheless dear." The repetition of φίλος at the beginning and end of the line underlines Polynices' affection for his brother.

7–8. **πόλιν ... παρηγορεῖτον**: "pacify, the two of you, the angry city"; παρηγορεῖτον: present imperative dual (second person).

8–9. **τοσόνδε γοῦν ... χθονὸς πατρῴας**: "this much at least of my native land." Polynices, who has been an enemy to Thebes, means just that part of his homeland where he will be buried.

9. **κεἰ**: crasis for καὶ εἰ.

10. **χερί**: = χειρί.

τίθησι ... ὀμμάτων ἔπι: understand χέρα; notice too the anastrophe, the throwing back of the accent to the first syllable, which occurs when a disyllabic preposition follows its noun.

12.6   Aristophanes, *Acharnians* 280–99: the Acharnian elders of the chorus are all set to stone Dicaeopolis for having made peace with the Spartans.

Χορός   Δικαιόπολις

Χο.   οὗτος αὐτός ἐστιν, οὗτος.
        βάλλε, βάλλε, βάλλε, βάλλε,
        παῖε, παῖε τὸν μιαρόν.
        οὐ βαλεῖς; οὐ βαλεῖς;

Δι.   Ἡράκλεις, τουτὶ τί ἐστι; τὴν χύτραν συντρίψετε.   5

Χο.   σὲ μὲν οὖν καταλεύσομεν, ὦ μιαρὰ κεφαλή.

Δι.   ἀντὶ ποίας αἰτίας, ὦχαρνέων γεραίτατοι;

Χο.   τοῦτ' ἐρωτᾷς; ἀναίσχυντος εἶ καὶ βδελυρὸς,
        ὦ προδότα τῆς πατρίδος, ὅστις ἡμῶν μόνος
        σπεισάμενος εἶτα δύνασαι πρὸς ἔμ' ἀποβλέπειν.   10

Δι.   ἀντὶ δ' ὧν ἐσπεισάμην οὐκ ἴστε. ἀλλ' ἀκούσατε.

Χο.   σοῦ γ' ἀκούσωμεν; ἀπολεῖ· κατά σε χώσομεν τοῖς
                          λίθοις.

Δι.   μηδαμῶς πρὶν ἄν γ' ἀκούσητ'· ἀλλ' ἀνάσχεσθ'
                            ὦγαθοί.

Χο.   οὐκ ἀνασχήσομαι· μηδὲ λέγε μοι σὺ λόγον·
        ὡς μεμίσηκά σε Κλέωνος ἔτι μᾶλλον, ὃν ἐ-   15
        γὼ κατατεμῶ ποθ' ἱππεῦσι καττύματα.
        σοῦ δ' ἐγὼ λόγους λέγοντος οὐκ ἀκούσομαι
                         μακρούς,
        ὅστις ἐσπείσω Λάκωσιν, ἀλλὰ τιμωρήσομαι.

Notes: 1. **οὗτος ... οὗτος**: "that's the very man there."
4. **οὐ βαλεῖς**: the question is almost an imperative = "come on, pelt him" (lit. "won't you pelt him?").
5. **Ἡράκλεις**: the vocative used in a mild oath.
τουτί: a stronger form of τοῦτο = "this here."
χύτραν: an earthenware pot that Dicaeopolis is carrying in procession.

6. **ὦ μιαρὰ κεφαλή**: "you foul creature."

7. **ὦχαρνέων γεραίτατοι**: "O elders of the Acharnians"; ὦχαρνέων = ὦ Ἀχαρνέων.

11. **ἀντὶ δ᾽ ὧν**: "for what reason."

12. **ἀκούσωμεν**: a deliberative subjunctive ("are we to listen to you").

κατά … χώσομεν: tmesis of καταχώσομεν, future (1st plural) of καταχώννυμι ("I heap up").

13. **ἀνάσχεσθ᾽**: aorist imperative (3rd plural) of ἀνέχομαι ("I hold back/have patience").

ὦγαθοί: = ὦ ἀγαθοί.

15. **μεμίσηκα**: "I have come to hate," therefore "I hate." The perfect tense indicates a present state that is the result of a past action.

Κλέωνος: Cleon was an Athenian politician, prominent during the first part of the Peloponnesian War. He is depicted by both Thucydides and Aristophanes as a vulgar and unscrupulous demagogue.

16. **ἱππεῦσι καττύματα**: in apposition to ὅν, lit. "as shoe soles for the Knights." In Athens the term "Knights" (ἱππεῖς) originally included all the richest citizens, but in his reform of the constitution in the early sixth century, Solon used it to refer specifically to the second highest census class, i.e., those wealthy enough to keep a horse. At the time of 'the production of *Acharnians*' in 425 BC, the Knights were powerful opponents of the populist Cleon, whose well-known associations with the leather trade explain the precise nature of the Acharnian elders' attack here. Aristophanes was to launch an even more vicious assault on Cleon the following year in his comedy *Knights*.

18. **ὅστις**: "you who."

12.7   Thucydides, *Histories* 2.12.2–3: the Spartans, already on the march against the Athenians, have sent a herald, Melesippus, to negotiate a surrender. The Athenians send him away without a hearing, and he predicts big trouble ahead.

> ἀποπέμπουσιν οὖν αὐτὸν πρὶν ἀκοῦσαι καὶ ἐκέλευον
> ἐκτὸς ὅρων εἶναι αὐθημερόν, τό τε λοιπὸν ἀναχωρήσαντας
> ἐπὶ τὰ σφέτερα αὐτῶν, ἤν τι βούλωνται, πρεσβεύεσθαι.
> ξυμπέμπουσί τε τῷ Μελησίππῳ ἀγωγούς, ὅπως μηδενὶ
> ξυγγένηται. ὁ δ᾽ ἐπειδὴ ἐπὶ τοῖς ὁρίοις ἐγένετο καὶ ἔμελλε   5
> διαλύσεσθαι, τοσόνδε εἰπὼν ἐπορεύετο ὅτι Ἥδε ἡ ἡμέρα
> τοῖς Ἕλλησι μεγάλων κακῶν ἄρξει.

Notes: 2–3. **τό τε λοιπὸν … πρεσβεύεσθαι**: the really significant command is contained in the participle ἀναχωρήσαντας = "and in future, if they wanted anything, to withdraw into their own territory before sending an embassy" (lit. "in future, if they wanted anything, to send an embassy after having withdrawn into their own territory").

6. **διαλύσεσθαι**: "to part company," future infinitive after μέλλω.
τοσόνδε: "just this."
ὅτι: used here colloquially to introduce direct speech; do not translate.

12.8 Xenophon, *Hellenica* 4.1.37–39: the Persian Pharnabazus gives a frank reply to Agesilaus the Spartan, who has just tried to persuade him to secede from the king of Persia and join in alliance with him.

Οὐκοῦν, ἔφη ὁ Φαρνάβαζος, ἁπλῶς ὑμῖν ἀποκρίνομαι
ἅπερ ποιήσω; Πρέπει γοῦν σοι. Ἐγὼ τοίνυν, ἔφη, ἐὰν
βασιλεὺς ἄλλον μὲν στρατηγὸν πέμπῃ, ἐμὲ δὲ ὑπήκοον
ἐκείνου τάττῃ, βουλήσομαι ὑμῖν καὶ φίλος καὶ σύμμαχος
εἶναι· ἐὰν μέντοι μοι τὴν ἀρχὴν προστάττῃ - τοιοῦτόν τι,   5
ὡς ἔοικε, φιλοτιμία ἐστίν -, εὖ χρὴ εἰδέναι ὅτι πολεμήσω
ὑμῖν ὡς ἂν δύνωμαι ἄριστα. ἀκούσας ταῦτα ὁ Ἀγησίλαος
ἐλάβετο τῆς χειρὸς αὐτοῦ καὶ εἶπεν· Εἴθ᾽, ὦ λῷστε σύ,
τοιοῦτος ὢν φίλος ἡμῖν γένοιο. ἐν δ᾽ οὖν, ἔφη, ἐπίστω, ὅτι
νῦν τε ἄπειμι ὡς ἂν δύνωμαι τάχιστα ἐκ τῆς σῆς χώρας,   10
τοῦ τε λοιποῦ, κἂν πόλεμος ᾖ, ἕως ἂν ἐπ᾽ ἄλλον ἔχωμεν
στρατεύεσθαι, σοῦ τε καὶ τῶν σῶν ἀφεξόμεθα. τούτων δὲ
λεχθέντων διέλυσε τὴν σύνοδον.

Notes: 1–2. **Οὐκοῦν ... ποιήσω**: "Do I then give you a straight answer as to what I shall do?"
2. **Πρέπει γοῦν σοι**: "It's certainly right that you should" (lit. "it certainly befits you"). Remember that the conventional way to indicate the beginning of direct speech in Greek is to start with a capital letter. In a conversational passage like this we can see at a glance where the changes in speaker occur.
5. **τοιοῦτόν τι**: "such a thing."
6. **φιλοτιμία**: "ambition."
εὖ χρὴ εἰδέναι: "you should be well assured"; εὖ goes with εἰδέναι and ὑμᾶς is understood with χρή.
8. **ὦ λῷστε σύ**: "you excellent fellow."
9. **ἐπίστω**: imperative (2nd singular) of ἐπίσταμαι.
11. **κἂν**: crasis of καὶ ἐάν.
ἔχωμεν: ἔχειν here, as regularly with an infinitive, means "to be able."

12.9 Euripides, *Electra* 1060–73: Electra tells her mother Clytemnestra, sister of Helen and of Castor and Pollux, a few home truths.

Ἠλέκτρα

λέγοιμ' ἄν· ἀρχὴ δ' ἥδε μοι προοιμίου·
εἴθ' εἶχες, ὦ τεκοῦσα, βελτίους φρένας.
τὸ μὲν γὰρ εἶδος αἶνον ἄξιον φέρειν
Ἑλένης τε καὶ σοῦ, δύο δ' ἔφυτε συγγόνω,
ἄμφω ματαίω Κάστορός τ' οὐκ ἀξίω.   5
ἡ μὲν γὰρ ἁρπασθεῖσ' ἑκοῦσ' ἀπώλετο,
σὺ δ' ἄνδρ' ἄριστον Ἑλλάδος διώλεσας,
σκῆψιν προτείνουσ', ὡς ὑπὲρ τέκνου πόσιν
ἔκτεινας· οὐ γάρ σ' ὡς ἔγωγ' ἴσασιν εὖ.
ἥτις, θυγατρὸς πρὶν κεκυρῶσθαι σφαγάς,   10
νέον τ' ἀπ' οἴκων ἀνδρὸς ἐξωρμημένου,
ξανθὸν κατόπτρῳ πλόκαμον ἐξήσκεις κόμης.
γυνὴ δ', ἀπόντος ἀνδρός ἥτις ἐκ δόμων
ἐς κάλλος ἀσκεῖ, διάγραφ' ὡς οὖσαν κακήν.

Notes: 1. **λέγοιμ' ἄν:** "I'll speak then." Electra takes advantage of the offer Clytemnestra has just made that she speak freely, without fear of recrimination.

ἀρχὴ ... προοιμίου: understand ἔσται ("and my preamble will begin like this").

3. **αἶνον ἄξιον φέρειν:** understand ἐστί = "deservedly wins praise" (lit. "is worthy to bring praise").

4. **ἔφυτε συγγόνω:** "in nature you're two of a kind" (lit. "you are by nature two sisters"). The intransitive aorist ἔφυν (from φύω, here 2nd plural) is used with present meaning. συγγόνω is nominative dual: Greek has no qualms about mixing dual and plural like this.

5. **ματαίω:** (here) "frivolous" or "wanton."

7. **ἄνδρ' ἄριστον Ἑλλάδος:** i.e., Agamemnon.

9. **γάρ:** the underlying sense is "[And people believed you], for. . . ."

10. **κεκυρῶσθαι:** perfect infinitive passive of κυρόω ("I sanction").

12. **ξανθὸν ... πλόκαμον ἐξήσκεις κόμης:** "were primping your blonde curls" (lit. "were decking out a golden lock of your hair").

14. **ἐς κάλλος ἀσκεῖ:** "beautifies herself" (lit. "adorns herself into beauty"); ἀσκεῖ = ἀσκεῖ ἑαυτήν.

διάγραφ': understand αὐτήν ("write her off").

12.10 Homer, *Iliad* 3.424–36: more home truths, Helen to Paris this time, after Aphrodite has delivered him from certain death in single combat with Menelaus.

τῇ ἄρα δίφρον ἑλοῦσα φιλομμειδὴς Ἀφροδίτη
ἀντί' Ἀλεξάνδροιο θεὰ κατέθηκε φέρουσα·
ἔνθα κάθιζ' Ἑλένη κούρη Διὸς αἰγιόχοιο
ὄσσε πάλιν κλίνασα, πόσιν δ' ἠνίπαπε μύθῳ·
Ἤλυθες ἐκ πολέμου· ὡς ὤφελες αὐτόθ' ὀλέσθαι   5
ἀνδρὶ δαμεὶς κρατερῷ, ὃς ἐμὸς πρότερος πόσις ἦεν.
ἦ μὲν δὴ πρίν γ' εὔχε' ἀρηϊφίλου Μενελάου
σῇ τε βίῃ καὶ χερσὶ καὶ ἔγχεϊ φέρτερος εἶναι·
ἀλλ' ἴθι νῦν προκάλεσσαι ἀρηΐφιλον Μενέλαον
ἐξαῦτις μαχέσασθαι ἐναντίον· ἀλλά σ' ἔγωγε   10
παύεσθαι κέλομαι, μηδὲ ξανθῷ Μενελάῳ
ἀντίβιον πόλεμον πολεμίζειν ἠδὲ μάχεσθαι
ἀφραδέως, μή πως τάχ' ὑπ' αὐτοῦ δουρὶ δαμήῃς.

Notes: 1. **τῇ ... ἑλοῦσα**: "taking then a stool for her," i.e., for Helen. ἑλοῦσα: nominative singular feminine of aorist participle (ἑλών) of αἱρέω.
2. **ἀντί' Ἀλεξάνδροιο**: the adverbial ἀντία (accusative neuter plural of ἀντίος) is used as a preposition with the genitive, = "facing Alexander." Alexander is an alternative name for Paris.
4. **ὄσσε πάλιν κλίνασα**: "turning aside her gaze." ὄσσε is dual (lit. "her two eyes").
ἠνίπαπε: aorist (third singular) of ἐνίπτω ("I rebuke").
5. **Ἤλυθες ἐκ πολέμου**: a hostile beginning ("So, you've come back from the war"); ἤλυθες = ἦλθες.
6. **ἀνδρὶ δαμεὶς κρατερῷ**: δαμείς is one of three possible aorist passive participles of δαμάζω. δμηθείς and δαμασθείς are also possible; ἀνδρί ... κρατερῷ is a dative of agent.
7. **εὔχε'**: = εὔχεο Homeric imperfect (second singular) of εὔχομαι ("you used to boast").
9. **προκάλεσσαι**: = προκάλεσαι, aorist imperative middle (second singular) of προκαλέω.
10–11. **ἀλλά ... κέλομαι**: "but my advice to you is to call a halt," harsh and wounding words, though some have thought them an indication of Helen's love for Paris reasserting itself.
13. **δουρί**: = δορί.
δαμήῃς: aorist subjunctive passive (second singular) of δαμάζω.

CHAPTER 13

Purpose Clauses

"I went to New York *(in order) to see the statue of Liberty.*" The italicized clause expresses purpose. (Such clauses are sometimes called final clauses.) Greek has three ways of doing this.

A. ἵνα, ὅπως, ὄφρα, ὡς, μή + SUBJUNCTIVE OR OPTATIVE.
The subjunctive is used in primary sequence, and the optative is generally found in historic sequence. If the subjunctive is used in historic sequence, a sense of immediacy is conveyed (see 13.2 below).

13.1 Homer, *Iliad* 2.381: Agamemnon tells the Greeks to eat and then to fight.

νῦν δ᾽ ἔρχεσθ᾽ ἐπὶ δεῖπνον ἵνα ξυνάγωμεν Ἄρηα.

Notes: 1. **ἔρχεσθ᾽**: plural imperative. *You* do this and then *we* can start ...
ξυνάγωμεν Ἄρηα: "we may begin [lit. gather together] fighting."
Ares, the god of war, is here used in metonymy to convey his sphere of influence.

13.2 Xenophon, *Anabasis* 1.4.18: By burning the boats, Abrocomas, one of the Persian king's key commanders, has made a vain attempt to prevent Cyrus, the pretender to the throne, from crossing over a river.

οἱ δὲ Θαψακηνοὶ ἔλεγον ὅτι οὐπώποθ᾽ οὗτος ὁ ποταμὸς
διαβατὸς γένοιτο πεζῇ εἰ μὴ τότε, ἀλλὰ πλοίοις, ἃ τότε
Ἀβροκόμας προϊὼν κατέκαυσεν, ἵνα μὴ Κῦρος διαβῇ.

Notes: 1. **οἱ Θαψακηνοί**: "the people of Thapsacus" (see map).
2. **διαβατός**: "fordable/crossable."
εἰ μὴ τότε: "except at that time."
3. **κατέκαυσεν**: aorist of κατακαίω.
διαβῇ: the subjunctive is used in historic sequence to convey
Abrocomas' thoughts at the moment when he makes the decision.

13.3   Lysias 1.4: the speaker has killed Eratosthenes. He claims in
the law court that he had no other motive for this than the fact that
the victim had seduced his wife.

> ἡγοῦμαι δέ, ὦ ἄνδρες, τοῦτό με δεῖν ἐπιδεῖξαι, ὡς
> ἐμοίχευεν Ἐρατοσθένης τὴν γυναῖκα τὴν ἐμὴν καὶ ἐκείνην
> τε διέφθειρε καὶ τοὺς παῖδας τοὺς ἐμοὺς ᾔσχυνε καὶ ἐμὲ
> αὐτὸν ὕβρισεν εἰς τὴν οἰκίαν τὴν ἐμὴν εἰσιών, καὶ οὔτε
> ἔχθρα ἐμοὶ καὶ ἐκείνῳ οὐδεμία ἦν πλὴν ταύτης, οὔτε   5
> χρημάτων ἕνεκα ἔπραξα ταῦτα, ἵνα πλούσιος ἐκ πένητος
> γένωμαι, οὔτε ἄλλου κέρδους οὐδενὸς πλὴν τῆς κατὰ τοὺς
> νόμους τιμωρίας.

Notes: 1. **ὦ ἄνδρες**: this refers to the jurors.
7. **γένωμαι**: this is in historic sequence. Why do you think it is in the
subjunctive?

13.4   Xenophon, *Memorabilia* 4.4.16: Socrates insists on the
importance of agreement among citizens. This goes beyond agreement in aesthetic matters.

> ἀλλὰ μὴν καὶ ὁμόνοιά γε μέγιστόν τε ἀγαθὸν δοκεῖ ταῖς
> πόλεσιν εἶναι καὶ πλειστάκις ἐν αὐταῖς αἵ τε γερουσίαι καὶ
> οἱ ἄριστοι ἄνδρες παρακελεύονται τοῖς πολίταις ὁμονοεῖν,
> καὶ πανταχοῦ ἐν τῇ Ἑλλάδι νόμος κεῖται τοὺς πολίτας
> ὀμνύναι ὁμονοήσειν, καὶ πανταχοῦ ὀμνύουσι τὸν ὅρκον   5
> τοῦτον· οἶμαι δ᾽ ἐγὼ ταῦτα γίγνεσθαι οὐχ ὅπως τοὺς
> αὐτοὺς χοροὺς κρίνωσιν οἱ πολῖται, οὐδ᾽ ὅπως τοὺς αὐτοὺς
> αὐλητὰς ἐπαινῶσιν, οὐδ᾽ ὅπως τοὺς αὐτοὺς ποιητὰς
> αἱρῶνται, οὐδ᾽ ἵνα τοῖς αὐτοῖς ἥδωνται, ἀλλ᾽ ἵνα τοῖς
> νόμοις πείθωνται. τούτοις γὰρ τῶν πολιτῶν ἐμμενόντων,   10

αἱ πόλεις ἰσχυρόταταί τε καὶ εὐδαιμονέσταται γίγνονται·
ἄνευ δὲ ὁμονοίας οὔτ᾽ ἂν πόλις εὖ πολιτευθείη οὔτ᾽ οἶκος
καλῶς οἰκηθείη.

Notes: 1. **ἀλλὰ μήν**: "and another point."
4. **νόμος κεῖται**: "the custom is established that" + accusative and
infinitive.
7. **κρίνωσιν**: judge best (in the choral competitions).
12. **οὔτ᾽ ἂν πόλις εὖ πολιτευθείη**: "neither would a city be well
governed." πολιτευθείη and οἰκηθείη are in the aorist passive optative.

13.5   Homer, *Iliad* 1.522–27: Zeus assents to Thetis' supplication
that he should assist the cause of her son Achilles but is afraid that
his wife Hera may notice. (She does!)

ἀλλὰ σὺ μὲν νῦν αὖτις ἀπόστιχε μή τι νοήσῃ
Ἥρη· ἐμοὶ δέ κε ταῦτα μελήσεται ὄφρα τελέσσω·
εἰ δ᾽ ἄγε τοι κεφαλῇ κατανεύσομαι ὄφρα πεποίθῃς·
τοῦτο γὰρ ἐξ ἐμέθεν γε μετ᾽ ἀθανάτοισι μέγιστον
τέκμωρ· οὐ γὰρ ἐμὸν παλινάγρετον οὐδ᾽ ἀπατηλὸν   5
οὐδ᾽ ἀτελεύτητον ὅ τί κεν κεφαλῇ κατανεύσω.

Notes: 2. **μελήσεται**: future of μέλει = it is a concern (to).
τελέσσω: subjunctive of τελέω.
3. **εἰ δ᾽ ἄγε**: "come on!"
τοι: = σοι.
πεποίθῃς: perfect subjunctive of πείθω: "you may be confident."
4–5. **τοῦτο γὰρ ἐξ ἐμέθεν γε μετ᾽ ἀθανάτοισι μέγιστον τέκμωρ**: "for
this [i.e., my nod] from *me* is the surest token among the immortal
gods."
5. **οὐ ... ἐμὸν**: i.e., "nothing from me (is)."
5–6. **παλινάγρετον ... ἀπατηλὸν ... ἀτελεύτητον**: "reversible,"
"false," "unfulfilled."
6. **ὅ τί**: "whatever (I nod, i.e., agree with a nod to.)"

13.6   Xenophon, *Cyropaedia* 1.2.3: the Persian laws ensure that the
vulgar cries of salesmen do not obtrude on the ears of the educated.

οἱ δὲ Περσικοὶ νόμοι προλαβόντες ἐπιμέλονται ὅπως τὴν
ἀρχὴν μὴ τοιοῦτοι ἔσονται οἱ πολῖται οἷοι πονηροῦ τινος ἢ

αἰσχροῦ ἔργου ἐφίεσθαι. ἐπιμέλονται δὲ ὧδε· ἔστιν αὐτοῖς
ἐλευθέρα ἀγορὰ καλουμένη, ἔνθα τά τε βασίλεια καὶ τἆλλα
ἀρχεῖα πεποίηται. ἐντεῦθεν τὰ μὲν ὤνια καὶ οἱ ἀγοραῖοι   5
καὶ αἱ τούτων φωναὶ καὶ ἀπειροκαλίαι ἀπελήλανται εἰς
ἄλλον τόπον, ὡς μὴ μιγνύηται ἡ τούτων τύρβη τῇ τῶν
πεπαιδευμένων εὐκοσμίᾳ.

Notes: 1. **προλαβόντες**: προλαμβάνω = I take advance measures.
1–2. **τὴν ἀρχήν**: "from the start."
2. **τοιοῦτοι ... οἷοι**: "of such a kind as to" + infinitive.
3. **ἐφίεσθαι**: "to desire" + genitive.
4. **ἐλευθέρα ἀγορὰ καλουμένη**: "what they call an open market."
5. **ἀρχεῖα**: "government buildings."
τὰ μὲν ὤνια καὶ οἱ ἀγοραῖοι: "the cheap salesmen with their wares,"
lit., "the market goods and the market men."
6. **ἀπειροκαλίαι**: "vulgar behavior."
7. **ἀπελήλανται**: perfect passive of ἀπελαύνω.
μὴ μιγνύηται ἡ τούτων τύρβη: lit. "their disorder may not be mingled
with."

B. FUTURE PARTICIPLE

13.7   Xenophon, *Anabasis* 1.1.3: Cyrus is falsely accused by Tissaphernes of plotting against his brother Artaxerxes. His mother saves
him from execution. The previous king was called Darius.

ἐπεὶ δὲ ἐτελεύτησε Δαρεῖος καὶ κατέστη εἰς τὴν βασιλείαν
Ἀρταξέρξης, Τισσαφέρνης διαβάλλει τὸν Κῦρον
πρὸς τὸν ἀδελφὸν ὡς ἐπιβουλεύοι αὐτῷ. ὁ δὲ πείθεται
καὶ συλλαμβάνει Κῦρον ὡς ἀποκτενῶν· ἡ δὲ μήτηρ
ἐξαιτησαμένη αὐτὸν ἀποπέμπει πάλιν ἐπὶ τὴν ἀρχήν.   5

Notes: 1. **κατέστη εἰς τὴν βασιλείαν**: "succeeded him as king" (lit. "to
the kingdom").
3. **ὡς ἐπιβουλεύοι αὐτῷ**: ὡς introduces the charge Tissaphernes makes
to Cyrus' brother; it does not begin a purpose clause. The optative is
used because it is in a clause of indirect statement in historic sequence.
(Though διαβάλλει is a present tense, it is a historic present, lending
vividness to a report of past time.)
5. **τὴν ἀρχήν**: "his sphere of rule," i.e., his province.

13.8   Thucydides, *Histories* 1.29.1: The Corinthians refuse to listen to the Corcyraeans' proposals for arbitration but sail to the attack.

> Κορίνθιοι δὲ οὐδὲν τούτων ὑπήκουον, ἀλλ᾽ ἐπειδὴ
> πλήρεις αὐτοῖς ἦσαν αἱ νῆες καὶ οἱ ξύμμαχοι παρῆσαν,
> προπέμψαντες κήρυκα πρότερον πόλεμον προεροῦντα
> Κερκυραίοις, ἄραντες ἑβδομήκοντα ναυσὶ καὶ πέντε
> δισχιλίοις τε ὁπλίταις ἔπλεον ἐπὶ τὴν Ἐπίδαμνον   5
> Κερκυραίοις ἐναντία πολεμήσοντες.

Notes: 3. **πρότερον**: "in advance", i.e., "before sailing out (αἴρω)".
πόλεμον προεροῦντα: "to declare war": προεροῦντα is the future participle of προλέγω.
5. **τὴν Ἐπίδαμνον**: Epidamnus was a city on the west coast of Northern Greece (see map); its possession was disputed between the Corinthians and Corcyraeans.
6. **ἐναντία**: "in opposition (to)".

C. RELATIVES WITH FUTURE INDICATIVE

13.9   Demosthenes, *Olynthiac* 1.2: Philip of Macedon is besieging Olynthus in North Greece. Demosthenes proposes that the Athenians should send help to the Olynthians.

> ὁ μὲν οὖν παρὼν καιρός, ὦ ἄνδρες Ἀθηναῖοι, μόνον
> οὐχὶ λέγει φωνὴν ἀφιεὶς ὅτι τῶν πραγμάτων ὑμῖν
> ἐκείνων αὐτοῖς ἀντιληπτέον ἐστίν, εἴπερ ὑπὲρ
> σωτηρίας αὐτῶν φροντίζετε· ἡμεῖς δ᾽ οὐκ οἶδ᾽ ὅντινά
> μοι δοκοῦμεν ἔχειν τρόπον πρὸς αὐτά. ἔστι δὴ τά γ᾽   5
> ἐμοὶ δοκοῦντα, ψηφίσασθαι μὲν ἤδη τὴν βοήθειαν,
> καὶ παρασκευάσασθαι τὴν ταχίστην ὅπως ἐνθένδε
> βοηθήσετε, ... πρεσβείαν δὲ πέμπειν, ἥτις ταῦτ᾽ ἐρεῖ καὶ
> παρέσται τοῖς πράγμασιν.

Notes: 1–2. **μόνον οὐχὶ ... φωνὴν ἀφιείς**: "almost with an audible voice," lit. "only not sending out a voice."
τῶν πραγμάτων ... ἐκείνων: "those affairs (of yours)," i.e., "your interests."

2–3. **ὑμῖν ... αὐτοῖς ἀντιληπτέον ἐστίν** + gen.: "you yourselves must take into your hands."

4–5. **ἡμεῖς δ᾽ οὐκ οἶδ᾽ ὅντινά μοι δοκοῦμεν ἔχειν τρόπον πρὸς αὐτά**: lit. "I am not sure what attitude to these things we seem to me to have," i.e., "our attitude to this is a puzzle to me."

7. **τὴν ταχίστην**: lit. "the quickest (way)," i.e., "as quickly as possible."

9. **παρέσται τοῖς πράγμασιν**: i.e., "keep a watch over events."

13.10 Demosthenes, *Olynthiac* 2.11: an excerpt from a further speech by Demosthenes on the same theme.

> φημὶ δὴ δεῖν ἡμᾶς τοῖς μὲν Ὀλυνθίοις βοηθεῖν, καὶ ὅπως
> τις λέγει κάλλιστα καὶ τάχιστα, οὕτως ἀρέσκει μοι· πρὸς
> δὲ Θετταλοὺς πρεσβείαν πέμπειν, ἣ τοὺς μὲν διδάξει
> ταῦτα, τοὺς δὲ παροξυνεῖ· καὶ γὰρ νῦν εἰσιν ἐψηφισμένοι
> Παγασὰς ἀπαιτεῖν καὶ περὶ Μαγνησίας λόγους ποιεῖσθαι.   5

Notes: 1–2. **ὅπως τις λέγει κάλλιστα καὶ τάχιστα**: "the best and speediest way that anyone can suggest," lit. "how anyone says best and speediest."
4. **εἰσιν ἐψηφισμένοι**: "they have voted."
5. **Παγασὰς ... Μαγνησίας**: Pagasae is a port and Magnesia a coastal area in Thessaly (in Northeastern Greece; see map).
λόγους ποιεῖσθαι: lit. "to make words," i.e., "to protest." Philip of Macedon has occupied Magnesia.

13.11 Sophocles, *Electra* 378–84: Chrysothemis tells her sister Electra that Clytemnestra and Aegisthus, the murderers of their father, Agamemnon, plan to shut her up in a dungeon unless she stops lamenting him.

Χρυσόθεμις

> ἀλλ᾽ ἐξερῶ σοι πᾶν ὅσον κάτοιδ᾽ ἐγώ.
> μέλλουσι γάρ σ᾽, εἰ τῶνδε μὴ λήξεις γόων,
> ἐνταῦθα πέμψειν ἔνθα μή ποθ᾽ ἡλίου
> φέγγος προσόψει, ζῶσα δ᾽ ἐν κατηρεφεῖ
> στέγῃ χθονὸς τῆσδ᾽ ἐκτὸς ὑμνήσεις κακά.   5
> πρὸς ταῦτα φράζου καί με μή ποθ᾽ ὕστερον
> παθοῦσα μέμψῃ· νῦν γὰρ ἐν καλῷ φρονεῖν.

Notes: 2. **λήξεις**: future of λήγω.

3. **ἐνταῦθα ... ἔνθα**: "there ... where."

μή: in what sense can what follows this word be seen as expressing purpose?

4. **προσόψει**: second person singular of the future of προσοράω = I look upon.

4–5. **ἐν κατηρεφεῖ στέγῃ**: "in a dungeon."

ἐκτός: governs χθονὸς τῆσδ'.

6. **πρὸς ταῦτα φράζου**: "in view of this, take thought."

6–7. **μή ... μέμψῃ**: "don't blame:" μή plus the aorist subjunctive is a strong prohibition.

7. **ἐν καλῷ**: "(it is) a good time."

CHAPTER 14

Result Clauses

ὥστε (*that, so that, as*), or sometimes ὡς, with the infinitive expresses a result that is a natural or likely consequence of the action or circumstances of the main verb. The subject of the infinitive is in the accusative if different from that of the main verb. It is either omitted or in the nominative if it is the same as the subject of the main verb. The negative is μή.

When the actual occurrence of the result is stressed, ὥστε is followed by the indicative. The negative is οὐ. In practice, however, the distinction between the two constructions is regularly blurred.

INFINITIVE CONSTRUCTION

14.1   Euripides, *Hecuba* 730: Agamemnon is amazed at Hecuba's delay in coming to bury her daughter Polyxena.

Ἀγαμέμνων

σὺ δὲ σχολάζεις, ὥστε θαυμάζειν ἐμέ.

Notes: 1. **σχολάζεις**: σχολάζω, basically "I have leisure time" or "I am at leisure," here more specifically means "I delay, take my time."

14.2   Lysias 12.4: Lysias asserts the long-term innocence of his family.

οὑμὸς πατὴρ Κέφαλος ἐπείσθη μὲν ὑπὸ Περικλέους εἰς
ταύτην τὴν γῆν ἀφικέσθαι, ἔτη δὲ τριάκοντα ᾤκησε,
καὶ οὐδενὶ πώποτε οὔτε ἡμεῖς οὔτε ἐκεῖνος δίκην οὔτε
ἐδικασάμεθα οὔτε ἐφύγομεν, ἀλλ᾽ οὕτως ᾠκοῦμεν
δημοκρατούμενοι ὥστε μήτε εἰς τοὺς ἄλλους ἐξαμαρτάνειν   5
μήτε ὑπὸ τῶν ἄλλων ἀδικεῖσθαι.

Notes: 1. **οὑμός** = ὁ ἐμός.
Κέφαλος: Lysias' father, Cephalus, a rich Syracusan in the munitions
business, was encouraged by Pericles, the great Athenian statesman,
to settle in Athens as a "resident alien" or "metic" (μέτοικος). When
the Thirty Tyrants came to power in 404 BC, bringing democratic
government to an end, Lysias and his brother Polemarchus were among
the rich metics selected for execution so that the Thirty could confiscate
their wealth. Lysias escaped, but Polemarchus was arrested and put
to death. Our passage comes close to the beginning of the speech that
Lysias later delivered in court against Eratosthenes, one of the Thirty.
3–4. **καὶ οὐδενί . . . ἐφύγομεν**: "and neither he nor we ever yet either
brought a lawsuit against anyone or were put on trial." Compound
negatives following another negative, whether simple or compound
(here οὔτε . . . οὔτε following οὐδενί, so all compound), reinforce the
negative sense. δίκην δικάζεσθαι (with dative) regularly means "to
bring a lawsuit against," and as a legal term φεύγειν means "to be a
defendant" or (with δίκην, as here) "to be put on trial."
5. **δημοκρατούμενοι** = "under the democracy" (lit. "living under a
democracy").

14.3   Plato, *Symposium* 215e–16a: Alcibiades describes the effect
made on him by hearing Socrates speak.

ὅταν γὰρ ἀκούω, πολύ μοι μᾶλλον ἢ τῶν κορυβαντιώντων
ἥ τε καρδία πηδᾷ καὶ δάκρυα ἐκχεῖται ὑπὸ τῶν λόγων
τῶν τούτου, ὁρῶ δὲ καὶ ἄλλους παμπόλλους τὰ αὐτὰ
πάσχοντας. Περικλέους δὲ ἀκούων καὶ ἄλλων ἀγαθῶν
ῥητόρων εὖ μὲν ἡγούμην λέγειν, τοιοῦτον δ᾽ οὐδὲν   5
ἔπασχον, οὐδ᾽ ἐτεθορύβητό μου ἡ ψυχὴ οὐδ᾽ ἠγανάκτει
ὡς ἀνδραποδωδῶς διακειμένου· ἀλλ᾽ ὑπὸ τουτουῒ τοῦ
Μαρσύου πολλάκις δὴ οὕτω διετέθην ὥστε μοι δόξαι
μὴ βιωτὸν εἶναι ἔχοντι ὡς ἔχω. καὶ ταῦτα, ὦ Σώκρατες, οὐκ
ἐρεῖς ὡς οὐκ ἀληθῆ.   10

Result Clauses 101

Notes: 1. **τῶν κορυβαντιώντων**: "(that) of those filled with Corybantic frenzy" (from κορυβαντιάω). The Corybants were a mythical group connected with the goddess Cybele. The drum and pipe music of their cult induced in worshippers a state of frenzy.

2–3. **ὑπὸ τῶν λόγων τῶν τούτου**: "at the sound of his speech."

5. **εὖ μὲν ἡγούμην λέγειν**: understand αὐτούς = "I considered that they spoke well."

6. **ἐτεθορύβητο**: pluperfect passive (3rd singular) of θορυβέω, "I throw into confusion."

7. **ὡς ἀνδραποδωδῶς διακειμένου**: understand ἐμοῦ = "at my being in a servile state." διάκειμαι, taking the place of the perfect passive of διάτιθημι, is used with an adverb to mean "I am in a certain state"; cf. later in the sentence οὕτω διετέθην (aorist passive of διατίθημι), "I was brought into such a state," and the comparable usage with ἔχω in ἔχοντι ὡς ἔχω.

7–8. **ὑπὸ τουτουῒ τοῦ Μαρσύου**: note the force of the deictic iota on τουτουῒ = "by this Marsyas here." Socrates is likened to Marsyas, a legendary satyr of such great musical skill that he challenged Apollo to a competition in playing the *aulos*. He lost, and, suspended from a tree, was flayed alive by the god.

8–9. **ὥστε μοι δόξαι μὴ βιωτὸν εἶναι**: "that life didn't seem to me worth living." Note here the use of the verbal adjective βιωτός (from βιόω).

14.4 Sophocles, *Antigone* 449–55: Antigone justifies herself to Creon for defying his edicts forbidding the burial of her brother Polynices.

Κρέων   Ἀντιγόνη

Κρ. καὶ δῆτ᾽ ἐτόλμας τούσδ᾽ ὑπερβαίνειν νόμους;

Ἀν. οὐ γάρ τί μοι Ζεὺς ἦν ὁ κηρύξας τάδε,
οὐδ᾽ ἡ ξύνοικος τῶν κάτω θεῶν Δίκη
τοιούσδ᾽ ἐν ἀνθρώποισιν ὥρισεν νόμους.
οὐδὲ σθένειν τοσοῦτον ᾠόμην τὰ σὰ   5
κηρύγμαθ᾽, ὥστ᾽ ἄγραπτα κἀσφαλῆ θεῶν
νόμιμα δύνασθαι θνητὰ γ᾽ ὄνθ᾽ ὑπερδραμεῖν.

Notes: 2. **γάρ**: (as often) = "yes, for …"
οὐ … τί: "in no way." τί here is so accented not because it is interrogative, but because of the enclitic μοι that follows.
3. **Δίκη**: the Justice here represented as "dwelling with the gods below" is their right to demand from the living such rituals, in particular burial, as will consecrate the dead to them.

5. **τοσοῦτον**: adverbial with σθένειν = "had so much power."
6–7. **ἄγραπτα κἀσφαλῆ** (= καὶ ἀσφαλῆ) **θεῶν νόμιμα**: "the unwritten and steadfast commandments of the gods."
7. **ὑπερδραμεῖν**: aorist infinitive of ὑπερτρέχω.

INDICATIVE CONSTRUCTION

14.5 *St. John's Gospel* 3.16: St. John encapsulates the essence of the Christian faith.

> οὕτω γὰρ ἠγάπησεν ὁ Θεὸς τὸν κόσμον, ὥστε τὸν υἱὸν
> αὐτοῦ τὸν μονογενῆ ἔδωκεν, ἵνα πᾶς ὁ πιστεύων εἰς αὐτὸν
> μὴ ἀπόληται ἀλλ' ἔχῃ ζωὴν αἰώνιον.

Notes: 1. **ἠγάπησεν**: ἀγαπάω and its related noun ἀγάπη are regularly used in the New Testament to denote both brotherly love between humans and the love of God for man and of man for God.
2. **ζωὴν αἰώνιον**: "everlasting life." ζωή, more common than βίος in the New Testament, is regularly used both of life in the physical sense and, as here, of the immortality that believers will receive in the future.

14.6 Xenophon, *Anabasis* 7.4.2–4: Xenophon's men, fighting with King Seuthes, discover how the weather dictates winter clothing in Thrace.

> αὐτὸς δὲ καὶ οἱ Ἕλληνες ἐστρατοπεδεύοντο ἀνὰ τὸ
> Θυνῶν πεδίον. οἱ δ' ἐκλιπόντες ἔφευγον εἰς τὰ ὄρη. ἦν
> δὲ χιὼν πολλὴ καὶ ψῦχος οὕτως ὥστε τὸ ὕδωρ ὃ ἐφέροντο
> ἐπὶ δεῖπνον ἐπήγνυτο καὶ ὁ οἶνος ὁ ἐν τοῖς ἀγγείοις, καὶ
> τῶν Ἑλλήνων πολλῶν καὶ ῥῖνες ἀπεκαίοντο καὶ ὦτα. καὶ   5
> τότε δῆλον ἐγένετο οὗ ἕνεκα οἱ Θρᾷκες τὰς ἀλωπεκᾶς
> ἐπὶ ταῖς κεφαλαῖς φοροῦσι καὶ τοῖς ὠσί, καὶ χιτῶνας οὐ
> μόνον περὶ τοῖς στέρνοις ἀλλὰ καὶ περὶ τοῖς μηροῖς, καὶ
> ζειρὰς μέχρι τῶν ποδῶν ἐπὶ τῶν ἵππων ἔχουσιν, ἀλλ' οὐ
> χλαμύδας.   10

Notes: 1. **αὐτός**: "he himself." This is the Thracian king, Seuthes II, who has recruited Xenophon and his mercenaries to help him in his raids on the Thyni and other local tribes.
1–2. **ἀνὰ τὸ Θυνῶν πεδίον**: "on the plain of the Thyni."

2. **οἱ δ′**: "and they," i.e., the Thyni.

5. **ἀπεκαίοντο**: "were frozen off." ἀποκαίειν, which literally means "to burn off," is here used to describe the effects of frostbite.

6. **ἀλωπεκᾶς**: "fox skins" (from ἀλωπεκῆ *sc.* δορά).

9. **ζειράς**: a ζειρά was an ankle-length cloak, as opposed to the χλαμύς, a short cloak or mantle extending no lower than the knee.

14.7 Thucydides, *Histories* 3.49.1–3: in 428 BC Mytilene, along with the rest of Lesbos except Methymna, revolted from Athens. The following year it was brought back to heel by an Athenian expedition, and in retribution the Assembly, influenced by Cleon, voted that the entire population be put to death or enslaved. On the next day, however, at the proposal of Diodotus, this edict was revoked, and, as here narrated, a fast trireme was dispatched to overtake the one already sent to carry out the massacre.

> τοιαῦτα δὲ ὁ Διόδοτος εἶπεν. ῥηθεισῶν δὲ τῶν γνωμῶν
> τούτων μάλιστα ἀντιπάλων πρὸς ἀλλήλας οἱ Ἀθηναῖοι
> ἦλθον μὲν ἐς ἀγῶνα ὅμως τῆς δόξης καὶ ἐγένοντο ἐν τῇ
> χειροτονίᾳ ἀγχώμαλοι, ἐκράτησε δὲ ἡ τοῦ Διοδότου. καὶ
> τριήρη εὐθὺς ἄλλην ἀπέστελλον κατὰ σπουδήν, ὅπως μὴ   5
> φθασάσης τῆς προτέρας εὕρωσι διεφθαρμένην τὴν πόλιν·
> προεῖχε δὲ ἡμέρᾳ καὶ νυκτὶ μάλιστα. παρασκευασάντων
> δὲ τῶν Μυτιληναίων πρέσβεων τῇ νηὶ οἶνον καὶ ἄλφιτα
> καὶ μεγάλα ὑποσχομένων, εἰ φθάσειαν, ἐγένετο σπουδὴ
> τοῦ πλοῦ τοιαύτη ὥστε ἤσθιόν τε ἅμα ἐλαύνοντες οἴνῳ καὶ   10
> ἐλαίῳ ἄλφιτα πεφυραμένα, καὶ οἱ μὲν ὕπνον ᾑροῦντο κατὰ
> μέρος, οἱ δὲ ἤλαυνον.

Notes: 1. **ῥηθεισῶν**: genitive plural feminine of the participle from ἐρρήθην, regularly used as the aorist passive of λέγω.

3. **ὅμως**: "after all"; i.e., in spite of the change of heart that had caused them to revisit the issue.

3–4. **ἐν τῇ χειροτονίᾳ ἀγχώμαλοι**: "nearly equal in the show of hands."

4. **ἡ τοῦ Διοδότου**: understand γνώμη.

6. **φθασάσης τῆς προτέρας**: "the earlier [ship] having got there first." φθάνειν, often used with a participle (see p. **125**), is here used on its own (as also in the next sentence) meaning "to arrive first."

7. **προεῖχε … μάλιστα:** "it had a head start of about (μάλιστα) a day and a night."

8. **τῶν Μυτιληναίων πρέσβεων:** these are Mytilenaean ambassadors present in Athens to treat for terms.

10. **ἐλαύνοντες:** "rowing."

10–11. **οἴνῳ καὶ ἐλαίῳ ἄλφιτα πεφυραμένα:** "barley-meal kneaded (φυράω) with wine and oil" into cakes known as οἰνοῦτται.

11–12. **κατὰ μέρος:** "in turn." Triremes usually hugged the shore and beached for meals and sleep, but not on this urgent occasion.

14.8 Euripides, *Phoenissae* 361–64: Polynices tells his mother of his fear of treachery at the hands of his brother as he came through Thebes.

Πολυνείκης

οὕτω δ᾽ ἐτάρβουν ἐς φόβον τ᾽ ἀφικόμην
μή τις δόλος με πρὸς κασιγνήτου κτάνη,
ὥστε ξιφήρη χεῖρ᾽ ἔχων δι᾽ ἄστεως
κυκλῶν πρόσωπον ἦλθον.

Notes: 1. **οὕτω … ἀφικόμην:** οὕτω should be taken with both verbs in this double expression of fear = "and I was so scared and became so fearful" (lit. "and I was so afraid and so came into [a state of] fear").
2. **πρὸς κασιγνήτου:** "at the hands of my brother."
3. **ξιφήρη χεῖρ᾽ ἔχων:** "with a sword in my hand" (lit. "having my hand armed with a sword").
4. **κυκλῶν πρόσωπον:** "looking all around me" (lit. "turning around my face").

PASSAGES INVOLVING BOTH CONSTRUCTIONS

14.9 Xenophon, *Anabasis* 2.2.17–18: the Greeks, setting up camp in the dark, cause panic and flight among the enemy.

οἱ μὲν οὖν πρῶτοι ὅμως τρόπῳ τινὶ ἐστρατοπεδεύσαντο,
οἱ δὲ ὕστεροι σκοταῖοι προσιόντες ὡς ἐτύγχανον ἕκαστοι
ηὐλίζοντο, καὶ κραυγὴν πολλὴν ἐποίουν καλοῦντες
ἀλλήλους, ὥστε καὶ τοὺς πολεμίους ἀκούειν· ὥστε οἱ μὲν
ἐγγύτατα τῶν πολεμίων καὶ ἔφυγον ἐκ τῶν σκηνωμάτων.   5

δῆλον δὲ τοῦτο τῇ ὑστεραίᾳ ἐγένετο· οὔτε γὰρ ὑποζύγιον
ἔτ’ οὐδὲν ἐφάνη οὔτε στρατόπεδον οὔτε καπνὸς οὐδαμοῦ
πλησίον.

Notes: 1. **ὅμως**: "nevertheless," i.e., despite the adverse conditions just
described before the passage begins.
2. **ὡς ἐτύγχανον ἕκαστοι**: "each as best he could" (lit. "just as each of
them chanced").
4. **ὥστε . . . ἀκούειν**: "so that the enemy too could hear." ὥστε +
infinitive, as always, expresses a natural consequence, here of the noise
the Greeks were making.
4–5. **ὥστε . . . καὶ ἔφυγον**: "as a result the nearest of the enemy actually
(καί) took to flight." Here ὥστε, as regularly at the beginning of a
sentence or after a colon, means "consequently, as a result." The usage
with the indicative, which stresses the occurrence of the result, is here
further strengthened by καί.

14.10   Lysias 3.6–8: the speaker, on trial in court, explains how a
boy to whom they were both attracted was the origin of the first violent encounter between himself and Simon, his accuser.

πυθόμενος γὰρ ὅτι τὸ μειράκιον ἦν παρ’ ἐμοί, ἐλθὼν
ἐπὶ τὴν οἰκίαν τὴν ἐμὴν νύκτωρ μεθύων, ἐκκόψας τὰς
θύρας εἰσῆλθεν εἰς τὴν γυναικωνῖτιν, ἔνδον οὐσῶν
τῆς τε ἀδελφῆς τῆς ἐμῆς καὶ τῶν ἀδελφιδῶν, αἳ οὕτω
κοσμίως βεβιώκασιν ὥστε καὶ ὑπὸ τῶν οἰκείων ὁρώμεναι   5
αἰσχύνεσθαι. οὗτος τοίνυν εἰς τοῦτο ἦλθεν ὕβρεως ὥστ’
οὐ πρότερον ἠθέλησεν ἀπελθεῖν, πρὶν αὐτὸν ἡγούμενοι
δεινὰ ποιεῖν οἱ παραγενόμενοι καὶ οἱ μετ’ αὐτοῦ ἐλθόντες,
ἐπὶ παῖδας κόρας καὶ ὀρφανὰς εἰσιόντα, ἐξήλασαν βίᾳ. καὶ
τοσούτου ἐδέησεν αὐτῷ μεταμελῆσαι τῶν ὑβρισμένων,   10
ὥστε ἐξευρὼν οὗ ἐδειπνοῦμεν ἀτοπώτατον πρᾶγμα καὶ
ἀπιστότατον ἐποίησεν, εἰ μή τις εἰδείη τὴν τούτου μανίαν.
ἐκκαλέσας γάρ με ἔνδοθεν, ἐπειδὴ τάχιστα ἐξῆλθον, εὐθύς
με τύπτειν ἐπεχείρησεν· ἐπειδὴ δὲ αὐτὸν ἠμυνάμην, ἐκστὰς
ἔβαλλέ με λίθοις. καὶ ἐμοῦ μὲν ἁμαρτάνει, Ἀριστοκρίτου   15
δέ, ὃς παρ’ ἐμὲ ἦλθε μετ’ αὐτοῦ, βαλὼν λίθῳ συντρίβει τὸ
μέτωπον.

Notes: 5. **καὶ ὑπὸ τῶν οἰκείων**: "even by their own kinsmen."

6. **εἰς τοῦτο ἦλθεν ὕβρεως**: "came to such a pitch of insolence."

10. **τοσούτου ἐδέησεν αὐτῷ μεταμελῆσαι τῶν ὑβρισμένων**: "so far was he from repenting of his outrageous behavior."

12. **εἰ μή τις εἰδείη τὴν τούτου μανίαν**: "unless one knew his madness," i.e., his actions would have seemed both strange and incredible only to those unaware of his madness.

13. **ἐπειδὴ τάχιστα**: "as soon as."

15–16. **ἁμαρτάνει . . . συντρίβει**: the historic presents add an extra vivid quality to the climax of the narrative.

16. **παρ' ἐμέ**: "to my place."

CHAPTER 15

Conditionals 1

OPEN CONDITIONS

Despite the presence of the word "if," conditional sentences can express facts. This is most obvious in axioms such as "If a triangle has two equal sides, it is an isosceles triangle." Compare "If you are working hard, I am delighted": the speaker is advancing this as a simple truth.

In such sentences Greek uses the appropriate tense of the indicative in the present and the past. Conditional clauses referring to the future inevitably contain a note of uncertainty. The regular construction here calls for ἐάν (or ἤν) + the subjunctive in the protasis (the if clause) and the future indicative in the apodosis (the main clause). In threats and emphatic statements (in which the speaker wishes to remove any note of uncertainty), εἰ + the future indicative is used in the if clause.

The negative in the "if" clause is always μή.

15.1 Homer, *Iliad* 1.564: Zeus tells his nagging wife, Hera, that the situation in which they find themselves will be fine with him.

εἰ δ᾽ οὕτω τοῦτ᾽ ἐστὶν, ἐμοὶ μέλλει φίλον εἶναι.

15.2 Plato, *Phaedrus* 228a: Socrates tells Phaedrus how well he knows him.

ὦ Φαῖδρε, εἰ ἐγὼ Φαῖδρον ἀγνοῶ, καὶ ἐμαυτοῦ
ἐπιλέλησμαι. ἀλλὰ γὰρ οὐδέτερά ἐστι τούτων.

Notes: 1. **καὶ ἐμαυτοῦ**: "myself too."
2. **ἐπιλέλησμαι**: perfect of ἐπιλανθάνομαι + gen. = I forget.
ἀλλὰ γάρ: "but the fact is that."
οὐδέτερά: "neither."

15.3   Demosthenes, *On the Liberty of the Rhodians* 23: the orator
urges the Athenians to imitate the Argives of old when faced by the
militaristic Lacedaemonians and not to show fear of a barbarian
queen.

εἶτ᾽ οὐκ αἰσχρόν, ὦ ἄνδρες Ἀθηναῖοι, εἰ τὸ μὲν Ἀργείων
πλῆθος οὐκ ἐφοβήθη τὴν Λακεδαιμονίων ἀρχὴν ἐν
ἐκείνοις τοῖς καιροῖς οὐδὲ τὴν ῥώμην, ὑμεῖς δ᾽ ὄντες
Ἀθηναῖοι βάρβαρον ἄνθρωπον, καὶ ταῦτα γυναῖκα,
φοβήσεσθε;   5

Notes: 1. **εἶτ᾽ οὐκ αἰσχρόν**: "then is it not disgraceful . . . ?" The sentence
is one long question.
2. **οὐκ**: in a small number of circumstances οὐ is found instead of μή in
the protasis of a conditional clause, but this is not regular Greek.
4. **βάρβαρον ἄνθρωπον, καὶ ταῦτα γυναῖκα**: "a barbarian human being,
and a woman at that": the word ἄνθρωπος is used contemptuously.

15.4   Xenophon, *Anabasis* 2.5.41: it is right that oath breakers such
as Clearchus should receive their just deserts.

Κλέαρχος μὲν τοίνυν εἰ παρὰ τοὺς ὅρκους ἔλυε τὰς
σπονδάς, τὴν δίκην ἔχει· δίκαιον γὰρ ἀπόλλυσθαι τοὺς
ἐπιορκοῦντας.

Notes: 1. **τοίνυν**: "well then."
2–3. **ἀπόλλυσθαι τοὺς ἐπιορκοῦντας**: "for oath breakers to perish."

15.5   Thucydides, *Histories* 3.54.3–4: the Plataeans tell the Spartans
that they have a fine record in fighting for the cause of Greece.

τὰ δ’ ἐν τῇ εἰρήνῃ καὶ πρὸς τὸν Μῆδον ἀγαθοὶ γεγενήμεθα,
τὴν μὲν οὐ λύσαντες νῦν πρότεροι, τῷ δὲ ξυνεπιθέμενοι
τότε ἐς ἐλευθερίαν τῆς Ἑλλάδος μόνοι Βοιωτῶν. καὶ γὰρ
ἠπειρῶταί τε ὄντες ἐναυμαχήσαμεν ἐπ’ Ἀρτεμισίῳ, μάχῃ
τε τῇ ἐν τῇ ἡμετέρᾳ γῇ γενομένῃ παρεγενόμεθα ὑμῖν   5
τε καὶ Παυσανίᾳ· εἴ τέ τι ἄλλο κατ’ ἐκεῖνον τὸν χρόνον
ἐγένετο ἐπικίνδυνον τοῖς Ἕλλησι, πάντων παρὰ δύναμιν
μετέσχομεν.

Notes: 1. **τὰ δ’ ἐν τῇ εἰρήνῃ καὶ πρὸς τὸν Μῆδον**: "both during the
peace and against the Persians" (lit. "the Mede").
2. **γεγενήμεθα**: perfect (1st plural) of γίγνομαι.
τὴν μὲν οὐ λύσαντες νῦν πρότεροι: "not being the first to break the
(peace) now": τήν looks back to τῇ εἰρήνῃ.
2–3. **τῷ δὲ ξυνεπιθέμενοι τότε ἐς ἐλευθερίαν τῆς Ἑλλάδος μόνοι
Βοιωτῶν**: "and being the only Boeotians then to join them in the
fight with (ξυνεπιθέμενοι) the Persians for the freedom of Greece":
τῷ looks back to τὸν Μῆδον. The Plataeans were in fact the only
Greeks who joined the Athenians to fight the Persians at Marathon
in 490 BC.
4. **Ἀρτεμισίῳ**: see map: the Greeks fought indecisively with the
Persians in a sea battle off this promontory in 480 BC.
4–5. **μάχῃ τε τῇ ἐν τῇ ἡμετέρᾳ γῇ γενομένῃ**: i.e., the battle of Plataea in
which the Greeks defeated the Persians on land in 479 BC. They were
led by the Spartan general Pausanias. γενομένῃ is the aorist participle
of γίγνομαι.
5. **παρεγενόμεθα**: "we were there in support" + dat.
7. **παρὰ δύναμιν**: "beyond our strength."

15.6 Xenophon, *Cyropaedia* 3.2.13: Cyrus nobly sends his Chal-
daean captives back home.

ἐγὼ οὖν ἀφίημι ὑμᾶς οἴκαδε τοὺς εἰλημμένους, καὶ
δίδωμι ὑμῖν σὺν τοῖς ἄλλοις Χαλδαίοις βουλεύσασθαι
εἴτε βούλεσθε πολεμεῖν ἡμῖν εἴτε φίλοι εἶναι. καὶ ἢν μὲν
πόλεμον αἱρῆσθε, μηκέτι ἥκετε δεῦρο ἄνευ ὅπλων, εἰ
σωφρονεῖτε.   5

Notes: 1. **εἰλημμένους**: perfect passive participle of λαμβάνω = I take, capture.

2. **δίδωμι ὑμῖν**: "I give you (the chance)."

4. **ἥκετε**: imperative.

15.7 Plato, *Republic* 5.473c–e: Socrates says that philosopher-kings are vital for the success of a happy state.

> ἐὰν μή, ἦν δ᾽ ἐγώ, ἢ οἱ φιλόσοφοι βασιλεύσωσιν ἐν ταῖς
> πόλεσιν ἢ οἱ βασιλῆς τε νῦν λεγόμενοι καὶ δυνάσται
> φιλοσοφήσωσι γνησίως τε καὶ ἱκανῶς, καὶ τοῦτο εἰς
> ταὐτὸν συμπέσῃ, δύναμίς τε πολιτικὴ καὶ φιλοσοφία, τῶν
> δὲ νῦν πορευομένων χωρὶς ἐφ᾽ ἑκάτερον αἱ πολλαὶ φύσεις   5
> ἐξ ἀνάγκης ἀποκλεισθῶσιν, οὐκ ἔστι κακῶν παῦλα, ὦ
> φίλε Γλαύκων, ταῖς πόλεσι, δοκῶ δ᾽ οὐδὲ τῷ ἀνθρωπίνῳ
> γένει, οὐδὲ αὕτη ἡ πολιτεία μή ποτε πρότερον φυῇ τε εἰς τὸ
> δυνατὸν καὶ φῶς ἡλίου ἴδῃ, ἣν νῦν λόγῳ διεληλύθαμεν.

Notes: 1. **ἦν δ᾽ ἐγώ**: "I said."

3. **γνησίως τε καὶ ἱκανῶς**: "seriously and adequately."

3–4. **καὶ τοῦτο εἰς ταὐτὸν συμπέσῃ, δύναμίς τε πολιτικὴ καὶ φιλοσοφία**: "and there is a conjunction of these two things [lit. this falls together into the same thing], political power and philosophical intelligence."

4–6. **τῶν δὲ ... ἀποκλεισθῶσιν**: "and the many natures of those who at present pursue [lit. travel toward] either apart (from the other) are compulsorily excluded," i.e., "and those who are by nature inclined at present to pursue either political power or philosophical intelligence but not both are compulsorily excluded."

6. **παῦλα**: "cessation (from)" + genitive.

7–8. **δοκῶ δ᾽ οὐδὲ τῷ ἀνθρωπίνῳ γένει**: "nor, I think, for the human race either."

8–9. **οὐδὲ ... μή ... φυῇ ... ἴδῃ**: οὐ (here οὐδὲ) μή + subjunctive expresses a strongly negative statement: "nor will this republic, which ..., ever develop." πρότερον: i.e., before political power and philosophical intelligence are combined.

φυῇ τε εἰς τὸ δυνατόν: "both develop into (the realm of) possibility."

9. **ἴδῃ**: aorist subjunctive of ὁράω.

ἣν νῦν λόγῳ διεληλύθαμεν: "which we have now been discussing in theory": the antecedent to the relative pronoun is ἡ πολιτεία (the constitution, republic).

15.8 Aristophanes, *Frogs* 584–88: Dionysus persuades his slave Xanthias to dress in his own Heracles costume since he suspects that the individual dressed in it is going to be beaten up. He promises the sulky Xanthias that he will never take it back.

Διόνυσος

οἶδ' οἶδ' ὅτι θυμοῖ, καὶ δικαίως αὐτὸ δρᾷς·
κἂν εἴ με τύπτοις, οὐκ ἂν ἀντείποιμί σοι.
ἀλλ' ἤν σε τοῦ λοιποῦ ποτ' ἀφέλωμαι χρόνου,
πρόρριζος αὐτός, ἡ γυνή, τὰ παιδία,
κάκιστ' ἀπολοίμην, κἀρχέδημος ὁ γλάμων.   5

Notes: 1. **θυμοῖ**: second person singular of θυμόομαι = I am angry.
2. **κἂν**: crasis: καὶ ἄν κἂν εἰ = καὶ εἰ.
τύπτοις … ἂν ἀντείποιμί: the optatives mean "you were to strike me" and "I wouldn't say no." You will be exercising this conditional construction on in Chapter 16.
3. **σε … ἀφέλωμαι**: "I take (it) away from you."
τοῦ λοιποῦ ποτ' … χρόνου: "any time in the future."
4. **πρόρριζος**: "root and branch," "utterly."
ἡ γυνή: "the wife."
5. **ἀπολοίμην**: "may I (and the others) perish!"
κἀρχέδημος ὁ γλάμων: "and blear-eyed Archedemus." We know nothing about this individual. It is characteristic of Aristophanes to work in gratuitous insults of his contemporaries.

15.9 Euripides, *Phoenissae* 1615–21: the blind Oedipus pleads with Creon not to cast him out of the land of Thebes.

Οἰδίπους

εἶεν· τί δράσω δῆθ' ὁ δυσδαίμων ἐγώ;
τίς ἡγεμών μοι ποδὸς ὁμαρτήσει τυφλοῦ;
ἥδ' ἡ θανοῦσα; ζῶσά γ' ἂν σάφ' οἶδ' ὅτι.
ἀλλ' εὔτεκνος ξυνωρίς; ἀλλ' οὐκ ἔστι μοι.

ἀλλ᾽ ἔτι νεάζων αὐτὸς εὕροιμ᾽ ἂν βίον;   5
πόθεν; τί μ᾽ ἄρδην ὧδ᾽ ἀποκτείνεις, Κρέον;
ἀποκτενεῖς γάρ, εἴ με γῆς ἔξω βαλεῖς.

Notes: 2. **ἡγεμών ... ποδὸς ... τυφλοῦ**: lit. "(as) leader of (my) blind foot."

3. **ἡ θανοῦσα**: i.e., his wife, Jocasta, who has committed suicide: her corpse lies on the stage (hence ἥδ᾽ = this here).

ζῶσά γ᾽ ἂν σάφ᾽ οἶδ᾽ ὅτι: "I know full well that she would have (done had) she been alive."

4. **εὔτεκνος ξυνωρίς**: "my lovely pair of sons": his sons Eteocles and Polynices have killed each other on the battle field. They too lie dead on the stage.

5. **ἀλλ᾽ ἔτι νεάζων αὐτὸς εὕροιμ᾽ ἂν βίον**: "but am I still young (and vigorous enough) to find my own livelihood?" lit. "but still being young (νεάζων), could I find ... ?"

6. **ἄρδην ὧδ᾽**: "so utterly."

15.10   Lysias 7.41: the speaker relates the tragic consequences that will ensue if he is driven into exile.

πάντων γὰρ ἀθλιώτατος ἂν γενοίμην, εἰ φυγὰς ἀδίκως
καταστήσομαι, ἄπαις μὲν ὢν καὶ μόνος, ἐρήμου δὲ τοῦ
οἴκου γενομένου, μητρὸς δὲ πάντων ἐνδεοῦς οὔσης,
πατρίδος δὲ τοιαύτης ἐπ᾽ αἰσχίσταις στερηθεὶς αἰτίαις,
πολλὰς μὲν ναυμαχίας ὑπὲρ αὐτῆς νεναυμαχηκώς,   5
πολλὰς δὲ μάχας μεμαχημένος, κόσμιον δ᾽ ἐμαυτὸν καὶ ἐν
δημοκρατίᾳ καὶ ἐν ὀλιγαρχίᾳ παρασχών.

Notes: 1. **ἂν γενοίμην**: "I would become."

2. **καταστήσομαι**: "I am reduced to becoming." We would expect an optative—"I were to be reduced ..."—instead of the future indicative. This adds immediacy to the terrible prospect that may await him.

3. **ἐνδεοῦς**: (genitive) "in need (of)."

4. **ἐπ᾽ αἰσχίσταις ... αἰτίαις**: "on disgraceful charges."

5. **αὐτῆς**: i.e., his fatherland.

7. **ἐν δημοκρατίᾳ καὶ ἐν ὀλιγαρχίᾳ**: Athens passed through both these forms of government at the end of the fifth century BC.

CHAPTER 16

Conditionals 2

UNREAL CONDITIONS

Unreal conditions, sometimes called unfulfilled (present and past) and remote (future), deal with hypothetical or unlikely sets of circumstances, signaled in English, generally, by the words "would" or "should."

Present: εἰ + imperfect indicative in the protasis; imperfect indicative + ἄν in the apodosis.

Past: εἰ + aorist indicative in the protasis; aorist indicative + ἄν in the apodosis.

Future: εἰ + optative (present or aorist) in the protasis; optative + ἄν in the apodosis.

NB. 1 The imperfect indicative, as well as referring to the present, may be used also to refer to a continuous or repeated act in the past. Context will usually make it clear which of the two possible meanings is intended.

2 The two halves of a conditional sentence may refer to different times. Greek simply uses the construction appropriate to each clause.

UNREAL CONDITIONS REFERRING TO PRESENT TIME

16.1 Xenophon, *Cyropaedia* 1.2.16: in his *Cyropaedia*, a pseudo-historical account of the life of Cyrus the Great, Xenophon attributes Persian fastidiousness about bodily functions to their modest diet and hard-work ethic.

αἰσχρὸν μὲν γὰρ ἔτι καὶ νῦν ἐστι Πέρσαις καὶ τὸ πτύειν
καὶ τὸ ἀπομύττεσθαι καὶ τὸ φύσης μεστοὺς φαίνεσθαι,
αἰσχρὸν δέ ἐστι καὶ τὸ ἰόντα ποι φανερὸν γενέσθαι ἢ
τοῦ οὐρῆσαι ἕνεκα ἢ καὶ ἄλλου τινὸς τοιούτου. ταῦτα δὲ
οὐκ ἂν ἐδύναντο ποιεῖν, εἰ μὴ καὶ διαίτῃ μετρίᾳ ἐχρῶντο   5
καὶ τὸ ὑγρὸν ἐκπονοῦντες ἀνήλισκον, ὥστε ἄλλῃ πῃ
ἀποχωρεῖν.

Notes: 1. **ἔτι καὶ νῦν**: "to this very day" (lit. "even now also").
τὸ πτύειν: "spitting." The neuter article is used with an infinitive to produce a verbal noun. This usage is known as the *articular infinitive*. There are several other examples in this passage, including one in the genitive case.
2. **τὸ ἀπομύττεσθαι**: "blowing the nose."
τὸ φύσης μεστοὺς φαίνεσθαι: "being clearly full of wind." The subject or complement of an infinitive, as μεστούς here, is regularly in the accusative, cf. ἰόντα later in the sentence.
3. **τὸ ἰόντα ποι φανερὸν γενέσθαι**: "openly going off" (lit. "being clear going somewhere").
4–5. **ταῦτα . . . ποιεῖν**: i.e., "this would be impossible for them."
6. **τὸ ὑγρὸν . . . ἀνήλισκον**: "disposed of their moisture." The verb ἀναλίσκω regularly means "I spend."
ἄλλῃ πῃ: "in some other way."

16.2   Lysias 2.78–80: "Age shall not weary them, nor the years condemn": Lysias praises those Athenians who died supporting Corinth against Sparta during the Corinthian War, 395–386 BC.

εἰ μὲν γὰρ οἷόν τε ἦν τοῖς τοὺς ἐν τῷ πολέμῳ κινδύνους
διαφυγοῦσιν ἀθανάτους εἶναι τὸν λοιπὸν χρόνον, ἄξιον ἦν
τοῖς ζῶσι τὸν ἄπαντα χρόνον πενθεῖν τοὺς τεθνεῶτας· νῦν
δὲ ἥ τε φύσις καὶ νόσων ἥττων καὶ γήρως, ὅ τε δαίμων ὁ τὴν
ἡμετέραν μοῖραν εἰληχὼς ἀπαραίτητος. ὥστε προσήκει   5
τούτους εὐδαιμονεστάτους ἡγεῖσθαι, οἵτινες ὑπὲρ
μεγίστων καὶ καλλίστων κινδυνεύσαντες οὕτω τὸν βίον
ἐτελεύτησαν, οὐκ ἐπιτρέψαντες περὶ αὑτῶν τῇ τύχῃ, οὐδ᾽

ἀναμείναντες τὸν αὐτόματον θάνατον, ἀλλ᾽ ἐκλεξάμενοι
τὸν κάλλιστον. καὶ γάρ τοι ἀγήρατοι μὲν αὐτῶν αἱ μνῆμαι,   10
ζηλωταὶ δὲ ὑπὸ πάντων ἀνθρώπων αἱ τιμαί· οἳ πενθοῦνται
μὲν διὰ τὴν φύσιν ὡς θνητοί, ὑμνοῦνται δὲ ὡς ἀθάνατοι διὰ
τὴν ἀρετήν.

Notes: 2. **τὸν λοιπὸν χρόνον**: "for evermore" (lit. "for the rest of
time"); cf. τὸν ἄπαντα χρόνον later in the sentence.
ἄξιον ἦν: "it would be appropriate." ἄν is often omitted when, as here,
an apodosis consists of an impersonal expression in the imperfect
indicative followed by an infinitive.
3. **τοὺς τεθνεῶτας**: accusative plural masculine of τεθνεώς, an
alternative form of τεθνηκώς, perfect participle of θνήσκω = "the dead."
3–4. **νῦν δέ**: "as it is, however" (lit. "but now"). These words are often
used to bring the reader back to reality after some hypothetical situation.
4. **νόσων ἥττων καὶ γήρως**: understand ἐστί = "is subject to illness and
old age" (lit. "lesser than diseases and old age"). γήρως is the genitive
of γῆρας, contracted from γήραος.
4–5. **ὅ τε δαίμων ... ἀπαραίτητος**: εἰληχώς is the perfect participle active
of λαγχάνω, "I receive by lot." The whole initial phrase, literally "the
deity who has received our fate by lot" means something like "the deity
who has been allotted charge of our fate." Understand ἐστί again with
ἀπαραίτητος.
8. **οὐκ ἐπιτρέψαντες ... τῇ τύχῃ**: ἐπιτρέπω + dative means "I rely upon."
10. **καὶ γάρ ... αἱ μνῆμαι**: the combination of particles καὶ γάρ τοι
regularly means "and in consequence." εἰσίν needs to be understood
after ἀγήρατοι μέν.
11. **οἵ**: this connecting relative pronoun, quite loosely linked with the
previous section, is best translated simply as "they."

16.3   Euripides, *Helen* 68–77: in *Helen* Euripides uses an alternative
version of the familiar story. In this only a phantom made from ether
goes with Paris to Troy and is responsible for the horrific bloodshed
there, while the real Helen is whisked off by Hermes to Egypt, there
to live in the royal palace and await reunion with Menelaus after
the war is over. In this short extract Teucer, the famous archer and
brother of Ajax, arrives in Egypt en route for Cyprus. He initially
wonders who is master of the imposing palace before him, and is
then disgusted at the sight of someone who, as he thinks, so closely
resembles the hated Helen.

Τεῦκρος

τίς τῶνδ᾽ ἐρυμνῶν δωμάτων ἔχει κράτος;
Πλούτῳ γὰρ οἶκος ἄξιος προσεικάσαι,
βασίλειά τ᾽ ἀμφιβλήματ᾽ εὔθριγκοί θ᾽ ἕδραι.
ἔα.
ὦ θεοί, τίν᾽ εἶδον ὄψιν; ἐχθίστης ὁρῶ   5
γυναικὸς εἰκὼ φόνιον, ἥ μ᾽ ἀπώλεσεν
πάντας τ᾽ Ἀχαιούς. θεοί σ᾽, ὅσον μίμημ᾽ ἔχεις
Ἑλένης, ἀποπτύσειαν. εἰ δὲ μὴ ᾽ν ξένῃ
γαίᾳ πόδ᾽ εἶχον, τῷδ᾽ ἂν εὐστόχῳ πτερῷ
ἀπόλαυσιν εἰκοῦς ἔθανες ἂν Διὸς κόρης.   10

Notes: 1. **ἔχει κράτος**: "holds sway over" (+ genitive).
2. **Πλούτῳ**: for Πλούτου οἴκῳ. Plutus was the god of wealth.
ἄξιος προσεικάσαι: "fit to be likened to." Note the active infinitive (lit.
"fit [for people] to liken to") where English naturally uses a passive.
3. **βασίλειά… ἕδραι**: the nouns in this line are an extension of the subject,
οἶκος. We might translate "with its…." εὔθριγκος ("beautifully corniced")
appears only here in Greek. ἕδραι are probably "chambers" or "rooms."
4. **ἔα**: an exclamation indicating both surprise and displeasure.
6. **εἰκώ**: the poetic form of εἰκόνα, accusative of εἰκών ("likeness" or
"image"). Cf. too εἰκοῦς (genitive) for εἰκόνος in the last line of this
extract.
φόνιον: φόνιος ("murderous") is here treated as an adjective of two
terminations, i.e., without a separate set of endings for the feminine.
7–8. **θεοί… ἀποπτύσειαν**: a wish = "May the gods…" ἀποπτύω,
literally "I spit out," means "I abominate." ὅσον μίμημ᾽ ἔχεις: "such a
likeness do you have" (lit. "how great a likeness…").
8–10. **εἰ δὲ μὴ… εἶχον,… ἔθανες ἄν**: the imperfect tense in the
protasis refers to present time, the aorist in the apodosis to the past. ᾽ν
= ἐν (by prodelision).
9. **πτερῷ**: literally "feather" or "wing"; here = "arrow."
10. **ἀπόλαυσιν**: accusative in apposition to the rest of the sentence = "as
a reward for."

UNREAL CONDITIONS REFERRING TO PAST TIME

16.4   Plato, *Apology* 32d: Socrates reflects that he would probably
have been executed by the Thirty Tyrants for failing to carry out
their instructions, had not their government collapsed soon after.

καὶ ἴσως ἂν διὰ ταῦτα ἀπέθανον, εἰ μὴ ἡ ἀρχὴ διὰ ταχέων
κατελύθη.

Notes: 1. **διὰ ταῦτα**: "for this reason." As he has just explained, Socrates
had previously refused to co-operate with the Thirty when they
ordered him, and four others, to arrest Leon of Salamis for execution.
διὰ ταχέων: an idiomatic alternative to ταχέως. The rule of the Thirty
Tyrants, established in Athens in 404 BC, lasted for less than a year.

16.5　Homer, *Iliad* 5.674–82: Odysseus is prevented from slaugh-
tering Sarpedon, leader of the Lycians. He goes on a killing spree,
stopped only by the arrival on the scene of Hector, the Trojan leader.

οὐδ᾽ ἄρ᾽ Ὀδυσσῆϊ μεγαλήτορι μόρσιμον ἦεν
ἴφθιμον Διὸς υἱὸν ἀποκτάμεν ὀξέϊ χαλκῷ·
τῷ ῥα κατὰ πληθὺν Λυκίων τράπε θυμὸν Ἀθήνη.
ἔνθ᾽ ὅ γε Κοίρανον εἷλεν Ἀλάστορά τε Χρομίον τε
Ἄλκανδρόν θ᾽ Ἅλιόν τε Νοήμονά τε Πρύτανίν τε.　　5
καί νύ κ᾽ ἔτι πλέονας Λυκίων κτάνε δῖος Ὀδυσσεὺς
εἰ μὴ ἄρ᾽ ὀξὺ νόησε μέγας κορυθαίολος Ἕκτωρ·
βῆ δὲ διὰ προμάχων κεκορυθμένος αἴθοπι χαλκῷ
δεῖμα φέρων Δαναοῖσι.

Notes: 1. **ἦεν**: Homeric imperfect (3rd singular) of εἰμί.
2. **ἴφθιμον Διὸς υἱόν**: this is Sarpedon, son of Zeus and Laodamia and
commander of the Lycian contingent of Priam's allies. He is later killed
by Patroclus.
ἀποκτάμεν: Homeric aorist infinitive active of ἀποκτείνω.
3. **τῷ**: "therefore."
κατά: + accusative (here) = "toward."
τράπε: strong aorist (3rd singular) of τρέπω.
4. **ὅ**: "he." Note this regular Homeric usage of the article as a
demonstrative, its original function.
5–6. **Κοίρανον … Πρύτανίν**: Coeranus, Alastor, Chromius,
Alcandrus, Halius, Noëmon, and Prytanis are all Lycian warriors.
7. **ὀξὺ**: here used adverbially = "sharply," i.e., "quickly."
8. **κεκορυθμένος**: "equipped"—perfect participle passive of
κορύσσω = "I equip" (originally with a helmet = κόρυς).
9. **Δαναοῖσι**: "the Danaans," a regular collective way of referring to the
Greeks.

16.6 Thucydides, *Histories* 8.96.3–4: the Athenians, in a state of panic after hearing news of rebellion in Euboea, fear a Peloponnesian attack on the Piraeus.

μάλιστα δ' αὐτοὺς καὶ δι' ἐγγυτάτου ἐθορύβει, εἰ οἱ
πολέμιοι τολμήσουσι νενικηκότες εὐθὺ σφῶν ἐπὶ τὸν
Πειραιᾶ ἐρῆμον ὄντα νεῶν πλεῖν· καὶ ὅσον οὐκ ἤδη
ἐνόμιζον αὐτοὺς παρεῖναι. ὅπερ ἄν, εἰ τολμηρότεροι ἦσαν,
ῥᾳδίως ἂν ἐποίησαν, καὶ ἢ διέστησαν ἂν ἔτι μᾶλλον τὴν   5
πόλιν ἐφορμοῦντες ἤ, εἰ ἐπολιόρκουν μένοντες, καὶ τὰς
ἀπ' Ἰωνίας ναῦς ἠνάγκασαν ἂν καίπερ πολεμίας οὔσας τῇ
ὀλιγαρχίᾳ τοῖς σφετέροις οἰκείοις καὶ τῇ ξυμπάσῃ πόλει
βοηθῆσαι· καὶ ἐν τούτῳ Ἑλλήσποντός τε ἂν ἦν αὐτοῖς καὶ
Ἰωνία καὶ αἱ νῆσοι καὶ τὰ μέχρι Εὐβοίας καὶ ὡς εἰπεῖν ἡ   10
Ἀθηναίων ἀρχὴ πᾶσα.

Notes: 1. **μάλιστα ... εἰ**: "what troubled them especially and most immediately was whether ...": essentially the whole εἰ clause is the subject of ἐθορύβει. δι' ἐγγυτάτου = ἐγγύτατα.
2. **εὐθὺ σφῶν**: "straight for them."
3. **ὅσον οὐκ**: "all but," "almost."
4. **ὅπερ ἄν**: the connecting relative pronoun is here strengthened by the suffix -περ. ἄν looks forward to ἂν ἐποίησαν.
εἰ ... ἦσαν: εἰμί has no aorist, so the imperfect is used to refer to the past as well as to the present; cf. ἂν ἦν αὐτοῖς near the end of the extract.
5. **διέστησαν ἂν ἔτι μᾶλλον**: "would have caused yet more division in" (lit. "would have divided still further").
6. **εἰ ἐπολιόρκουν μένοντες**: "if they had stayed and blockaded it" (lit. "if, staying, they had blockaded it"). The imperfect indicative here refers to continuous past time, not to the present.
7–8. **τῇ ὀλιγαρχίᾳ**: i.e., the oligarchic council of the Four Hundred, in power in Athens in 411 BC. As is clear here, the fleet in Ionia had remained resolutely democratic in its sympathies.
10. **τὰ μέχρι Εὐβοίας**: "everywhere as far as Euboea."
ὡς εἰπεῖν: "virtually."

UNREAL CONDITIONS REFERRING TO FUTURE TIME

16.7 Aeschylus, *Agamemnon* 34–39: the watchman on Agamemnon's palace roof looks forward to his master's return, and, in famous words, hints darkly that all is not well within the house.

Φύλαξ

γένοιτο δ᾽ οὖν μολόντος εὐφιλῆ χέρα
ἄνακτος οἴκων τῇδε βαστάσαι χερί.
τὰ δ᾽ ἄλλα σιγῶ· βοῦς ἐπὶ γλώσσῃ μέγας
βέβηκεν· οἶκος δ᾽ αὐτός, εἰ φθογγὴν λάβοι,
σαφέστατ᾽ ἂν λέξειεν· ὡς ἑκὼν ἐγὼ   5
μαθοῦσιν αὐδῶ κοὐ μαθοῦσι λήθομαι.

Notes: 1. **γένοιτο δ᾽ οὖν**: "Well, at any rate, may it come about [for
me]." The optative γένοιτο expresses a wish, while δ᾽ οὖν indicates that
the watchman is leaving out a thought to which he doesn't want to give
voice, namely that troubles are in store for Agamemnon on his return.
μολόντος: participle, here in the genitive singular, of ἔμολον, used as
aorist of βλώσκω = "I come/go."
εὐφιλῆ χέρα: object of βαστάσαι.
3. **τὰ δ᾽ ἄλλα σιγῶ**: the verb is here used transitively to mean "I am
silent about/say nothing of."
3–4. **βοῦς ἐπὶ γλώσσῃ μέγας βέβηκεν**: a proverbial expression for
keeping a secret. βέβηκεν: (here) "has stepped upon," perfect active
(third singular) of βαίνω.
5. **ἑκών**: to be taken both with αὐδῶ and λήθομαι: those who are in the
know will understand his hints, but others will not ("for I choose to speak"
[lit. speak willingly] to those who know, but to forget to those who don't").
6. **κοὐ**: crasis for καὶ οὐ.
λήθομαι: = (ἐπι)λανθάνομαι.

16.8   Homer, *Iliad* 2.483–92: Homer appeals to the Muses for
inspiration before embarking on the Catalogue of Ships.

ἔσπετε νῦν μοι Μοῦσαι Ὀλύμπια δώματ᾽ ἔχουσαι—
ὑμεῖς γὰρ θεαί ἐστε πάρεστέ τε ἴστέ τε πάντα,
ἡμεῖς δὲ κλέος οἶον ἀκούομεν οὐδέ τι ἴδμεν—
οἵ τινες ἡγεμόνες Δαναῶν καὶ κοίρανοι ἦσαν·
πληθὺν δ᾽ οὐκ ἂν ἐγὼ μυθήσομαι οὐδ᾽ ὀνομήνω,   5
οὐδ᾽ εἴ μοι δέκα μὲν γλῶσσαι, δέκα δὲ στόματ᾽ εἶεν,
φωνὴ δ᾽ ἄρρηκτος, χάλκεον δέ μοι ἦτορ ἐνείη,
εἰ μὴ Ὀλυμπιάδες Μοῦσαι Διὸς αἰγιόχοιο
θυγατέρες μνησαίαθ᾽ ὅσοι ὑπὸ Ἴλιον ἦλθον·
ἀρχοὺς αὖ νηῶν ἐρέω νῆάς τε προπάσας.   10

Notes: 1. **ἔσπετε**: aorist imperative (plural) of ἐνέπω.

2–3. **ὑμεῖς . . . ἴδμεν**: these two lines, which highlight the omniscience of the Muses, are a parenthesis between ἔσπετε . . . μοι ("Tell me") and the indirect question which naturally follows (οἵ τινες . . . ἦσαν). πάρεστέ = "are present" (i.e., everywhere); κλέος: normally means "glory" but here something like "report/rumor"; οἶον: "only," from οἶος = "alone"; ἴδμεν: Homeric form of ἴσμεν (first pl. of οἶδα).

5. **οὐκ ἂν ἐγὼ μυθήσομαι . . . μνησαίαθ'**: with apparent fluidity of construction Homer starts with an apodosis using ἄν with the aorist subjunctive, interrupts this with οὐδ' εἴ + optative ("not even if"), and then has εἰ μή + optative in the protasis. For translation purposes the whole is most simply treated as a remote future ("I could not . . . , not even if . . . , unless the Muses were to remind me . . ."); μυθήσομαι is a Homeric aorist subjunctive with omicron for omega; αἰγιόχοιο: Homeric genitive; μνησαίαθ' = μνήσαιντο.

8. **Ὀλυμπιάδες Μοῦσαι**: "Olympian Muses." Ὀλυμπιάς is a specifically feminine form of Ὀλύμπιος -ον.

9. **ὑπὸ Ἴλιον**: "to Ilios."

10. **αὖ**: "in turn."

νηῶν . . . νῆας: Homeric forms of νεῶν and ναῦς.

16.9 Herodotus, *Histories* 2.173.2–4: "All work and no play . . .": the Egyptian king Amasis gives a clever answer to his friends who are concerned about his daily drinking and merrymaking.

> ἀχθεσθέντες δὲ τούτοισι οἱ φίλοι αὐτοῦ ἐνουθέτεον
> αὐτὸν τοιάδε λέγοντες. Ὦ βασιλεῦ, οὐκ ὀρθῶς σεωυτοῦ
> προέστηκας, ἐς τὸ ἄγαν φαῦλον προάγων σεωυτόν.
> σὲ γὰρ ἐχρῆν ἐν θρόνῳ σεμνῷ σεμνὸν θωκέοντα δι'
> ἡμέρης πρήσσειν τὰ πρήγματα, καὶ οὕτω Αἰγύπτιοί τ'   5
> ἂν ἠπιστέατο ὡς ὑπ' ἀνδρὸς μεγάλου ἄρχονται, καὶ
> ἄμεινον σὺ ἂν ἤκουες· νῦν δὲ ποιέεις οὐδαμῶς βασιλικά.
> ὁ δ' ἀμείβετο τοῖσιδε αὐτούς. Τὰ τόξα οἱ ἐκτημένοι,
> ἐπεὰν μὲν δέωνται χρᾶσθαι, ἐντανύουσι· ἐπεὰν δὲ
> χρήσωνται, ἐκλύουσι. εἰ γὰρ δὴ τὸν πάντα χρόνον   10
> ἐντεταμένα εἴη, ἐκραγείη ἄν, ὥστε ἐς τὸ δέον οὐκ ἂν ἔχοιεν
> αὐτοῖσι χρᾶσθαι. οὕτω δὲ καὶ ἀνθρώπου κατάστασις· εἰ
> ἐθέλοι κατεσπουδάσθαι αἰεὶ μηδὲ ἐς παιγνίην τὸ μέρος
> ἑωυτὸν ἀνιέναι, λάθοι ἂν ἤτοι μανεὶς ἢ ὅ γε ἀπόπληκτος

γενόμενος· τὰ ἐγὼ ἐπιστάμενος μέρος ἑκατέρῳ νέμω.   15
ταῦτα μὲν τοὺς φίλους ἀμείψατο.

Notes: 1. **ἀχθεσθέντες**: aorist participle from ἄχθομαι ("having been annoyed").
τούτοισι: "this," i.e., Amasis' lifestyle.
2–3. **σεωυτοῦ προέστηκας**: "you order your life" (lit. "yourself").
προέστηκα (perfect of προΐστημι) + genitive = "I govern, direct, manage."
3. **ἐς τὸ ἄγαν φαῦλον προάγων σεωυτόν**: "indulging in excessive levity" (lit. "bringing yourself into what is excessively trivial").
4. **σὲ ... ἐχρῆν**: "you ought" (lit. "it behooved you").
ἐν θρόνῳ σεμνῷ σεμνὸν θωκέοντα: the polyptoton (repetition of the same word in different cases) highlights the behavior the Egyptians would like to see in their king ("sitting in state on a stately throne").
4–5. **δι' ἡμέρης**: "all day long."
5–7. **καὶ οὕτω ... ἂν ἤκουες**: the single word οὕτω ("thus" = "if this were so") functions as the protasis in this unreal present condition.
ἂν ἠπιστέατο (= ἠπίσταντο): "would know"; ἄμεινον ἂν ἤκουες: "you would have a better reputation" (lit. "would hear better [of yourself]").
7. **νῦν δέ**: "but as it is" (cf. on passage 16.3 above).
ποιέεις οὐδαμῶς βασιλικά: "your behavior is in no way regal" (lit. "in no way do you do royal things").
8. **τοῖσιδε**: understand λόγοις.
οἱ ἐκτημένοι: "Those who own." κτάομαι (I acquire) has both κέκτημαι and ἔκτημαι as perfects.
9. **ἐπεάν**: = ἐπειδάν.
9–10. **ἐπεὰν δὲ χρήσωνται**: "whenever they have used them."
11. **ἐντεταμένα**: perfect participle passive of ἐντείνω ("I stretch, string" [a bow]).
ἐκραγείη: aorist optative passive (3rd singular) of ἐκρήγνυμι.
ἐς τὸ δέον: "when needed."
οὐκ ἂν ἔχοιεν: ἔχω here, as often with an infinitive, means "I am able."
13. **κατεσπουδάσθαι**: perfect infinitive, expressing a permanent state, of κατασπουδάζομαι ("I am serious") = "to live a serious life."
τὸ μέρος: adverbial accusative = "in turn."
14–15. **λάθοι ἄν ... γενόμενος**: "would without knowing it become a madman or a simpleton." λανθάνω with a participle means "I escape notice." μανείς: aorist participle of μαίνομαι ("I am/become mad"); ὅ γε: there is no need to translate this repetition of the subject.
16. **ταῦτα μὲν τοὺς φίλους ἀμείψατο**: ἀμείβομαι ("I reply") here has two accusatives. The more normal construction is the accusative of the person with a dative of the words spoken, as above.

CHAPTER 17

Participles 2

THE GENITIVE ABSOLUTE

In our first section on these verbal adjectives (see Chapter 7), all the participles agreed with the subject or an object of a verb or with a noun or pronoun. In the first five excerpts below, however, the participial phrase (the noun + the participle) is independent of the structure of the rest of the sentence. The technical term for this is *absolute* (from the Latin word for "loosed from" or "set free from," i.e., "independent"). In these circumstances, the genitive is regularly used. Hence "genitive absolute."

17.1 Homer, *Iliad* 12.392–3: Sarpedon is distressed by Glaucus' departure.

> Σαρπήδοντι δ' ἄχος γένετο Γλαύκου ἀπιόντος,
> αὐτίκ' ἐπεί τ' ἐνόησεν.

Notes: 2. **αὐτίκ' ἐπεί τ'**: "as soon as."

17.2 Xenophon, *Anabasis* 3.3.1: at Xenophon's urging, the Greeks break camp.

> τούτων λεχθέντων ἀνέστησαν καὶ ἀπελθόντες κατέκαιον
> τὰς ἁμάξας καὶ τὰς σκηνάς, τῶν δὲ περιττῶν ὅτου μὲν
> δέοιτό τις μετεδίδοσαν ἀλλήλοις, τὰ δὲ ἄλλα εἰς τὸ πῦρ
> ἐρρίπτουν. ταῦτα ποιήσαντες ἠριστοποιοῦντο.

Notes: 1. **ἀνέστησαν**: "(those assembled) got up."
2–3. **τῶν δὲ περιττῶν ὅτου μὲν δέοιτό τις**: "whatever anybody needed of less than vital (literally, superfluous) items …": δέοιτό is in the optative because it is in an indefinite clause (see Chapter 19).
4. **ἐρρίπτουν**: imperfect (3rd plural) of ῥιπτέω, an alternative form of ῥίπτω.

17.3   Herodotus 1.30.1: Solon arrives at Croesus' palace, where he is hospitably received and shown its treasures.

> ἀπικόμενος δὲ ἐξεινίζετο ἐν τοῖσι βασιληίοισι ὑπὸ τοῦ
> Κροίσου· μετὰ δὲ ἡμέρῃ τρίτῃ ἢ τετάρτῃ κελεύσαντος
> Κροίσου, τὸν Σόλωνα θεράποντες περιῆγον κατὰ τοὺς
> θησαυρούς, καὶ ἐπεδείκνυσαν πάντα ἐόντα μεγάλα τε καὶ
> ὄλβια.   5

Notes: 2. **μετὰ δὲ ἡμέρῃ τρίτῃ**: "and on the third day after (his arrival)."
3–4. **κατὰ τοὺς θησαυρούς**: "on a tour of the treasures."

17.4   Xenophon, *Anabasis* 1.2.22: Cyrus goes up into the mountains and then descends into a fertile plain.

> Κῦρος δ' οὖν ἀνέβη ἐπὶ τὰ ὄρη οὐδενὸς κωλύοντος, καὶ
> εἶδε τὰς σκηνὰς οὗ οἱ Κίλικες ἐφύλαττον. ἐντεῦθεν δὲ
> κατέβαινεν εἰς πεδίον μέγα καὶ καλόν, ἐπίρρυτον, καὶ
> δένδρων παντοδαπῶν σύμπλεων καὶ ἀμπέλων· πολὺ δὲ καὶ
> σήσαμον καὶ μελίνην καὶ κέγχρον καὶ πυροὺς καὶ κριθὰς   5
> φέρει. ὄρος δ' αὐτὸ περιεῖχεν ὀχυρὸν καὶ ὑψηλὸν πάντη ἐκ
> θαλάττης εἰς θάλατταν.

Notes: 3. **ἐπίρρυτον**: "well-watered."
4. **σύμπλεων**: (accusative) "full of" + genitive.
5. **σήσαμον καὶ μελίνην καὶ κέγχρον καὶ πυροὺς καὶ κριθὰς**: "sesame, millet, panic (a type of millet), wheat and barley."
6. **αὐτό**: i.e., the plain.
ὀχυρόν: "formidable."
πάντη: "on all sides."

17.5   Euripides, *Hecuba* 303–5: Odysseus repeats to Hecuba that it is necessary to sacrifice her daughter Polyxena since the ghost of Achilles has demanded this.

Ὀδυσσεύς

ἃ δ᾽ εἶπον εἰς ἅπαντας οὐκ ἀρνήσομαι,
Τροίας ἁλούσης ἀνδρὶ τῷ πρώτῳ στρατοῦ
σὴν παῖδα δοῦναι σφάγιον ἐξαιτουμένῳ.

Notes: 1. **οὐκ ἀρνήσομαι**: "I shall not disown" what I said …
2. **ἁλούσης**: aorist participle (genitive singular feminine) of
ἁλίσκομαι = I am taken.
3. **σφάγιον ἐξαιτουμένῳ**: "as a sacrificial victim since he asks for
(this)."

ACCUSATIVE ABSOLUTE

The accusative absolute is used with impersonal verbs.

17.6   Plato, *Protagoras* 358d: Socrates says that it is not in human
nature to choose evil over good or the greater evil over the lesser.

οὐδ᾽ ἔστι τοῦτο, ὡς ἔοικεν, ἐν ἀνθρώπου φύσει, ἐπὶ ἃ
οἴεται κακὰ εἶναι ἐθέλειν ἰέναι ἀντὶ τῶν ἀγαθῶν· ὅταν τε
ἀναγκασθῇ δυοῖν κακοῖν τὸ ἕτερον αἱρεῖσθαι, οὐδεὶς τὸ
μεῖζον αἱρήσεται, ἐξὸν τὸ ἔλαττον.

Notes: 2–3. **ὅταν τε ἀναγκασθῇ**: "whenever he is compelled": indefinite
construction (see Chapter 19).
3. **δυοῖν κακοῖν**: "of two evils": genitive plural dual.
4. **ἐξόν**: "it being possible (to choose)."

17.7   Plato, *Alcibiades* 1.115a–b: is it good or bad to risk your life to
help a comrade in battle?

Σωκράτης   Ἀλκιβιάδης

Σωκ.   τί δ᾽ αὖ τὰ καλά; πότερον πάντα ἀγαθά, ἢ τὰ μέν, τὰ
δ᾽ οὔ;

Ἀλκ.   οἴομαι ἔγωγε, ὦ Σώκρατες, ἔνια τῶν καλῶν κακὰ
εἶναι.

Σωκ.   ἦ καὶ αἰσχρὰ ἀγαθά;   5

Ἀλκ.   ναί.

Σωκ.　ἆρα λέγεις τὰ τοιάδε, οἷον πολλοὶ ἐν πολέμῳ
βοηθήσαντες ἑταίρῳ ἢ οἰκείῳ τραύματα ἔλαβον
καὶ ἀπέθανον, οἱ δ᾽ οὐ βοηθήσαντες, δέον, ὑγιεῖς
ἀπῆλθον;　　　　　　　　　　　　　　　　　10

Ἀλκ.　πάνυ μὲν οὖν.

Σωκ.　οὐκοῦν τὴν τοιαύτην βοήθειαν καλὴν μὲν λέγεις
κατὰ τὴν ἐπιχείρησιν τοῦ σῶσαι οὓς ἔδει; τοῦτο δ᾽
ἐστὶν ἀνδρεία· ἢ οὔ;

Ἀλκ.　ναί.　　　　　　　　　　　　　　　　　15

Notes: 1. **τί δ᾽ αὖ τὰ καλά;**: "and then again, what of noble things?"
1–2. **τὰ μέν, τὰ δ᾽ οὔ;**: "are some but not others?"
5. **ἦ καὶ αἰσχρὰ ἀγαθά;**: "and some disgraceful things are good?"
7. **ἆρα λέγεις τὰ τοιάδε, οἷον**: i.e., "do you mean something like when…."
8. **οἰκείῳ**: "relative."
11. **πάνυ μὲν οὖν**: "certainly."
12. **οὐκοῦν…λέγεις;** "so don't you call…?"
13. **κατὰ τὴν ἐπιχείρησιν τοῦ σῶσαι**: "in respect of the attempt to save
(literally, of saving) …"

VERBS USED WITH PARTICIPLES

Various verbs, e.g., τυγχάνω (happen, am just now), λανθάνω
(escape the notice of, am secretly) and φθάνω (anticipate, am first)
are used with participles.

17.8　Homer, *Iliad* 24.477–84: Priam, king of Troy, slips into Achilles' hut unnoticed by him and his comrades. The Trojan has come
to plead for the return of the body of his son Hector, who has been
killed by Achilles.

τοὺς δ᾽ ἔλαθ᾽ εἰσελθὼν Πρίαμος μέγας, ἄγχι δ᾽ ἄρα
στὰς

χερσὶν Ἀχιλλῆος λάβε γούνατα καὶ κύσε χεῖρας

δεινὰς ἀνδροφόνους, αἵ οἱ πολέας κτάνον υἷας.

ὡς δ᾽ ὅτ᾽ ἂν ἄνδρ᾽ ἄτη πυκινὴ λάβῃ, ὅς τ᾽ ἐνὶ πάτρῃ

φῶτα κατακτείνας ἄλλων ἐξίκετο δῆμον　　　　　5

ἀνδρὸς ἐς ἀφνειοῦ, θάμβος δ᾽ ἔχει εἰσορόωντας,

ὡς Ἀχιλεὺς θάμβησεν ἰδὼν Πρίαμον θεοειδέα·
θάμβησαν δὲ καὶ ἄλλοι, ἐς ἀλλήλους δὲ ἴδοντο.

Notes: 1. **ἔλαθ’:** aorist of λανθάνω.
2. **Ἀχιλλῆος . . . γούνατα:** "the knees of Achilles."
3. **ἀνδροφόνους:** "man-slaying."
πολέας . . . υἷας: "many (of his) sons."
4. **ὡς δ’ ὅτ’ ἂν ἄνδρ’ ἄτη πυκινὴ λάβῃ:** "as when strong folly takes hold of a man."
5–6. **ἄλλων ἐξίκετο δῆμον ἀνδρὸς ἐς ἀφνειοῦ:** "he has come to a community of other men to (the house) of a rich man."
6. **εἰσορόωντας:** "those looking on."
8. **ἴδοντο:** "they looked."

17.9   Herodotus 4.136.1–2: the Scythians sympathize with the soldiers abandoned by the Persian king Darius and beat him to the bridge over the Istros.

ἡμέρης δὲ γενομένης γνόντες οἱ ὑπολειφθέντες ὡς
προδεδομένοι εἶεν ὑπὸ Δαρείου, χεῖράς τε προετείνοντο
τοῖσι Σκύθησι καὶ ἔλεγον τὰ κατήκοντα· οἱ δὲ ὡς ἤκουσαν
ταῦτα τὴν ταχίστην συστραφέντες, αἵ τε δύο μοῖραι τῶν
Σκυθέων καὶ ἡ μία καὶ Σαυρομάται καὶ Βουδῖνοι καὶ   5
Γελωνοί, ἐδίωκον τοὺς Πέρσας ἰθὺ τοῦ Ἴστρου. ἅτε δὲ
τοῦ Περσικοῦ μὲν τοῦ πολλοῦ ἐόντος πεζοῦ στρατοῦ καὶ
τὰς ὁδοὺς οὐκ ἐπισταμένου, ὥστε οὐ τετμημένων τῶν
ὁδῶν, τοῦ δὲ Σκυθικοῦ ἱππότεω καὶ τὰ σύντομα τῆς ὁδοῦ
ἐπισταμένου, ἁμαρτόντες ἀλλήλων, ἔφθησαν πολλῷ οἱ   10
Σκύθαι τοὺς Πέρσας ἐπὶ τὴν γέφυραν ἀπικόμενοι.

Notes: 2. **προδεδομένοι εἶεν:** (perfect passive optative) "they had been betrayed."
χεῖράς τε προετείνοντο: "stretched out their arms" (a sign of surrender).
3. **τὰ κατήκοντα:** i.e., "the present crisis," lit. "the things fitting (the situation)."
4. **τὴν ταχίστην συστραφέντες:** "having very quickly formed a single unit." The two divisions (μοῖραι) of the Scythian army were joined by one comprising Sauromatae, Budini and Geloni.

6. **ἰθὺ τοῦ Ἴστρου**: "straight for the Ister," i.e., the Danube.

6–7. **ἅτε ... τοῦ Περσικοῦ μὲν τοῦ πολλοῦ ἐόντος πεζοῦ στρατοῦ**: "inasmuch as the greater part of the Persian army was traveling on foot."

8–9. **ὥστε οὐ τετμημένων τῶν ὁδῶν**: literally, "inasmuch as the roads had not been cut (in the ground)," i.e., "in the absence of regular roads." ὥστε here = ἅτε.

9–10. **τοῦ ... Σκυθικοῦ ἱππότεω καὶ τὰ σύντομα τῆς ὁδοῦ ἐπισταμένου**: 'the Scythian force being on horseback and knowing the shortcuts''.

10. **ἁμαρτόντες ἀλλήλων**: "having missed each other": the Scythians had arrived at the river without encountering the Persian army.

10–11. **ἔφθησαν πολλῷ οἱ Σκύθαι τοὺς Πέρσας ἐπὶ τὴν γέφυραν ἀπικόμενοι**: lit. "the Scythians anticipated [aorist of φθάνω] the Persians by much (time) having arrived at the bridge," i.e., "the Scythians got to the bridge (τὴν γέφυραν) long before the Persians."

17.10 Plato, *Euthydemus* 272d–e: Socrates explains how he came to encounter two foreign teachers of wisdom at the gymnasium.

Κρίτων   Σωκράτης

Κρ. πρῶτον δέ μοι διήγησαι τὴν σοφίαν τοῖν ἀνδροῖν τίς
ἐστιν, ἵνα εἰδῶ ὅτι καὶ μαθησόμεθα.

Σωκ. οὐκ ἂν φθάνοις ἀκούων· ὡς οὐκ ἂν ἔχοιμί γε εἰπεῖν
ὅτι οὐ προσεῖχον τὸν νοῦν αὐτοῖν, ἀλλὰ πάνυ καὶ
προσεῖχον καὶ μέμνημαι, καί σοι πειράσομαι ἐξ   5
ἀρχῆς ἅπαντα διηγήσασθαι. κατὰ θεὸν γάρ τινα
ἔτυχον καθήμενος ἐνταῦθα, οὗπερ σύ με εἶδες, ἐν τῷ
ἀποδυτηρίῳ μόνος, καὶ ἤδη ἐν νῷ εἶχον ἀναστῆναι·
ἀνισταμένου δέ μου ἐγένετο τὸ εἰωθὸς σημεῖον τὸ
δαιμόνιον. πάλιν οὖν ἐκαθεζόμην....   10

Notes: 1. **διήγησαι**: aorist imperative.
1–2. **τὴν σοφίαν τοῖν ἀνδροῖν τίς ἐστιν**: literally, "the wisdom of the two men what it is": cf. "I know thee who thou art." τοῖν ἀνδροῖν: is in the genitive of the dual.
2. **εἰδῶ**: subjunctive of οἶδα.
ὅτι: "what (it is)."
3. **οὐκ ἂν φθάνοις ἀκούων**: "you wouldn't get in first listening," i.e., "you'll hear at once."

4. **οὐ προσεῖχον τὸν νοῦν αὐτοῖν**: "I didn't pay attention to the two of them." αὐτοῖν is the dative of the dual.

5. **προσεῖχον**: supply τὸν νοῦν.

6. **κατὰ θεὸν γάρ τινα**: i.e., "by some divine providence."

7–8. **ἐν τῷ ἀποδυτηρίῳ**: "in the changing room."

9–10. **τὸ εἰωθὸς σημεῖον τὸ δαιμόνιον**: "my usual divine sign." Socrates believed that he was the recipient of a divine sign that could guide his conduct. Plato says that it always told him what *not* to do. Here it must have instructed him not to get up and leave.

CHAPTER 18

Verbs of Fearing, Precaution and Preventing

VERBS OF FEARING

Fears for the future are expressed by μή (negative μή οὐ) followed by the subjunctive in primary sequence and by the optative in historic sequence. By the so-called vivid construction the subjunctive may also be used in historic sequence.

Fears for the present and past are similarly introduced by μή and μὴ οὐ. The verb is in the appropriate tense of the indicative.

Verbs of fearing may also be followed by an infinitive, as in English.

The normal verbs of fearing are φοβέομαι and δείδω, the latter appearing most commonly in its aorist ἔδεισα and its two perfects δέδοικα and δέδια, both of which are used with present meaning.

18.1   (I) Euripides, *Medea* 37: Medea's nurse fears for the future.

Τροφός

δέδοικα δ᾽ αὐτὴν μή τι βουλεύσῃ νέον.

Notes: 1. **αὐτήν**: "her," i.e., Medea. The pronoun anticipates the subject of the subordinate clause.
νέον: "new" in a bad sense, i.e., "untoward," even "evil."

(II) Xenophon, *Anabasis* 1.10.9: in the closing stages of the Battle of Cunaxa (401 BC) the Greeks are afraid that they will be hacked to pieces by the forces of Artaxerxes.

ἐπεὶ δ᾽ ἦσαν κατὰ τὸ εὐώνυμον τῶν Ἑλλήνων κέρας,
ἔδεισαν οἱ Ἕλληνες μὴ προσάγοιεν πρὸς τὸ κέρας καὶ
περιπτύξαντες ἀμφοτέρωθεν αὐτοὺς κατακόψειαν.

Notes: 1. **ἦσαν**: the subject, "they" are the Persian forces of Artaxerxes.
κατά: "opposite."
2. **προσάγοιεν πρός**: "advance against."
3. **περιπτύξαντες**: "enfolding," i.e., "outflanking,"

(III) Aristophanes, *Clouds* 492–93: Socrates, director of the
φροντιστήριον, or "Thinkery," finds Strepsiades a disappointing
pupil. He threatens a beating.

Σωκράτης

ἄνθρωπος ἀμαθὴς οὑτοσὶ καὶ βάρβαρος.
δέδοικά σ᾽ ὦ πρεσβῦτα μὴ πληγῶν δέει.

Notes: 1. **ἄνθρωπος ... οὑτοσί**: the so-called deictic iota strengthens
the demonstrative pronoun ("this fellow here").
2. **σ᾽**: again the pronoun, as object of the verb of fearing, anticipates the
subject of the subordinate clause.
δέει: present tense (2nd singular) of δέομαι (I need), which takes the
genitive.

(IV) Thucydides, *Histories* 3.53.2: the Plataeans have sur-
rendered their city to the Spartans after a siege. Contrary to
their expectation they have been put on trial for their earlier
opposition, and in the course of the proceedings begin to suspect
that they will not get the fair treatment they had hoped for.

νῦν δὲ φοβούμεθα μὴ ἀμφοτέρων ἅμα ἡμαρτήκαμεν.

Notes: 1. **μὴ ... ἡμαρτήκαμεν**: "that we have been disappointed in both
matters at the same time," i.e., the expectation that they wouldn't be
put on trial, and the hope that, if they were, they would be treated fairly.

(V) Thucydides, *Histories* 1.136.1: Themistocles, pursued by both
Athenians and Spartans, seeks refuge on the island of Corcyra
(modern Corfu). The Corcyraeans, however, are afraid to keep
him.

ὁ δὲ Θεμιστοκλῆς προαισθόμενος φεύγει ἐκ
Πελοποννήσου ἐς Κέρκυραν, ὢν αὐτῶν εὐεργέτης.
δεδιέναι δὲ φασκόντων Κερκυραίων ἔχειν αὐτὸν ὥστε
Λακεδαιμονίοις καὶ Ἀθηναίοις ἀπεχθέσθαι, διακομίζεται
ὑπ᾽ αὐτῶν ἐς τὴν ἤπειρον τὴν καταντικρύ.   5

Notes: 1. **προαισθόμενος**: "forewarned" (lit. "perceiving in advance").
φεύγει: historic present.
3. **δεδιέναι**: infinitive of δέδια, perfect of δείδω (see above).
3–4. **ὥστε . . . ἀπεχθέσθαι**: this clause expresses what the result would
be of their keeping Themistocles = "as they would become hateful to
the Spartans and Athenians."

18.2   Euripides, *Medea* 282–89: Creon, king of Corinth, explains
why he fears Medea.

Κρέων

δέδοικά σ᾽, οὐδὲν δεῖ παραμπίσχειν λόγους,
μή μοί τι δράσῃς παῖδ᾽ ἀνήκεστον κακόν.
συμβάλλεται δὲ πολλὰ τοῦδε δείγματα·
σοφὴ πέφυκας καὶ κακῶν πολλῶν ἴδρις,
λυπῇ δὲ λέκτρων ἀνδρὸς ἐστερημένη.   5
κλύω δ᾽ ἀπειλεῖν σ᾽, ὡς ἀπαγγέλλουσί μοι,
τὸν δόντα καὶ γήμαντα καὶ γαμουμένην
δράσειν τι. ταῦτ᾽ οὖν πρὶν παθεῖν φυλάξομαι.

Notes: 1. **δέδοικά σ᾽**: as often (see 1 [I] and 1 [III] above), the subject of
the subordinate clause is anticipated as object of the verb of fearing.
οὐδὲν δεῖ: "there's no point in."
2. **μή . . . κακόν**: note the two accusatives after δράω ("I do something
[to] someone"), as also in lines 7 and 8 below. μοί is technically an ethic
dative, indicating someone who will be affected by the action in question
(lit. "that you will do some irreparable harm to my daughter *on me*").
3. **συμβάλλεται . . . δείγματα**: "and there's a lot of evidence to support
this [fear]" (lit. "and many pieces of evidence of this are brought
together").
4. **σοφή**: "clever" rather than "wise."
πέφυκας: intransitive perfect (2nd singular) of φύω, with present
meaning = "you are (by nature)."

7. **τὸν δόντα ... γαμουμένην**: "(to) the giver (Creon himself), the marrier (Jason) and the married (the princess Glauce)."

8. **φυλάξομαι**: "I shall guard against."

18.3 Xenophon, *Anabasis* 1.7.6: Cyrus reassures the Greeks that he does have at his disposal the means to reward them all richly, should he be victorious over his brother King Artaxerxes.

> ἀκούσας ταῦτα ἔλεξεν ὁ Κῦρος· Ἀλλ᾽ ἔστι μὲν ἡμῖν, ὦ
> ἄνδρες, ἀρχὴ πατρῴα πρὸς μὲν μεσημβρίαν μέχρι οὗ διὰ
> καῦμα οὐ δύνανται οἰκεῖν ἄνθρωποι, πρὸς δὲ ἄρκτον
> μέχρι οὗ διὰ χειμῶνα· τὰ δ᾽ ἐν μέσῳ τούτων πάντα
> σατραπεύουσιν οἱ τοῦ ἐμοῦ ἀδελφοῦ φίλοι. ἢν δ᾽ ἡμεῖς   5
> νικήσωμεν, ἡμᾶς δεῖ τοὺς ἡμετέρους φίλους τούτων
> ἐγκρατεῖς ποιῆσαι. ὥστε οὐ τοῦτο δέδοικα, μὴ οὐκ ἔχω
> ὅ τι δῶ ἑκάστῳ τῶν φίλων, ἂν εὖ γένηται, ἀλλὰ μὴ οὐκ   crown
> ἔχω ἱκανοὺς οἷς δῶ. ὑμῶν δὲ τῶν Ἑλλήνων καὶ στέφανον
> ἑκάστῳ χρυσοῦν δώσω. οἱ δὲ ταῦτα ἀκούσαντες αὐτοί τε   10
> ἦσαν πολὺ προθυμότεροι καὶ τοῖς ἄλλοις ἐξήγγελλον.

Notes: 1. **Ἀλλ᾽ ἔστι μὲν ἡμῖν**: "but we have available to us," a possessive dative.

2. **μέχρι οὗ**: "up to where."

2–3. **διὰ καῦμα**: "on account of the burning heat."

4. **διὰ χειμῶνα**: "on account of the wintry cold"; οὐ δύνανται οἰκεῖν ἄνθρωποι is understood.

5. **σατραπεύουσιν**: "rule as satraps." Satraps were Persian provincial governors.

ἢν: = ἐάν; cf. too ἄν in line 5.

8. **ὅ τι δῶ**: "something to give."

ἂν εὖ γένηται: "if things go well."

9. **ἱκανούς**: understand φίλους.

18.4 Homer, *Odyssey* 5.299–307: Odysseus, caught in a savage storm at sea, wonders what is to become of him.

> ὤ μοι ἐγὼ δειλός, τί νύ μοι μήκιστα γένηται;
> δείδω μὴ δὴ πάντα θεὰ νημερτέα εἶπεν,
> ἥ μ᾽ ἔφατ᾽ ἐν πόντῳ, πρὶν πατρίδα γαῖαν ἱκέσθαι,

ἄλγε' ἀναπλήσειν· τὰ δὲ δὴ νῦν πάντα τελεῖται.
οἵοισιν νεφέεσσι περιστέφει οὐρανὸν εὐρὺν   5
Ζεύς, ἐτάραξε δὲ πόντον, ἐπισπέρχουσι δ' ἄελλαι
παντοίων ἀνέμων. νῦν μοι σῶς αἰπὺς ὄλεθρος.
τρὶς μάκαρες Δαναοὶ καὶ τετράκις, οἳ τότ' ὄλοντο
Τροίῃ ἐν εὐρείῃ χάριν Ἀτρεΐδῃσι φέροντες.

Notes: 1. **ὤ μοι ἐγὼ δειλός**: "Ah me, wretched as I am!"
μήκιστα: "at the last."
2. **θεά**: i.e., Calypso, as Odysseus was setting out from her island on his raft.
4. **ἄλγε' ἀναπλήσειν**: "that I would receive a full measure of woes."
ἀναπλήσειν is future infinitive of ἀναπίμπλημι (lit. "I fill up").
6. **ἐπισπέρχουσι**: "rage furiously."
7. **νῦν … ὄλεθρος**: understand ἐστίν; σῶς: "assured."
8. **τρὶς … τετράκις**: understand εἰσίν.

18.5   *St. Matthew's Gospel* 1.19–22: Joseph, aware that Mary is with child, wishes to break off their engagement; but an angel appears in a dream and assures him that Mary's pregnancy is of divine origin, and that her son, Jesus, will be the savior of his people.

Ἰωσὴφ δὲ ὁ ἀνὴρ αὐτῆς, δίκαιος ὢν καὶ μὴ θέλων αὐτὴν
δειγματίσαι, ἐβουλήθη λάθρα ἀπολῦσαι αὐτήν. ταῦτα δὲ
αὐτοῦ ἐνθυμηθέντος, ἰδού, ἄγγελος Κυρίου κατ' ὄναρ
ἐφάνη αὐτῷ λέγων, Ἰωσήφ, υἱὸς Δαυείδ, μὴ φοβηθῇς
παραλαβεῖν Μαρίαμ τὴν γυναῖκά σου· τὸ γὰρ ἐν αὐτῇ   5
γεννηθὲν ἐκ πνεύματός ἐστιν ἁγίου. τέξεται δὲ υἱὸν καὶ
καλέσεις τὸ ὄνομα αὐτοῦ Ἰησοῦν, αὐτὸς γὰρ σώσει τὸν
λαὸν αὐτοῦ ἀπὸ τῶν ἁμαρτιῶν αὐτῶν.

Notes: 1. **αὐτῆς**: i.e., Mary.
μὴ θέλων: μή is regularly used with the participle in NT Greek, particularly in a conditional, causal (as here) or concessive sense.
2. **δειγματίσαι**: aorist infinitive active of δειγματίζω ("I make an example of").
ἀπολῦσαι: ἀπολύω is regularly used for "divorcing" a wife or bethrothed.
4. **υἱὸς Δαυείδ**: "son of David." Joseph, Mary's fiancé, traced his ancestry back to King David.

7. **καλέσεις**: from καλέσω, future of καλέω. In Attic Greek a contracted future, καλῶ, is the norm.

Ἰησοῦν: "Jesus." The original Hebrew form of the word means "God is salvation".

VERBS OF PRECAUTION

The most common verbs in question are ὁράω (I see to it), σκοπέω/ -έομαι (I see to it), εὐλαβέομαι (I take care), ἐπιμελέομαι (I take care), φυλάττομαι (I am on my guard) and φροντίζω (I take heed).

They are regularly followed by ὅπως (negative ὅπως μή) with the future indicative, even in historic sequence, where the alternative future optative is only occasionally found.

The present or aorist subjunctive or optative, as in final clauses, sometimes replaces the future indicative.

μή or μὴ οὐ with the subjunctive or optative (without ὅπως) are sometimes found in negative clauses after verbs of precaution.

If the verb of precaution is a second person imperative, it is regularly omitted; e.g., ὅπως τοῦτο ποιήσεις = *See that you do this.*

18.6   (I) Isocrates 2.37: the Athenian Isocrates gives good advice to Nicocles, king of Salamis in Cyprus.

> ἐν πᾶσι τοῖς ἔργοις μέμνησο τῆς βασιλείας, καὶ φρόντιζε
> ὅπως μηδὲν ἀνάξιον τῆς τιμῆς ταύτης πράξεις.

Notes: 1. **μέμνησο τῆς βασιλείας**: "remember you are a king" (lit. "remember your kingship").
2. **τῆς τιμῆς ταύτης**: "of this office."

(II) Sophocles, *Trachiniae* 1129: Heracles demands loyalty from his son, Hyllus.

Ἡρακλῆς

> λέγ', εὐλαβοῦ δὲ μὴ φανῇς κακὸς γεγώς.

Notes: 1. **μὴ φανῇς κακὸς γεγώς**: "that you don't prove a bad/disloyal son"; γεγώς = γεγονώς.

(III) Demosthenes, *De Falsa Legatione* 92: Demosthenes assures his rival Aeschines that no one blames him for the war with Philip.

ὅπως τοίνυν περὶ τοῦ πολέμου μηδὲν ἐρεῖς· οὐδεὶς γὰρ
οὐδὲν αἰτιᾶται περὶ αὐτοῦ σε.

Notes: 1. **ὅπως … μηδὲν ἐρεῖς**: the imperative of a verb of precaution is
understood before the ὅπως clause (see above), giving the instruction a
strong sense of urgency.
2. **οὐδέν**: (after the preceding negative) "at all."

18.7   Xenophon, *Anabasis* 1.3.11: the Spartan Clearchus, diplomatically dealing with a mutiny among the Greek forces following Cyrus
against his brother, King Artaxerxes, is pretending to side with his
men. Now that they have seceded, he says, they must look out for
themselves and their own safety.

ἐμοὶ οὖν δοκεῖ οὐχ ὥρα εἶναι ἡμῖν καθεύδειν οὐδ᾽ ἀμελεῖν
ἡμῶν αὐτῶν, ἀλλὰ βουλεύεσθαι ὅ τι χρὴ ποιεῖν ἐκ τούτων.
καὶ ἕως γε μένομεν αὐτοῦ σκεπτέον μοι δοκεῖ εἶναι ὅπως
ὡς ἀσφαλέστατα μενοῦμεν, εἴ τε ἤδη δοκεῖ ἀπιέναι, ὅπως
ὡς ἀσφαλέστατα ἄπιμεν, καὶ ὅπως τὰ ἐπιτήδεια ἕξομεν·   5
ἄνευ γὰρ τούτων οὔτε στρατηγοῦ οὔτε ἰδιώτου ὄφελος
οὐδέν.

Notes: 2. **ἐκ τούτων**: "under the present circumstances."
3. **σκεπτέον μοι δοκεῖ εἶναι**: "it seems to me we must see to it that."
For verbal adjectives and their use, see Chapter 21.
6–7. **οὔτε … ὄφελος οὐδέν**: understand ἐστί = "neither general nor private
is of any use" (lit. "there is no advantage of either general or private");
ἰδιώτης, normally a "private citizen," here means a "private soldier."

VERBS OF PREVENTING, HINDERING, FORBIDDING AND DENYING

These verbs, all of which contain some kind of negative sense, are
followed by the infinitive, which itself is often preceded by a redundant μή. When the verb of preventing is negatived itself, or is part
of a question expecting the answer *no*, it is usually followed by μὴ
οὐ with the infinitive. κωλύω, however, whether negatived or not, is
usually followed by the simple infinitive without μή.

Also found with the infinitive after these verbs are (i) τὸ μή (or just τό) and τὸ μὴ οὔ, and (ii) τοῦ μή (or just τοῦ) and τοῦ μὴ οὔ (very rare).

The main verbs in question are κωλύω ("I hinder/prevent"), εἴργω ("I hinder/prevent"), ἐμποδών εἰμι ("I hinder/prevent"), ἀπαγορεύω ("I forbid"), ἀπεῖπον ("I forbade"), οὐκ ἐάω ("I do not allow/forbid"), (ἀπ)αρνέομαι ("I deny") and ἀμφισβητέω ("I dispute/disagree").

18.8 (I) Herodotus, *Histories* 2.20.2: in the course of his discussion of the inundation of the Nile, Herodotus mentions, and rejects, three contemporary Greek explanations of the phenomenon. The first two of them, he makes clear (our passage deals with just the first), have little to recommend them.

> τῶν ἡ ἑτέρη μὲν λέγει τοὺς ἐτησίας ἀνέμους εἶναι αἰτίους
> πληθύειν τὸν ποταμόν, κωλύοντας ἐς θάλασσαν ἐκρέειν
> τὸν Νεῖλον.

Notes: 1. **τῶν ἡ ἑτέρη**: "one of these two"; τῶν is a connecting relative. **τοὺς ἐτησίας ἀνέμους**: the "etesian" or seasonal winds blow in summer, normally from the northwest.
1–2. **αἰτίους πληθύειν τὸν ποταμόν**: "responsible for the river being full"; αἰτίους is followed by an accusative and infinitive.

(II) Sophocles, *Antigone* 441–43: Creon asks for, and gets, a straight answer.

Κρέων   Ἀντιγόνη

Κρ. σὲ δή, σὲ τὴν νεύουσαν εἰς πέδον κάρα,
        φῂς ἢ καταρνεῖ μὴ δεδρακέναι τάδε;
Ἀντ. καὶ φημὶ δρᾶσαι κοὐκ ἀπαρνοῦμαι τὸ μή.

Notes: 1. **σὲ δή, σέ**: "You there, you"; an understood καλῶ explains the accusative.
3. **κοὐκ**: crasis for καὶ οὐκ.
τὸ μή: here for the more normal (i.e., after a negative) τὸ μὴ οὔ (δρᾶσαι).

(III) Plato, *Hippias Minor* 369d: Socrates (ironically) admits the superior wisdom of Hippias.

ὦ Ἱππία, ἐγώ τοι οὐκ ἀμφισβητῶ μὴ οὐχὶ σὲ εἶναι
σοφώτερον ἢ ἐμέ.

Notes: 1. **οὐχί**: a longer form of οὐ (cf. the Modern Greek ὄχι = "no").

18.9 Thucydides, *Histories* 3.1: Peloponnesian activity in Attica during the summer of 428 BC.

τοῦ δ᾽ ἐπιγιγνομένου θέρους Πελοποννήσιοι καὶ οἱ
ξύμμαχοι ἅμα τῷ σίτῳ ἀκμάζοντι ἐστράτευσαν ἐς τὴν
Ἀττικήν· ἡγεῖτο δὲ αὐτῶν Ἀρχίδαμος ὁ Ζευξιδάμου
Λακεδαιμονίων βασιλεύς. καὶ ἐγκαθεζόμενοι ἐδήουν
τὴν γῆν· καὶ προσβολαί, ὥσπερ εἰώθεσαν, ἐγίγνοντο τῶν   5
Ἀθηναίων ἱππέων ὅπῃ παρείκοι, καὶ τὸν πλεῖστον ὅμιλον
τῶν ψιλῶν εἶργον τὸ μὴ προεξιόντας τῶν ὅπλων τὰ ἐγγὺς
τῆς πόλεως κακουργεῖν. ἐμμείναντες δὲ χρόνον οὗ εἶχον τὰ
σιτία ἀνεχώρησαν καὶ διελύθησαν κατὰ πόλεις.

Notes: 2. **ἅμα τῷ σίτῳ ἀκμάζοντι**: "just when the corn was ripening," i.e., about the middle of May.
3. **Ἀρχίδαμος ὁ Ζευξιδάμου**: Archidamus, son of Zeuxidamus, was King of Sparta for more than forty years, c. 464–427 BC. Despite his opposition to the war, he led invasions into Attica on three occasions, in 432, 430, and 428 BC.
5. **ὥσπερ εἰώθεσαν**: "as were customary," i.e., "as usual."
6. **ὅπῃ παρείκοι**: "wherever it was practicable," a regular impersonal usage.
7. **τῶν ὅπλων**: (here) = τοῦ στρατοπέδου.
8. **τὰ ἐγγὺς τῆς πόλεως**: "the districts near the city."
ἐμμείναντες etc.: the subject is once again "the Peloponnesians."
9. **διελύθησαν κατὰ πόλεις**: "dispersed to their several cities."

18.10 Euripides, *Phoenissae* 1172–86: a messenger tells of the spectacular death of Capaneus, one of the Seven against Thebes.

Ἄγγελος

Καπανεὺς δὲ πῶς εἴποιμ᾽ ἂν ὡς ἐμαίνετο;
μακραύχενος γὰρ κλίμακος προσαμβάσεις
ἔχων ἐχώρει, καὶ τοσόνδ᾽ ἐκόμπασε
μηδ᾽ ἂν τὸ σεμνὸν πῦρ νιν εἰργαθεῖν Διὸς

τὸ μὴ οὐ κατ᾽ ἄκρων περγάμων ἑλεῖν πόλιν.   5
καὶ ταῦθ᾽ ἅμ᾽ ἠγόρευε καὶ πετρούμενος
ἀνεῖρφ᾽ ὑπ᾽ αὐτὴν ἀσπίδ᾽ εἱλίξας δέμας,
κλίμακος ἀμείβων ξέστ᾽ ἐνηλάτων βάθρα.
ἤδη δ᾽ ὑπερβαίνοντα γεῖσα τειχέων
βάλλει κεραυνῷ Ζεύς νιν· ἐκτύπησε δὲ   10
χθών, ὥστε δεῖσαι πάντας· ἐκ δὲ κλιμάκων
ἐσφενδονᾶτο χωρὶς ἀλλήλων μέλη,
κόμαι μὲν εἰς Ὄλυμπον, αἷμα δ᾽ ἐς χθόνα,
χεῖρες δὲ καὶ κῶλ᾽ ὡς κύκλωμ᾽ Ἰξίονος
εἱλίσσετ᾽· ἐς γῆν δ᾽ ἔμπυρος πίπτει νεκρός.   15

Notes: 2. **μακραύχενος ... κλίμακος προσαμβάσεις**: "a long scaling ladder" (lit. "the ascents of a long-necked ladder").
3. **τοσόνδ᾽ ἐκόμπασε**: "made this great boast" (lit. "boasted so much").
4. **εἰργαθεῖν**: εἴργαθον is a poetic alternative for εἶρξα, aorist active of εἴργω.
5. **κατ᾽ ἄκρων περγάμων**: "from its topmost citadel." Πέργαμα, originally the citadel of Troy, came to be used of any citadel.
7. **ἀνεῖρφ᾽**: = ἀνεῖρπε, imperfect (third singular) of ἀνέρπω ("I creep up").
εἱλίξας: "having curled up" (aorist participle active of ἑλίσσω).
8. **κλίμακος ... βάθρα**: "going up the smooth rungs of the ladder" (lit. "exchanging [one for another] the smooth steps of the rungs of the ladder").
9. **γεῖσα τειχέων**: "cornice of the walls."
12. **ἐσφενδονᾶτο**: "were hurled as from a sling."
13. **εἰς Ὄλυμπον**: lit. "into Olympus," i.e., "up to heaven."
14. **κύκλωμ᾽ Ἰξίονος**: Ixion was a legendary king of Thessaly, punished for various offenses by being attached to a fiery wheel, revolving throughout eternity.

CHAPTER 19

Indefinite Sentences

"I like whatever you do." Here "ever" in "whatever" makes the clause in which it appears indefinite. We are not talking about a specific action but *any* action. In Greek, verbs in primary (i.e., present or future) time in an indefinite clause are in the subjunctive with ἄν or κέ(ν). Verbs in historic (i.e., past) time are in the optative without ἄν or κέ(ν).

Negative μή.

Note the coalescing forms for ὅταν (for ὅτε ἄν), ἐπειδάν (for ἐπειδὴ ἄν), ἐάν, or ἤν (for εἰ ἄν).

19.1 Xenophon, *Cyropaedia* 1.1.2: while men do not always obey their rulers, cattle do what their masters want them to.

πορεύονταί τε γὰρ αἱ ἀγέλαι ᾗ ἂν αὐτὰς εὐθύνωσιν οἱ
νομεῖς, νέμονταί τε χωρία ἐφ᾽ ὁποῖα ἂν αὐτὰς ἐπάγωσιν,
ἀπέχονταί τε ὧν ἂν αὐτὰς ἀπείργωσι· καὶ τοῖς καρποῖς
τοίνυν τοῖς γιγνομένοις ἐξ αὐτῶν ἐῶσι τοὺς νομέας
χρῆσθαι οὕτως ὅπως ἂν αὐτοὶ βούλωνται.   5

Notes: 1. ᾗ: "where."
εὐθύνωσιν: εὐθύνω = I guide.
3–4. **τοῖς καρποῖς ... τοῖς γιγνομένοις ἐξ αὐτῶν**: "the profits that accrue from them." **τοίνυν**: "furthermore."

19.2   Homer, *Iliad* 9.312–3: Achilles tells Odysseus that he is going to be completely frank in what he will say to him.

ἐχθρὸς γάρ μοι κεῖνος ὁμῶς Ἀΐδαο πύλησιν
ὅς χ᾽ ἕτερον μὲν κεύθῃ ἐνὶ φρεσίν, ἄλλο δὲ εἴπῃ.

Notes: 1. **ὁμῶς Ἀΐδαο πύλησιν**: "like the gates of Hades."
2. **χ᾽**: = κε = ἄν.

19.3   Lysias 12.41: the orator concludes that birds of a feather stick together.

πολλάκις οὖν ἐθαύμασα τῆς τόλμης τῶν λεγόντων ὑπὲρ
αὐτοῦ, πλὴν ὅταν ἐνθυμηθῶ ὅτι τῶν αὐτῶν ἐστιν αὐτούς τε
πάντα τὰ κακὰ ἐργάζεσθαι καὶ τοὺς τοιούτους ἐπαινεῖν.

Notes: 1. **ἐθαύμασα**: plus genitive = "I have wondered *at*."
2. **αὐτοῦ**: i.e., Eratosthenes, the defendant.
τῶν αὐτῶν ἐστιν αὐτούς τε: "it is (characteristic) of the same people both themselves . . ." (plus infinitive).

19.4   Sophocles, *Antigone* 574–81: King Creon makes it clear to the Chorus that he is determined to execute his son's fiancée Antigone.

Χορός   Κρέων

Χορ. ἦ γὰρ στερήσεις τῆσδε τὸν σαυτοῦ γόνον;
Κρ.   Ἅιδης ὁ παύσων τούσδε τοὺς γάμους ἔφυ.
Χορ. δεδογμέν᾽, ὡς ἔοικε, τήνδε κατθανεῖν.
Κρ.   καὶ σοί γε κἀμοί. μὴ τριβὰς ἔτ᾽, ἀλλά νιν
         κομίζετ᾽ εἴσω, δμῶες· ἐκ δὲ τοῦδε χρὴ   5
         γυναῖκας εἶναι τάσδε μηδ᾽ ἀνειμένας.
         φεύγουσι γάρ τοι χοἰ θρασεῖς, ὅταν πέλας
         ἤδη τὸν Ἅιδην εἰσορῶσι τοῦ βίου.

Notes: 1. **ἦ γάρ**: "are you really going to . . ."
τῆσδε: i.e., of Antigone.
2. **Ἅιδης . . . ἔφυ**: "Hades (i.e., death) is the one who . . ."
3. **δεδογμέν᾽**: "it has been decided that" followed by the accusative and infinitive.

4. **καὶ σοί γε κἀμοί**: "(it has been decided) both for you and for me."
μὴ τριβὰς ἔτ': "no further delays!"
5–6. **ἐκ δὲ τοῦδε χρὴ γυναῖκας εἶναι τάσδε μηδ᾽ ἀνειμένας**: "from now on these girls (τάσδε) must be (proper) women and not roaming loose."
7. **τοι**: "you know."
χοἰ: καὶ οἱ in crasis: "even the ..."
7–8. **πέλας ... τοῦ βίου**: "near their life," i.e., "closing in on their life."
8. **ἤδη**: "actually."

19.5 Xenophon, *Cyropaedia* 5.3.55: Cyrus shows true leadership qualities on the march.

> αὐτὸς δὲ παρελαύνων τὸν ἵππον εἰς τὸ πρόσθεν ἥσυχος
> κατεθεᾶτο τὰς τάξεις. καὶ οὓς μὲν ἴδοι εὐτάκτως καὶ σιωπῇ
> ἰόντας, προσελαύνων αὐτοῖς τίνες τε εἶεν ἠρώτα καὶ ἐπεὶ
> πύθοιτο ἐπῄνει· εἰ δέ τινας θορυβουμένους αἴσθοιτο,
> τὸ αἴτιον τούτου σκοπῶν κατασβεννύναι τὴν ταραχὴν   5
> ἐπειρᾶτο.

Notes: 1. **παρελαύνων τὸν ἵππον εἰς τὸ πρόσθεν**: "riding his horse to the front."
3. **προσελαύνων**: "riding up (to them)."
5. **κατασβεννύναι**: lit. "to quench," i.e., to "calm."

19.6 Thucydides, *Histories* 2.34.3–5: the customs the Athenians observe for the burial of their dead in war.

> ἐπειδὰν δὲ ἡ ἐκφορὰ ᾖ, λάρνακας κυπαρισσίνας ἄγουσιν
> ἄμαξαι, φυλῆς ἑκάστης μίαν· ἔνεστι δὲ τὰ ὀστᾶ ἧς ἕκαστος
> ἦν φυλῆς. μία δὲ κλίνη κενὴ φέρεται ἐστρωμένη τῶν
> ἀφανῶν, οἳ ἂν μὴ εὑρεθῶσιν ἐς ἀναίρεσιν. ξυνεκφέρει δὲ ὁ
> βουλόμενος καὶ ἀστῶν καὶ ξένων, καὶ γυναῖκες πάρεισιν αἱ   5
> προσήκουσαι ἐπὶ τὸν τάφον ὀλοφυρόμεναι. τιθέασιν οὖν ἐς
> τὸ δημόσιον σῆμα, ὅ ἐστιν ἐπὶ τοῦ καλλίστου προαστείου
> τῆς πόλεως, καὶ αἰεὶ ἐν αὐτῷ θάπτουσι τοὺς ἐκ τῶν
> πολέμων, πλήν γε τοὺς ἐν Μαραθῶνι· ἐκείνων δὲ διαπρεπῆ
> τὴν ἀρετὴν κρίναντες αὐτοῦ καὶ τὸν τάφον ἐποίησαν.   10

Notes: 1. **ἡ ἐκφορά**: "the funeral procession."
λάρνακας κυπαρισσίνας: "coffins of cypress wood."
2. **φυλῆς ἑκάστης μίαν**: "one for each tribe."
2–3. **ἔνεστι δὲ τὰ ὀστᾶ ἧς ἕκαστος ἦν φυλῆς**: i.e., each man's bones (τὰ ὀστᾶ) are in his own tribe's coffin.
3. **ἐστρωμένη**: "dressed."
3–4. **τῶν ἀφανῶν**: "of (i.e., for) the missing."
4. **εὑρεθῶσιν**: aorist passive subjunctive of εὑρίσκω.
ἐς ἀναίρεσιν: i.e., "to be taken up for burial."
ξυνεκφέρει: "joins in the procession."
5–6. **γυναῖκες … αἱ προσήκουσαι**: "the women of the families (of the dead)."
7. **τὸ δημόσιον σῆμα**: "the public cemetery."
ἐπὶ τοῦ καλλίστου προαστείου: "in the most beautiful suburb."
9–10. **ἐκείνων δὲ διαπρεπῆ τὴν ἀρετὴν κρίναντες**: "judging their valor exceptional." Ten thousand Athenians and one thousand Plataeans had defeated a vast Persian army at Marathon in 490 BC. The funeral mound can still be seen there.
10. **καί**: i.e., as well as burning the bodies.

19.7 Demosthenes, *De Corona* 235: Demosthenes points out that the enemy's king, Philip of Macedon, is totally in charge of his own situation. He does not have to cope with the problems of a democracy.

> τὰ μὲν τῆς πόλεως οὕτως ὑπῆρχεν ἔχοντα, καὶ οὐδεὶς ἂν
> ἔχοι παρὰ ταῦτ' εἰπεῖν ἄλλ' οὐδέν· τὰ δὲ τοῦ Φιλίππου,
> πρὸς ὃν ἦν ἡμῖν ὁ ἀγών, σκέψασθε πῶς. πρῶτον μὲν ἦρχε
> τῶν ἀκολουθούντων αὐτὸς αὐτοκράτωρ, ὃ τῶν εἰς τὸν
> πόλεμον μέγιστόν ἐστιν ἁπάντων· εἶθ' οὗτοι τὰ ὅπλ' εἶχον   5
> ἐν ταῖς χερσὶν ἀεί· ἔπειτα χρημάτων ηὐπόρει καὶ ἔπραττεν
> ἃ δόξειεν αὐτῷ, οὐ προλέγων ἐν τοῖς ψηφίσμασιν, οὐδ' ἐν
> τῷ φανερῷ βουλευόμενος, οὐδ' ὑπὸ τῶν συκοφαντούντων
> κρινόμενος, οὐδὲ γραφὰς φεύγων παρανόμων, οὐδ'
> ὑπεύθυνος ὢν οὐδενί, ἀλλ' ἁπλῶς αὐτὸς δεσπότης,   10
> ἡγεμών, κύριος πάντων.

Notes: 1. **τὰ … τῆς πόλεως οὕτως ὑπῆρχεν ἔχοντα**: "such were the resources of the city," lit. "the things of the city were being like this." The city referred to here is Athens.

1–2. **ἂν ἔχοι**: "would be able."

2. **τά**: i.e., "the resources."

3. **πῶς**: "how (his resources are/stand)."

4. **τῶν ἀκολουθούντων**: "his followers."

ὅ: "a thing which is."

5–6. **οὗτοι τὰ ὅπλ᾽ εἶχον ἐν ταῖς χερσὶν ἀεί**: i.e., he had a standing army.

6. **χρημάτων ηὐπόρει**: "he had plenty of money."

7–8. **οὐ προλέγων ἐν τοῖς ψηφίσμασιν, οὐδ᾽ ἐν τῷ φανερῷ βουλευόμενος**: "not giving notice by publishing [lit. in] decrees, or deliberating in public."

9. **κρινόμενος**: "being accused."

γραφὰς φεύγων παρανόμων: "being indicted for illegal measures."

10. **ὑπεύθυνος**: "dependent on" plus dative.

19.8 Thucydides, *Histories* 1.99.3: the city-states in Athens' empire made it more difficult for themselves to revolt by contributing money to the empire rather than keeping up their navies.

> ὧν αὐτοὶ αἴτιοι ἐγένοντο οἱ ξύμμαχοι· διὰ γὰρ τὴν
> ἀπόκνησιν ταύτην τῶν στρατειῶν οἱ πλείους αὐτῶν,
> ἵνα μὴ ἀπ᾽ οἴκου ὦσι, χρήματα ἐτάξαντο ἀντὶ τῶν νεῶν
> τὸ ἱκνούμενον ἀνάλωμα φέρειν, καὶ τοῖς μὲν Ἀθηναίοις
> ηὔξετο τὸ ναυτικὸν ἀπὸ τῆς δαπάνης ἣν ἐκεῖνοι   5
> ξυμφέροιεν, αὐτοὶ δέ, ὁπότε ἀποσταῖεν, ἀπαράσκευοι καὶ
> ἄπειροι ἐς τὸν πόλεμον καθίσταντο.

Notes: 1. **ὧν**: "of/for these things," i.e., for the growth of Athenian power.

1–2. **διὰ γὰρ τὴν ἀπόκνησιν ταύτην τῶν στρατειῶν**: "because of their reluctance to go on campaigns," lit. "because of this shrinking from campaigns."

3–4. **χρήματα ἐτάξαντο ἀντὶ τῶν νεῶν τὸ ἱκνούμενον ἀνάλωμα φέρειν**: "it was arranged for them [lit. "they were arranged"] to pay (φέρειν) the contribution which fell to them (as) money instead of ships."

4–5. **καὶ τοῖς ... Ἀθηναίοις ηὔξετο τὸ ναυτικὸν ἀπὸ τῆς δαπάνης**: lit. "and for the Athenians the fleet was increased/developed from the income ..."

6. **ἀποσταῖεν**: intransitive aorist optative of ἀφίστημι: "they revolted."

6–7. **ἀπαράσκευοι καὶ ἄπειροι ἐς τὸν πόλεμον καθίσταντο**: "they found themselves short of resources and inexperienced in war."

19.9 Homer, *Iliad* 1.163–71: Achilles tells Agamemnon, who has threatened to take away his prize in war, that he gets less of a share than Agamemnon though he has done most to deserve a prize. He says that he will sail off home to Phthia.

οὐ μὲν σοί ποτε ἶσον ἔχω γέρας ὁππότ' Ἀχαιοὶ
Τρώων ἐκπέρσωσ' εὖ ναιόμενον πτολίεθρον·
ἀλλὰ τὸ μὲν πλεῖον πολυάϊκος πολέμοιο
χεῖρες ἐμαὶ διέπουσ'· ἀτὰρ ἤν ποτε δασμὸς ἵκηται,
σοὶ τὸ γέρας πολὺ μεῖζον, ἐγὼ δ' ὀλίγον τε φίλον τε   5
ἔρχομ' ἔχων ἐπὶ νῆας, ἐπεί κε κάμω πολεμίζων.
νῦν δ' εἶμι' Φθίηνδ', ἐπεὶ ἦ πολὺ φέρτερόν ἐστιν
οἴκαδ' ἴμεν σὺν νηυσὶ κορωνίσιν, οὐδέ σ' ὀΐω
ἐνθάδ' ἄτιμος ἐὼν ἄφενος καὶ πλοῦτον ἀφύξειν.

Notes: 2. **ἐκπέρσωσ' εὖ ναιόμενον πτολίεθρον**: "sack a well-settled city."
3–4. **ἀλλὰ τὸ μὲν πλεῖον πολυάϊκος πολέμοιο χεῖρες ἐμαὶ διέπουσ'**: "but my hands bear the brunt of tumultuous war."
4. **ἤν ποτε**: "whenever."
δασμός: "distribution."
6. **κάμω πολεμίζων**: "I am weary with fighting." κάμω is the aorist subjunctive of κάμνω.
7. **Φθίηνδ'**: "to Phthia."
φέρτερόν: "better."
8. **κορωνίσιν**: "curving."
8–9. **οὐδέ σ' ὀΐω ... ἄφενος καὶ πλοῦτον ἀφύξειν**: "and I do not intend to acquire possessions and wealth for you."

19.10 Xenophon, *Agesilaos* 7.3: the king of Sparta treats his political opponents with nobility.

ὃς καὶ πρὸς τοὺς διαφόρους ἐν τῇ πόλει ὥσπερ πατὴρ
πρὸς παῖδας προσεφέρετο. ἐλοιδορεῖτο μὲν γὰρ ἐπὶ τοῖς
ἁμαρτήμασιν, ἐτίμα δ' εἴ τι καλὸν πράττοιεν, παρίστατο δ'
εἴ τις συμφορὰ συμβαίνοι, ἐχθρὸν μὲν οὐδένα ἡγούμενος
πολίτην, ἐπαινεῖν δὲ πάντας ἐθέλων, σῴζεσθαι δὲ πάντας   5
κέρδος νομίζων, ζημίαν δὲ τιθεὶς εἰ καὶ ὁ μικροῦ ἄξιος

ἀπόλοιτο· εἰ δ᾽ ἐν τοῖς νόμοις ἡρεμοῦντες διαμένοιεν, δῆλος
ἦν εὐδαίμονα μὲν αἰεὶ ἔσεσθαι τὴν πατρίδα λογιζόμενος,
ἰσχυρὰν δὲ τότε ὅταν οἱ Ἕλληνες σωφρονῶσιν.

Notes: 1. **ὅς**: connecting relative: "he," i.e., Agesilaus.
καὶ πρὸς τοὺς διαφόρους: "even toward his political opponents."
3. **παρίστατο**: "he stood by them."
5–6. **σῴζεσθαι δὲ πάντας κέρδος νομίζων**: "considering it a gain that all should be kept safe."
6. **ὁ μικροῦ ἄξιος**: lit. "the man worthy of little."
7. **ἡρεμοῦντες**: "being at rest," i.e., "without disturbance."
7–8. **δῆλος ἦν ... τὴν πατρίδα λογιζόμενος**: "he clearly reckoned [lit. was clear reckoning] that the fatherland (was) ..."

CHAPTER 20

Temporal Clauses

PRESENT AND PAST

Temporal clauses that relate to the past or present have their verbs in the indicative, unless they are indefinite (see Chapter 19).

The conjunctions that regularly introduce them are:

referring to the same time as the main verb

ὅτε, ὁπότε, ἡνίκα	when, at the time when
ἕως, μέχρι (οὗ), ὅσον (χρόνον)	as long as
ἕως, ἐν ᾧ	while

referring to time before the main verb:

ἐπεί, ἐπειδή, ὡς	when, after
ἐπει/ἐπειδὴ τάχιστα, ἐπεὶ πρῶτον	as soon as
ἐξ οὗ, ἀφ' οὗ	(ever) since, since the time when

FUTURE

Temporal clauses referring to the future use the indefinite construction, i.e., the subjunctive with ἄν in primary sequence, the optative without ἄν in historic sequence.

20.1 (1) Demosthenes, *Olynthiac* 1.20: Demosthenes urges the Athenians to take in hand the matter of financing the war against Philip.

καὶ ἕως ἐστὶ καιρός, ἀντιλάβεσθε τῶν πραγμάτων.

Notes: 1. **ἀντιλάβεσθε**: aorist imperative (2nd plural) of
ἀντιλαμβάνομαι (+ genitive) = I take hold of/take in hand.

(II) Xenophon, *Anabasis* 1.6.5: Xenophon introduces Clearchus'
report to his friends about the trial of the traitor, Orontas.

> ἐπεὶ δ᾽ ἐξῆλθεν, ἀπήγγειλε τοῖς φίλοις τὴν κρίσιν τοῦ
> Ὀρόντα ὡς ἐγένετο.

Notes: 1. **ἐπεὶ δ᾽ ἐξῆλθεν**: the subject is Clearchus, one of the leaders
of the Greek mercenaries in Cyrus' expedition against his brother,
Artaxerxes.
1–2. **τὴν κρίσιν ... ὡς ἐγένετο**: the subject of the indirect question
appears as object of the introductory verb = ὡς ἐγένετο ἡ κρίσις τοῦ
Ὀρόντα; Ὀρόντα is genitive of Ὀρόντας.

(III) Sophocles, *Antigone* 91: Antigone assures her sister Ismene
that she will not give up her determination to bury her brother,
Polynices, until she has no strength left.

Ἀντιγόνη

> οὐκοῦν, ὅταν δὴ μὴ σθένω, πεπαύσομαι.

Notes: 1. **οὐκοῦν**: "Well, then."
ὅταν δή: "when, and only when" (lit. "when indeed").
πεπαύσομαι: future perfect middle (1st singular) = "I shall stop
forthwith."

20.2 Thucydides, *Histories* 2.21.1–2: the Athenians get panicky as
Peloponnesian forces draw closer to Athens (431 BC).

> Ἀθηναῖοι δέ, μέχρι μὲν οὖ περὶ Ἐλευσῖνα καὶ τὸ Θριάσιον
> πεδίον ὁ στρατὸς ἦν, καί τινα ἐλπίδα εἶχον ἐς τὸ ἐγγυτέρω
> αὐτοὺς μὴ προϊέναι, μεμνημένοι καὶ Πλειστοάνακτα τὸν
> Παυσανίου Λακεδαιμονίων βασιλέα, ὅτε ἐσβαλὼν τῆς
> Ἀττικῆς ἐς Ἐλευσῖνα καὶ Θριῶζε στρατῷ Πελοποννησίων   5
> πρὸ τοῦδε τοῦ πολέμου τέσσαρσι καὶ δέκα ἔτεσιν
> ἀνεχώρησε πάλιν ἐς τὸ πλέον οὐκέτι προελθών (δι᾽ ὃ δὴ
> καὶ ἡ φυγὴ αὐτῷ ἐγένετο ἐκ Σπάρτης δόξαντι χρήμασι

πεισθῆναι τὴν ἀναχώρησιν)· ἐπειδὴ δὲ περὶ Ἀχαρνὰς εἶδον
τὸν στρατὸν ἑξήκοντα σταδίους τῆς πόλεως ἀπέχοντα,   10
οὐκέτι ἀνασχετὸν ἐποιοῦντο, ἀλλ᾽ αὐτοῖς, ὡς εἰκός,
γῆς τεμνομένης ἐν τῷ ἐμφανεῖ, ὃ οὔπω ἑοράκεσαν οἵ γε
νεώτεροι, οὐδ᾽ οἱ πρεσβύτεροι πλὴν τὰ Μηδικά, δεινὸν
ἐφαίνετο καὶ ἐδόκει τοῖς τε ἄλλοις καὶ μάλιστα τῇ νεότητι
ἐπεξιέναι καὶ μὴ περιορᾶν.   15

Notes: 1–2. **περὶ Ἐλευσῖνα καὶ τὸ Θριάσιον πεδίον**: the Thriasian
plain, named after Thria, one of the Attic demes (local districts), is in
western Attica, immediately to the west of Athens. Its main town was
Eleusis, home of the famous Eleusinian Mysteries.

2. **ὁ στρατός**: i.e., the Peloponnesian army, referred to later in the
sentence by the plural αὐτούς.

καί τινα ἐλπίδα εἶχον: the main clause of this sentence resumes here
("had also some hope").

3–4. **μεμνημένοι καὶ Πλειστοάνακτα ... ὅτε**: "remembering too the
time when Pleistoanax"; Pleistoanax, really the subject of the
ὅτε clause, appears as object of the introductory participle
μεμνημένοι.

4–5. **ἐσβαλὼν ... Θριῶζε**: "having invaded Attica as far as Eleusis and
Thria" (lit. "having invaded Eleusis and Thria in Attica"); Θριῶζε: = ἐς
Θρίαν. This earlier invasion took place in 445 BC. As here described,
Pleistoanax on that occasion prematurely withdrew his forces from
Attica and was subsequently exiled on suspicion of having accepted an
Athenian bribe. He was eventually recalled in 426 BC.

6. **τοῦδε τοῦ πολέμου**: i.e., the Peloponnesian War.

7. **ἐς τὸ πλέον**: "any further."

8. **ἡ φυγή**: "exile."

8–9. **χρήμασι πεισθῆναι τὴν ἀναχώρησιν**: "to have been bribed to
withdraw." τὴν ἀναχώρησιν is an internal accusative.

9. **περὶ Ἀχαρνάς**: Acharnae was the largest of the Attic demes, some six
miles north of Athens.

11. **οὐκέτι ἀνασχετὸν ἐποιοῦντο**: "they considered it no longer
tolerable."

12. **ὅ**: "something that."

13. **πλὴν τὰ Μηδικά**: "except in the Persian Wars."

20.3 Euripides, *Hecuba* 10–27: the ghost of Polydorus, Priam's
youngest son, tells of his murder in Thrace at the hands of his
father's guest-friend.

Πολυδώρου εἴδωλον

πολὺν δὲ σὺν ἐμοὶ χρυσὸν ἐκπέμπει λάθρᾳ
πατήρ, ἵν’, εἴ ποτ’ Ἰλίου τείχη πέσοι,
τοῖς ζῶσιν εἴη παισὶ μὴ σπάνις βίου.
νεώτατος δ’ ἦ Πριαμιδῶν, ὃ καί με γῆς
ὑπεξέπεμψεν· οὔτε γὰρ φέρειν ὅπλα   5
οὔτ’ ἔγχος οἷός τ’ ἦ νέῳ βραχίονι.
ἕως μὲν οὖν γῆς ὄρθ’ ἔκειθ’ ὁρίσματα
πύργοι τ’ ἄθραυστοι Τρωικῆς ἦσαν χθονὸς
Ἕκτωρ τ’ ἀδελφὸς οὑμὸς εὐτύχει δορί,
καλῶς παρ’ ἀνδρὶ Θρῃκὶ πατρῴῳ ξένῳ   10
τροφαῖσιν ὥς τις πτόρθος ηὐξόμην, τάλας·
ἐπεὶ δὲ Τροία θ’ Ἕκτορός τ’ ἀπόλλυται
ψυχή, πατρῷα θ’ ἑστία κατεσκάφη,
αὐτὸς δὲ βωμῷ πρὸς θεοδμήτῳ πίτνει
σφαγεὶς Ἀχιλλέως παιδὸς ἐκ μιαιφόνου,   15
κτείνει με χρυσοῦ τὸν ταλαίπωρον χάριν
ξένος πατρῷος καὶ κτανὼν ἐς οἶδμ’ ἁλὸς
μεθῆχ’, ἵν’ αὐτὸς χρυσὸν ἐν δόμοις ἔχῃ.

Notes: 1. **ἐκπέμπει**: historic present.
3. **σπάνις βίου**: "shortage of livelihood/sustenance."
4. **ἦ**: = ἦν.
Πριαμιδῶν: "of the sons of Priam." Adding the suffix -ίδης is one of the commonest ways to form a patronymic.
4. **ὃ καί**: "for which reason also"; ὅ is an accusative of respect.
7. **ὄρθ’ ἔκειθ’**: "remained secure" (lit. "were set upright").
9. **οὑμός**: crasis for ὁ ἐμός.
10–11. **καλῶς … τροφαῖσιν … ηὐξόμην**: "I was nurtured and grew up well" (lit. "I grew up well with nurture").
15. **ἐκ**: (here) "at the hands of."
16. **χρυσοῦ … χάριν**: "for the sake of the gold."
18. **μεθῆχ’**: aorist active (3rd singular) of μεθίημι.

20.4 Arrian, *Anabasis* 5.18.6: admiring his nobility, Alexander resolves to save Porus, the Indian king, and sends messengers to him.

καὶ Ἀλέξανδρος μέγαν τε αὐτὸν καὶ γενναῖον ἄνδρα
ἰδὼν ἐν τῇ μάχῃ σῶσαι ἐπεθύμησε. πέμπει δὴ παρ᾽ αὐτὸν
πρῶτα μὲν Ταξίλην τὸν Ἰνδόν· καὶ Ταξίλης προσιππεύσας
ἐφ᾽ ὅσον οἱ ἀσφαλὲς ἐφαίνετο τῷ ἐλέφαντι ὃς ἔφερε τὸν
Πῶρον ἐπιστῆσαί τε ἠξίου τὸ θηρίον (οὐ γὰρ εἶναί οἱ ἔτι   5
φεύγειν) καὶ ἀκοῦσαι τῶν παρ᾽ Ἀλεξάνδρου λόγων. ὁ δὲ
ἰδὼν ἄνδρα ἐχθρὸν ἐκ παλαιοῦ τὸν Ταξίλην ἐπιστρέψας
ἀνήγετο ὡς ἀκοντίσων· καὶ ἂν καὶ κατέκανε τυχόν,
εἰ μὴ ὑποφθάσας ἐκεῖνος ἀπήλασεν ἀπὸ τοῦ Πώρου
πρόσω τὸν ἵππον. Ἀλέξανδρος δὲ οὐδὲ ἐπὶ τῷδε τῷ Πώρῳ   10
χαλεπὸς ἐγένετο, ἀλλ᾽ ἄλλους τε ἐν μέρει ἔπεμπε καὶ δὴ
καὶ Μερόην ἄνδρα Ἰνδόν, ὅτι φίλον εἶναι ἐκ παλαιοῦ
τῷ Πώρῳ τὸν Μερόην ἔμαθεν. Πῶρος δὲ ὡς τὰ παρὰ
τοῦ Μερόου ἤκουσε καὶ ἐκ τοῦ δίψους ἅμα ἐκρατεῖτο,
ἐπέστησέ τε τὸν ἐλέφαντα καὶ κατέβη ἀπ᾽ αὐτοῦ· ὡς δὲ   15
ἔπιέ τε καὶ ἀνέψυξεν, ἄγειν αὐτὸν σπουδῇ ἐκέλευσεν παρὰ
Ἀλέξανδρον.

Notes: 1–2. **μέγαν … μάχῃ**: "seeing that he (i.e., Porus) had played a
great and noble part in the battle" (lit. "seeing him both a great and a
noble man in the battle").

2. **πέμπει**: historic present.

4. **ἐφ᾽ ὅσον οἱ ἀσφαλὲς ἐφαίνετο**: "as close as seemed safe to him"; οἱ =
αὐτῷ, as also in line 5.

5–6. **οὐ γὰρ εἶναί οἱ ἔτι φεύγειν**: understand ἔφη after οὐ γάρ; εἶναι =
ἐξεῖναι.

7. **ἐκ παλαιοῦ**: "from of old," as also in line 8.

ἐπιστρέψας: here intransitive.

8. **ἀνήγετο**: ἀνάγομαι, which usually means "I put out to sea," is here
used with ὡς and future participle meaning "I make ready to."

κατέκανε: κατακαίνω (used only in aorist κατέκανον) = κατακτείνω.

τυχόν: "perhaps."

9–10. **ἀπὸ τοῦ Πώρου πρόσω**: "some distance away from Porus."

10. **οὐδὲ ἐπὶ τῷδε**: "not even in these circumstances."

11. **ἐν μέρει**: "in turn."

16–17. **ἄγειν … Ἀλέξανδρον**: "told Meroes to take him swiftly
to Alexander"; σπουδῇ should be taken with ἄγειν, and Meroes
understood as the object of ἐκέλευσεν.

20.5 Xenophon, *Anabasis* 7.2.31: the Thracian king, Seuthes, who wishes to enlist Xenophon and his mercenaries, explains at a meeting what use he purposes to make of them.

μετὰ ταῦτα δ᾽ ἐπεὶ εἰσῆλθον οὓς ἔδει, πρῶτον Ξενοφῶν
ἐπήρετο Σεύθην ὅ τι δέοιτο χρῆσθαι τῇ στρατιᾷ. ὁ
δὲ εἶπεν ὧδε. Μαισάδης ἦν πατήρ μοι, ἐκείνου δὲ ἦν
ἀρχὴ Μελανδῖται καὶ Θυνοὶ καὶ Τρανίψαι. ἐκ ταύτης
οὖν τῆς χώρας, ἐπεὶ τὰ Ὀδρυσῶν πράγματα ἐνόσησεν,   5
ἐκπεσὼν ὁ πατὴρ αὐτὸς μὲν ἀποθνῄσκει νόσῳ, ἐγὼ δ᾽
ἐξετράφην ὀρφανὸς παρὰ Μηδόκῳ τῷ νῦν βασιλεῖ. ἐπεὶ
δὲ νεανίσκος ἐγενόμην, οὐκ ἐδυνάμην ζῆν εἰς ἀλλοτρίαν
τράπεζαν ἀποβλέπων· καὶ ἐκαθεζόμην ἐνδίφριος αὐτῷ
ἱκέτης δοῦναί μοι ὁπόσους δυνατὸς εἴη ἄνδρας, ὅπως   10
καὶ τοὺς ἐκβαλόντας ἡμᾶς εἴ τι δυναίμην κακὸν ποιοίην
καὶ ζῴην μὴ εἰς τὴν ἐκείνου τράπεζαν ἀποβλέπων. ἐκ
τούτου μοι δίδωσι τοὺς ἄνδρας καὶ τοὺς ἵππους οὓς
ὑμεῖς ὄψεσθε ἐπειδὰν ἡμέρα γένηται. καὶ νῦν ἐγὼ ζῶ
τούτους ἔχων, λῃζόμενος τὴν ἐμαυτοῦ πατρῴαν χώραν.   15
εἰ δέ μοι ὑμεῖς παραγένοισθε, οἶμαι ἂν σὺν τοῖς θεοῖς
ῥᾳδίως ἀπολαβεῖν τὴν ἀρχήν. ταῦτ᾽ ἐστὶν ἃ ἐγὼ ὑμῶν
δέομαι.

Notes: 1. **οὓς ἔδει**: understand ἐκεῖνοι = "those who had to."
2. **ὅ τι**: "in what way" (lit. "in respect of what").
3–4. **ἐκείνου δὲ ἦν ἀρχή**: "and his kingdom embraced" (lit. "was").
4. **Μελανδῖται … Τρανίψαι**: the Melanditae, Thyni, and Tranipsae were all local Thracian tribes.
5. **τὰ Ὀδρυσῶν πράγματα**: the Odrysae or Odrysians were a strong Thracian tribe who, uniting with other local tribes, created a powerful kingdom during the fifth century BC.
ἐνόσησεν: "fell into a bad state" (lit. "fell ill").
8–9. **εἰς ἀλλοτρίαν τράπεζαν ἀποβλέπων**: "looking toward someone else's table" = "dependent on another's charity."
9–10. **ἐνδίφριος αὐτῷ ἱκέτης**: "on the same seat with him, begging him"; the infinitive δοῦναι depends on the idea of "asking" contained in ἱκέτης (lit. "a suppliant").

11. **εἴ τι δυναίμην κακόν**: "whatever harm I could."
13. **δίδωσι**: historic present.
16. **σὺν τοῖς θεοῖς**: i.e., "with the help of the gods."

UNTIL AND BEFORE

ἕως, μέχρι (οὗ), ἔστε, ἄχρι(ς) οὗ and ὄφρα (Homer) mean *until*. They are used with the indicative when a definite or known time is referred to, with the indefinite construction when they refer to a time not fixed or known, i.e., in the future.

After a negative main verb, when *before* can be substituted for *until* with no change of meaning, πρίν is regularly used instead of the other conjunctions, with the same constructions.

After a positive main verb πρίν regularly takes the infinitive and means *before*. πρότερον ἤ can be used in just the same way.

20.6 (I) I *Corinthians* 11.26: St. Paul explains to the Corinthians that the commemoration of the Last Supper is a memorial of Christ's death until his second coming.

ὁσάκις γὰρ ἂν ἐσθίητε τὸν ἄρτον τοῦτον καὶ τὸ ποτήριον πίνητε, τὸν θάνατον τοῦ Κυρίου καταγγέλλετε, ἄχρις οὗ ἂν ἔλθῃ.

Notes: 1. **ὁσάκις**: "as often as."

(II) Homer, *Odyssey* 5.55–58: Hermes arrives at Calypso's cave.

ἀλλ' ὅτε δὴ τὴν νῆσον ἀφίκετο τηλόθ' ἐοῦσαν,
ἤιεν, ὄφρα μέγα σπέος ἵκετο, τῷ ἔνι νύμφη
ναῖεν ἐυπλόκαμος· τὴν δ' ἔνδοθι τέτμεν ἐοῦσαν.

Notes: 1. **ἐοῦσαν**: = οὖσαν, as also in line 3.
2. **ἤιεν**: = ἤει(ν), imperfect (third singular) of εἶμι (I shall go). **τῷ ἔνι**: = ἐν ᾧ.
3. **τέτμεν**: "he found"; ἔτετμον is an Homeric strong aorist, with no present in use, meaning "I reached/came up to/found." It occurs both with and without the augment.

(III) Isocrates 1.24: Isocrates gives the Cyprian Demonicus good advice about friendship.

μηδένα φίλον ποιοῦ, πρὶν ἂν ἐξετάσῃς πῶς κέχρηται τοῖς
πρότερον φίλοις· ἔλπιζε γὰρ αὐτὸν καὶ περὶ σὲ γενέσθαι
τοιοῦτον, οἷος καὶ περὶ ἐκείνους γέγονε.

Notes: 1. **κέχρηται**: "has treated," a common meaning of χράομαι.
2. **καὶ περὶ σέ**: "in your case also."

(IV) Thucydides, *Histories* 2.93.1: Cnemus and Brasidas, along
with other Peloponnesian leaders, propose a surprise naval attack
on the Piraeus (429 BC).

πρὶν δὲ διαλῦσαι τὸ ἐς Κόρινθόν τε καὶ τὸν Κρισαῖον
κόλπον ἀναχωρῆσαν ναυτικόν, ὁ Κνῆμος καὶ ὁ Βρασίδας
καὶ οἱ ἄλλοι ἄρχοντες τῶν Πελοποννησίων ἀρχομένου τοῦ
χειμῶνος ἐβούλοντο διδαξάντων Μεγαρέων ἀποπειρᾶσαι
τοῦ Πειραιῶς τοῦ λιμένος τῶν Ἀθηναίων· ἦν δὲ ἀφύλακτος   5
καὶ ἄκλῃστος εἰκότως διὰ τὸ ἐπικρατεῖν πολὺ τῷ ναυτικῷ.

Notes: 1–2. **τὸ . . . ἀναχωρῆσαν ναυτικόν**: "the fleet that had retired";
τὸν Κρισαῖον κόλπον: the Crisaean Gulf is an inlet on the northern
shore of the Gulf of Corinth, close to the Phocian town of Crisa.
4. **διδαξάντων Μεγαρέων**: genitive absolute = "at the suggestion of
the Megarians."
6. **ἄκλῃστος**: "unlocked," i.e., by a chain across the harbor mouth.
εἰκότως . . . τῷ ναυτικῷ: "quite reasonably, on account of their [i.e., the
Athenians'] great naval superiority."

20.7 Aeschylus, *Persae* 421–28: a messenger recounts to Atossa,
mother of King Xerxes, details of the Persian defeat at the Battle of
Salamis.

Ἄγγελος

ἀκταὶ δὲ νεκρῶν χοιράδες τ᾽ ἐπλήθυον,
φυγῇ δ᾽ ἀκόσμῳ πᾶσα ναῦς ἠρέσσετο,
ὅσαιπερ ἦσαν βαρβάρου στρατεύματος.
τοὶ δ᾽ ὥστε θύννους ἤ τιν᾽ ἰχθύων βόλον
ἀγαῖσι κωπῶν θραύμασίν τ᾽ ἐρειπίων   5
ἔπαιον, ἐρράχιζον· οἰμωγὴ δ᾽ ὁμοῦ

κωκύμασιν κατεῖχε πελαγίαν ἅλα,
ἕως κελαινῆς νυκτὸς ὄμμ' ἀφείλετο.

Notes: 1. **χοιράδες**: "reefs," literally piglike (cf. χοῖρος, a pig) rocks in the water.
4. **τοὶ δ'**: "but they" (i.e., the Greeks), the only instance of this epic usage in the dialogue of Greek tragedy.
5. **ἀγαῖσι . . . ἐρειπίων**: "with splinters of oars and fragments of wreckage."
6. **ἔπαιον, ἐρράχιζον**: the understood object is ἡμᾶς.
ὁμοῦ: probably here a preposition (with dative) = "along with shrieks."
7. **κατεῖχε**: (of sound) "filled."
πελαγίαν ἅλα: "the salt-sea."
8. **ἀφείλετο**: "took [it] away," i.e., "brought it to an end."

20.8 Xenophon, *Anabasis* 5.7.3–5: Xenophon speaks forthrightly to his men when they suspect him of intending to found a new city by the River Phasis rather than taking them home to Greece as quickly as possible.

ἐπεὶ δὲ ᾐσθάνετο Ξενοφῶν, ἔδοξεν αὐτῷ ὡς τάχιστα
ξυναγαγεῖν αὐτῶν ἀγοράν, καὶ μὴ ἐᾶσαι ξυλλεγῆναι
αὐτομάτους· καὶ ἐκέλευσε τὸν κήρυκα ξυλλέξαι ἀγοράν.
οἱ δ᾽ ἐπεὶ τοῦ κήρυκος ἤκουσαν, ξυνέδραμον καὶ μάλα
ἑτοίμως. ἐνταῦθα Ξενοφῶν τῶν μὲν στρατηγῶν οὐ   5
κατηγόρει, ὅτι ἦλθον πρὸς αὐτόν, λέγει δὲ ὧδε· Ἀκούω
τινὰ διαβάλλειν, ὦ ἄνδρες, ἐμὲ ὡς ἐγὼ ἄρα ἐξαπατήσας
ὑμᾶς μέλλω ἄγειν εἰς Φᾶσιν. ἀκούσατε οὖν μου πρὸς θεῶν,
καὶ ἐὰν μὲν ἐγὼ φαίνωμαι ἀδικεῖν, οὐ χρή με ἐνθένδε
ἀπελθεῖν πρὶν ἂν δῶ δίκην· ἂν δ᾽ ὑμῖν φαίνωνται ἀδικεῖν οἱ   10
ἐμὲ διαβάλλοντες, οὕτως αὐτοῖς χρῆσθε ὥσπερ ἄξιον.

Notes: 2. **ἀγοράν**: "an assembly."
4–5. **καὶ μάλα ἑτοίμως**: "and very readily at that."
5–6. **τῶν μὲν στρατηγῶν . . . πρὸς αὐτόν**: Xenophon had, in fact, been in favor of staying and founding a city, but had earlier abandoned the plan because of its unpopularity with his men. Just before this passage, however, some of his generals had come to him in an attempt to resurrect the notion. Judging the mood of the moment, he says nothing of this.

7–8. ὡς ἐγὼ ἄρα . . . Φᾶσιν: the particle ἄρα, which needn't be translated, shows that Xenophon is shedding doubt on the accuracy of the charge against him. The River Phasis (the modern Rioni) rises in the Caucasus mountains and flows down into the Black Sea.

10. ἄν: = ἐάν.

11. οὕτως . . . ὥσπερ ἄξιον: "just as they deserve."

20.9 Euripides, *Medea* 1021–39: Medea reflects that she will now have no joy of her children.

Μήδεια

ὦ τέκνα τέκνα, σφῷν μὲν ἔστι δὴ πόλις
καὶ δῶμ᾽, ἐν ᾧ λιπόντες ἀθλίαν ἐμὲ
οἰκήσετ᾽ αἰεὶ μητρὸς ἐστερημένοι·
ἐγὼ δ᾽ ἐς ἄλλην γαῖαν εἶμι δὴ φυγάς,
πρὶν σφῷν ὀνάσθαι κἀπιδεῖν εὐδαίμονας,   5
πρὶν λουτρὰ καὶ γυναῖκα καὶ γαμηλίους
εὐνὰς ἀγῆλαι λαμπάδας τ᾽ ἀνασχεθεῖν.
ὦ δυστάλαινα τῆς ἐμῆς αὐθαδίας.
ἄλλως ἄρ᾽ ὑμᾶς, ὦ τέκν᾽, ἐξεθρεψάμην,
ἄλλως δ᾽ ἐμόχθουν καὶ κατεξάνθην πόνοις,   10
στερρὰς ἐνεγκοῦσ᾽ ἐν τόκοις ἀλγηδόνας.
ἦ μήν ποθ᾽ ἡ δύστηνος εἶχον ἐλπίδας
πολλὰς ἐν ὑμῖν, γηροβοσκήσειν τ᾽ ἐμὲ
καὶ κατθανοῦσαν χερσὶν εὖ περιστελεῖν,
ζηλωτὸν ἀνθρώποισι· νῦν δ᾽ ὄλωλε δὴ   15
γλυκεῖα φροντίς. σφῷν γὰρ ἐστερημένη
λυπρὸν διάξω βίοτον ἀλγεινόν τ᾽ ἐμόν.
ὑμεῖς δὲ μητέρ᾽ οὐκέτ᾽ ὄμμασιν φίλοις
ὄψεσθ᾽, ἐς ἄλλο σχῆμ᾽ ἀποστάντες βίου.

Notes: 1. **σφῷν:** dative of σφῷι ("you two"), the 2nd person dual pronoun; the genitive has exactly the same form, as in lines 5 and 16.

5. **ὀνάσθαι:** aorist infinitive of ὀνίναμαι (+ genitive) = "I have enjoyment of."

κἀπιδεῖν: crasis for καὶ ἐπιδεῖν.

6. **λουτρά**: the pre-nuptial bath is something regularly associated with both the mother of the bride and the mother of the bridegroom. So too the raising of torches (λαμπάδες) in the wedding procession.

7. **ἀγῆλαι**: aorist infinitive active of ἀγάλλω ("I adorn").

ἀνασχεθεῖν: an alternative aorist infinitive of ἀνέχω (from ἀνέσχεθον).

8. **τῆς ἐμῆς αὐθαδίας**: a genitive of cause explaining why Medea is δυστάλαινα.

9. **ἄλλως ἄρ'**: "in vain, then."

10. **κατεξάνθην πόνοις**: "was torn by toils"; καταξαίνω (lit. "I card wool") is frequently used meaning "I tear in shreds."

11. **στερρὰς ... ἀλγηδόνας**: "cruel pains."

12–13. **ἐλπίδας πολλάς**: followed by the future infinitives γηροβοσκήσειν and περιστελεῖν in an indirect statement = "many hopes ... that you (understand ὑμᾶς) would ..."

15. **ζηλωτὸν ἀνθρώποισι**: neuter in apposition to what precedes = "something for people to envy."

19. **ἐς ἄλλο σχῆμ' ἀποστάντες βίου**: "removed to a different sphere of life," a nicely ambiguous remark, as Medea might be referring to her sons' "new life" with their father and his new bride, but really means their life in Hades after she has murdered them.

CHAPTER 21

Impersonal Verbs and Verbal Adjectives

IMPERSONAL VERBS

In English impersonal verbs are frequently used of the weather, e.g., "it's raining" or "it's snowing", as well as in other contexts, e.g., "it upsets me that. . . ."

The most common impersonal verbs in Greek are used either with the accusative and the infinite or the dative and the infinitive.

For the accusative absolute with impersonal verbs, see p. 124–125.

21.1   Xenophon, *Anabasis* 3.2.15: Xenophon says that his men have been brave when fighting for Cyrus, the pretender to the Persian throne. Now that it's a matter of their own safety, they must show much more commitment.

> καὶ τότε μὲν δὴ περὶ τῆς Κύρου βασιλείας ἄνδρες ἦτε
> ἀγαθοί· νῦν δ' ὁπότε περὶ τῆς ὑμετέρας σωτηρίας ὁ
> ἀγών ἐστι, πολὺ δήπου ὑμᾶς προσήκει καὶ ἀμείνονας καὶ
> προθυμοτέρους εἶναι.

Notes: 3. **ὑμᾶς προσήκει**: "it is fitting that you . . .": the accusative is used as the subject of the infinitive εἶναι. προσήκει is generally used with the dative.

21.2   Plato, *Crito* 44c: Socrates asks Crito why they should care about the view of most people that his friends should enable him to escape from prison when those of good judgment will understand the truth of the situation.

> ἀλλὰ τί ἡμῖν, ὦ μακάριε Κρίτων, οὕτω τῆς τῶν πολλῶν
> δόξης μέλει; οἱ γὰρ ἐπιεικέστατοι, ὧν μᾶλλον ἄξιον
> φροντίζειν, ἡγήσονται αὐτὰ οὕτω πεπρᾶχθαι ὥσπερ ἂν
> πραχθῇ.

Notes: 2. **οἱ γὰρ ἐπιεικέστατοι**: "the most reasonable people."
3. **φροντίζειν**: "to think about" + genitive.
3–4. **ὥσπερ ἂν πραχθῇ**: "just as things (understand αὐτὰ) would have been done": singular verb with neuter plural subject. Translate: "just as they really will be done."

21.3   Xenophon, *Cyropaedia* 7.2.28: King Croesus explains to Cyrus that his wife has all the advantages of her royal status but none of the responsibilities.

> καὶ ὁ Κῦρος εἶπε· τίς δὴ ὁ ἔχων ταύτην τὴν μακαρίαν
> βιοτήν; ἡ ἐμὴ γυνή, εἶπεν, ὦ Κῦρε· ἐκείνη γὰρ τῶν μὲν
> ἀγαθῶν καὶ τῶν μαλακῶν καὶ εὐφροσυνῶν πασῶν ἐμοὶ τὸ
> ἴσον μετεῖχε, φροντίδων δὲ ὅπως ταῦτα ἔσται καὶ πολέμου
> καὶ μάχης οὐ μετῆν αὐτῇ.   5

Notes: 3. **τῶν μαλακῶν καὶ εὐφροσυνῶν πασῶν**: "the luxury and all the good cheer."
4. **φροντίδων δὲ ὅπως ταῦτα ἔσται**: "in/of the anxieties about how these things will happen."

21.4   Andocides 4.17: the outrageous treatment of the painter Agatharchos by Alcibiades.

> ὃς εἰς τοσοῦτον ἐλήλυθε τόλμης, ὥστε πείσας Ἀγάθαρχον
> τὸν γραφέα συνεισελθεῖν οἴκαδε τὴν οἰκίαν ἐπηνάγκασε
> γράφειν, δεομένου δὲ καὶ προφάσεις ἀληθεῖς λέγοντος,
> ὡς οὐκ ἂν δύναιτο ταῦτα πράττειν ἤδη διὰ τὸ συγγραφὰς
> ἔχειν παρ᾽ ἑτέρων, προεῖπεν αὐτῷ δήσειν, εἰ μὴ πάνυ   5
> ταχέως γράφοι. ὅπερ ἐποίησε· καὶ οὐ πρότερον ἀπηλλάγη,

πρὶν ἀποδρὰς ᾤχετο τετάρτῳ μηνί, τοὺς φύλακας λαθών,
ὥσπερ παρὰ βασιλέως. οὕτω δ᾽ ἀναίσχυντός ἐστιν,
ὥστε προσελθὼν ἐνεκάλει αὐτῷ ὡς ἀδικούμενος, καὶ
οὐχ ὧν ἐβιάσατο μετέμελεν αὐτῷ, ἀλλ᾽ ὅτι κατέλιπε   10
τὸ ἔργον ἠπείλει, καὶ οὔτε τῆς δημοκρατίας οὔτε τῆς
ἐλευθερίας οὐδὲν ἦν ὄφελος· οὐδὲν γὰρ ἧττον ἐδεδέκει τῶν
ὁμολογουμένων δούλων.

Notes: 1. **ὅς**: connecting relative, i.e., "he," referring to Alcibiades.
εἰς τοσοῦτον … τόλμης: "to such a pitch of impudence."
3. **δεομένου δὲ καὶ προφάσεις ἀληθεῖς λέγοντος**: "and when he
pleaded with him and gave genuine reasons."
4–5. **διὰ τὸ συγγραφὰς ἔχειν παρ᾽ ἑτέρων**: "because he had
commitments to other people."
5. **προεῖπεν αὐτῷ δήσειν**: "he threatened him with imprisonment," lit.
"that he would put him in bonds."
6–7. **οὐ πρότερον ἀπηλλάγη, πρὶν ἀποδρὰς ᾤχετο**: "he didn't get out
before he ran off" (lit. "he went running…").
8. **παρὰ βασιλέως**: "from the king (of Persia)."
9. **ἐνεκάλει**: "he accused" plus dative.
10. **οὐχ ὧν ἐβιάσατο μετέμελεν αὐτῷ**: "and he wasn't sorry about his
violent methods."
κατέλιπε: i.e., Agatharchos had left it unfinished.
12. **οὐδὲν ἦν ὄφελος**: "there was no help in" plus genitive: i.e.,
democracy and freedom were of no avail.
12–13. **οὐδὲν γὰρ ἧττον ἐδεδέκει τῶν ὁμολογουμένων** δούλων: "for
he had bound him in chains (δέω) no less than (i.e., just like) men
acknowledged to be slaves."

VERBAL ADJECTIVES

a). The verbal adjective ending in –τός usually has a passive meaning.

21.5 Euripides, *Medea* 238–43: Medea says that if a woman
embarking on marriage is able to manage married life well her situation is to be envied, but if not. …

Μήδεια

ἐς καινὰ δ᾽ ἤθη καὶ νόμους ἀφιγμένην
δεῖ μάντιν εἶναι, μὴ μαθοῦσαν οἴκοθεν,

ὅπως ἄριστα χρήσεται ξυνευνέτῃ.
κἂν μὲν τάδ᾽ ἡμῖν ἐκπονουμέναισιν εὖ
πόσις ξυνοικῇ μὴ βίᾳ φέρων ζυγόν,   5
ζηλωτὸς αἰών· εἰ δὲ μή, θανεῖν χρεών.

Notes: 1. **ἐς καινὰ δ᾽ ἤθη**: "to/among new characteristics."
2. **δεῖ**: understand αὐτήν.
3. **χρήσεται ξυνευνέτῃ**: "she will manage (χράομαι + dat.) her bedfellow."
4–5. **κἂν . . . τάδ᾽ ἡμῖν ἐκπονουμέναισιν εὖ πόσις ξυνοικῇ**: "and if our husband lives together with us as we work successfully at this."
5. **μὴ βίᾳ φέρων ζυγόν**: "if he doesn't bear [lit. not bearing] the yoke (of marriage) by force": i.e., the husband bears the yoke of marriage because he wants to.
6. **ζηλωτὸς**: "enviable."
χρεών: "(it is) necessary."

b). Verbal adjectives ending in –τέος are passive and express obligation: "to be done," "must be done," etc.

21.6   Demosthenes, *Philippic* 3.70: the orator tells the Athenians that they must equip themselves militarily to defend their freedom.

καὶ ἡμεῖς τοίνυν, ὦ ἄνδρες Ἀθηναῖοι, ἕως ἐσμὲν σῷοι,
πόλιν μεγίστην ἔχοντες, ἀφορμὰς πλείστας, ἀξίωμα
κάλλιστον, τί ποιῶμεν; πάλαι τις ἡδέως ἂν ἴσως ἐρωτήσας
κάθηται. ἐγὼ νὴ Δί᾽ ἐρῶ, καὶ γράψω δέ, ὥστ᾽ ἂν
βούλησθε χειροτονήσετε. αὐτοὶ πρῶτον ἀμυνόμενοι καὶ   5
παρασκευαζόμενοι, τριήρεσι καὶ χρήμασι καὶ στρατιώταις
λέγω· καὶ γὰρ ἂν ἅπαντες δήπου δουλεύειν συγχωρήσωσιν
οἱ ἄλλοι, ἡμῖν γ᾽ ὑπὲρ τῆς ἐλευθερίας ἀγωνιστέον.

Notes: 1. **τοίνυν**: "so."
2. **ἀφορμὰς πλείστας**: "most ample resources."
3. **ποιῶμεν**: deliberative subjunctive.
3–4. **πάλαι τις ἡδέως ἂν ἴσως ἐρωτήσας κάθηται**: "perhaps someone is sitting (here) who would gladly have asked that question ages ago."

4–5. **γράψω δέ, ὥστ᾽ ἂν βούλησθε χειροτονήσετε**: "and I shall propose a motion with the result that you can vote on it if (ἄν) you want."

5–6. **αὐτοὶ πρῶτον ἀμυνόμενοι καὶ παρασκευαζόμενοι**: "to begin with ourselves (we must) take defensive measures and prepare ourselves" (lit. "[we must begin] by first of all ourselves defending ourselves and preparing ourselves").

6–7. **τριήρεσι . . . λέγω**: "I mean with triremes, etc."

7. **ἂν ἅπαντες**: "if all the other (Greeks)."

δήπου: "I suppose"

δουλεύειν συγχωρήσωσιν: "agree to be slaves."

8. **ἡμῖν**: dative of the agent. Note that that the verbal adjectives ending in –τέος can be used flexibly, both impersonally (as in our passage) and with a subject: compare ὠφελητέον ἐστιν ἡμῖν τὴν πόλιν and ὠφελητέα ἐστιν ἡμῖν ἡ πόλις.

ἀγωνιστέον: verbal adjective from ἀγωνίζομαι = I fight, contend.

CHAPTER 22

Additional Prose Passages

22.1 Herodotus, *Histories* 1.8: King Candaules asks Gyges to check out the beauty of his wife.

οὗτος δὴ ὦν ὁ Κανδαύλης ἠράσθη τῆς ἑωυτοῦ γυναικός,
ἐρασθεὶς δὲ ἐνόμιζέ οἱ εἶναι γυναῖκα πολλὸν πασέων
καλλίστην. ὥστε δὲ ταῦτα νομίζων, ἦν γάρ οἱ τῶν
αἰχμοφόρων Γύγης ὁ Δασκύλου ἀρεσκόμενος μάλιστα,
τούτῳ τῷ Γύγῃ καὶ τὰ σπουδαιέστερα τῶν πρηγμάτων   5
ὑπερετίθετο ὁ Κανδαύλης καὶ δὴ καὶ τὸ εἶδος τῆς γυναικὸς
ὑπερεπαινέων. χρόνου δὲ οὐ πολλοῦ διελθόντος (χρῆν
γὰρ Κανδαύλῃ γενέσθαι κακῶς) ἔλεγε πρὸς τὸν Γύγην
τοιάδε. 'Γύγη, οὐ γὰρ σε δοκέω πείθεσθαι μοι λέγοντι περὶ
τοῦ εἴδεος τῆς γυναικός (ὦτα γὰρ τυγχάνει ἀνθρώποισι   10
ἐόντα ἀπιστότερα ὀφθαλμῶν), ποίεε ὅκως ἐκείνην θεήσεαι
γυμνήν.' ὃ δ' ἀμβώσας εἶπε 'δέσποτα, τίνα λέγεις λόγον
οὐκ ὑγιέα, κελεύων με δέσποιναν τὴν ἐμὴν θεήσασθαι
γυμνήν; ἅμα δὲ κιθῶνι ἐκδυομένῳ συνεκδύεται καὶ τὴν
αἰδῶ γυνή. πάλαι δὲ τὰ καλὰ ἀνθρώποισι ἐξεύρηται, ἐκ   15
τῶν μανθάνειν δεῖ· ἐν τοῖσι ἓν τόδε ἐστί, σκοπέειν τινὰ τὰ
ἑωυτοῦ. ἐγὼ δὲ πείθομαι ἐκείνην εἶναι πασέων γυναικῶν
καλλίστην, καὶ σέο δέομαι μὴ δέεσθαι ἀνόμων.'

Notes: 3–4. ἦν... οἱ... **Γύγης ὁ Δασκύλου ἀρεσκόμενος μάλιστα**:
Gyges, the son of Dascylus and a favorite of Candaules, is introduced
in parenthesis. **τῶν αἰχμοφόρων**: "among [lit. of] his personal guards."
5–6. **τὰ σπουδαιέστερα τῶν πρηγμάτων ὑπερετίθετο**: "used to
discuss the more important of his concerns."
6. **καὶ δὴ καί**: "in particular."
7–8. **χρῆν γὰρ Κανδαύλῃ γενέσθαι κακῶς**: lit. "it was fated (necessary)
to turn out badly for Candaules," i.e., "Candaules was destined to come
to a bad end." He persisted in his extraordinarily rash behavior.
10. **ὦτα**: nom. plur. of οὖς.
11–12. **ποίεε ὅκως ἐκείνην θεήσεαι γυμνήν**: lit. "see to it [lit. make,
bring about] that you may see her naked," i.e., "find a way to see her
naked."
12. **ἀμβώσας**: "shouting."
14–15. **ἅμα δὲ κιθῶνι ἐκδυομένῳ συνεκδύεται καὶ τὴν αἰδῶ γυνή**:
lit. "at the same time as her clothes being put off, a woman puts off her
modesty as well."
15. **τὰ καλὰ ἀνθρώποισι ἐξεύρηται**: "good principles have been
established [lit. found, devised] for men."

22.2 Herodotus, *Histories* 2.68: Herodotus on the nature of the
crocodile.

> τῶν δὲ κροκοδείλων φύσις ἐστὶ τοιήδε. τοὺς
> χειμεριωτάτους μῆνας τέσσερας ἐσθίει οὐδέν, ἐὸν δὲ
> τετράπουν χερσαῖον καὶ λιμναῖόν ἐστι. τίκτει μὲν γὰρ ᾠὰ
> ἐν γῇ καὶ ἐκλέπει, καὶ τὸ πολλὸν τῆς ἡμέρης διατρίβει ἐν
> τῷ ξηρῷ, τὴν δὲ νύκτα πᾶσαν ἐν τῷ ποταμῷ· θερμότερον   5
> γὰρ δή ἐστι τὸ ὕδωρ τῆς τε αἰθρίης καὶ τῆς δρόσου. πάντων
> δὲ τῶν ἡμεῖς ἴδμεν θνητῶν τοῦτο ἐξ ἐλαχίστου μέγιστον
> γίνεται· τὰ μὲν γὰρ ᾠὰ χηνέων οὐ πολλῷ μέζονα τίκτει,
> καὶ ὁ νεοσσὸς κατὰ λόγον τοῦ ᾠοῦ γίνεται, αὐξανόμενος
> δὲ γίνεται καὶ ἐς ἑπτακαίδεκα πήχεας καὶ μέζων ἔτι.   10
> ἔχει δὲ ὀφθαλμοὺς μὲν ὑός, ὀδόντας δὲ μεγάλους καὶ
> χαυλιόδοντας κατὰ λόγον τοῦ σώματος. γλῶσσαν
> δὲ μοῦνον θηρίων οὐκ ἔφυσε, οὐδὲ κινέει τὴν κάτω
> γνάθον, ἀλλὰ καὶ τοῦτο μοῦνον θηρίων τὴν ἄνω γνάθον
> προσάγει τῇ κάτω. ἔχει δὲ καὶ ὄνυχας καρτεροὺς καὶ   15
> δέρμα λεπιδωτὸν ἄρρηκτον ἐπὶ τοῦ νώτου. τυφλὸν δὲ ἐν

ὕδατι, ἐν δὲ τῇ αἰθρίῃ ὀξυδερκέστατον. ἅτε δὴ ὦν ἐν ὕδατι
δίαιταν ποιεύμενον, τὸ στόμα ἔνδοθεν φορέει πᾶν μεστὸν
βδελλέων. τὰ μὲν δὴ ἄλλα ὄρνεα καὶ θηρία φεύγει μιν, ὁ δὲ
τροχίλος εἰρηναῖόν οἱ ἐστι ἅτε ὠφελεομένῳ πρὸς αὐτοῦ·   20
ἐπεὰν γὰρ ἐς τὴν γῆν ἐκβῇ ἐκ τοῦ ὕδατος ὁ κροκόδειλος
καὶ ἔπειτα χάνῃ (ἔωθε γὰρ τοῦτο ὡς ἐπίπαν ποιέειν πρὸς
τὸν ζέφυρον), ἐνθαῦτα ὁ τροχίλος ἐσδύνων ἐς τὸ στόμα
αὐτοῦ καταπίνει τὰς βδέλλας· ὁ δὲ ὠφελεύμενος ἥδεται καὶ
οὐδὲν σίνεται τὸν τροχίλον.   25

Notes: 1. **φύσις ἐστὶ τοιήδε**: "the nature is as follows."

2. **χειμεριωτάτους**: "most wintry" or "mid-winter."

2–3. **ἐὸν δὲ ... λιμναῖον ἐστί**: the neuter gender of the participle and
two adjectives reflects the subject of ἐσθίει (*it eats*), i.e., τὸ θηρίον.

4–5. **ἐν τῷ ξηρῷ**: the neuter τὸ ξηρόν is here used to refer to "the dry
land." The feminine ἡ ξηρά (understood γῆ) is also found.

6. **τῆς τε αἰθρίης καὶ τῆς δρόσου**: genitive of comparison. Here,
though not always, αἰθρίη refers to the clear, cold air of night.

6–7. **πάντων δὲ τῶν ἡμεῖς ἴδμεν θνητῶν**: "of all the mortal creatures
which we know." τῶν is a relative pronoun (= ὧν) and is attracted into
the genitive case, and θνητῶν, really part of the antecedent, is attracted
into the relative clause; ἴδμεν = ἴσμεν.

7–8. **ἐξ ἐλαχίστου μέγιστον γίνεται**: lit. "becomes biggest from
smallest." Herodotus means that no other animal becomes so big
from such a small beginning; γίνεται (and twice in the next sentence) =
γίγνεται.

8. **χηνέων**: i.e., χηνέων ᾠῶν, a genitive of comparison with μέζονα
(= μείζονα). The Attic form of χήνεος ("of a goose") is χήνειος.

9. **κατὰ λόγον**: + genitive, both here and in the next sentence, = "in
proportion to."

9–10. **αὐξανόμενος ... ἑπτακαίδεκα πήχεας**: "but it grows to a length
of even seventeen cubits," i.e., approximately 25 feet. In fact crocodiles
don't normally grow beyond a length of 20 feet, though there are
occasional records of larger specimens.

10. **μέζων**: = μείζων.

13. **οὐκ ἔφυσε**: a gnomic aorist = "it does not grow." Herodotus is
mistaken here: crocodiles do have tongues, but they are very small.

14. **καὶ τοῦτο**: "in this regard also."

14–15. **τὴν ἄνω γνάθον προσάγει τῇ κάτω**: again not true: the
crocodile moves its lower jaw quite normally.

16–17. τυφλὸν δὲ ἐν ὕδατι: understand ἐστί. Yet another misconception of Herodotus: the crocodile can see as well in water as on land.

17. ἐν δὲ τῇ αἰθρίῃ: "in the open air," i.e., out of the water.

17–18. ἅτε ... ἐν ὕδατι δίαιταν ποιεύμενον: "because it spends its life in the water"; see Chapter 7 for this use of the participle.

18. φορέει: = ἔχει.

19. βδελλέων: apparently there are no leeches in the Nile, so Herodotus is wrong again!

20. εἰρηναῖόν οἱ ἐστὶ: "is at peace with it." Note the neuter adjective, lit. "is a thing at peace with it."

πρὸς αὐτοῦ: "by it."

21. ἐπεάν: Ionic for ἐπήν = ἐπεί ἄν.

22. ἔωθε: = εἴωθε.

22–23. ὡς ἐπίπαν: "as a general rule."

πρὸς τὸν ζέφυρον: i.e., "to catch the west wind," presumably for cooling purposes.

23. ἐνθαῦτα: = ἐνταῦθα.

24. καταπίνει: "gobbles down."

22.3 Thucydides, *Histories*, 6.57: Hipparchus, the brother of the Athenian tyrant Hippias, is murdered by Harmodius and Aristogiton. Neither escapes with his life.

καὶ ὡς ἐπῆλθεν ἡ ἑορτή, Ἱππίας μὲν ἔξω ἐν τῷ Κεραμεικῷ
καλουμένῳ μετὰ τῶν δορυφόρων διεκόσμει ὡς ἕκαστα
ἐχρῆν τῆς πομπῆς προϊέναι, ὁ δὲ Ἁρμόδιος καὶ ὁ
Ἀριστογείτων ἔχοντες ἤδη τὰ ἐγχειρίδια ἐς τὸ ἔργον
προῇσαν. καὶ ὡς εἶδόν τινα τῶν ξυνωμοτῶν σφίσι   5
διαλεγόμενον οἰκείως τῷ Ἱππίᾳ (ἦν δὲ πᾶσιν εὐπρόσοδος
ὁ Ἱππίας), ἔδεισαν καὶ ἐνόμισαν μεμηνῦσθαί τε καὶ ὅσον
οὐκ ἤδη ξυλληφθήσεσθαι. τὸν λυπήσαντα οὖν σφᾶς καὶ
δι᾽ ὅνπερ πάντα ἐκινδύνευον ἐβούλοντο πρότερον, εἰ
δύναιντο, προτιμωρήσασθαι, καὶ ὥσπερ εἶχον ὥρμησαν   10
ἔσω τῶν πυλῶν, καὶ περιέτυχον τῷ Ἱππάρχῳ παρὰ τὸ
Λεωκόρειον καλούμενον, καὶ εὐθὺς ἀπερισκέπτως
προσπεσόντες καὶ ὡς ἂν μάλιστα δι᾽ ὀργῆς ὁ μὲν
ἐρωτικῆς, ὁ δὲ ὑβρισμένος, ἔτυπτον καὶ ἀποκτείνουσιν
αὐτόν. καὶ ὁ μὲν τοὺς δορυφόρους τὸ αὐτίκα διαφεύγει   15

ὁ Ἀριστογείτων, ξυνδραμόντος τοῦ ὄχλου, καὶ ὕστερον
ληφθεὶς οὐ ῥᾳδίως διετέθη· Ἁρμόδιος δὲ αὐτοῦ παραχρῆμα
ἀπόλλυται.

Notes: 1. **ἡ ἑορτή**: the Great Panathenaea. The Panathenaea was a
festival held in Athens every summer in honor of Athena, the city's
patron goddess. For three out of four years it was a two-day event,
known as the Lesser Panathenaea, but every fourth year it was
celebrated with particular magnificence, for a week, and was known
as the Great Panathenaea. The climax of the festival was a procession
(cf. ἕκαστα . . . τῆς πομπῆς later in the sentence) along the Panathenaic
Way, up to the Parthenon, where a new robe, the πέπλος, was presented
to Athena's statue.

Ἱππίας: eldest son of Pisistratus, and tyrant of Athens from 527 to
510 BC.

ἔξω: i.e., outside the city walls.

ἐν τῷ Κεραμεικῷ: "in the Ceramicus" or "Potters' Quarter," an area of
ancient Athens northwest of the Agora.

2–3. **ὡς ἕκαστα . . . προϊέναι**: "how each element of the procession should
go forward."

3–4. **ὁ δὲ Ἁρμόδιος καὶ ὁ Ἀριστογείτων**: two Athenian lovers who, in
514 BC, plotted to kill the tyrant Hippias and his brother Hipparchus.
Hipparchus had made sexual overtures to Harmodius, causing
Aristogiton to plot against him in jealousy; Harmodius then joined
his partner in the conspiracy when the rejected Hipparchus publicly
insulted his sister.

4–5. **ἐς τὸ ἔργον προῇσαν**: "came forward to (do) the deed," i.e., to put
their conspiracy into effect.

5. **τινα τῶν ξυνωμοτῶν σφίσι**: "one of their fellow conspirators."

7. **μεμηνῦσθαί**: perfect infinitive passive of μηνύω (I disclose).

7–8. **καὶ ὅσον οὐκ ἤδη ξυλληφθήσεσθαι**: "and were all but already
about to be arrested."

10. **ὥσπερ εἶχον**: "just as they were."

11–12. **τὸ Λεωκόρειον**: the Leocorium was a small sanctuary, situated
in the western part of the Agora, in the city center, and dedicated to the
daughters of Leos, who were said to have been sacrificed to rescue the
city from a plague.

13–14. **καὶ ὡς ἂν . . . ὑβρισμένος**: "as they would in extreme anger, the
one sexually jealous, the other insulted." Thucydides gives extra point
to the balancing ὁ μέν and ὁ δέ by varying an adjective agreeing with
ὀργῆς (ἐρωτικῆς) with a participle (ὑβρισμένος.).

14. **ἀποκτείνουσιν**: the sudden change to the historic present here vividly highlights the moment of Hipparchus' murder.

15–16. **ὁ μὲν … ὁ Ἀριστογείτων**: "one of them, Aristogiton." **τὸ αὐτίκα**: "for the moment."

16. **ξυνδραμόντος τοῦ ὄχλου**: lit. "the crowd having gathered" = "through the crowd that had gathered."

17. **οὐ ῥᾳδίως**: "in no gentle way."
αὐτοῦ παραχρῆμα: "right there on the spot."

22.4 Thucydides, *Histories* 8.1: news of the disaster that has befallen their fleet and army in Sicily arrives in Athens.

ἐς δὲ τὰς Ἀθήνας ἐπειδὴ ἠγγέλθη, ἐπὶ πολὺ μὲν ἠπίστουν
καὶ τοῖς πάνυ τῶν στρατιωτῶν ἐξ αὐτοῦ τοῦ ἔργου
διαπεφευγόσι καὶ σαφῶς ἀγγέλλουσι, μὴ οὕτω γε ἄγαν
πανσυδὶ διεφθάρθαι· ἐπειδὴ δὲ ἔγνωσαν, χαλεποὶ μὲν
ἦσαν τοῖς ξυμπροθυμηθεῖσι τῶν ῥητόρων τὸν ἔκπλουν,   5
ὥσπερ οὐκ αὐτοὶ ψηφισάμενοι, ὠργίζοντο δὲ καὶ τοῖς
χρησμολόγοις τε καὶ μάντεσι καὶ ὁπόσοι τι τότε αὐτοὺς
θειάσαντες ἐπήλπισαν ὡς λήψονται Σικελίαν. πάντα δὲ
πανταχόθεν αὐτοὺς ἐλύπει τε καὶ περιειστήκει ἐπὶ τῷ
γεγενημένῳ φόβος τε καὶ κατάπληξις μεγίστη δή. ἅμα   10
μὲν γὰρ στερόμενοι καὶ ἰδίᾳ ἕκαστος καὶ ἡ πόλις ὁπλιτῶν
τε πολλῶν καὶ ἱππέων καὶ ἡλικίας οἵαν οὐχ ἑτέραν ἑώρων
ὑπάρχουσαν ἐβαρύνοντο· ἅμα δὲ ναῦς οὐχ ὁρῶντες ἐν
τοῖς νεωσοίκοις ἱκανὰς οὐδὲ χρήματα ἐν τῷ κοινῷ οὐδ᾽
ὑπηρεσίας ταῖς ναυσὶν ἀνέλπιστοι ἦσαν ἐν τῷ παρόντι   15
σωθήσεσθαι, τούς τε ἀπὸ τῆς Σικελίας πολεμίους
εὐθὺς σφίσιν ἐνόμιζον τῷ ναυτικῷ ἐπὶ τὸν Πειραιᾶ
πλευσεῖσθαι, ἄλλως τε καὶ τοσοῦτον κρατήσαντας, καὶ
τοὺς αὐτόθεν πολεμίους τότε δὴ καὶ διπλασίως πάντα
παρεσκευασμένους κατὰ κράτος ἤδη καὶ ἐκ γῆς καὶ ἐκ   20
θαλάσσης ἐπικείσεσθαι, καὶ τοὺς ξυμμάχους σφῶν μετ᾽
αὐτῶν ἀποστάντας. ὅμως δὲ ὡς ἐκ τῶν ὑπαρχόντων ἐδόκει
χρῆναι μὴ ἐνδιδόναι …

Notes: 1. **ἠγγέλθη**: lit., "it was announced" (impersonal use of the passive), i.e., "the news came."

ἐπὶ πολύ: "for a long time."

2. **πάνυ**: those who had "actually . . ."

3–4. **μὴ οὕτω γε ἄγαν πανσυδὶ διεφθάρθαι**: μή introduces what they disbelieved: "that their forces had been so utterly destroyed."

5. **τοῖς ξυμπροθυμηθεῖσι . . . τὸν ἔκπλουν**: "with those . . . who had taken part in advocating the expedition."

8. **θειάσαντες**: lit. "being inspired," i.e., "by their prophecies."

9–10. **περιειστήκει . . . φόβος τε καὶ κατάπληξις μεγίστη δή**: lit. "fear and the greatest consternation . . . stood round them," i.e., "they were plunged into fear and terrible consternation."

12–13. **ἡλικίας οἵαν οὐχ ἑτέραν ἑώρων ὑπάρχουσαν**: lit. "of youth of the kind that they did not see another being available," i.e., "of young men for whom they could see no replacement."

15. **ὑπηρεσίας**: "crews."

ἐν τῷ παρόντι: "in the present situation."

16. **σωθήσεσθαι**: "that they would be saved" after ἀνέλπιστοι.

18. **πλευσεῖσθαι**: future infinitive of πλέω.

ἄλλως τε καί: "especially."

τοσοῦτον κρατήσαντας: "having won such a great victory."

19. **αὐτόθεν**: lit. "from the same place (as themselves)," i.e., "from home."

19–20. **διπλασίως πάντα παρεσκευασμένους**: "doubly prepared in all respects."

20. **κατὰ κράτος**: "in full force."

21–22. **τοὺς ξυμμάχους σφῶν μετ᾽ αὐτῶν ἀποστάντας**: "their own allies revolting (from them and joining) with them (i.e., the enemy)."

22. **ὡς ἐκ τῶν ὑπαρχόντων**: "as far as lay in their power."

22.5 Xenophon, *Hellenica*, 4.2.10–12: when the Spartans advance against a combined force from several other states, Timolaus the Corinthian uses examples from the natural world to encourage the allies to make an early attack.

> ἐπεὶ δ᾽ ἐξῇσαν μὲν οἱ Λακεδαιμόνιοι, συνειλεγμένοι
> δ᾽ ἦσαν οἱ ἐναντίοι, συνελθόντες ἐβουλεύοντο πῶς ἂν
> τὴν μάχην συμφορώτατα σφίσιν αὐτοῖς ποιήσαιντο.
> Τιμόλαος μὲν δὴ Κορίνθιος ἔλεξεν· Ἀλλ᾽ ἐμοὶ δοκεῖ, ἔφη,
> ὦ ἄνδρες σύμμαχοι, ὅμοιον εἶναι τὸ τῶν Λακεδαιμονίων   5
> πρᾶγμα οἷόνπερ τὸ τῶν ποταμῶν. οἵ τε γὰρ ποταμοὶ
> πρὸς μὲν ταῖς πηγαῖς οὐ μεγάλοι εἰσὶν ἀλλ᾽ εὐδιάβατοι,

ὅσῳ δ᾽ ἂν πορρωτέρω γίγνωνται, ἐπεμβάλλοντες ἕτεροι
ποταμοὶ ἰσχυρότερον αὐτῶν τὸ ῥεῦμα ποιοῦσι, καὶ οἱ
Λακεδαιμόνιοι ὡσαύτως, ἔνθεν μὲν ἐξέρχονται, αὐτοὶ 10
μόνοι εἰσί, προϊόντες δὲ καὶ παραλαμβάνοντες τὰς πόλεις
πλείους τε καὶ δυσμαχώτεροι γίγνονται. ὁρῶ δ᾽ ἔγωγε,
ἔφη, καὶ ὁπόσοι σφῆκας ἐξαιρεῖν βούλονται, ἐὰν μὲν
ἐκθέοντας τοὺς σφῆκας πειρῶνται θηρᾶν, ὑπὸ πολλῶν
τυπτομένους· ἐὰν δ᾽ ἔτι ἔνδον ὄντων τὸ πῦρ προσφέρωσι, 15
πάσχοντας μὲν οὐδέν, χειρουμένους δὲ τοὺς σφῆκας. ταῦτ᾽
οὖν ἐνθυμούμενος ἡγοῦμαι κράτιστον εἶναι μάλιστα μὲν
ἐν αὐτῇ, εἰ δὲ μή, ὅτι ἐγγύτατα τῆς Λακεδαίμονος τὴν
μάχην ποιεῖσθαι.

Notes: 1. **ἐξῇσαν**: note the imperfect = "when the Spartans were
[already] marching out."
2. **οἱ ἐναντίοι**: these include the Thebans, Corinthians, and Argives,
all of whom have been paid by the Persians to start this war, so that the
Spartan king, Agesilaus, may be deflected from his military activity in
Asia Minor. The Athenians, even though not bribed by the Persians,
have sent a force as well.
6. **οἱόνπερ**: picks up the earlier ὅμοιον = "the same as."
8. **ὅσῳ δ᾽ ἂν πορρωτέρω γίγνωνται**: "the further on they go."
ἐπεμβάλλοντες: "flowing in besides."
10. **ὡσαύτως**: "in just the same way."
ἔνθεν: "at the place from which."
12–13. **ὁρῶ δ᾽ ἔγωγε . . . καί**: "and again I see" (lit. "and I for my part see
also").
13. **ἐξαιρεῖν**: (here) "to get rid of."
14. **ἐκθέοντας**: "as they rush forth," i.e., from their nest.
15. **τυπτομένους**: "are struck" i.e., "stung."
18. **ἐν αὐτῇ**: = ἐν αὐτῇ τῇ Λακεδαίμονι.
ὅτι ἐγγύτατα: = ὡς ἐγγύτατα ("as close as possible").

22.6 Xenophon, *Memorabilia* 2.1.21–22: the sophist Prodicus tells
how Heracles was confronted at a crossroads by two women, beautiful in very different ways, who invited him to make an important
choice in life style.

φησὶ γὰρ Ἡρακλέα, ἐπεὶ ἐκ παίδων εἰς ἥβην ὡρμᾶτο,
ἐν ᾗ οἱ νέοι ἤδη αὐτοκράτορες γιγνόμενοι δηλοῦσιν

εἴτε τὴν δι᾽ ἀρετῆς ὁδὸν τρέψονται ἐπὶ τὸν βίον εἴτε
τὴν διὰ κακίας, ἐξελθόντα εἰς ἡσυχίαν καθῆσθαι
ἀποροῦντα ποτέραν τῶν ὁδῶν τράπηται· καὶ φανῆναι   5
αὐτῷ δύο γυναῖκας προσιέναι μεγάλας, τὴν μὲν ἑτέραν
εὐπρεπῆ τε ἰδεῖν καὶ ἐλευθέριον φύσει, κεκοσμημένην
τὸ μὲν σῶμα καθαρότητι, τὰ δὲ ὄμματα αἰδοῖ, τὸ δὲ
σχῆμα σωφροσύνῃ, ἐσθῆτι δὲ λευκῇ, τὴν δ᾽ ἑτέραν
τεθραμμένην μὲν εἰς πολυσαρκίαν τε καὶ ἁπαλότητα,   10
κεκαλλωπισμένην δὲ τὸ μὲν χρῶμα ὥστε λευκοτέραν τε
καὶ ἐρυθροτέραν τοῦ ὄντος δοκεῖν φαίνεσθαι, τὸ δὲ σχῆμα
ὥστε δοκεῖν ὀρθοτέραν τῆς φύσεως εἶναι, τὰ δὲ ὄμματα
ἔχειν ἀναπεπταμένα, ἐσθῆτα δὲ ἐξ ἧς ἂν μάλιστα ὥρα
διαλάμποι· κατασκοπεῖσθαι δὲ θαμὰ ἑαυτήν, ἐπισκοπεῖν   15
δὲ καὶ εἴ τις ἄλλος αὐτὴν θεᾶται, πολλάκις δὲ καὶ εἰς τὴν
ἑαυτῆς σκιὰν ἀποβλέπειν.

Notes: 1. **φησί**: the subject is Prodicus.
ἐκ παίδων: i.e., "from childhood."
3. **τρέψονται**: lit. "they will turn (to + acc.)": here, "they will travel along."
5. **καὶ φανῆναι**: "and (Prodicus says) that it appeared that ..." + acc. + inf.
7. **ἐλευθέριον**: a two-termination adjective, i.e., one with no separate feminine form: here it is in the feminine.
8. **καθαρότητι**: "with purity."
10. **τεθραμμένην**: perfect passive participle of τρέφω.
πολυσαρκίαν: "fleshiness."
ἁπαλότητα: "softness."
11–12. **κεκαλλωπισμένην ... τὸ μὲν χρῶμα ὥστε λευκοτέραν τε καὶ ἐρυθροτέραν τοῦ ὄντος δοκεῖν φαίνεσθαι**: "her face made up [lit. beautified as to her complexion] so as to seem to appear more white and more pink than she really was" (lit. "than the reality").
12–13. **τὸ δὲ σχῆμα ὥστε δοκεῖν ὀρθοτέραν τῆς φύσεως εἶναι**: lit. "and (beautified) as to her posture so as to appear more upright than nature (i.e., than she really was)."
14. **ἀναπεπταμένα**: "wide open."
14–15. **ἐξ ἧς ἂν μάλιστα ὥρα διαλάμποι**: lit. "from which her beauty could most shine through": she wears a see-through dress.
15. **κατασκοπεῖσθαι**: "(she appeared) to look at ..."

22.7   Plato, *Apology*, 22a–c: in his quest to find those wiser than himself, Socrates is far from impressed by the poets he talks to.

μετὰ γὰρ τοὺς πολιτικοὺς ᾖα ἐπὶ τοὺς ποιητὰς τούς τε
τῶν τραγῳδιῶν καὶ τοὺς τῶν διθυράμβων καὶ τοὺς
ἄλλους, ὡς ἐνταῦθα ἐπ᾽ αὐτοφώρῳ καταληψόμενος
ἐμαυτὸν ἀμαθέστερον ἐκείνων ὄντα. ἀναλαμβάνων
οὖν αὐτῶν τὰ ποιήματα ἅ μοι ἐδόκει μάλιστα   5
πεπραγματεῦσθαι αὐτοῖς, διηρώτων ἂν αὐτοὺς τί
λέγοιεν, ἵν᾽ ἅμα τι καὶ μανθάνοιμι παρ᾽ αὐτῶν.
αἰσχύνομαι οὖν ὑμῖν εἰπεῖν, ὦ ἄνδρες, τἀληθῆ· ὅμως
δὲ ῥητέον. ὡς ἔπος γὰρ εἰπεῖν ὀλίγου αὐτῶν ἅπαντες οἱ
παρόντες ἂν βέλτιον ἔλεγον περὶ ὧν αὐτοὶ   10
ἐπεποιήκεσαν. ἔγνων οὖν αὖ καὶ περὶ τῶν ποιητῶν
ἐν ὀλίγῳ τοῦτο, ὅτι οὐ σοφίᾳ ποιοῖεν ἃ ποιοῖεν, ἀλλὰ
φύσει τινὶ καὶ ἐνθουσιάζοντες ὥσπερ οἱ θεομάντεις
καὶ οἱ χρησμῳδοί· καὶ γὰρ οὗτοι λέγουσι μὲν πολλὰ
καὶ καλά, ἴσασιν δὲ οὐδὲν ὧν λέγουσι. τοιοῦτόν τί μοι   15
ἐφάνησαν πάθος καὶ οἱ ποιηταὶ πεπονθότες, καὶ ἅμα
ἠσθόμην αὐτῶν διὰ τὴν ποίησιν οἰομένων καὶ τἆλλα
σοφωτάτων εἶναι ἀνθρώπων ἃ οὐκ ἦσαν. ἀπῇα οὖν καὶ
ἐντεῦθεν τῷ αὐτῷ οἰόμενος περιγεγονέναι ᾧπερ καὶ
τῶν πολιτικῶν.   20

Notes: 2. **τῶν διθυράμβων**: the dithyramb was a hymn to Dionysus, sung by dancers to the accompaniment of the αὐλός.

3. **ὡς**: with the future participle (καταληψόμενος) to express purpose = "in order to catch myself."

ἐπ᾽ αὐτοφώρῳ: "red-handed" or "in the very act."

5–6. **μάλιστα πεπραγματεῦσθαι αὐτοῖς**: "to be their most perfect works" (lit. "to have been most elaborated by them"); note the dative of the agent (αὐτοῖς) with a perfect passive.

6. **διηρώτων ἄν**: "I would ask," a common use of ἄν with the imperfect to denote repeated action.

9. **ῥητέον**: understand ἐστί = "it must be told."

9–10. **ὡς ἔπος . . . εἰπεῖν ὀλίγου . . . ἅπαντες οἱ παρόντες**: "virtually (ὡς ἔπος . . . εἰπεῖν) nearly (ὀλίγου = ὀλίγου δεῖν) all those present."

αὐτῶν... ἂν βέλτιον ἔλεγον: αὐτῶν is a genitive of comparison to be taken with βέλτιον, and ἂν... ἔλεγον is a regular past potential usage = "would have spoken better than they."

10. περὶ ὧν: = περὶ ἐκείνων ἅ, a case of relative attraction (see Chapter 8).

12. ἐν ὀλίγῳ: understand χρόνῳ.

13. φύσει τινί: "by a sort of instinct."

15. ἴσασιν δέ: "but understand."

15–16. τοιοῦτόν... πεπονθότες: "it was clear to me that the poets too had experienced some such thing" (lit. "the poets also were clear to me having experienced some such experience"). Note this use of φαίνομαι with a participle.

17. καὶ τἆλλα: "in other respects also."

18. ἀνθρώπων: depends on σοφωτάτων = "the wisest of men."
ἃ οὐκ ἦσαν: understand σοφοί "in which (accusative of respect) they were not (wise)."

19–20. τῷ αὐτῷ... τῶν πολιτικῶν: "thinking that I had been superior in precisely the same way as I had been also to the politicians."

22.8   Plato, *Phaedo* 117e–18a: the last moments of Socrates, who has been condemned to death by drinking hemlock. His last words are to his old friend Crito.

> ὁ δὲ περιελθών, ἐπειδή οἱ βαρύνεσθαι ἔφη τὰ σκέλη,
> κατεκλίνη ὕπτιος—οὕτω γὰρ ἐκέλευεν ὁ ἄνθρωπος—
> καὶ ἅμα ἐφαπτόμενος αὐτοῦ οὗτος ὁ δοὺς τὸ φάρμακον,
> διαλιπὼν χρόνον ἐπεσκόπει τοὺς πόδας καὶ τὰ σκέλη,
> κἄπειτα σφόδρα πιέσας αὐτοῦ τὸν πόδα ἤρετο εἰ   5
> αἰσθάνοιτο, ὁ δ᾽ οὐκ ἔφη. καὶ μετὰ τοῦτο αὖθις τὰς
> κνήμας· καὶ ἐπανιὼν οὕτως ἡμῖν ἐπεδείκνυτο ὅτι ψύχοιτό
> τε καὶ πήγνυτο. καὶ αὖθις ἥπτετο καὶ εἶπεν ὅτι, ἐπειδὰν
> πρὸς τῇ καρδίᾳ γένηται αὐτῷ, τότε οἰχήσεται. ἤδη οὖν
> σχεδόν τι αὐτοῦ ἦν τὰ περὶ τὸ ἦτρον ψυχόμενα, καὶ   10
> ἐκκαλυψάμενος—ἐνεκεκάλυπτο γάρ—εἶπεν—ὃ δὴ
> τελευταῖον ἐφθέγξατο—Ὦ Κρίτων, ἔφη, τῷ Ἀσκληπιῷ
> ὀφείλομεν ἀλεκτρυόνα· ἀλλὰ ἀπόδοτε καὶ μὴ ἀμελήσητε.
> Ἀλλὰ ταῦτα, ἔφη, ἔσται, ὁ Κρίτων· ἀλλ᾽ ὅρα εἴ τι ἄλλο λέγεις.
> ταῦτα ἐρομένου αὐτοῦ οὐδὲν ἔτι ἀπεκρίνατο, ἀλλ᾽ ὀλίγον   15
> χρόνον διαλιπὼν ἐκινήθη τε καὶ ὁ ἄνθρωπος ἐξεκάλυψεν

αὐτόν, καὶ ὃς τὰ ὄμματα ἔστησεν· ἰδὼν δὲ ὁ Κρίτων
συνέλαβε τὸ στόμα καὶ τοὺς ὀφθαλμούς.

Notes: 2. **ὁ ἄνθρωπος**: i.e., the jailer administering the hemlock.
7–8. **ψύχοιτό τε καὶ πήγνυτο**: "he was growing cold and rigid" (lit.
"was being fixed").
10. **σχεδόν τι**: "pretty nearly."
ψυχόμενα: "growing cold."
11. **ἐκκαλυψάμενος—ἐνεκεκάλυπτο γάρ**: "uncovering himself—for
he had been covered": Socrates had covered his head.
12–13. **τῷ Ἀσκληπιῷ ὀφείλομεν ἀλεκτρυόνα**: Socrates' wish to
sacrifice a cock to Asclepius, the god of healing, presumably reflects his
gratitude at being released from the disease of life.
16–17. **ἐξεκάλυψεν αὐτόν**: Socrates has covered himself again.
17. **ὅς**: "he," i.e., Socrates.

22.9 Lucian, *Vera Historia* 2, 35–36: some travelers put in at
Ogygia, the island of Calypso, and deliver a letter from Odysseus.

τριταῖοι δ᾽ ἐκεῖθεν τῇ Ὠγυγίᾳ νήσῳ προσσχόντες
ἀπεβαίνομεν. πρότερον δ᾽ ἐγὼ λύσας τὴν ἐπιστολὴν
ἀνεγίνωσκον τὰ γεγραμμένα. ἦν δὲ τοιάδε· Ὀδυσσεὺς
Καλυψοῖ χαίρειν. Ἴσθι με, ὡς τὰ πρῶτα ἐξέπλευσα παρὰ
σοῦ τὴν σχεδίαν κατασκευασάμενος, ναυαγίᾳ χρησάμενον   5
μόλις ὑπὸ Λευκοθέας διασωθῆναι εἰς τὴν τῶν Φαιάκων
χώραν, ὑφ᾽ ὧν ἐς τὴν οἰκείαν ἀποπεμφθεὶς κατέλαβον
πολλοὺς τῆς γυναικὸς μνηστῆρας ἐν τοῖς ἡμετέροις
τρυφῶντας. ἀποκτείνας δὲ ἅπαντας ὑπὸ Τηλεγόνου
ὕστερον τοῦ ἐκ Κίρκης μοι γενομένου ἀνῃρέθην, καὶ   10
νῦν εἰμι ἐν τῇ Μακάρων νήσῳ πάνυ μετανοῶν ἐπὶ
τῷ καταλιπεῖν τὴν παρὰ σοὶ δίαιταν καὶ τὴν ὑπὸ σοῦ
προτεινομένην ἀθανασίαν. ἢν οὖν καιροῦ λάβωμαι,
ἀποδρὰς ἀφίξομαι πρὸς σέ. ταῦτα μὲν ἐδήλου ἡ ἐπιστολή,
καὶ περὶ ἡμῶν, ὅπως ξενισθῶμεν. ἐγὼ δὲ προελθὼν ὀλίγον   15
ἀπὸ τῆς θαλάττης εὗρον τὸ σπήλαιον τοιοῦτον οἷον
Ὅμηρος εἶπεν, καὶ αὐτὴν ταλασιουργοῦσαν. ὡς δὲ τὴν
ἐπιστολὴν ἔλαβεν καὶ ἐπελέξατο, πρῶτα μὲν ἐπὶ πολὺ

ἐδάκρυεν, ἔπειτα δὲ παρεκάλει ἡμᾶς ἐπὶ ξένια καὶ εἰστία
λαμπρῶς καὶ περὶ τοῦ Ὀδυσσέως ἐπυνθάνετο καὶ περὶ   20
τῆς Πηνελόπης, ὁποία τε εἴη τὴν ὄψιν καὶ εἰ σωφρονοίη,
καθάπερ Ὀδυσσεὺς πάλαι περὶ αὐτῆς ἐκόμπαζεν· καὶ ἡμεῖς
τοιαῦτα ἀπεκρινάμεθα, ἐξ ὧν εἰκάζομεν εὐφρανεῖσθαι
αὐτήν.

Notes: 1. **τριταῖοι δ᾽ ἐκεῖθεν**: "on the third day from there."
προσσχόντες: προσέχω is used either with εἰς + accusative, or, as here,
with the dative, to mean "I put in to."
2. **πρότερον**: (here) "first," i.e., before doing anything else.
λύσας τὴν ἐπιστολήν: "having opened the letter," i.e., having untied
the scroll that contained it.
3. **ἀνεγίνωσκον**: = ἀνεγίγνωσκον.
3–4. **Ὀδυσσεὺς Καλυψοῖ χαίρειν**: "Odysseus to Calypso, greeting."
4. **Ἴσθι**: imperative of οἶδα = "Know that ..."
ὡς τὰ πρῶτα: "as soon as."
6. **ὑπὸ Λευκοθέας**: "by Leucothea," a sea goddess.
6–7. **τὴν τῶν Φαιάκων χώραν**: the island of Scheria, as depicted in
Books 6–8 of the *Odyssey*.
8. **ἐν τοῖς ἡμετέροις**: understand δώμασι or δόμοις.
9. **ὑπὸ Τηλεγόνου**: Telegonus was Odysseus' son by the nymph Circe,
and the unwitting killer of his father.
10. **ἀνῃρέθην**: "I was killed."
11. **τῇ Μακάρων νήσῳ**: the "Island" or "Islands of the Blest" were
mythical islands in the Ocean stream, beyond the Pillars of Hercules,
where specially favored mortals spent a blissful afterlife.
11–12. **μετανοῶν ἐπὶ τῷ καταλιπεῖν**: "repenting having left behind."
13. **ἤν**: = ἐάν.
14. **ἀποδράς**: aorist participle of ἀποδιδράσκω ("I run away").
15. **ὅπως ξενισθῶμεν**: "that we should be entertained."
16–17. **τοιοῦτον οἷον Ὅμηρος εἶπεν**: "just as Homer described it," cf.
Odyssey 5, 55ff.
21. **τὴν ὄψιν**: accusative of respect ("in appearance").
23–24. **τοιαῦτα ἀπεκρινάμεθα, ἐξ ὧν εἰκάζομεν εὐφρανεῖσθαι αὐτήν**:
"gave such answers as we reckoned would please her" (lit. "answered
such things as we reckoned she would be pleased by").

22.10 *The Acts of the Apostles* 9.1–12: Saul of Tarsus, the future St.
Paul, is converted from his persecution of Christianity on the road
to Damascus and the Lord arranges that Ananias, a Christian in
Damascus, should help him.

ὁ δὲ Σαῦλος, ἔτι ἐνπνέων ἀπειλῆς καὶ φόνου εἰς τοὺς
μαθητὰς τοῦ κυρίου, προσελθὼν τῷ ἀρχιερεῖ ᾐτήσατο
παρ᾽ αὐτοῦ ἐπιστολὰς εἰς Δαμασκὸν πρὸς τὰς συναγωγάς,
ὅπως ἐάν τινας εὕρῃ τῆς ὁδοῦ ὄντας, ἄνδρας τε καὶ
γυναῖκας, δεδεμένους ἀγάγῃ εἰς Ἰερουσαλήμ. ἐν δὲ τῷ   5
πορεύεσθαι ἐγένετο αὐτὸν ἐγγίζειν τῇ Δαμασκῷ, ἐξαίφνης
τε αὐτὸν περιήστραψεν φῶς ἐκ τοῦ οὐρανοῦ, καὶ πεσὼν
ἐπὶ τὴν γῆν ἤκουσεν φωνὴν λέγουσαν αὐτῷ Σαούλ Σαούλ,
τί με διώκεις; εἶπεν δέ Τίς εἶ, κύριε; ὁ δέ Ἐγώ εἰμι Ἰησοῦς
ὃν σὺ διώκεις· σκληρόν σοι πρὸς κέντρα λακτίζειν. ἀλλὰ   10
ἀνάστηθι καὶ εἴσελθε εἰς τὴν πόλιν, καὶ λαληθήσεταί
σοι ὅτι σε δεῖ ποιεῖν. οἱ δὲ ἄνδρες οἱ συνοδεύοντες αὐτῷ
ἱστήκεισαν ἐνεοί, ἀκούοντες μὲν τῆς φωνῆς μηδένα δὲ
θεωροῦντες. ἠγέρθη δὲ Σαῦλος ἀπὸ τῆς γῆς, ἀνεῳγμένων
δὲ τῶν ὀφθαλμῶν αὐτοῦ οὐδὲν ἔβλεπεν· χειραγωγοῦντες   15
δὲ αὐτὸν εἰσήγαγον εἰς Δαμασκόν. καὶ ἦν ἡμέρας τρεῖς μὴ
βλέπων, καὶ οὐκ ἔφαγεν οὐδὲ ἔπιεν.

ἦν δέ τις μαθητὴς ἐν Δαμασκῷ ὀνόματι Ἀνανίας, καὶ εἶπεν
πρὸς αὐτὸν ἐν ὁράματι ὁ κύριος Ἀνανία. ὁ δὲ εἶπεν Ἰδοὺ
ἐγώ, κύριε. ὁ δὲ κύριος πρὸς αὐτόν Ἀνάστα, πορεύθητι ἐπὶ   20
τὴν ῥύμην τὴν καλουμένην Εὐθεῖαν καὶ ζήτησον ἐν οἰκίᾳ
Ἰούδα Σαῦλον ὀνόματι Ταρσέα, ἰδοὺ γὰρ προσεύχεται, καὶ
εἶδεν ἄνδρα ἐν ὁράματι Ἀνανίαν ὀνόματι εἰσελθόντα καὶ
ἐπιθέντα αὐτῷ τὰς χεῖρας ὅπως ἀναβλέψῃ.

Notes: 1. **ἐνπνέων ἀπειλῆς καὶ φόνου**: "breathing threats and murder."
The genitives are used because Saul was full of threats and murder,
which he then breathed forth.
2. **τῷ ἀρχιερεῖ**: "the high priest."
3. **συναγωγάς**: transliteration of this word should lead to its meaning.
4. **τῆς ὁδοῦ**: "of/belonging to the Way," i.e., Christianity.
5. **Ἰερουσαλήμ**: note how the words *Jerusalem* and (later in the
passage) *Jesus* and *Judas* appear in Greek.
7. **περιήστραψεν**: "flashed around."
10. **πρὸς ... λακτίζειν**: "to kick against" + acc.: supply "it is" with σκληρόν.
11–12. **λαληθήσεταί σοι**: "it will be spoken to you," i.e., "you will be told."

12. **συνοδεύοντες**: "traveling with."

13. **ἱστήκεισαν ἐνεοί**: "stood speechless."

15. **χειραγωγοῦντες**: it should be possible to work out the meaning of this word by splitting up its two main parts.

19. **ἐν ὁράματι**: "in a vision."

20. **Ἀνάστα**: "rise."

21. **τὴν ῥύμην τὴν καλουμένην Εὐθεῖαν**: "the street called Straight."

22. **Ἰούδα**: genitive: "of Judas."

CHAPTER 23

Additional Verse Passages

23.1 Homer, *Iliad* 6, 466–84: Hector with his wife and son.

ὣς εἰπὼν οὗ παιδὸς ὀρέξατο φαίδιμος Ἕκτωρ·
ἂψ δ᾽ ὁ πάϊς πρὸς κόλπον ἐϋζώνοιο τιθήνης
ἐκλίνθη ἰάχων, πατρὸς φίλου ὄψιν ἀτυχθείς,
ταρβήσας χαλκόν τε ἰδὲ λόφον ἱππιοχαίτην,
δεινὸν ἀπ᾽ ἀκροτάτης κόρυθος νεύοντα νοήσας.   5
ἐκ δ᾽ ἐγέλασσε πατήρ τε φίλος καὶ πότνια μήτηρ·
αὐτίκ᾽ ἀπὸ κρατὸς κόρυθ᾽ εἵλετο φαίδιμος Ἕκτωρ,
καὶ τὴν μὲν κατέθηκεν ἐπὶ χθονὶ παμφανόωσαν·
αὐτὰρ ὅ γ᾽ ὃν φίλον υἱὸν ἐπεὶ κύσε πῆλέ τε χερσὶν,
εἶπε δ᾽ ἐπευξάμενος Διί τ᾽ ἄλλοισίν τε θεοῖσι·   10
Ζεῦ ἄλλοι τε θεοὶ δότε δὴ καὶ τόνδε γενέσθαι
παῖδ᾽ ἐμὸν ὡς καὶ ἐγώ περ ἀριπρεπέα Τρώεσσιν,
ὧδε βίην τ᾽ ἀγαθόν, καὶ Ἰλίου ἶφι ἀνάσσειν·
καί ποτέ τις εἴποι ᾽πατρός γ᾽ ὅδε πολλὸν ἀμείνων᾽
ἐκ πολέμου ἀνιόντα· φέροι δ᾽ ἔναρα βροτόεντα   15
κτείνας δήϊον ἄνδρα, χαρείη δὲ φρένα μήτηρ.
ὣς εἰπὼν ἀλόχοιο φίλης ἐν χερσὶν ἔθηκε
παῖδ᾽ ἑόν· ἡ δ᾽ ἄρα μιν κηώδεϊ δέξατο κόλπῳ
δακρυόεν γελάσασα.

Notes: 1. **οὗ**: genitive of the possessive pronoun ὅς ἥ ὅν = "his." Cf. also ὃν φίλον υἱόν in l.9 and παῖδ᾽ ἑόν in 18.

2–3. **ἂψ . . . ἐκλίνθη**: "shrank back."

3. **ἀτυχθείς**: aorist participle of ἀτύζομαι, here used transitively = "dismayed at."

5. **δεινόν**: adverbial with νεύοντα = "nodding dreadfully."

ἀπ᾽ ἀκροτάτης κόρυθος: "from the very top of the helmet."

6. **ἐκ . . . ἐγέλασσε**: tmesis for ἐξεγέλασσε (Attic ἐξεγέλασε).

7. **ἀπὸ . . . εἵλετο**: tmesis for ἀφείλετο.

8. **τήν**: the article, as regularly in Homer, is used as a demonstrative = "it."

9. **κύσε πῆλέ τε**: from κυνέω ("I kiss") and πάλλω ("I swing").

10. **εἶπε δ᾽**: δέ is used here simply to indicate the beginning of the main clause.

11–12. **δότε δὴ . . . Τρώεσσιν**: "grant that this child of mine also, just like me, may prove pre-eminent (ἀριπρεπέα) among the Trojans."

13. **ὧδε βίην τ᾽ ἀγαθόν**: "and as valiant (ἀγαθόν) in might." Note βίην, accusative of respect.

καὶ Ἰλίου ἶφι ἀνάσσειν: "and that he may rule mightily over Ilios" (i.e., Troy). ἀνάσσειν is a second infinitive after δότε.

14–15. **καί ποτέ τις εἴποι . . . ἀνιόντα**: "and some day may some man say of him as he comes back from war." The optative εἴποι, like φέροι and χαρείη in the next two lines, introduces a wish. ἀνιόντα is accusative agreeing with αὐτόν, the understood object of εἴποι.

16. **φρένα**: an accusative of respect ("at heart").

18. **μιν**: = αὐτόν.

19. **δακρυόεν γελάσασα**: δακρυόεν is used adverbially = "laughing tearfully" or "laughing through her tears."

23.2   Homer, *Odyssey* 22.1–21: Odysseus removes his beggar's disguise of rags and starts shooting his bow at the suitors for the hand of his wife, Penelope. His first victim is Antinous, the leading suitor.

αὐτὰρ ὁ γυμνώθη ῥακέων πολύμητις Ὀδυσσεύς,
ἆλτο δ᾽ ἐπὶ μέγαν οὐδόν, ἔχων βιὸν ἠδὲ φαρέτρην
ἰῶν ἐμπλείην, ταχέας δ᾽ ἐκχεύατ᾽ ὀϊστοὺς
αὐτοῦ πρόσθε ποδῶν, μετὰ δὲ μνηστῆρσιν ἔειπεν·
'οὗτος μὲν δὴ ἄεθλος ἀάατος ἐκτετέλεσται·   5
νῦν αὖτε σκοπὸν ἄλλον, ὃν οὔ πώ τις βάλεν ἀνήρ,
εἴσομαι, αἴ κε τύχωμι, πόρῃ δέ μοι εὖχος Ἀπόλλων.'
ἦ καὶ ἐπ᾽ Ἀντινόῳ ἰθύνετο πικρὸν ὀϊστόν.

ἦ τοι ὁ καλὸν ἄλεισον ἀναιρήσεσθαι ἔμελλε,
χρύσεον ἄμφωτον, καὶ δὴ μετὰ χερσὶν ἐνώμα,   10
ὄφρα πίοι οἴνοιο· φόνος δέ οἱ οὐκ ἐνὶ θυμῷ
μέμβλετο· τίς κ᾽ οἴοιτο μετ᾽ ἀνδράσι δαιτυμόνεσσι
μοῦνον ἐνὶ πλεόνεσσι, καὶ εἰ μάλα καρτερὸς εἴη,
οἷ τεύξειν θάνατόν τε κακὸν καὶ κῆρα μέλαιναν;
τὸν δ᾽ Ὀδυσεὺς κατὰ λαιμὸν ἐπισχόμενος βάλεν ἰῷ,   15
ἀντικρὺ δ᾽ ἁπαλοῖο δι᾽ αὐχένος ἤλυθ᾽ ἀκωκή.
ἐκλίνθη δ᾽ ἑτέρωσε, δέπας δέ οἱ ἔκπεσε χειρὸς
βλημένου, αὐτίκα δ᾽ αὐλὸς ἀνὰ ῥῖνας παχὺς ἦλθεν
αἵματος ἀνδρομέοιο· θοῶς δ᾽ ἀπὸ εἷο τράπεζαν
ὦσε ποδὶ πλήξας, ἀπὸ δ᾽ εἴδατα χεῦεν ἔραζε·   20
σῖτός τε κρέα τ᾽ ὀπτὰ φορύνετο.

Notes: 1. **γυμνώθη ῥακέων**: "stripped himself of his rags."
2. **ἆλτο**: "leaped."
3. **ἰῶν ἐμπλείην**: "full of arrows."
ἐκχεύατ᾽: "he poured forth."
5. **οὗτος . . . ἄεθλος ἄατος**: "this destructive contest." Odysseus has already won a contest with the suitors by shooting an arrow through the handles of twelve axes.
6–7. **σκοπὸν ἄλλον . . . εἴσομαι**: "I shall aim at [lit. I shall know] another target."
7. **πόρῃ δέ μοι εὖχος Ἀπόλλων**: "and Apollo grants my prayer."
8. **ἦ**: "he spoke."
10. **ἄμφωτον**: "two-handled," lit. "two-eared."
12. **μέμβλετο**: "had been a concern": pluperfect passive of μέλει.
ἀνδράσι δαιτυμόνεσσι: "banqueting men," "banqueters."
15. **ἐπισχόμενος** : "having taken aim."
κατὰ λαιμόν: "in the throat."
17. **ἐκλίνθη δ᾽ ἑτέρωσε**: "he lurched [lit. was bent] to one side."
18. **βλημένου**: genitive absolute: "when (he) had been hit."
αὐλὸς . . . παχύς: "a thick jet."
19. **αἵματος ἀνδρομέοιο**: "of life-blood."
ἀπὸ εἷο: "from himself."
20. **ἀπὸ . . . εἴδατα χεῦεν ἔραζε**: lit. "he poured his food onto the ground."
21. **κρέα . . . ὀπτά**: "roasted meat."
φορύνετο: "were befouled": singular verb; one of the subjects is neuter plural, and the food and drink are seen as one concept.

23.3   Sophocles, *Ajax* 541–59: Ajax with his wife and son.

Τέκμησσα   Αἴας

Τε.   ὦ παῖ, πατὴρ καλεῖ σε. δεῦρο προσπόλων
ἄγ᾽ αὐτὸν ὅσπερ χερσὶν εὐθύνων κυρεῖς.

Αἰ.   ἕρποντι φωνεῖς ἢ λελειμμένῳ λόγων;

Τε.   καὶ δὴ κομίζει προσπόλων ὅδ᾽ ἐγγύθεν.

Αἰ.   αἶρ᾽ αὐτόν, αἶρε δεῦρο· ταρβήσει γὰρ οὒ   5
νεοσφαγῆ τοῦτόν γε προσλεύσσων φόνον,
εἴπερ δικαίως ἔστ᾽ ἐμὸς τὰ πατρόθεν.
ἀλλ᾽ αὐτίκ᾽ ὠμοῖς αὐτὸν ἐν νόμοις πατρὸς
δεῖ πωλοδαμνεῖν κἀξομοιοῦσθαι φύσιν.
ὦ παῖ, γένοιο πατρὸς εὐτυχέστερος,   10
τὰ δ᾽ ἄλλ᾽ ὅμοιος· καὶ γένοι᾽ ἂν οὐ κακός.
καίτοι σε καὶ νῦν τοῦτό γε ζηλοῦν ἔχω,
ὁθούνεκ᾽ οὐδὲν τῶνδ᾽ ἐπαισθάνει κακῶν·
ἐν τῷ φρονεῖν γὰρ μηδὲν ἥδιστος βίος,
ἕως τὸ χαίρειν καὶ τὸ λυπεῖσθαι μάθῃς.   15
ὅταν δ᾽ ἵκῃ πρὸς τοῦτο, δεῖ σ᾽ ὅπως πατρὸς
δείξεις ἐν ἐχθροῖς, οἷος ἐξ οἵου 'τράφης.
τέως δὲ κούφοις πνεύμασιν βόσκου, νέαν
ψυχὴν ἀτάλλων, μητρὶ τῇδε χαρμονήν.

Notes: 1–2. **δεῦρο . . . ὅσπερ**: lit. "bring him here, (you) of the servants who . . ." = "bring him here, whichever of you servants . . ."

3. **ἕρποντι . . . λόγων**: Ajax means no more than "Is he coming, or has he failed to obey you?" He actually says, considerably more pompously, "Do you speak to one coming [ἕρπω doesn't have to mean "crawl"], or to one left behind by your command?"

4. **καὶ δὴ . . . προσπόλων ὅδ᾽**: "Yes, indeed; this servant here" (lit. "this one here of the servants").

7. **τὰ πατρόθεν**: "on his father's side."

8. **ὠμοῖς . . . ἐν νόμοις πατρός**: "in his father's harsh ways."

8–9. **αὐτὸν . . . φύσιν**: αὐτόν is both object of πωλοδαμνεῖν and subject of the passive ἐξομοιοῦσθαι and φύσιν is an accusative of respect = lit. "it is necessary to break him in . . . and that he be made like him (i.e., his father) in nature."

10. **γένοιο**: a wish = "may you be."

11. **τὰ δ᾽ ἄλλ᾽** : "but in everything else."

καὶ γένοι᾽ ἂν οὐ κακός: "if so, you'll turn out a fine man." καί, literally "and," means something like "and in that case," and the potential γένοι᾽ ἄν expresses an understated future (lit. "you'll be likely to turn out").

12. **ζηλοῦν ἔχω**: "I have cause to envy."

13. **ὁθούνεκ᾽**: picks up τοῦτο in the previous clause, i.e., "to envy you this, (namely) that . . ."

14. **ἐν τῷ φρονεῖν . . . μηδὲν ἥδιστος βίος**: ἐστί should be understood with ἥδιστος βίος, and μηδέν is object of φρονεῖν = "life is sweetest when you feel nothing" (lit. "in feeling nothing").

15. **τὸ χαίρειν καὶ τὸ λυπεῖσθαι**: "(the meaning of) joy and sorrow."

16. **δεῖ σ᾽ ὅπως**: "you must see to it that."

17. **οἷος ἐξ οἵου ᾽τράφης**: "the stuff you're made of" (lit. "what type of man you were brought up, [and] from what type of [father]").

18–19. **νέαν ψυχὴν ἀτάλλων**: "nurturing your young life."

23.4   Euripides, *Hippolytus* 1–22: the goddess of love Cypris (Aphrodite) explains why she will punish Hippolytus, whose devotion is to Artemis, goddess of hunting. He is the illegitimate son of Theseus by the Amazon Hippolyta.

Κύπρις

πολλὴ μὲν ἐν βροτοῖσι κοὐκ ἀνώνυμος
θεὰ κέκλημαι Κύπρις οὐρανοῦ τ᾽ ἔσω·
ὅσοι τε Πόντου τερμόνων τ᾽ Ἀτλαντικῶν
ναίουσιν εἴσω, φῶς ὁρῶντες ἡλίου,
τοὺς μὲν σέβοντας τἀμὰ πρεσβεύω κράτη,   5
σφάλλω δ᾽ ὅσοι φρονοῦσιν εἰς ἡμᾶς μέγα.
ἔνεστι γὰρ δὴ κἀν θεῶν γένει τόδε·
τιμώμενοι χαίρουσιν ἀνθρώπων ὕπο.
δείξω δὲ μύθων τῶνδ᾽ ἀλήθειαν τάχα·
ὁ γάρ με Θησέως παῖς, Ἀμαζόνος τόκος,   10
Ἱππόλυτος, ἁγνοῦ Πιτθέως παιδεύματα
μόνος πολιτῶν τῆσδε γῆς Τροζηνίας
λέγει κακίστην δαιμόνων πεφυκέναι·
ἀναίνεται δὲ λέκτρα κοὐ ψαύει γάμων,
Φοίβου δ᾽ ἀδελφὴν Ἄρτεμιν, Διὸς κόρην,   15

τιμᾷ, μεγίστην δαιμόνων ἡγούμενος,
χλωρὰν δ᾽ ἀν᾽ ὕλην παρθένῳ ξυνὼν ἀεὶ
κυσὶν ταχείαις θῆρας ἐξαιρεῖ χθονός,
μείζω βροτείας προσπεσὼν ὁμιλίας.
τούτοισι μέν νυν οὐ φθονῶ· τί γάρ με δεῖ;   20
ἃ δ᾽ εἰς ἔμ᾽ ἡμάρτηκε τιμωρήσομαι
Ἱππόλυτον ἐν τῇδ᾽ ἡμέρᾳ·

Notes: 1. **πολλὴ … κοὐκ ἀνώνυμος**: "mighty and of high renown" (lit. not anonymous).

3–4. **Πόντου τερμόνων τ᾽ Ἀτλαντικῶν … εἴσω**: "between [lit. inside] the Black Sea and the Atlantic boundaries," i.e., the Pillars of Atlas (the Straits of Gibraltar).

6. **ὅσοι φρονοῦσιν … μέγα**: "all those who are arrogant" (lit. think big).

7. **κἀν**: = καὶ ἐν.

11. **ἁγνοῦ Πιτθέως παιδεύματα**: "the ward of holy Pittheus." Pittheus was Theseus' grandfather and king of the Trozenian land.

13. **πεφυκέναι**: "(that I) am."

14. **ἀναίνεται … λέκτρα**: "he shuns the bed (of love)."

17. **παρθένῳ ξυνών**: "being with the maiden," i.e., the goddess Artemis, daughter of Zeus and sister of Phoebus Apollo.

18. **κυσὶν ταχείαις**: note the feminine adjective; these are bitches. **ἐξαιρεῖ**: "gets rid" of something or someone (acc.) from (gen.).

19. **μείζω βροτείας προσπεσὼν ὁμιλίας**: lit. "having fallen upon greater (things) than mortal companionship," i.e., "having fallen in with a companionship greater than mortal." μείζω is accusative neuter plural; βροτείας ὁμιλίας is genitive of comparison.

20. **τούτοισι**: "for these things," i.e., "for this reason."

21. **ἃ δ᾽ εἰς ἔμ᾽ ἡμάρτηκε**: "for his sins [lit. what he has sinned] against me."

23.5 Sophocles, *Antigone*, 781–800: after Haemon has argued with his father about whether his fiancée Antigone should be spared, the chorus sing a hymn to Love, as if acknowledging that Haemon, even if disloyal to his country and his father, is at least under the influence of an irresistible deity.

Χορός

Ἔρως ἀνίκατε μάχαν,
Ἔρως, ὃς ἐν κτήμασι πίπτεις,

ὃς ἐν μαλακαῖς παρειαῖς
νεάνιδος ἐννυχεύεις,¶
φοιτᾷς δ᾽ ὑπερπόντιος ἔν τ᾽   5
ἀγρονόμοις αὐλαῖς·
καί σ᾽ οὔτ᾽ ἀθανάτων φύξιμος οὐδεὶς
οὔθ᾽ ἁμερίων σέ γ᾽ ἀν-
θρώπων. ὁ δ᾽ ἔχων μέμηνεν.

σὺ καὶ δικαίων ἀδίκους   10
φρένας παρασπᾷς ἐπὶ λώβᾳ,
σὺ καὶ τόδε νεῖκος ἀνδρῶν
ξύναιμον ἔχεις ταράξας·
νικᾷ δ᾽ ἐναργὴς βλεφάρων
ἵμερος εὐλέκτρου   15
νύμφας, τῶν μεγάλων πάρεδρος ἐν ἀρχαῖς
θεσμῶν. ἄμαχος γὰρ ἐμ-
παίζει θεός, Ἀφροδίτα.

Notes: It is beyond the scope of this volume to go into the detail of
lyric meters. Suffice it to say here that the rhythms of these two
stanzas are fundamentally aeolo-choriambic, i.e., based around the
metrical unit of the choriamb (- ᴗ ᴗ -), as in, e.g., ἐν μαλακαῖς (l.3) or
ἀγρονόμοις (l.6).

1. **ἀνίκατε μάχαν**: "unconquered in battle." Note in both words that
long α has replaced η, the most obvious feature of the literary Doric in
which the lyric sections of Greek drama are conventionally written.

2. **ἐν κτήμασι πίπτεις**: "fall upon possessions"; ἐν … πίπτεις is for
ἐμπίπτεις, and the idea is that love can cause the destruction of men's
wealth and property.

5-6. **ἔν τ᾽ ἀγρονόμοις αὐλαῖς**: "and among dwellings in the fields."

7. **σ᾽ … φύξιμος οὐδείς**: "no one can avoid you."

8-9. **ἁμερίων … ἀνθρώπων**: "of men that last but a day," i.e., "of mortal
men."

9. **μέμηνεν**: from μέμηνα, perfect of μαίνομαι with present meaning =
"is mad."

10-11. **σὺ … παρασπᾷς**: ἀδίκους should be taken proleptically, i.e., "you
wrest aside the minds even of just men (so that they become) unjust."

11. **ἐπὶ λώβᾳ**: Doric for ἐπὶ λώβῃ = "to their ruin."

12-13. **καὶ τόδε νεῖκος ἀνδρῶν ξύναιμον**: "this strife of kinsmen also."
Note the hypallage or transferred epithet (ξύναιμον with νεῖκος rather

than ξυναίμων with ἀνδρῶν). The verbal reminiscence of Haemon's name in ξύναιμον is surely deliberate.

13. ἔχεις ταράξας: "you have stirred up," a periphrastic perfect.

14–16. νικᾷ ... νύμφας: "victorious is the desire shining clearly in the eyes of the young bride ready for marriage," as we might say, in the young bride's "bedroom eyes"; νύμφας is the Doric genitive of νυμφή.

16–17. τῶν μεγάλων ... θεσμῶν: "enthroned in power (ἐν ἀρχαῖς) by the side of the great laws." The "great laws" are the unwritten principles of loyalty to country and obedience to parents. The poet's point is that love can be just as powerful—or more so—than these.

17–18. ἐμπαίζει: "mocks [us]" or "plays her games."

18. Ἀφροδίτα: as the hymn began with Eros, so it ends with Aphrodite, thus bringing together the two gods interchangeably seen as responsible for love and all its impulses.

23.6 Euripides, *Medea* 1251–70: Medea is about to kill her children. The appalled chorus lament the futility of her coming to Greece and having a family.

Χορός

ἰὼ Γᾶ τε καὶ παμφαὴς
ἀκτὶς Ἀλίου, κατίδετ᾽ ἴδετε τὰν
ὀλομέναν γυναῖκα, πρὶν φοινίαν
τέκνοις προσβαλεῖν χέρ᾽ αὐτοκτόνον·
σᾶς γὰρ χρυσέας ἀπὸ γονᾶς   5
ἔβλαστεν, θεοῦ δ᾽ αἷμα χαμαὶ πίτνειν
φόβος ὑπ᾽ ἀνέρων.
ἀλλά νιν, ὦ φάος διογενές, κάτειρ-
γε κατάπαυσον, ἔξελ᾽ οἴκων τάλαι-
ναν φονίαν τ᾽ Ἐρινὺν ὑπ᾽ ἀλαστόρων.   10

μάταν μόχθος ἔρρει τέκνων,
μάταν ἄρα γένος φίλιον ἔτεκες, ὦ
κυανεᾶν λιποῦσα Συμπληγάδων
πετρᾶν ἀξενωτάταν ἐσβολάν.
δειλαία, τί σοι φρενοβαρὴς   15
χόλος προσπίτνει καὶ ζαμενὴς φόνου

φόνος ἀμείβεται;
χαλεπὰ γὰρ βροτοῖς ὁμογενῆ μιά-
σματ᾽, ἕπεται δ᾽ ἅμ᾽ αὐτοφόνταις ξυνῳδὰ θεόθεν πίτνοντ᾽ ἐπὶ δόμοις ἄχη.   20

Notes: The meter of this choral song is dochmiac, a rhythm very well adapted to high emotion. The basic metrical unit (in which x can be long or short) is x - - x –, but any of the long syllables can be resolved into two shorts.

1. **Γᾶ:** = Γῆ: in the Doric dialect which is a feature of the choral lyrics of Greek tragedy, alpha is often used when Attic would have used eta. This will not be commented on again.

2. **κατίδετ᾽:** "look down upon."

3. **ὀλομέναν:** "accursed."

4. **αὐτοκτόνον:** "kin-destroying."

5–6. **σᾶς ... χρυσέας ἀπὸ γονᾶς ἔβλαστεν:** "they were born from your golden seed." Medea is the granddaughter of the Sun, and thus her children are from the Sun's seed.

6–7. **θεοῦ ... αἶμα χαμαὶ πίτνειν φόβος ὑπ᾽ ἀνέρων:** "it is frightening [lit. (there is) fear] for the blood of a god to fall on the ground at the hands of men"; ἀνέρων = ἄνδρων.

9. **ἔξελ᾽:** aorist imperative of ἐξαιρέω.

9–10. **τάλαιναν φονίαν τ᾽ Ἐρινὺν ὑπ᾽ ἀλαστόρων:** "a Fury (made) wretched and murderous by demons."

11. **μάταν μόχθος ἔρρει τέκνων:** "(your [i.e., Medea's]) labor over (your children) is gone in vain," i.e., "was for nothing."

13–14. **κυανεᾶν λιποῦσα Συμπληγάδων πετρᾶν ἀξενωτάταν ἐσβολάν:** "you who left the most inhospitable mouth of the dark-blue Symplegades (the Clashing Rocks)." In Doric, feminine genitive plurals end in alpha nu and not omega nu: hence πετρᾶν.

15. **φρενοβαρής:** "that weighs on the mind."

16–17. **ζαμενὴς φόνου φόνος ἀμείβεται:** "does raging murder follow upon murder?"

18–19. **ὁμογενῆ μιάσματ᾽:** (neuter plural) "pollution arising from the slaying of kin."

19–20. **ἕπεται ... ἅμ᾽ αὐτοφόνταις ξυνῳδὰ ... ἄχη:** lit. "appropriate (harmonious) griefs follow along with kin murderers," i.e., "murderers are dogged by woes harmonious with their deeds."

23.7 Aristophanes, *Frogs*, 1198–1221: in a competition to decide which of them is the better poet, Aeschylus sets about destroying Euripides' prologues with a little oil-flask.

Αἰσχύλος   Εὐριπίδης   Διόνυσος

Αἰ. καὶ μὴν μὰ τὸν Δί᾽ οὐ κατ᾽ ἔπος γέ σου κνίσω
τὸ ῥῆμ᾽ ἕκαστον, ἀλλὰ σὺν τοῖσιν θεοῖς
ἀπὸ ληκυθίου σου τοὺς προλόγους διαφθερῶ.

Εὐ. ἀπὸ ληκυθίου σὺ τοὺς ἐμούς; **Αἰ.** ἑνὸς μόνου.
ποιεῖς γὰρ οὕτως ὥστ᾽ ἐναρμόττειν ἅπαν,   5
καὶ κῳδάριον καὶ ληκύθιον καὶ θύλακον,
ἐν τοῖς ἰαμβείοισι. δείξω δ᾽ αὐτίκα.

Εὐ. ἰδού, σὺ δείξεις; **Αἰ.** φημί. **Εὐ.** καὶ δὴ χρὴ λέγειν.
Αἴγυπτος, ὡς ὁ πλεῖστος ἔσπαρται λόγος,
ξὺν παισὶ πεντήκοντα ναυτίλῳ πλάτῃ   10
Ἄργος κατασχών—**Αἰ.** ληκύθιον ἀπώλεσεν.

Δι. τουτὶ τί ἦν τὸ ληκύθιον; οὐ κλαύσεται;
λέγ᾽ ἕτερον αὐτῷ πρόλογον, ἵνα καὶ γνῶ πάλιν.

Εὐ. Διόνυσος, ὃς θύρσοισι καὶ νεβρῶν δοραῖς
καθαπτὸς ἐν πεύκαισι Παρνασσὸν κάτα   15
πηδᾷ χορεύων—**Αἰ.** ληκύθιον ἀπώλεσεν.

Δι. οἴμοι πεπλήγμεθ᾽ αὖθις ὑπὸ τῆς ληκύθου.

Εὐ. ἀλλ᾽ οὐδὲν ἔσται πρᾶγμα· πρὸς γὰρ τουτονὶ
τὸν πρόλογον οὐχ ἕξει προσάψαι λήκυθον.
'οὐκ ἔστιν ὅστις πάντ᾽ ἀνὴρ εὐδαιμονεῖ·   20
ἢ γὰρ πεφυκὼς ἐσθλὸς οὐκ ἔχει βίον,
ἢ δυσγενὴς ὤν—**Αἰ.** ληκύθιον ἀπώλεσεν.

Δι. Εὐριπίδη—**Εὐ.** τί ἔσθ᾽; **Δι.** ὑφέσθαι μοι δοκεῖ·
τὸ ληκύθιον γὰρ τοῦτο πνευσεῖται πολύ.

Notes: 1. **καὶ μὴν μὰ τὸν Δί᾽**: "Well now, by Zeus."
κατ᾽ ἔπος γέ: "just word by word."
1–2. **σου . . . τὸ ῥῆμ᾽ ἕκαστον**: "each phrase of yours."
3. **ἀπὸ ληκυθίου**: "with a little oil-flask."
4. **ἀπὸ ληκυθίου σὺ τοὺς ἐμούς;**: understand διαφθερεῖς.
5–7. **ὥστ᾽ ἐναρμόττειν ἅπαν . . . ἐν τοῖς ἰαμβείοισι**: "that everything . .
. fits into your iambics."
8. **ἰδού, σὺ δείξεις;**: very scornful = "Ah look! You're going to show us,
are you?"
φημί: "Yes, I am."

καὶ δή: "Well, then."

9–11. Ἄἴγυπτος . . . κατασχών: these are the opening lines of Euripides' lost play *Archelaus*. Since, however, in later times the play is known to have started with different words, it seems likely that the version we have here was the original one and that it was altered later, either by Euripides himself or by another hand; ὡς . . . λόγος: "as the widely-circulated report has been spread abroad." ἔσπαρται is the perfect passive (third singular) of σπείρω; ναυτίλῳ πλάτῃ: lit. "with ship's oar" = "by ship."

12. τουτί: = τοῦτο with the deictic iota ("this here little oil-flask").

οὐ κλαύσεται;: "will he (i.e., Aeschylus) not lament?" = "he'll regret this."

13. γνῶ: aorist subjunctive (third singular) of γιγνώσκω.

14–16. Διόνυσος . . . χορεύων: the prologue of Euripides' *Hypsipyle*; καθαπτός: "equipped."

17. οἴμοι πεπλήγμεθ': "Ah me! We are smitten . . ." Dionysus' first person plural here, in this mock-tragic reminiscence of Agamemnon's dying cry (cf. Aesch., *Agamemnon* 1345), shows that he is firmly on Euripides' side. Despite this support, clearly seen from the very beginning of the play, it is Aeschylus who is eventually chosen as victor.

18. οὐδὲν ἔσται πρᾶγμα: "it won't matter."

19. οὐχ ἕξει: "he won't be able."

20–22. οὐκ ἔστιν . . . δυσγενὴς ὤν: the beginning of the prologue of Euripides' *Stheneboea*; πάντ' . . . εὐδαιμονεῖ : "is happy in everything." πάντ(α) is an accusative of respect; ἐσθλός: "noble"; βίον: "livelihood."

23. ὑφέσθαι μοι δοκεῖ: "it seems best to me to lower sail," i.e., to take care.

24. πνευσεῖται πολύ: "is going to blow a gale." πνευσεῖται is Doric for πνεύσεται.

23.8 Aristophanes, *Clouds* 1–18: Strepsiades can't sleep for worrying about the debts that his son, a horse-racing enthusiast, has built up.

Στρεψιάδης

ἰοὺ ἰού·
ὦ Ζεῦ βασιλεῦ τὸ χρῆμα τῶν νυκτῶν ὅσον·
ἀπέραντον. οὐδέποθ' ἡμέρα γενήσεται;
καὶ μὴν πάλαι γ' ἀλεκτρυόνος ἤκουσ' ἐγώ·
οἱ δ' οἰκέται ῥέγκουσιν· ἀλλ' οὐκ ἂν πρὸ τοῦ.   5

ἀπόλοιο δῆτ᾽, ὦ πόλεμε, πολλῶν οὕνεκα,
ὅτ᾽ οὐδὲ κολάσ᾽ ἔξεστί μοι τοὺς οἰκέτας.
ἀλλ᾽ οὐδ᾽ ὁ χρηστὸς οὑτοσὶ νεανίας
ἐγείρεται τῆς νυκτός, ἀλλὰ πέρδεται
ἐν πέντε σισύραις ἐγκεκορδυλημένος.   10
ἀλλ᾽ εἰ δοκεῖ ῥέγκωμεν ἐγκεκαλυμμένοι.
ἀλλ᾽ οὐ δύναμαι δείλαιος εὕδειν δακνόμενος
ὑπὸ τῆς δαπάνης καὶ τῆς φάτνης καὶ τῶν χρεῶν
διὰ τουτονὶ τὸν υἱόν. ὁ δὲ κόμην ἔχων
ἱππάζεταί τε καὶ ξυνωρικεύεται   15
ὀνειροπολεῖ θ᾽ ἵππους· ἐγὼ δ᾽ ἀπόλλυμαι
ὁρῶν ἄγουσαν τὴν σελήνην εἰκάδας·
οἱ γὰρ τόκοι χωροῦσιν.

Notes: 1. **ἰοὺ ἰού**: a cry of distress.

2. **τὸ χρῆμα τῶν νυκτῶν ὅσον**: lit. "how great is the business of the nights," i.e., "how these nights drag on!"

4. **καὶ μήν**: "and yet."

5. **οὐκ ἂν πρὸ τοῦ**: "they would not (have snored) before this," i.e., "they would not have behaved like this before." Athens was at war and slaves who felt ill-treated would find it comparatively easy to escape and find refuge with her enemies.

7. **κολάσ᾽**: κολάσαι (aorist infinitive).
ἔξεστί: "it is possible."

8. **οὐδ(έ)**: the point is that Strepsiades is awake while his son most decidedly is not. Simply translate "not."

9. **πέρδεται**: "he farts."

10. **ἐν πέντε σισύραις ἐγκεκορδυλημένος**: "swathed in five goat-hair cloaks."

11. **ἀλλ᾽ εἰ δοκεῖ**: lit. "but if it seems good," i.e., "well, all right then."

13. **τῆς φάτνης**: lit. "a manger," but here referring to a stable of horses.

14. **κόμην**: i.e., "long hair."

15. **ξυνωρικεύεται**: "drives a two-horse chariot."

16. **ὀνειροπολεῖ θ᾽ ἵππους**: "and dreams horses."

17. **ἄγουσαν τὴν σελήνην εἰκάδας**: lit. "the moon going through its twenties," i.e., "the (lunar) month nearing its end." Interest on the money borrowed to fund his son's expensive habit had to be paid at the end of the month.

18. **οἱ ... τόκοι χωροῦσιν**: i.e., "the interest mounts up." οἱ τόκοι is plural, which explains the number of the verb (lit. "go").

23.9   Theocritus 11.17–37: the Cyclops, a one-eyed giant, woos the extremely resistant nymph Galatea.

ἀλλὰ τὸ φάρμακον εὗρε, καθεζόμενος δ᾽ ἐπὶ πέτρας
ὑψηλᾶς ἐς πόντον ὁρῶν ἄειδε τοιαῦτα.
Ὦ λευκὰ Γαλάτεια, τί τὸν φιλέοντ᾽ ἀποβάλλῃ;
λευκοτέρα πακτᾶς ποτιδεῖν, ἁπαλωτέρα ἀρνός,
μόσχω γαυροτέρα, σφριγανωτέρα ὄμφακος ὠμᾶς.	5
φοιτῇς δ᾽ αὖθ᾽ οὕτως, ὅκκα γλυκὺς ὕπνος ἔχῃ με,
οἴχῃ δ᾽ εὐθὺς ἰοῖσ᾽, ὅκκα γλυκὺς ὕπνος ἀνῇ με,
φεύγεις δ᾽ ὥσπερ ὄις πολιὸν λύκον ἀθρήσασα.
ἠράσθην μὲν ἔγωγα τεοῦς, κόρα, ἁνίκα πρᾶτον
ἦνθες ἐμᾷ σὺν ματρὶ θέλοισ᾽ ὑακίνθινα φύλλα	10
ἐξ ὄρεος δρέψασθαι, ἐγὼ δ᾽ ὁδὸν ἁγεμόνευον.
παύσασθαι δ᾽ ἐσιδών τυ καὶ ὕστερον οὐδέ τί πα νῦν
ἐκ τήνω δύναμαι· τὶν δ᾽ οὐ μέλει, οὐ μὰ Δί᾽ οὐδέν.
γινώσκω, χαρίεσσα κόρα, τίνος ὤνεκα φεύγεις·
ὤνεκά μοι λασία μὲν ὀφρῦς ἐπὶ παντὶ μετώπῳ	15
ἐξ ὠτὸς τέταται ποτὶ θὤτερον ὣς μία μακρά,
εἷς δ᾽ ὀφθαλμὸς ὕπεστι, πλατεῖα δὲ ῥὶς ἐπὶ χείλει.
ἀλλ᾽ οὗτος τοιοῦτος ἐὼν βοτὰ χίλια βόσκω,
κἠκ τούτων τὸ κράτιστον ἀμελγόμενος γάλα πίνω·
τυρὸς δ᾽ οὐ λείπει μ᾽ οὔτ᾽ ἐν θέρει οὔτ᾽ ἐν ὀπώρᾳ,	20
οὐ χειμῶνος ἄκρω· ταρσοὶ δ᾽ ὑπεραχθέες αἰεί.

Notes: 1. **τὸ φάρμακον**: "the medicine," i.e., for love.
εὗρε: the Cyclops is the subject.
4. **πακτᾶς ποτιδεῖν**: "than cream-cheese to look at": note the Doric form **ποτιδεῖν** (Attic πακτᾶς προσιδεῖν): Theocritus came from Syracuse. **ἀρνός**: "than a lamb," a genitive of comparison.
5. **μόσχω γαυροτέρα, σφριγανωτέρα ὄμφακος ὠμᾶς**: "more skittish than a calf, more plump than ripening grapes." μόσχω is a Doric genitive.
6. **φοιτῇς δ᾽ αὖθ᾽ οὕτως, ὅκκα**: "you come immediate in this way, when ..." αὖθι = αὐτίκα.
7. **ἰοῖσ᾽**: "going" (Attic ἰοῦσα).
9. **τεοῦς**: = τευ = Attic σου.

ἁνίκα: = Attic ἡνίκα.

πρᾶτον: Attic πρῶτον.

10. ἦνθες: = Attic ἦλθες: "you came."

ἐμᾷ: = Attic ἐμῇ.

ὑακίνθινα φύλλα: "hyacinth plants."

11. ἁγεμόνευον: "I led the way (along...)"

12–13. παύσασθαι δ᾽ ἐσιδών τυ ... ἐκ τήνω δύναμαι: lit. "after I saw you, from then on (ἐκ τήνω) I cannot stop (loving you)." The negative comes from οὐδέ. τυ = Attic σε. καὶ ὕστερον οὐδέ τί πᾳ νῦν: i.e., "neither later nor in any way now."

13. τίν: = Attic σοί.

οὐ μὰ Δί᾽: "no, by Zeus": the three negatives add emphasis to the Cyclops' comment that she doesn't care a fig for his devotion.

14. γινώσκω: Attic γιγνώσκω.

τίνος ὥνεκα: "why."

15. ὥνεκά: "because."

16. ἐξ ὠτὸς τέταται ποτὶ θὥτερον: "stretches [lit. has been stretched] from one ear to the other."

ὡς μία μακρά: "a single long one."

18. βοτά: "grazing animals."

19. κἠκ: καί ἐκ.

ἀμελγόμενος: "milking."

21. χειμῶνος ἄκρω: "in the depths of winter."

ταρσοὶ ... ὑπεραχθέες αἰεί: "my crates are always over-burdened."

23.10 Callimachus, *Epigrammata* 2: "They told me Heraclitus": Callimachus muses that even though his old friend Heraclitus has died, his poetry will live on.

εἶπέ τις, Ἡράκλειτε, τεὸν μόρον, ἐς δέ με δάκρυ
  ἤγαγεν, ἐμνήσθην δ᾽ ὁσσάκις ἀμφότεροι
ἥλιον ἐν λέσχῃ κατεδύσαμεν· ἀλλὰ σὺ μέν που,
  ξεῖν᾽ Ἁλικαρνησεῦ, τετράπαλαι σποδιή·
αἱ δὲ τεαὶ ζώουσιν ἀηδόνες, ᾗσιν ὁ πάντων   5
  ἁρπακτὴς Ἀίδης οὐκ ἐπὶ χεῖρα βαλεῖ.

Notes: 1. Ἡράκλειτε: not the pre-Socratic philosopher of that name, but a poet of the third century BC, some two hundred years later. τεόν: Ionic for σόν. Cf. too τεαί in line 5.

2–3. ἐμνήσθην ... κατεδύσαμεν: the famous version of this poem by William Johnson Cory (1823–1892) captures in memorable words the idea of "setting the sun in conversation": "*I wept as I remembered how often you and I / had tired the sun with talking and sent him down the sky*"; ὁσσάκις is Ionic for ὁσάκις ("how often").

3. **ἀλλὰ σὺ μέν που**: "now you, I suppose."

4. **ξεῖν᾽ Ἁλικαρνησεῦ**: "my friend from Halicarnassus." Both these words have Ionic forms. In Attic they would be ξέν᾽ Ἁλικαρνασσεῦ.

τετράπαλαι σποδιή: understand εἶ, i.e., "are long, long ago a heap of ashes." τετράπαλαι literally means "four times long ago," and σποδίη is Ionic for σποδία.

5. **αἱ δὲ τεαὶ . . . ἀηδόνες**: "your nightingales" i.e., your poems.

6. **ἐπὶ . . . βαλεῖ**: tmesis for ἐπιβαλεῖ.

APPENDICES

The Greek Writers

Aeschylus (525–456 BC)

The earliest of the three great Attic writers of tragedy, and the true founder of the genre, Aeschylus was born at Eleusis, took part in the Persian Wars, and eventually died at Gela in Sicily. Six of his eighty to ninety plays survive, including the sole trilogy to have come down to us, the *Oresteia*, comprising *Agamemnon, Choephoroe* and *Eumenides*. His death is said to have been caused by an eagle dropping a tortoise on his bald head, thinking that it was a stone on which he could break open the shell.

Andocides (c. 440–c. 390 BC)

A member of an established aristocratic Athenian family, Andocides, although not a trained or professional orator, has left us three speeches (it is now generally believed that the *In Alcibiadem* is of separate authorship), two of them related to his own involvement in the Mutilation of the Herms and profanation of the Eleusinian Mysteries in 415 BC (cf. Chapter 8.8). All are conspicuous for their clarity of expression and eloquent persuasiveness.

Antiphon (c. 480–411 BC)

The earliest of the surviving Attic orators, he gained a fine reputation as a *logographos*, a writer of speeches for others to deliver on their own behalf. He was involved in the oligarchic revolution and the establishment of the rule of the Four Hundred in Athens in 411, and was put to death by the restored democracy. His speech *On the Murder of Herodes* is the most famous of his surviving works.

Appian (active c. 160 AD)

Originally a native of Alexandria, Appian practiced as a lawyer in Rome and wrote narratives, in Greek, of Roman victories up until the accession of the emperor Vespasian in 69 AD. Of his twenty-five books, nine survive complete, and we have substantial fragments of a number of others as well.

Aristophanes (c. 485–c. 385 BC)

Beyond the facts that he was born in Athens and may have lived or owned property on Aegina, virtually nothing is known of the life of Aristophanes, the greatest of the writers of Old Attic Comedy. Eleven of his plays survive, extracts from four of them featuring in this volume. Aristophanic comedy is famous for its colorful and imaginative language, and for the exaggerated and satirical nature of its humor.

Arrian (c. 86–c. 160 AD)

A Greek from Nicomedia, Flavius Arrianus was an officer in the Roman army, suffect consul in 129 or 130, and governor of Cappadocia from 131 to 137 AD. He retired to Athens and was archon there in 145–46. The most famous of his various surviving works are the *Anabasis Alexandri*, seven books narrating the campaigns of Alexander the Great. An eighth book, the *Indica*, describes in a pretty wooden imitation of the language and style of Herodotus the land and customs of India.

Callimachus (310/305–240 BC)

Born in Cyrene in North Africa, Callimachus spent most of his life in Alexandria, producing for King Ptolemy II Philadelphus of Egypt a catalogue, in 120 volumes, of all the books in the famous library there. Of his more than eight hundred works, only six hymns and some sixty epigrams survive intact. His enthusiasm for the small scale in literature is well exemplified by one of his most famous fragments, which states that "a big book is a big evil": μέγα βιβλίον μέγα κακόν.

Demosthenes (384–322 BC)

Born in Athens, the son of a wealthy manufacturer of swords and cutlery, Demosthenes was to become the greatest of all the Attic orators. Orphaned at the age of seven, in 364 he successfully prosecuted his guardian for the mismanagement of his property, overcoming the problem of a weak voice, it is said, by practicing speaking aloud with pebbles in his mouth or on the sea shore, to accustom himself to the noise and confusion of the Athenian lawcourts. Sixty-one surviving speeches are attributed to him, not all of them necessarily authentic. These include both private orations delivered in the lawcourts and some great civic speeches on public policy, particularly on the necessity of opposing the encroaching power of Philip of Macedon, father of Alexander the Great. The most famous of these is *De Corona*, delivered against Aeschines, Demosthenes' great political adversary, in 330 BC. Demosthenes' patriotic opposition to the power of Macedon was ultimately unsuccessful, and in 322, rather than submit to being taken alive for execution at the behest of Antipater, Alexander's successor, he allegedly sucked poison concealed in the end of his pen and died.

Euripides (c. 485–406 BC)

The youngest of the three great Athenian tragedians, Euripides was much affected by the intellectual issues of his age, but seems to have played no prominent part in the civic life of his home state. In all he wrote more than ninety plays, of which some eighteen still survive. His brand of tragedy is characterized by a more subversive tone than that of either Aeschylus or Sophocles: prominence is given to unconventional views, to women, or to slaves; and heroes, down on their luck, may be dressed in rags and lament their plight in ordinary words and terms that are all too human. Aristotle quotes Sophocles

as having remarked that he represented people as they should be,
Euripides as they are. The story goes that after the Athenian disaster
in Sicily in 413, some prisoners won their freedom by being able to
quote passages from Euripides' plays.

Herodotus (c. 490–325 BC)

Herodotus was the first great Greek historian, who wrote in his
Histories an account of the wars between the Persians and the
Greeks at the beginning of the fifth century BC. Born in the Ionian
city of Halicarnassus, he had a keen interest in the ways of life not
only of Greeks but also of Asians and Egyptians. Cicero dubbed
him "the father of history."

Homer (active c. 750 BC)

About the life of the poet whom we call Homer, and whom we
regard as the author of the great epics that stand on the threshold
of Western literature, the *Iliad* and the *Odyssey*, we know absolutely
nothing for certain. Right from ancient times people have wanted
to know more about who Homer was, where he came from, when he
lived, and whether, indeed, he was one or two people, or even more.
Not to get bogged down in the historical details of this so-called
Homeric question, it is fair to say that today scholars generally agree
that the two monumental poems were each conceived as a unity by
a single poet (or perhaps by two poets), in Ionia, in the latter part of
the eighth century BC, and at or near the end of a long tradition of
oral poetry, whereby poetic accounts of what Homer himself would
call the κλέα ἀνδρῶν, the glorious deeds of the heroes of old, were
passed down orally from generation to generation in a language that
was a strange literary amalgam of different dialects, from different
parts of the Greek world and from various periods of history.

Isocrates (436–338 BC)

The Athenian Isocrates was the first significant orator to treat
rhetorical prose as a work of art. His political writings were chiefly
devoted to the cause of Greek unity. Among his other works are

a wonderful *Encomium of Helen*, "proving" that the woman who caused the Trojan War had nothing to apologize for.

Lucian (c. 115–after 180 AD)

Born at Samasota on the River Euphrates in Syria, Lucian wrote about eighty prose pieces in various forms, i.e., essays, speeches, letters, dialogues, and stories, mainly satirical in content. He had a delightful sense of the fantastic.

Lysias (c. 458–c. 380 BC)

Lysias, an Athenian orator, was a member of a metic (resident alien) family from Syracuse. As a metic, he could not appear in the law court in person, but he proved a highly successful ghost-writer for Athenian citizens in cases ranging from murder and treason to adultery and embezzlement.

Menander (342–c. 292 BC)

The Athenian Menander was the greatest writer of Attic New Comedy. His plays were lost in the seventh and eighth centuries AD, but in the twentieth century numerous papyrus finds have brought to light one complete play and substantial fragments of others. The Alexandrian scholar Aristophanes of Byzantium is quoted as exclaiming, "O Menander and Life, which of you copied the other!"

New Testament

The excerpts from books of the Bible are, of course, from the Greek New Testament. The Gospel writers, Matthew, Mark, Luke and John, have provided most of our passages, including the extract from the *Acts of the Apostles* (written by St Luke), but there is also one example of St. Paul's writing, from his *First Epistle to the Corinthians*.

Pindar (518–after 446 BC)

Pindar was a Greek lyric poet who was born in Boeotia near Thebes. Writing in the literary Dorian dialect, he composed poems celebrating victories at the four Greek Panhellenic Games (Olympian, Pythian,

Nemean, and Isthmian). He achieved great fame both in his lifetime and afterwards. When Alexander the Great sacked Thebes in 335 BC, he ordered that Pindar's house should be spared.

Plato (427–347 BC)

The greatest of the Greek philosophers, the Athenian Plato, was a pupil of Socrates and most of his works are cast as dialogues between that philosopher and a vast range of interlocutors. His influence on the history of philosophy has been immense. He founded the Academy in Athens, a school not only of philosophy but also of science and math. Over the door was the inscription ἀγεωμέτρητος μηδεὶς εἰσίτω ("Let no-one ignorant of geometry enter here").

Sophocles (c. 496–406/405 BC)

One of the three great Attic writers of tragedy, Sophocles also served as an Athenian general. Seven of his tragedies and a substantial fragment of a comic play survive. The poet Shelley had a volume of Sophocles in his pocket when he was drowned in 1822.

Theocritus (active c. 275 BC)

A Sicilian poet who lived in the first half of the third century BC, Theocritus was the creator of the genre of pastoral poetry. The poet John Dryden considered that his Doric dialect had "an incomparable sweetness in its clownishness."

Thucydides (c. 500–c. 399 BC)

The great Athenian historian wrote his History of the Peloponnesian War between Athens and her allies and Sparta and hers. He played a part in the war as an unsuccessful general and was exiled. His bleak analysis of human motivation has been enormously influential. He described his history as a κτῆμα ἐς αἰεί, "a possession for ever."

Vitruvius (c. 80/70–after 15 BC)

Vitruvius was a Roman engineer and architect of the first century BC. He saw military service under Julius Caesar. His treatise in ten books *On Architecture* is dedicated to the first Roman emperor, Augustus.

Xenophon (c. 428–c. 354 BC)

The Athenian Xenophon is best known as a historian. His *Anabasis* (*Journey Upland*) covers the expedition of ten thousand Greeks who had gone to Persia to support Cyrus, an aspirant to the Persian throne. Cyrus was killed and the Greeks found themselves adrift on the huge Asian land mass; but, operating under Xenophon's inspiring leadership, they eventually saw the prospect of safety when, with a cry of θάλαττα θάλαττα ("The sea! The sea!"), they caught sight of the sea that would enable them to sail home to Greece. An uncomprehending student of Socrates, Xenophon wrote on a number of subjects, including the education of Cyrus the Great, King of Persia from 559 to 529 BC.

Dialect

SOME KEY FEATURES OF HOMERIC DIALECT

The Greek after the equation marks is Attic.

1 The augment may be omitted—λῦσε = ἔλῦσε (he loosed), βῆ = ἔβη (he went).

2 Nominative singular: Attic -ᾱ always appears as -η: θύρη (door), χώρη (country). But N.B. θεά (goddess): there is no Attic equivalent.

3 Genitive singular in -οιο: δώροιο = δώρου (of a gift); also in -ᾱο, -εω: Ἀτρείδᾱο and Ἀτρείδεω = Ἀτρείδου (of the son of Atreus).

4 Dative plural:

(a) Where Attic has -αις we find -ῃς or -ῃσι: θύρῃσι = θύραις (doors), πύλῃσι = πύλαις (gates); τῇς and τῇσι = ταῖς (definite article, relative pronoun).

(b) 2nd declension words can end -οισι: δώροισι = δώροις (gifts).

(c) 3rd declension words can end -(σ)σι or -εσσι: πόδεσσι and ποσσί = ποσί (feet); βελέεσσι, βέλεσσι and βέλεσι = βέλεσι (missiles).

The moveable nu can be added to all of these.

5 The definite article:

(a) most commonly means "he," "she," "it," "they," or "this," "that."

(b) οἱ and αἱ appear also as τοί and ταί.

(c) Forms identical with the definite article are used as the relative pronoun, though the masculine nominative singular of the relative is ὅς as in Attic.

6 The use of the enclitics οἱ (to him, to her) and τοι (to you, sing.).

7 Active infinitives often end in -μεν or its extended form -μεναι: ἀκουέμεναι = ἀκούειν (to hear); τεθνάμεν(αι) = τεθνάναι (to be dead); ἔμεν, ἔμμεν, ἔμεναι, ἔμμεναι = εἶναι (to be).

8 Homer generally does not contract verbs ending in -έω, -άω, and -όω, which would contract in Attic.

9 κεν (κε, κ') can be used as well as ἄν, with the same force.

10 Tmesis, i.e., the separation of a preposition that is the prefix to a verb, from that verb: πρὸς μῦθον ἔειπεν = μῦθον προσεῖπεν (he addressed a word).

11 Particles frequently used in Homer:

ἄρα, ἄρ, ῥα	so, next (for transition)
δή	indeed (for emphasis, often of time)
ἦ	truly, certainly (for emphasis)
περ	just, even (for emphasis); although
τε	and; you know, let me tell you (to show that a comment is generalizing)
τοι	I tell you (for assertion); can also = σοι (to you)

SOME KEY FEATURES OF HERODOTUS' IONIC DIALECT

The Greek after the equation marks is Attic.

1 Herodotus often has η where Attic has ᾱ (especially after ε, ι, ρ): ἡμέρη = ἡμέρᾱ (day); πρῆγμα = πρᾶγμα (business, affair).

2 Herodotus uses -έω for the genitive singular of nouns like νεηνίης (= νεᾱνίᾱς, young man): νεηνίεω = νεᾱνίου.

3 Herodotus uses -έων for the genitive plural of nouns like τῑμή, θάλασσα, χώρη, κριτής: Περσέων = Περσῶν (of the Persians). (This is contracted in Attic.)

4 Dative plurals of the first and second declensions end in -σι: ἀγροῖσι (fields), τοῖσι (definite article), τούτοισι (these).

5 Herodotus uses σσ where Attic has ττ: θάλασσα = θάλαττα (sea), πρήσσω = πρᾱττω (I do).

6 Herodotus can have:

ει for Attic ε: ξεῖνος = ξένος (foreigner, guest, host)
ου for Attic ο: μοῦνος = μόνος (alone)
ηϊ for Attic ει: οἰκήϊος = οἰκεῖος (private, home-grown).

7 Herodotus often does not contract verbs ending in -έω which would contract in Attic: φιλέω = φιλῶ (I like), ποιέειν = ποιεῖν (to make). νόος (mind) does not contract.

8 Herodotus often does not contract nouns that have contracted forms in Attic, e.g., γένος (race): gen. sg. γένεος = γένους, nom. and acc. pl. γένεα = γένη. Compare σεο = σου (of you).

9 Herodotus can have ευ in place of Attic εο or ου: σευ (for σεο = σου, of you), μευ = μου (of me), ποιεύμενα (for ποιεόμενα = ποιούμενα, things being done), ποιεῦμεν = ποιοῦμεν (we do).

10 Herodotus uses forms identical with the definite article as the relative pronoun, though the masculine nom. singular of the relative is ὅς as in Attic.

11 With a few exceptions, there were no "h" sounds in Ionic. Thus aspiration is often omitted: ἀπικνέομαι = ἀφικνέομαι (I arrive); μετίημι = μεθίημι (I let go).

12 The following Herodotean forms are well worth noting:

Herodotus		Attic
ἐμεωυτόν (acc.)	myself	ἐμαυτόν
ἑωυτόν (acc.)	himself	ἑαυτόν
ἐών, ἐοῦσα, ἐόν	being	ὤν, οὖσα, ὄν

κοῖος (ὁκοῖος)	of what kind	ποῖος (ὁποῖος)
κότε (ὁκότε)	when	πότε (ὁπότε)
κῶς (ὅκως)	how	πῶς (ὅπως)
μιν (acc.—enclitic)	him, her	no comparable form
οἱ (dat.—enclitic)	to him, to her, to it	rare in Attic[1]
ὦν	therefore	οὖν

NEW TESTAMENT GREEK[2]

The Greek of the New Testament differs significantly from that of Plato or Xenophon. But it is not (as was once thought) a special variety of Greek used by Jews of the Near East, or by the Holy Spirit. On the whole, it reflects the everyday Greek of the first century AD.

Because of the political and commercial power of Athens, as well as the prestige of its literature, Attic became the dominant Greek dialect in the late fifth century BC. It gradually evolved (with an admixture of Ionic elements) into the so-called Koinē (ἡ κοινὴ διάλεκτος = the common dialect) of the Hellenistic period. The main catalyst was the fourth-century rise of Macedon under Philip the Second and his son Alexander the Great. The Macedonians were anxious to assert their Greekness (Demosthenes called them barbarians; 3.16, 3.24, etc.), but their own language (apparently unintelligible to other Greeks) lacked the cultural prestige to match their imperial ambitions. "Great Attic," already dominant outside its region of origin, met the need. As Alexander moved eastward through the former Persian empire to the borders of India, founding (according to tradition) seventy cities, this form of Greek was from the outset employed as the official language. It became the universal vernacular of the eastern Mediterranean, a form of Greek simplified and modified to be a suitable vehicle for ordinary people of many races.

The New Testament comes to us in Greek. However, the main language of Jesus and his disciples was Aramaic (a Semitic language

---

1 Except as an indirect reflexive
2 This section was written by Dr John Taylor

related to Hebrew), and the gospel writers give several direct quotations of this. But the culture of Palestine was multilingual. Hebrew was widely spoken around Jerusalem. The inscription on the cross "Jesus of Nazareth, the King of the Jews" was written in Hebrew, Latin, and Greek (*John* 19:20).

Some key features of New Testament Greek:

1. There is a general simplification of both accidence and syntax.

2. In accidence, difficulties and irregularities are frequently ironed out: unusual forms of comparative adjectives are made regular; third declension adjectives are rare; monosyllabic nouns (irregular in declension) are replaced; verbs in -μι are given the endings of verbs in -ω; first (regular) aorist endings often replace 2nd aorists; middle verbs are often replaced by active verbs with reflexive pronouns; the optative is rare; the dual number has disappeared.

3. ἵνα has acquired new roles: it now introduces result clauses, indirect statements and third person direct commands.

4. Purpose is often expressed by the infinitive or by the genitive singular of the definite article with the infinitive: μέλλει γὰρ ὁ Ἡρώδης ζητεῖν τὸ παιδίον, τοῦ ἀπολέσαι αὐτό (*Matt.* 2:13): "for Herod intends to seek the young child (in order) to destroy him."

5. Prepositions are used where the case alone would have sufficed in classical Attic. There are changes in the cases that prepositions take (the accusative advancing at the expense of others). Pronouns are used when the sense would be clear without them. Diminutive forms are used apparently with the same sense as the nouns of which they are diminutives, e.g., βιβλαρίδιον (book), diminutive of βίβλος.

6. There are about nine hundred words (about 10 percent of the total vocabulary) not found in classical authors.

7. There are numerous Semitic idioms, e.g., ἐγένετο introducing another verb (traditionally translated "it came to pass that…").

8. The narrative is generally without complication and clauses tend to follow one after another in a straightforward manner.

Two Important Greek Meters

Most of the verse passages in this collection are written in either the Homeric hexameter or the iambic trimeter. The following fundamental principles of quantity are common to both.

QUANTITY

The scansion of Greek verse is based on quantity, i.e., on whether syllables are light or heavy, not on accent as in English.

Syllable division: in a Greek word, if a vowel is preceded by a consonant, then that consonant will belong to the same syllable, so πατέρα is to be read as πα-τέ-ρα and λήγουσι as λή-γου-σι. If there is a consonant cluster within a word, the syllabic division will normally fall within it, the second of the consonants naturally going with the following vowel: πάντες = πάν-τες, ἔργον = ἔρ-γον, τύραννος = τύ-ραν-νος.

(a) All syllables are heavy if they contain a long vowel or diphthong, e.g., **μῆ**-νιν – ἄ-**ει**-δε. (Note that all vowels with a circumflex accent are long.) For the purposes of scansion, heavy syllables are marked with a macron -, light syllables with the symbol ˘;

(b) If a short vowel is followed by two consonants, whether in the same or in different words, or by the "double consonants" ζ, ξ, ψ, the syllable is heavy, e.g., ἐ-ρί-**σαν**-τε.

anceps: syllable is either long or short

(c) Exception to rule (b): if a short vowel is followed by a combination of a mute consonant (i.e., β, γ, δ, κ, χ, π, φ, τ, θ) and a liquid (i.e., λ, ρ) or nasal (μ, ν) consonant (in that order), the syllable may be scanned either light or heavy. The combinations are πλ, φλ, κλ, χλ, τλ, θλ, κμ, τμ, θμ, πν, φν, κν, χν, θν, τν, πρ, φρ, βρ, κρ, χρ, γρ, τρ, θρ, δρ. This is a matter of syllable division. With the word πατρός (of a father), the division πατρ-ός will lead to the first syllable being heavy, while the division πα-τρός will cause it to be light. In Homer, the syllable ending in (or followed by) these combinations is almost always heavy. In comedy, light syllables are the rule. In tragedy both light and heavy are found.

THE HOMERIC HEXAMETER

The verse of Homeric and all classical epic poetry is the dactylic hexameter, which consists of six successive feet, each scanned – ‿‿ (a dactyl), except that

(a) The sixth dactyl is reduced to two syllables;
(b) Each pair of light syllables may be replaced by a single heavy;
(c) The final syllable of the line may be light or heavy.

The basic scheme is

```
1      2      3      4      5      6

– ‿ ‿ | – ‿ ‿ | – ‿ ‿ | – ‿ ‿ | – ‿ ‿ | – ‿
```

Almost all lines in Homer have a break between words, which we call a *caesura* (*cutting*) in the third foot or fourth foot. If this comes after the heavy syllable it is called a *strong caesura*, and if after the first light one it is called a *weak caesura*. The first line of the *Iliad* has a strong caesura and scans:

$$- \cup \cup | - \cup \cup | - \| - | - \cup \cup | - \cup \cup | - x$$

μῆνιν ἄειδε θεὰ Πηληϊάδεω Ἀχιλῆος (*Iliad* 1.1)

("Sing, goddess, of the anger of Achilles, son of Peleus")

The symbol x = an *anceps*, i.e., a "doubtful" syllable that may be either light or heavy.

Identify the weak caesura in the following line, the first line of the *Odyssey*:

ἄνδρα μοι ἔννεπε, μοῦσα, πολύτροπον, ὃς μάλα πολλά

("Tell me, Muse, of the resourceful man, who [wandered] very much …")

ELISION

A final short α, ε, ο (and occasionally ι) followed by a vowel in the next word may be elided (struck out), e.g., ἄλγε᾽ ἔθηκε where the α at the end of ἄλγεα has been elided. When the first open vowel is left in, both vowels should be scanned. We call such a succession of vowels at the end and beginning of words without elision *hiatus*.

Note:

(a) If the meter demands it, a short vowel can be scanned long, e.g.:
ὣς ἔφατ᾽, ἔδεισεν δ᾽ ὁ γέρων καὶ ἐπείθετο μύθῳ (*Iliad* 1.33)
("Thus he spoke and the old man was afraid and obeyed his word.")
Here the first epsilon in ἔδεισεν, though naturally short, must be scanned long.

(b) By a process we call *correption*, a long vowel or diphthong, standing in hiatus, may be scanned as short. This applies e.g., to καί in *Iliad* 1.33:
ὣς ἔφατ᾽, ἔδεισεν δ᾽ ὁ γέρων καὶ ἐπείθετο μύθῳ (*Iliad* 1.33)

(c) By a process we call *synizesis*, two vowels either within a word or in successive words may be treated as coalescing into a single heavy syllable, for example εω in Πηληϊάδεω in *Iliad* 1.1 (quoted above) and ἢ οὐκ at *Iliad* 9.537. The heavy syllable can be made light by correption, e.g., χρυσέῳ ἀνὰ σκήπτρῳ ("on a golden staff," *Iliad* 1.15 at the start of the line), where the vowels έῳ in χρυσέῳ coalesce into one heavy syllable by synizesis and are then shortened/made light by correption.

THE IAMBIC TRIMETER

The normal meter for the spoken parts of Greek drama is the iambic trimeter. In its simplest form an iambic line is traditionally[1] regarded as consisting of six feet, each of which is one iambus (◡ –). Two feet together produce one iambic *metron*. Each line has therefore three iambic *metra*, hence the name ."iambic trimeter"

A completely iambic line looks like this:

◡ – | ◡ – | ◡ – | ◡ – | ◡ – | ◡ ⏑

ἐκεῖνος εἶ σύ, βούλομαι γὰρ εἰδέναι, (Eur. *Her.* 945; ch. 8.9)

("Are you that man, for I want to know . . .")

This basic scheme permits the following simple variations:

(a) the final syllable of the line may be light rather than heavy;

(b) a spondee (– –) is allowed in the first, third, or fifth foot.

– – | ◡ – | – – | ◡ – | – – | ◡ ◡

πρῶτον μὲν ἤρξω τοῦ λόγου ψευδῶς, ξένε, (Eur. *Suppl.* 403; ch. 2.6)

("First of all, you began your speech falsely, stranger.")

Further, on the assumption that two light syllables are equivalent to one heavy, in tragedy the following so-called resolutions are permitted:

(c) a tribrach (◡ ◡ ◡) is allowed in any of the first four feet;

(d) a dactyl (– ◡ ◡) is allowed in the first or third foot;

(e) an anapaest (◡ ◡ –) can regularly occur in the first foot, but may also appear in any foot at all in order to accommodate a proper name.

Accordingly the whole scheme of the tragic trimeter is as follows:

---

1 Contemporary scholarship largely rejects the division of the trimeter into six feet, preferring to concentrate on the three *metra*. We believe that those just beginning their study of meter will find the traditional analysis a more helpful introduction.

```
⏑ –   |  ⏑ –  |  ⏑ –  |  ⏑ –  |  ⏑ –  |  ⏑ –
– –   |      |  – –  |      |  – –  |  ⏑ ⏑
⏑ ⏑ ⏑ | ⏑ ⏑ ⏑ | ⏑ ⏑ ⏑ | ⏑ ⏑ ⏑ |
– ⏑ ⏑ |      | – ⏑ ⏑ |      |
⏑ ⏑ – |      |      |      |
```

The comic trimeter allows of even more variations: both tribrach and anapaest can appear in any of the first five feet, the dactyl in the first, third, or fifth.

A break between words in the middle of a foot is known as a caesura (see above). It is normal, when scanning, to indicate the principal caesura in the third or fourth foot.

```
⏑   ⏑   ⏑  | ⏑ –  | ⏑  – | ⏑ ‖ –  | ⏑  – | ⏑   –
```

Ἕλενος ἀριστόμαντις, ὃς λέγει σαφῶς, (Soph. *Phil.* 1338; ch. 4.2)
("the excellent seer, Helenus, who says clearly . . .")

Some Literary Terms

ALLITERATION the recurrence of the same or a similar consonant (cf. *assonance*), especially at the beginning of words or syllables:

τὸν δὲ ταύρῳ χαλκέῳ καυτῆρα νηλέα νόον

ἐχθρὰ Φάλαριν κατέχει παντᾷ φάτις. (Pindar, *Pythians* 1.95–96)

Universal condemnation seizes hold of Phalaris, the man of pitiless spirit who burned men in his bronze bull.

The use of alliteration imparts emphasis, and the effect this creates depends on the meaning of the words emphasized.

ANADIPLOSIS the repetition (literally "doubling") of one or several words, e.g., Byron's "The Isles of Greece, the Isles of Greece, Where burning Sappho loved and sung" (*Don Juan*, Canto 3).

Θῆβαι δέ, Θῆβαι πόλις ἀστυγείτων, μεθ᾽ ἡμέραν μίαν ἐκ μέσης τῆς Ἑλλάδος ἀνήρπασται. (Aeschines 3.133)

Thebes, Thebes, a neighbouring city, has been uprooted from the midst of Greece in the course of a single day.

ANAPHORA the repetition of a word or phrase in two or more successive clauses:

οὗτοι γὰρ πολλοὺς μὲν τῶν πολιτῶν εἰς τοὺς πολεμίους ἐξήλασαν, πολλοὺς δ᾽ ἀδίκως ἀποκτείναντες ἀτάφους ἐποίησαν, πολλοὺς δ᾽ ἐπιτίμους ὄντας ἀτίμους κατέστησαν. (Lysias 12.21)

For these men drove many of the citizens out to the enemy, many they
killed unjustly and left unburied, and many who had civic rights they
deprived of them.

ANTITHESIS the contrasting of ideas emphasized by the arrangement
of words:

ὡς **τρὶς** ἂν παρ' ἀσπίδα | στῆναι θέλοιμ' ἂν μᾶλλον ἢ τεκεῖν
ἄπαξ.
(Euripides, *Medea* 250–51)
since I would rather stand three times in the battle line than give birth
once.

APOSIOPESIS a device in which the speaker breaks off before com-
pleting the sentence:

εἴπερ γάρ κ' ἐθέλησιν Ὀλύμπιος ἀστεροπητής | ἐξ ἑδέων
στυφελίξαι... (Homer, *Iliad* 1.580–81)
for if the Olympian lightning-sender wishes to smash us from our
seats...
Here something like "what can we do about it?" must be understood.

APOSTROPHE the author "turns away" (ἀποστρέφεται) from his narrative (told in the third person) to address one of his characters:

οὐδὲ σέθεν, Μενέλαε, θεοὶ μάκαρες λελάθοντο | ἀθάνατοι.
(Homer, *Iliad* 4.127–28)
and you, Menelaus, the gods, the blessed immortals, did not forget.
Homer and other poets appear to use this device to express sympathy
for their characters.

ASSONANCE the occurrence of similar vowel sounds in words close to
each other (cf. *alliteration*):

κατῆγεν ἦγεν ἦγεν ἐς μέλαν πέδον. (Euripides, *Bacchae* 1065)
he pulled the branch down, down, down, to the black ground.
πάθει μάθος. (Aeschylus, *Agamemnon* 177)
through suffering (comes) knowledge.

ASYNDETON the omission of conjunctions (such as "and" or "but")
where these would usually occur:

προσπεσόντες ἐμάχοντο, ἐώθουν ἐωθοῦντο, ἔπαιον ἐπαίοντο.
(Xenophon, *Education of Cyrus* 7.1.38)
falling upon them, they fought, they pushed (and) were pushed, they
struck (and) were struck.

BATHOS the juxtaposition of the intense or important and the trivial:
in Aristophanes' *Birds*, Basileia (Royalty) is the keeper of the thunderbolt of Zeus, of good counsel, good sense, the dockyards, abuse, the
paymaster and the three-obol bits (1538–41).

CHIASMUS (ADJECTIVE **CHIASTIC**) a pair of balanced phrases where
the order of the elements of the second reverses that of the first:

ἓν ... σῶμ' ἔχων καὶ ψυχὴν μίαν (Demosthenes 19.227)
having a single body and a single soul
This patterning can be represented with crossing diagonal lines like the
Greek letter chi:

CLOSURE the sense of completion or resolution at the conclusion of a
literary work or part of a literary work. Often conclusions deny us this
sense of completion. For example, at the end of Homer's *Odyssey*, the
peace that has been established by the hero on his island by his slaughter of the suitors is a disconcertingly uneasy one.

ELLIPSIS the shortening of a sentence or phrase by the omission of
words that can be understood:

ἐξ ὀνύχων λέοντα (Alcaeus 113)
(to judge) a lion by its claws

ENALLAGE AND HYPALLAGE (in practice these terms cannot be
distinguished) the use of the transferred epithet, i.e., transferring an
adjective from the word to which it properly applies to another word in
the same phrase:

νεῖκος ἀνδρῶν ξύναιμον (Sophocles, *Antigone* 794)
kindred strife of men (for strife of kindred men)

ENJAMBEMENT (single-word enjambement) running a sentence over the end of a line of verse and then ending it after the first word of the new line, lending emphasis to that word:

πίπτει πρὸς οὖδας μυρίοις οἰμώγμασιν | Πενθεύς. (Euripides, *Bacchae* 1112–13)
He fell to the ground with innumerable cries of sorrow, did Pentheus.

EUPHEMISM the substitution of a mild or roundabout expression for one considered improper or too harsh or blunt: εὐφρόνη (the kindly time) for "night," Εὐμενίδες (the kindly ones) for the Furies, ἀριστερός (better) for "left," the unlucky side.

HENDIADYS a single idea expressed through two nouns or verbs:

ἐν ἁλὶ κύμασί τε (Euripides, *Helen* 226)
in the sea and the waves (for in the waves of the sea)
The word "hendiadys" is Greek for "one by means of two."

HYPERBATON the dislocation of normal word order, by way of displacing one part of one clause into another; the effect is often impossible to reproduce in a literal English translation of the Greek:

σὺ δὲ αὐτός, ὦ πρὸς θέων, Μένων, τί φῂς ἀρετὴν εἶναι; (Plato, *Meno* 71d)
but you yourself, by the gods, O Meno, what do you say that virtue is?
Here the hyperbaton seems to reflect the informality and emphasis of conversation: "Now you yourself, Meno—come on—what's your opinion?"

HYPERBOLE the use of exaggerated terms, not to be taken literally (cf. *litotes*). Thus μύριοι, which literally means "ten thousand", can (with the accentuation μυρίοι) mean "countless" or "infinite."

HYSTERON PROTERON the reversal of the normal (temporal) order of events:

εἵματά τ᾽ ἀμφιέσασα θυώδεα καὶ λούσασα (Homer, *Odyssey* 5.264)
having dressed him in fragrant robes and washed him

Clearly he was washed first. By his order Homer lays emphasis on what he describes first, which seems to him to be the more important action.

IRONY the expression of one's meaning by using words of the opposite meaning in order to make one's remarks forceful.

DRAMATIC IRONY occurs when a character in a play uses words that have a different meaning for the speaker and for the audience, who know the truth of the situation. This is a device that is employed with particular force by Sophocles. For example, in *Oedipus Tyrannus* he makes highly effective use of the fact that the blind seer Teiresias can see the truth while Oedipus, despite his gift of sight, cannot.

SOCRATIC IRONY the refusal to claim expertise, frequently employed by Socrates to provoke or confuse those in discussion with him.

JUXTAPOSITION the placing of words next to each other for effect (see also *oxymoron*):

δημοβόρος βασιλεύς (Homer, *Iliad* 1.231)
king who feeds on his people

LIMINALITY the use of location, especially involving passing through doors or gates, to make a symbolic point. In Euripides' play, Medea comes out of the house, to which her female role has confined her, to deliver the most assertive feminist manifesto in ancient literature (214).

LITOTES the use of understatement, involving a negative, to emphasize one's meaning (cf. *hyperbole*). Thus, οὐκ ὀλίγοι "not a few" can mean "many" and οὐκ ἀφανής (not obscure) can mean "famous." Cf. οὐδ᾿ οὕτω κακῶς (and not so badly), the words of a man who threw a tile at a dog but hit his stepmother (Plutarch, *Septem Sapientium Convivium* 147c).

METAPHOR the application of a word or phrase to something it does not apply to literally, indicating a comparison, for example "a sea (κλύδων) of troubles":

φωνῇ γὰρ ὁρῶ, τὸ φατιζόμενον. (Sophocles, *Oedipus at Colonus* 138)

for I see by sound, as the saying is.

METONYMY a form of expression by which people or things can take their name from something with which they are associated. Thus θέατρον "a theater" can be used of spectators, ἵππος "a horse" of cavalry, and ἰχθύες "fish" of a fish market. In poetic texts, the names of gods are frequently used to denote their areas of control. Thus Dionysus or Bacchus can mean "wine," Aphrodite "love," etc.; cf. *synecdoche.*

ONOMATOPOEIA words or combinations of words, the sound of which suggests their sense, for example, βρεκεκεκέξ κοάξ κοάξ (the croaking of frogs) in Aristophanes' *Frogs* (209). In the following hexameter line, the rhythm, with its smoothly running light syllables, imitates the rolling of Sisyphus' stone:

αὖτις ἔπειτα πέδονδε κυλίνδετο λᾶας ἀναιδής. (Homer, *Odyssey* 11.598)

then down again to the plain rolled the shameless stone.

OXYMORON the juxtaposition (see above) of two words of contradictory meaning to emphasize the contradiction:

νόμον ἄνομον (Aeschylus, *Agamemnon* 1142)

a discordant song

The word *oxymoron* is Greek for "sharp-blunt" and is an oxymoron itself.

PARADOX a statement that apparently contradicts itself but in fact makes a meaningful point:

εἰ γὰρ ὤφελον, ὦ Κρίτων, οἷοί τ᾽ εἶναι οἱ πολλοὶ τὰ μέγιστα κακὰ ἐργάζεσθαι, ἵνα οἷοί τ᾽ ἦσαν καὶ ἀγαθὰ τὰ μέγιστα. (Plato, *Crito* 44d)

if only, Crito, the majority were able to do the greatest evils, so that they might have been able to do the greatest good deeds as well.

PARONOMASIA a punning play on words:

οὐ γὰρ τὸν τρόπον ἀλλὰ τὸν τόπον μετήλλαξεν. (Aeschines 3.78)
for he changed not his disposition but his position.

PERIPHRASIS a circumlocutory or roundabout way of saying things.
Thus in verse, βλέπειν φάος can mean "to see the light (of day),"
i.e., "to be alive."

PERSONIFICATION the representation of an idea or thing as having
human characteristics. Death is frequently personified in Greek literature, and indeed appears as an actual character in Euripides' *Alcestis*.

PLEONASM the use of words that are superfluous to the literal
meaning:

κεῖτο μέγας μεγαλωστί. (Homer, *Iliad* 16.776)
he lay huge at his huge length.

PROLEPSIS the use of an adjective to anticipate its result; i.e., the
adjective will not be applicable until the action of the verb that controls
it has been completed:

τοῦτον τρέφειν τε καὶ αὔξειν μέγαν (Plato, *Republic* 565c)
to rear and to exalt this man into greatness

σὲ Θῆβαί γ᾽ οὐκ ἐπαίδευσαν κακόν. (Sophocles, *Oedipus at
Colonus* 919)
and yet, Thebes did not train you to be base.

SIMILE a figure of speech in which one thing is compared explicitly
with another; in English, the words "like" or "as" often indicate a simile. In Homer, for example, human beings are frequently compared to
animals or birds. The simile is a notable feature of epic; hence the term
"epic simile."

SYLLEPSIS an expression in which the same word is used in two
phrases in two different ways but makes literal sense in both, e.g., "she
went home in a flood of tears and a sedan chair" (Charles Dickens, *The
Pickwick Papers*) and "Miss Nipper shook her head and a tin canister,
and began unasked to make the tea" (Dickens, *Dombey and Son*):

χρήματα τελοῦντες τούτοις … καὶ χάριτας (Plato, *Crito* 48c)
paying (*literally*) money and paying (*metaphorically*) thanks to his men
Cf. *zeugma.*

SYNECDOCHE a form of expression in which the part is used to imply the whole. Thus δόρυ "plank" can mean "ship," while the other meaning of δόρυ "the shaft of a spear" can lead to "spear" and "war." Cf. *metonymy.*

TAUTOLOGY repeating the same thing in different ways:
ἀγὼν μέγας, | πλήρης στεναγμῶν οὐδὲ δακρύων κενός. (Euripides, *Hecuba* 229–30)
a great contest, full of groans and not empty of tears.

ZEUGMA a figure of speech in which a verb or adjective is applied to two nouns, though it is literally applicable to only one of them, e.g., "with tearful eyes and mind" (cf. *syllepsis*):
οὔτε φωνῶν οὔτε του μορφὴν βροτῶν ὄψει. (Aeschylus, *Prometheus Bound* 21)
you will know (literally, see) neither voice nor form of any of mortals.
The Greek word ζεῦγμα means "a yoking."

Vocabulary

This vocabulary provides an almost complete list of the words used in *A Little Greek Reader*. Readers should be aware that (1) rare words glossed in the notes on passages are not necessarily included; (2) proper names appearing in the titles of passages or in the notes are not usually repeated; (3) irregular futures and aorists, and occasionally other tenses, are routinely provided, though not in the case of compound verbs (which are printed with a hyphen between the prefix and the verb itself); and (4) long α, ι, and υ are marked with a macron in headwords, except where they have a circumflex accent or an iota subscript, but short vowels are never marked.

A

Ἄδμητος ου ὁ Admetus

ἀγαθός ή όν good; brave, strong; noble; honest

— τὸ ἀγαθόν the good, good fortune; welfare; benefit, interest

ἀγάλλω ἀγαλῶ ἤγηλα adorn

Ἀγαμέμνων ονος ὁ Agamemnon

ἄγᾱν too much

ἀγανακτέω be annoyed or discontented

ἀγαπάω love

ἀγγεῖον ου τό jar, pitcher

ἀγγέλλω ἀγγελῶ ἤγγειλα ἠγγέλθην announce, report; tell, order

ἄγγελος ου ὁ/ἡ messenger; envoy; angel

ἄγε, ἄγετε come on!

ἀγέλη ης ἡ herd, flock

ἀγή ῆς ἡ fragment

ἀγήρᾱτος ον imperishable

Ἀγησίλᾱος ου ὁ Agesilaus

ἅγιος ᾱ ον holy, sacred, venerable

ἀγκάλη ης ἡ (bent) arm

ἀγνοέω not to know

ἁγνός ή όν sacred

ἀγνώς ῶτος unknown, strange; not knowing, ignorant

ἄγνω(σ)τος ον unknown; unrecognizable

ἀγορά ᾶς ἡ meeting, assembly; marketplace, market

ἀγορεύω speak, say

ἄγραπτος ον unwritten

ἀγραυλέω live in the open air

ἀγρονόμος ον in the countryside

ἀγρός οῦ ὁ field; farm; country

ἀγρυπνίᾱ ᾶς ἡ sleeplessness

ἄγχι + *gen* near

ἀγχώμαλος ον nearly equal

ἄγω ἄξω ἤγαγον ἦχθην lead away, off, on, toward; conduct, bring

ἀγωγός οῦ ὁ/ἡ guide

ἀγών ῶνος ὁ contest; struggle, conflict

ἀδαμάντινος η ον of steel, steely

ἀδεής ές fearless; with impunity

ἄδεια ας ἡ fearlessness, security

ἀδελφή ῆς ἡ sister

ἀδελφιδῆ ῆς ἡ niece

ἀδελφός οῦ ὁ brother

ἀδελφός ή όν of a brother

ἄδηλος ον unseen, invisible

ἀδικέω act unjustly *or* lawlessly, do wrong; be wrong; injure, wrong, maltreat; *pass* be wrong

ἀδίκημα ατος τό, **ἀδικίᾱ** ᾶς ἡ, **ἀδίκιον** ου τό wrong, injury; offense

ἄδικος ον unjust, unlawful; dishonest

ἀεί, αἰεί always
ἀείδω, ᾄδω ᾄσομαι ᾖσα ᾔσθην sing
ἀέκων ουσα ον against one's will, involuntary, unwilling
ἄελλα ης ἡ storm, whirlwind
ἄζομαι stand in awe (of), dread, revere, worship
ἀηδών όνος ἡ nightingale
ἀθανασίᾱ ᾶς ἡ immortality
ἀθάνατος ον immortal, everlasting
ἄθεος ον godless, atheist
Ἀθῆναι ων αἱ Athens
 —Ἀθήνᾱζε to Athens
 —Ἀθήνησι(ν) in Athens
 —Ἀθήνηθεν from Athens
Ἀθηναῖος ᾱ ον Athenian
ἄθλιος ᾱ ον miserable, wretched
ἄθραυστος ον unshattered
ἀθρέω look at, observe
ἀθῷος ον unpunished; unhurt
αἰγίοχος ον aegis-bearing
Αἰγύπτιος ᾱ ον Egyptian
αἰδέομαι αἰδέσομαι ᾐδέσθην respect
Ἀΐδης ου ὁ Hades
αἰδοῖος ᾱ ον respectable
αἰδώς οῦς ἡ shame; modesty
αἰεί always, ever
αἰθήρ έρος ὁ/ἡ the upper air, sky
Αἰθίοψ οπος ὁ an Ethiopian
αἴθομαι burn, blaze
αἴθοψ οπος sparkling, shining
αἰθρίᾱ ᾶς ἡ bright, clear sky, clear air
αἷμα ατος τό blood
αἶνος ου ὁ praise
αἴξ, αἶξ αἰγός ὁ/ἡ goat
αἱρέω αἱρήσω εἷλον ᾕρέθην take, seize; catch; capture; *mid* take *or*
 seize for oneself; enjoy; choose, prefer
αἴρω ἀρῶ ἦρα ἤρθην raise, lift; *act intr* set out, put to sea

αἶσα ης ἡ fate, destiny

αἰσθάνομαι αἰσθήσομαι ᾐσθόμην feel, perceive; notice, observe; know, understand

Αἰσχίνης ου ὁ Aeschines

αἰσχρός ά όν ugly; shameful

αἰσχύνη ης ἡ shame

αἰσχύνω αἰσχυνῶ ᾔσχῡνα ᾐσχύνθην shame; disgrace; *pass* be *or* get ashamed

αἰτέω ask, ask for; beg for; *mid* ask for oneself

αἰτίᾱ ᾱς ἡ cause, reason; charge, blame

αἰτιάομαι accuse

αἴτιος ᾱ ον causing, responsible (for), guilty (of)
   —**τὸ αἴτιον** the cause

αἰχμάλωτος ον prisoner of war; captive

αἰών ῶνος ὁ/ἡ life

αἰώνιος (ᾱ) ον eternal

ἀκαχίζω trouble, grieve

ἀκλεής ές without fame, obscure

ἄκληστος ον not shut, unlocked

ἀκμάζω flourish, be in the prime of life

ἀκολουθέω follow, attend

ἀκοντίζω throw (a spear)

ἄκοσμος ον disorderly

ἀκούω ἀκούσομαι ἤκουσα ἠκούσθην + *acc* (of the sound) + *gen* (of the person who makes it) hear, hear from

ἀκρῑβής ές exact, accurate

ἀκρόπολις εως ἡ acropolis; citadel

ἄκρος ᾱ ον extreme, upper; topmost

ἀκτή ῆς ἡ coast, shore, beach

ἀκτίς ῖνος ἡ ray, beam; light

ἀκωκή ῆς ἡ point

ἄκων ουσα ον against one's will, involuntary, unwilling

ἀλγεινός ή όν painful, grievous; unpleasant

ἀλγηδών όνος ἡ, **ἄλγος**, εος τό pain, grief, sorrow

ἄλεισον ου τό cup

ἀλεκτρυών όνος ὁ cock

Ἀλέξανδρος ου ὁ Alexander

ἀλήθεια ᾱς ἡ truth

ἀληθής ές true; sincere, frank; real, genuine, proper; actual

ἀλήτης ου ὁ wanderer

Ἁλικαρνασσεύς έως ὁ man of Halicarnassus

ἁλίσκομαι ἁλώσομαι ἑάλων be taken, caught, captured

Ἀλκμήνη ης ἡ Alcmena

ἀλλά but, yet, however; why, well, certainly, well then

ἀλλήλους *acc pron* one another

ἄλλος η ο another, the other, other, different

ἄλλοτε at another time

ἀλλότριος ᾱ ον belonging to others

ἄλλως otherwise; in vain; besides

　—**ἄλλως τε καί** especially, above all

ἄλοχος ου ἡ wife

ἅλς ἁλός ἡ salt

ἄλφιτον ου τό barley meal; bread

ἀλωπεκῆ ἡ, **ἀλωπεκίς** ίδος ἡ fox skin

ἅμα together, at the same time, together with + *dat*

ἀμαθής ές ignorant, unlearned, unlettered

ἄμαξα ης ἡ wagon

ἁμαρτάνω ἁμαρτήσομαι ἥμαρτον ἡμαρτήθην miss, err, make a
　mistake, do wrong, lose

ἁμάρτημα ατος τό, **ἁμαρτίᾱ** ᾱς ἡ transgression, sin, error

ἄμαχος ον without fighting; unconquerable

ἀμείβομαι reply, answer

ἀμείβω change; exchange

ἀμείνων ον better, abler, nobler; stronger, more valiant

ἀμέλει *adv* never mind; of course

ἀμελέω be careless, heedless; neglect

ἀμήχανος ον helpless; impossible; unconquerable; inflexible

ἄμπελος ου ἡ vine

ἀμύνω keep off, ward off X *acc* from Y *dat*; defend + *dat*; *mid* defend
　oneself; resist

ἀμφί *prep* + *acc* round, about, at, near

ἀμφι-βαίνω encompass; bestride; protect

ἀμφίβλημα ατος τό enclosing wall

ἀμφίπολος ον attending, serving; servant

ἀμφισ-βητέω contradict, dispute

ἀμφότερος ᾱ ον both, either

ἀφοτέρωθεν from *or* on both sides

ἄμφω ἀμφοῖν both

ἀνά upward, above; *prep* + *acc* through, throughout, along

ἀνα-βαίνω go up, mount, ascend

ἀνα-βλέπω look up *or* back (upon); regain sight

ἀνα-γιγνώσκω read

ἀναγκάζω compel, force, urge, ask; persuade

ἀναγκαῖος (ᾱ) ον necessary; inevitable

ἀνάγκη ης ἡ necessity

ἀν-άγομαι put out to sea; set about a thing, make ready to

ἀνα-δύομαι rise, emerge

ἀνάεδνος ον without bridal gifts

ἀν-αιρέω take *or* lift up; give an oracle; kill; *mid* lift up for oneself; take up

ἀναισχυντίᾱ ᾱς ἡ impudence

ἀναίσχυντος ον impudent, shameless

ἀνα-λαμβάνω take *or* lift up

ἀνᾱλίσκω ἀνᾱλώσω ἀνήλωσα ἀνηλώθην spend, consume, use up, waste

ἀνα-μένω await; wait, stay; delay; endure

ἄναξ ἄνακτος ὁ lord, king, prince, ruler

ἀνάξιος (ᾱ) ον unworthy, not deserving; undeserved

ἀνα-πείθω persuade

ἀνα-πίμπλημι fill up, fulfill

ἀνάσσω rule, reign; be lord *or* master of + *gen*

ἀνα-στενάζω groan aloud

ἀνασχετός όν tolerable

ἀνα-τίθημι set up, dedicate

ἀνα-χωρέω retire, retreat, withdraw

ἀναχώρησις εως ἡ a going back, withdrawal, retreat

ἀνα-ψύχω cool, refresh; *act intr* recover oneself, revive; *pass* recover

ἀνδραποδώδης ες slavish; servile, base

ἀνδρείᾱ ᾶς ἡ manliness, courage
ἄν-ειμι go up, rise; return
ἀνελεύθερος ον ignoble, servile
ἀνέλπιστος ον without hope, despairing
ἄνεμος ου ὁ wind, storm
ἀν-έρπω creep upward
ἀν-έρχομαι go up, rise; come; come back, return, come home
ἄνευ *prep + gen* without
ἀν-ευρίσκω discover
ἀν-έχω *act tr* hold *or* lift up; restrain; *mid* hold up; hold out; bear; keep one's temper
ἀνήκεστος ον incurable, irreparable
ἀνήρ ἀνδρός ὁ man
ἀνθ-άπτομαι + *gen* take hold of
ἄνθρωπος ου ὁ human being, man
   —ἡ **ἄνθρωπος** woman, female slave
ἀνιάω distress, grieve
ἀν-ίημι *act tr* send up; let loose, let go, relax, dismiss; incite
ἀνίκητος ον unconquered; invincible
ἀν-ίστημι *act intr and pass* get up
ἀν-οίγνῡμι open
ἄνομος ον lawless, wicked
ἀντ-έχω hold out
ἀντί *prep + gen* in return for, instead of, for
ἀντίβιος ᾱ ον hostile, opposing, face to face
ἀντικρύ straight
ἀντι-λαμβάνω take *or* receive in turn *or* in return; *mid* take hold of, lay claim to, seize
ἀντι-λέγω speak against, deny
ἀντίος ᾱ ον opposite, confronting
ἀντίπαλος ον contrary
ἄνω upward, on high, above
ἄξιος ᾱ ον worthy; due; right and proper
ἀξιόω see fit, think worthy; request
ἀξίωμα ατος τό reputation
ἀπ-αγγέλλω report, announce, relate

ἀπ-άγω lead off *or* away; remove

ἄπαις (gen ἄπαιδος) childless

ἀπ-αλλάσσω set free, release, remove; *pass* go away, depart

ἁπαλός ή όν soft

ἀπ-αμείβομαι answer

ἀπάνευθε(ν) *adv* from afar; far off; aside, apart; *prep + gen* without

ἀπαντάω come *or* go to meet, meet

ἀπαραίτητος ον not to be moved by prayer; inexorable

ἀπ-αρνέομαι deny

ἅπᾱς ἅπᾱσα ἅπαν all, all together; whole, entire

ἀπ-ειλέω threaten, menace; boast; promise

ἄπ-ειμι shall go away, leave; shall return

ἀπ-είργω keep away

ἀπ-ελαύνω, ἀπελάω trick away, drive away, expel

ἀπέραντος ον infinite, endless

ἀπερίσκεπτος ον inconsiderate, reckless

ἀπ-έρχομαι go away, depart

ἀπ-εχθάνομαι be *or* become hated

ἀπέχθεια ᾱς ή enmity, hatred

ἀπ-έχω hold off; be distant *or* far from + *gen*; *mid* abstain from, desist

ἀπιστέω not believe; disbelieve + *dat*

ἄπιστος ον unreliable; incredible; unbelieving

ἁπλόος η ον, ἁπλοῦς ῆ οῦν onefold, single; plain; sincere

ἁπλῶς plainly, simply; in a word

ἀπό *prep + gen* from, away from

ἀπο-βαίνω step off, alight, dismount, land; turn out, come to pass, happen; *tr* disembark

ἀπο-βάλλω throw off; drive away

ἀπο-βλέπω look at, regard

ἀπο-διδράσκω run away

ἀπο-δίδωμι give away *or* back, give; return

ἀπο-θνήσκω die; be killed

ἄποινα ων τά ransom

ἀπο-καίω burn off, freeze off

ἀπο-κομίζω carry away *or* back

ἀπο-κρίνομαι answer
ἀπο-κτείνῡμι = ἀποκτείνω
ἀπο-κτείνω kill
ἀπο-λαμβάνω cut off; regain
ἀπόλαυσις εως ἡ enjoyment
ἀπο-λείπω leave, relinquish; leave behind
ἀπ-όλλῡμι, ἀπολλύω ruin, destroy; kill; lose; *mid and pass* be
   ruined, destroyed *or* lost; perish, die
ἀπο-λογέομαι defend *or* justify oneself; make a defense
Ἀπόλλων ωνος ὁ Apollo
ἀπο-λύω set free, deliver; dismiss, acquit
ἀπο-μύττομαι blow one's nose
ἀπο-πειράω *and pass* try, prove, make trial of
ἀπο-πέμπω send away *or* back; dismiss
ἀπόπληκτος ον disabled by a stroke; simple
ἀπο-πτύω spit out; abominate
ἀπορέω be embarrassed, at a loss *or* helpless
ἀπορίᾱ ᾱς ἡ helplessness, lack
ἀπο-στίχω go away
ἀπο-στέλλω send away
ἀπο-στερέω deprive (of)
ἀπο-χωρέω go away; retreat
ἅπτω fasten, attach; kindle; *mid* touch, grasp, lay hold of + *gen*
ἀπ-ωθέω drive away *or* back; repel
ἄρα then (logical); so then, after all (of realization)
ἀράομαι pray
Ἀργεῖος ᾱ ον Argive
ἀργός όν lazy, idle
Ἄργος ους τό Argos
ἀργύριον ου τό silver; money
ἀργυρότοξος ον with silver bow
ἀρέσκω *aor* ἤρεσα + *dat* please; *pass* be agreeable *or* pleasing
ἀρετή ῆς ἡ bravery, valor; virtue
ἀρηίφιλος ον loved by Ares
ἀριθμός οῦ ὁ number; amount, quantity; a counting, muster
ἀριπρεπής ές eminent, splendid

Ἀριστογείτων ονος ὁ Aristogiton

Ἀριστόκριτος ου ὁ Aristocritus

ἀριστοποιέομαι have one's breakfast

ἄριστος η ον best, noblest

Ἀρκαδίᾱ ᾱς ἡ Arcadia

ἀρκέω keep *or* ward off; help, assist, defend + *dat*

ἄρκτος ου ὁ/ἡ bear; the north

ἁρμάμαξα ης ἡ covered carriage

Ἁρμόδιος ου ὁ Harmodius

ἁρπάζω snatch, seize, rob, plunder

ἁρπακτής οῦ ὁ robber

ἄρρηκτος ον unbreakable, not to be broken *or* tired

ἄρτι just now; lately, the other day

ἀρτίως just now; lately, the other day

ἄρτος ου ὁ bread

ἀρχαῖος ᾱ ον ancient, old

ἀρχή ῆς ἡ beginning; leadership, power, rule, government; empire, kingdom

ἀρχός οῦ ὁ leader

ἄρχω ἄρξω ἦρξα ἤρχθην + *gen* be the first, lead on; begin; be at the head (of), rule; *pass* be ruled; *mid* begin

ἄρχων οντος ὁ leader, ruler, chief; archon, magistrate

ἀσκέω adorn

Ἀσκλήπιος ου ὁ Asclepius (god of healing)

ἄσμενος η ον willing, ready, glad

ἀσπάζομαι greet

ἀσπίς ίδος ἡ shield

Ἀσσύριος ᾱ ον Assyrian

ἀστός οῦ ὁ citizen

ἄστυ εως *or* εος τό city; town (as opposed to country)

ἀσφαλής ές steadfast; safe, certain

ἀτάλλω rear, foster

ἀτάρ but, yet, however

ἄτε + *participle* inasmuch as

ἀτέχνως plainly, simply

ἀτῑμάω hold in low esteem, dishonor, despise

ἄτῑμος ον unhonored, despised

ἄτοπος ον strange, unusual

Ἀτρεῖδαι ων οἱ sons of Atreus

ἀτρεκής ές exact, true

Ἀττική ῆς ἡ, **Ἀτθίς** ίδος (γῆ) ἡ Attica

ἀτύζω alarm, harass; *pass* be frightened *or* benumbed

αὖ again, once more; on the other hand; further; in turn

αὐγή ῆς ἡ brightness, brilliance; ray, beam; eye, glance

αὐθᾰδίᾱ ᾱς ἡ complacency; arrogance; obstinacy

αὐθήμερον on the same day

αὖθι there, on the spot

αὖθις again

αὔλειος ον belonging to the courtyard

αὐλή ῆς ἡ courtyard; dwelling

αὐλητής οῦ ὁ flute player

αὐλίζομαι camp (in the open air); bivouac

αὐλών ῶνος ἡ hollow way; canal

αὐξάνω, αὔξω αὐξήσω ηὔξησα ηὐξήθην increase, enlarge; *pass* grow

αὐτάρ but, however

αὖτε in turn

αὐτίκα straight away, instantly, directly

αὖτις back

αὐτόθι on the spot, there, here

αὐτοκράτωρ ορ independent; complete master; in control of oneself

αὐτόματος (η) ον self-moved; of one's own will, natural

αὐτόνομος ον independent

αὐτός ἡ ὁ self, oneself; by oneself; *in acc, gen and dat only* him, her, it

—**ὁ αὐτός** ἡ αὐτή τὸ αὐτό the same

αὐτοῦ in the same place; there, here

αὐτόφωρος ον caught in the very act; convicted by the facts

αὐχήν ένος ὁ neck, throat

ἀφ-αιρέω take off, away *or* from; remove; diminish

ἀφανής ές unseen, invisible

ἄφθονος ον abundant, plentiful

ἀφ-ίημι send off *or* away
ἀφ-ικνέομαι arrive at, come to; return; befall
ἀφ-ίστημι make revolt; *act intr and pass* go away; stand aloof; revolt
ἀφραδής ές foolish, silly, thoughtless, senseless
Ἀφροδίτη ης ἡ Aphrodite
ἀφύλακτος ον unguarded; careless, heedless
Ἀχαιοί ῶν οἱ Achaeans
Ἀχαρναί ῶν αἱ Acharnae
— Ἀχαρνεύς έως ὁ man of Acharnae
ἄχθομαι be burdened *or* annoyed; be sad *or* angry
ἄχος εος τό pain, sorrow, grief
ἄχρι(ς) *prep + gen* until; *conj* until
ἄψ back; again

B

Βαβυλών ῶνος ἡ Babylon
Βαβυλώνιος ᾱ ον Babylonian
βαδίζω step, page, walk, come, go
βάθος ους τό depth; height
βάθρον ου τό step, stair
βαίνω -βήσομαι -έβην walk, tread, go, step
βακχεύω celebrate the rites of Bacchus; be in ecstasy
βάλλω βαλῶ ἔβαλον ἐβλήθην throw, cast, hurl; hit, strike, pelt
βάρβαρος ον barbarous; foreign; uncivilized, barbarian
βαρύνω weigh down, distress
βαρύς εῖα ύ heavy, burdensome, oppressive; weighty
βασιλείᾱ ᾱς ἡ kingdom, monarchy; kingship
βασίλειος (ᾱ) ον kingly, royal, princely
— τὸ βασίλειον, τὸ βασίληιον royal palace
βασιλεύς έως ὁ king, prince; *without def art* the king of Persia
βασιλεύω be king, rule
βασιλικός ή όν kingly, royal, princely
βαστάζω touch, lift up
βδέλλα ης leech
βδελυρός ά όν disgusting

βελόνη ης needle
βέλος ους τό missile
βελτίων ον better, braver, nobler
βένθος ους τό depth
βίᾱ ᾱς ἡ strength, force
βίος ου ὁ life, livelihood
βιός οῦ ὁ bow
βιοτή ῆς ἡ **βίοτος** ου ὁ life
βιόω βιώσομαι ἐβιων live
βλέπω see
βλέφαρον ου τό eyelid, eye
βλώσκω μολοῦμαι ἔμολον go; come
βοή ῆς ἡ shout
βοηθέω + *dat* come to the rescue (of); help
βόλος ου ὁ draft (of fish)
βόσκω feed, pasture; *pass and mid* be fed
βότηρ ῆρος ὁ shepherd
βούλευμα ατος τό resolution; decree; plan; wish; counsel
βουλεύω, **βουλεύομαι** take counsel; plan, devise; consider;
   determine, resolve
βουλή ῆς ἡ council
βούλομαι βουλήσομαι ἐβουλήθην will, wish, want; be willing *or*
   resolved; prefer; choose
βοῦς βοός ὁ/ἡ cow, ox
Βρᾱσίδᾱς ου ὁ Brasidas
βραχίων ονος ὁ arm, shoulder
βραχύς εῖα ύ short
βρέτας εος τό statue
βρέφος ους τό newborn child, baby
βροτόεις εσσα εν bloody
βροτός ου ὁ/ἡ mortal; man
βρῶσις εως ἡ food
βύβλος ου ἡ papyrus roll
Βυζάντιον ου τό Byzantium
βωμός οῦ ὁ altar

Γ

γαῖα ᾱς ἡ land

γάλα ακτος τό milk

γαμέω γαμῶ ἔγημα *male subj* marry; *mid female subj* marry, be given in marriage to + *dat*

γαμήλιος ον belonging to a wedding or marriage

γάμος ου ὁ wedding

γάρ for; since, as; why, what; if only!

γαστήρ γαστρός ἡ belly, stomach

γε at least, at any rate, even, just, of course, indeed

γέγονα *perf. of* γίγνομαι

γεῖσον ου τό cornice, coping

γελάω γελάσομαι ἐγέλασα laugh, smile

γενεά ᾱς ἡ birth; generation

γενναῖος ᾱ ον high-born, noble, generous

γεννάω engender; beget, bring forth

γέννημα ατος τό product, fruit

γεραιός ά όν old, aged; old man

γέρας αος/ως τό gift of honor; reward

γερουσίᾱ ᾱς ἡ council of elders

γέρων οντος ὁ old; old man

γεύομαι + *gen* taste, eat

γῆ γῆς ἡ earth, land

γῆρας αος/ως τό old age

γηροβοσκέω feed *or* tend in old age

γίγνομαι γενήσομαι ἐγενόμην become, grow; be born, come into being; happen, occur

γιγνώσκω γνώσομαι ἔγνων ἐγνώσθην perceive, gain knowledge (of); know; learn; think; recognize

γλαφυρός ά όν hollow

γλυκύς εῖα ύ sweet; delightful, lovely; kind

γλῶσσα ης ἡ, **γλῶττα** ης ἡ tongue, language

γναθμός οῦ ὁ jaw

γνώμη ης ἡ mind, judgment; opinion; intention; advice, proposal

γνώριμος ον known, familiar

Γόγγυλος ου ὁ Gongylus

γόνος ου ὁ son

γόος ου ὁ lament

γοῦν at least, at any rate; of course; for instance; yet, indeed

γραῖα ᾶς ἡ old woman; old

γράμμα ατος τό letter of the alphabet

γραφεύς έως ὁ painter

γραφή ῆς ἡ indictment

γράφω engrave; write; paint

γυμνός ή όν naked

γυναικωνῖτις ιδος ἡ women's apartment

γυνή γυναικός ἡ woman, lady; wife

Δ

δαιμόνιος ᾶ ον divine, godlike; unfortunate; wonderful; *in voc* sir, madam

δαίμων ονος ὁ/ἡ divine being, deity

δαίνῡμι give a feast; *mid* eat, feast

δάκνω δήξομαι ἔδακον ἐδήχθην bite

δάκρυ υος τό, **δάκρυον** ου τό tear

δακρυόεις εσσα εν tearful; weeping

δακρ́ω weep; shed tears; weep for

δακτύλιος ου ὁ ring

δαμάζω δαμάσω ἐδάμασα tame; subdue, overpower

Δαναοί ῶν οἱ Danaans = Greeks

δαπάνη ης ἡ expense

δάς δᾳδός ἡ torch

δέ but; but on the other hand; further; thus; then

δεῖ δεήσει ἐδέησε *impers + acc of person* one must, one ought; it is necessary, right

    —**τὸ δέον, τὰ δέοντα** what is needed

δειγματίζω expose to shame; make a show of

δείδω δείσομαι ἔδεισα *pf (with pres meaning)* δέδοικα be afraid, fear; be alarmed

δείκνῡμι δείξω ἔδειξα ἐδείχθην show, point out, exhibit, display; demonstrate

δείλαιος α ον wretched

δειλός ή όν timid, cowardly; vile, worthless; unhappy, luckless
δεῖμα ατος τό fear, terror, horror
δεινός ή όν terrible, frightful, dangerous; shocking
δειπνέω dine
δεῖπνον ου τό meal; dinner
δέκα ten
δέμας ατος τό body, figure, stature
δέμνιον ου τό bed; bedstead, mattress
δένδρον ου τό tree
δεξίος ά όν on the right-hand side
　—**ἡ δεξιά** the right hand
δέομαι + gen need, ask for, want
δέπας τό cup
δέρμα ατος τό hide, skin
δεσμός οῦ ὁ (but in pl both οἱ δεσμοί and τὰ δεσμά) fetter, bond, thong
δεσμωτήριον ου τό prison
δέσποινα ης ἡ mistress, lady
δεσπότης ου ὁ lord, master, owner
δεῦρο, δευρί to here
δεύτερος ᾱ ον second
δέχομαι take, accept, receive
δέω δήσω ἔδησα bind
δέω δεήσω ἐδέησα ἐδεήθην + gen want, lack
δή indeed
δήϊος hostile
δῆλος η ον visible, evident, plain, clear
δηλόω manifest, show, signify; explain, prove
　—**δηλοῖ** it is clear
δημοκρατέομαι live in a democracy
δημοκρατίᾱ ᾱς ἡ democracy
δῆμος ου ὁ people; democracy
δηόω destroy, waste, plunder
δήπου certainly
δῆτα then
διά + acc through; on account of, because of, by reason of; + gen through, right through

δια-βαίνω cross
δια-βάλλω slander, accuse falsely
διαβολή ῆς ἡ slander
δια-γράφω cross out; strike out, reject
δια-δίδωμι hand over; distribute
διαθήκη ης ἡ arrangement; covenant
δίαιτα ης ἡ life; mode of life; diet
διά-κειμαι be in a certain condition *or* state
δια-κομίζω carry over *or* across
δια-κοσμέω set in order, arrange
δια-λάμπω shine through *or* forth
δια-λέγομαι talk (with), converse
δια-λείπω leave an interval
δια-λύω dissolve, disband
δια-μένω remain, continue
δια-νοέομαι consider, reflect
δια-πλέω sail through *or* across
δια-πράσσω accomplish, bring about
δια-σκοπιάομαι spy out
δια-σῴζω preserve; bring safely
δια-τίθημι arrange, manage, treat; *mid* dispose of
διατριβή ῆς ἡ pastime, haunt
δια-τρίβω rub away; stay, live
δια-φεύγω flee through; escape, avoid
δια-φθείρω fut διαφθερῶ destroy, ruin, corrupt; bribe
διαφορά ᾶς ἡ different, conflict
διδάσκαλος ου ὁ teacher, master
διδάσκω διδάξω ἐδίδαξα ἐδιδάχθην teach somebody (acc)
    something (acc), instruct; show; *mid* have (someone) taught
δίδωμι δώσω ἔδωκα ἐδόθην give, present, grant
δι-έρχομαι go *or* pass through
δι-ερωτάω question continually
δι-ηγέομαι explain, describe, narrate
διθύραμβος ου ὁ dithyramb (a kind of lyric poetry)
δι-ίστημι separate, divide; set at variance
δικάζω judge, administer justice
δίκαιος ᾱ ον just; righteous, honest; lawful, right

δικαιοσύνη ης ή, **δικαιότης** ητος ή justice; administration of justice

δικαστήριον ου τό law court

δικαστής οῦ ὁ judge, juror

δίκη ης ή right, law, justice; judgment; lawsuit; penalty
 —**δίκην δίδωμι** pay the penalty

διογενής born from Zeus

δι-όλλῡμι destroy *or* ruin completely; forget; *pass* perish completely

Διόνῡσος ου ὁ Dionysus

δι-ορύσσω dig through

δῖος ᾱ ον brilliant; noble; divine, goodly

δίπτυχος ον twofold, two

δίς twice, double

δισχίλιοι αι α two thousand

δίφρος ου ὁ chariot; chair, stool

δίψος ους τό thirst

διώκω pursue, chase; persecute

δμώς ωός ὁ slave

δοκέω δόξω ἔδοξα think, suppose; seem, appear
 —**δοκεῖ** it seems, it seems good

δόλος ου ὁ deceit, treachery; trick, stratagem

δόμος ου ὁ house, building; hall; home

δόξα ης ή opinion; reputation; glory, splendor, fame

δορά ᾶς ή hide, skin

Δόρκις εως ή Dorcis

δόρυ δόρατος τό shaft of a spear; spear

δορυφόρος ου ὁ spear bearer; bodyguard

δουλεύω be a slave, serve

δοῦλος ου ὁ slave

δοῦναι aor infin of δίδωμι

δουπέω make a thud

δράω δράσω ἔδρασα ἐδράσθην be active; do, perform, accomplish

δρέπομαι pluck

δρόσος ου ή dew

δύναμαι δυνήσομαι ἐδυνήθην be able (to)
δύναμις εως ἡ ability; power, strength
δυνάστης ου ὁ ruler
δυνατός ή όν able; powerful
δυσγενής ές of low birth
δυσδαίμων ον ill-fated
δύσκολος ον peevish, discontented; difficult
δύσμαχος ον hard to fight with
δυστάλᾱς αινα αν most unhappy
δύστηνος ον unhappy; wretched, abominable
δύω sink
δῶμα ατος τό dwelling, house; palace; hall
δωμάτιον ου τό room, bedchamber

E

ἔᾱ ha! ah! aha!
ἐάν if
ἑαυτόν ήν όν himself, herself, itself; oneself; *pl* themselves
ἐάω ἐάσω εἴασα εἰάθην let, allow; let *or* leave alone *or* unnoticed; omit
ἑβδμήκοντα seventy
ἐγ-γίγνομαι be born in
ἐγγίζω approach, draw near
ἐγ-γράφω write in
ἐγγύθεν from close at hand
ἐγγύς near, in the neighborhood
　　—**ἐγγύτερος** *comp*
　　—**ἐγγύτατος** *sup*
ἐγείρω ἐγερῶ ἤγειρα ἠγέρθην awaken; raise; *pass* wake up
ἐγ-καθέζομαι sit down in, encamp in
ἐγ-καλέω accuse
ἐγ-καλύπτω wrap up
ἐγκρατής ές having mastery over
ἐγκύπτω stoop; peep
ἐγχειρίδιον ου τό dagger; knife
ἔγχος ους τό spear, lance; weapon, sword

ἐγώ I, myself

—ἔγωγε I for my part, for myself

ἕδος ους τό seat, chair; abode, dwelling; temple

ἕδρᾱ ᾱς ἡ seat, chamber, room

ἐέλδωρ τό wish

ἐθέλω ἐθελήσω ἠθέλησα be willing, wish, want, desire

ἐθίζω accustom; *pass* be accustomed

εἰ if, whether

εἰδέναι *infin of* οἶδα

εἶδον *aor from* ὁράω

εἶδος ους τό appearance, shape, form; beauty

εἰδώς *participle of* οἶδα

εἶἐν well then

εἴθε if only!

εἰκάζω guess, conjecture

εἴκελος η ον + *dat* like

εἰκός ότος probably, likely, natural, reasonable

εἴκοσι twenty

εἰκοστός ή όν the twentieth

εἰκότως probably, naturally, of course, fairly, reasonably

εἰκών όνος ἡ likeness, image

εἶλον *aor from* αἱρέω

εἰμι ἔσομαι *imperf.* ἦν be

εἶμι (*pres. with future meaning in indicative*) go, come

εἶπον *aor from* λέγω

εἴργω enclose; prohibit, hinder, prevent

εἰρηναῖος ᾱ ον peaceful

εἰς, ἐς + *acc.* into, toward; against; for the purpose of

εἷς μία ἕν one, one alone, a single one

εἰσανα-βαίνω go up into

εἰσ-αφικνέομαι arrive at

εἰσ-βάλλω *act tr* throw into; *act intr* throw oneself into; invade, make an inroad, enter

εἰσ-δύνω enter, slip into

εἴσ-ειμι shall come *or* go into, enter

εἰσ-έρχομαι enter

εἰσ-οράω look into, on *or* at; behold; perceive

εἰσ-πίπτω fall into, rush into; invade, attack, fall upon; be thrown into

εἰσ-πορεύομαι go into, enter

εἴσω, ἔσω inside; within

εἶτα then

εἴτε ... εἴτε whether ... or

εἴωθα be accustomed

ἐκ, ἐξ + *gen.* out of, from, from among; on the part of

ἕκαστος η ον each

ἑκάτερος ᾱ ον each of (the) two, either; *pl* both, both parties

ἐκ-βαίνω come *or* step out, leave; depart from

ἐκ-βάλλω throw *or* cast out; expel, banish

ἐκ-γελάω laugh loudly

ἐκεῖ there

ἐκεῖθεν from there

ἐκεῖνος η ο that

ἐκεῖσε to there

ἑκηβόλος ον shooter, archer (of Apollo)

ἐκ-θέω run out; make a sally

ἐκ-καλέω call out, summon forth

ἐκ-καλύπτω uncover

ἐκκλησίᾱ ᾱς ἡ assembly of citizens *or* soldiers

ἐκ-κλίνω bend aside; avoid; *intr* turn away; give way; withdraw

ἐκ-κόπτω knock out; cut off *or* down, fell; break down

ἐκ-λέγω, ἐκ-λέγομαι pick out, choose; speak out

ἐκ-λείπω leave out, omit; forsake, abandon; *intr* disappear; run short

ἐκ-λέπω hatch

ἐκ-λύω loose, release, unstring

ἐκ-πέμπω send out

ἐκ-πέρθω destroy utterly

ἐκ-πίπτω fall out of; fall from, depart from; be banished *or* driven out of

ἐκ-πλέω sail out

ἐκ-πλήσσω strike out, drive away

ἐκποδών out of the way

ἐκ-πολιορκέω take by siege *or* assault, overpower

ἐκ-πονέω work out, work off, work hard

ἐκ-ρέω flow out; vanish

ἐκ-ρήγνῡμι break out *or* off; *act intr and pass* break

ἐκ-τελέω finish, bring to an end

ἐκτός + *gen* outside

ἐκ-τρέφω feed, rear, bring up

Ἕκτωρ ορος ὁ Hector

ἐκφαίνω reveal

ἐκ-χέω pour out, shed, spill; *pass* stream out

ἑκών οῦσα όν voluntary, willing; on purpose

ἔλαιον ου τό olive oil

ἔλαιος ου ὁ wild olive tree

ἐλάσσων ον lesser

Ἐλάτειᾱ ᾱς ἡ Elatea

ἐλαύνω ἐλῶ (άω) ἤλασα ἠλάθην drive, drive on; *intr* drive, ride, row, march, advance

ἐλάχιστος η ον smallest, least, shortest

ἔλδωρ τό wish

ἐλεέω have pity (upon), pity

Ἑλένη ης ἡ Helen

Ἕλενος ου ὁ Helenus

ἐλευθερίᾱ ᾱς ἡ freedom, liberty

ἐλευθέριος ᾱ ον noble-minded, noble

ἐλεύθερος ᾱ ον free, independent; free-spirited

ἐλευθερόω set free, release, acquit

Ἐλευσίς ῖνος ἡ Eleusis

ἐλέφᾱς αντος ὁ elephant

ἐλίσσω turn round; roll *or* whirl round; wind *or* wrap round; coil oneself

Ἑλλήσποντος ου ὁ Hellespont

Ἕλλην ηνος ὁ a Greek

Ἑλληνίς ίδος ἡ a Greek woman

ἐλπίζω ἐλπιῶ ἤλπισα hope, expect

ἐλπίς ίδος ἡ hope, expectation

ἐμαυτόν ήν όν *acc* myself

ἐμ-βάλλω throw, put *or* lay in; throw upon; *intr* make an invasion; attack

ἐμ-μένω + *dat* stay in; remain steadfast; abide by

ἐμός ή όν my, mine

ἐμ-παίζω mock, jest; play *or* sport in

ἔμπειρος ον expert

ἐμ-πίπτω fall in *or* upon; attack

ἐμ-πνέω breathe

ἔμπνοος ον, **ἔμπνους** ουν breathing, alive

ἔμπυρος ον in *or* on the fire, scorched

ἐμφανής ές conspicuous, visible; manifest; known, public

ἔμφρων ον in one's right mind; prudent

ἔμψῡχος ον having a soul in one, alive

ἐν + *dat* in, at, on; between, among; during, within; by means of, with, through; upon, by dint of

ἔναντα face to face

ἐναντίος ᾱ ον opposite, facing; opposing

ἔναρα ων τά armor; spoils

ἐναργής ές visible; manifest

ἐν-αρμόττω fit in; be convenient

ἐν-δίδωμι surrender; give up

ἐνδίφριος ον ὁ sitting on the same seat with + *dat*

ἔνδοθεν from within

ἔνδοθι inside, within

ἔνδον within, at home

ἔν-ειμι be within, in, on *or* at

ἔνεκα + *gen.* on account of, for the sake of

ἐνέπω speak, tell, relate; address, accost

ἐνήλατον ου τό rung

ἔνθα there; where; then

ἐνθάδε here

ἔνθεν from there; from where

ἐνθένδε from here, henceforth

ἔνθεος ον inspired

ἐν-θουσιάζω be inspired

ἐν-θῡμέομαι take to heart; consider, ponder, deliberate

ἐνί + *dat* in

ἐνιαυτός οὖ ὁ year

ἔνιοι αι α some, several

ἐνίπτω rebuke, reprove, blame; tell

ἐννέπω speak, tell, relate; address, accost

ἐν-νοέω have in mind, consider; plan, intend, think; perceive, observe

ἐν-νυχεύω pass the night in

ἐν-όρνῡμι arouse (in); *mid* arise

ἔνος η ον old

ἐν-τανύω stretch, string (a bow)

ἐνταῦθα there; here; then; thereupon

ἐν-τείνω stretch *or* strain in; bend

ἐντεῦθεν from there

ἐν-τίθημι put in

ἐντολή ῆς ἡ commandment

ἐν-τρέπω turn round; *pass* pay attention (to)

ἐν-τυγχάνω + *dat* encounter, fall in with; meet

ἐξ-αγγέλλω report, send word

ἐξ-αιρέω remove; destroy; drive away

ἐξ-αιτέομαι beg for oneself

ἐξ-αμαρτάνω make a mistake; transgress

ἐξαπατάω deceive, cheat

ἐξαπιναῖος (ᾱ) ον sudden

ἐξ-απόλλῡμι *act tr* kill, destroy utterly; *act intr and mid* perish

ἐξ-αρτάω hang on; *pass* be fastened *or* attached to, be hung upon

ἐξ-αρτύω prepare, equip, fit out

ἐξ-ασκέω adorn, deck out; train *or* teach thoroughly

ἐξ-αυδάω speak out

ἐξαῦτις once again; back

ἔξ-εστι it is allowed *or* possible

　　—ἐξόν it being possible

ἐξ-ελαύνω drive out, expel, chase; *intr* set out, march out *or* on

ἐξ-εργάζομαι finish, accomplish, do

ἐξ-έρχομαι go *or* come out

ἐξ-ετάζω ἐξετάσω ἐξήτασα ἐξητάσθην search; examine, test

ἐξ-ευρίσκω find, discover; devise

ἐξήκοντα sixty

ἐξῆς in order, one after the other, successively

ἐξ-ίστημι *act tr* put out of its place *or* away; alter; *act intr and mid* +
  gen step *or* stand aside from, retire (from)

ἐξ-ομοιόω make like; *pass* become like

ἐξ-ονομάζω call by name; speak out, utter

ἐξ-ορμάω *act tr* start, get going; send out; *act intr and pass* set out,
  go away

ἔξω + *gen* on the outside, outside; beyond; far from

ἔοικα be *or* look like; seem, have the appearance (of)

ἑορτή ῆς ἡ festival, feast, holiday

ἑός ἑή ἑόν his, hers; his *or* her own

ἐπ-άγω lead *or* drive to

ἐπ-αινέω praise

ἐπ-αισθάνομαι perceive, feel

ἐπ-αναγκάζω force, compel

ἐπαν-έρχομαι go up

ἐπ-εγείρω arouse, awaken

ἐπεί when, after, since

ἐπειδή when, since

ἔπ-ειμι go *or* come to *or* upon; approach, advance against, attack

ἔπειτα thereupon, thereafter, then, from then on

ἐπ-ελπίζω lead to hope

ἐπεμ-βάλλω put on besides; flow in besides

ἐπέξ-ειμι go out against

ἐπεξ-έρχομαι go out against, advance against

ἐπ-ερέφω roof (a building)

ἐπ-έρχομαι go *or* come up, toward, forward *or* on; approach, attack

ἐπ-ερωτάω question, ask; inquire of; consult

ἐπ-εύχομαι pray to; invoke

ἐπί + *acc* to, for, at, extending over, toward, up to; against; + *gen* on,
  upon, at; + *dat* on, in, at; on the grounds of, for the purpose of

ἐπι-βάλλω throw, cast *or* lay upon

ἐπι-βουλεύω + *dat* plot against

ἐπι-γίγνομαι come after; follow, elapse; happen

ἐπι-δείκνῡμι show

ἐπι-δημέω be at home

ἐπι-διώκω pursue further

ἐπι-θῡμέω + *gen* desire, long for, wish, covet

ἐπί-κειμαι attack

ἐπι-κηρύσσω proclaim publicly

ἐπι-κρατέω prevail, conquer; rule

Ἐπικυδίδας ου ὁ Epicydidas

ἐπι-λανθάνομαι *usu* + *gen* forget; forget willfully

ἐπι-λέγω say at *or* besides, add; name; *mid* collect; read

ἐπι-μελέομαι, ἐπι-μέλομαι + *gen* take care of, pay attention to

ἐπι-ορκέω break an oath

ἐπίπᾶν on the whole, generally

ἐπι-σκοπέω look

ἐπι-σκώπτω laugh *or* mock at; jest

ἐπι-σπέρχω rage furiously

ἐπίσταμαι ἐπιστήσομαι *imperf* ἠπιστάμην understand, know

ἐπι-στέλλω send to, send a message; command

ἐπιστολή ῆς ἡ letter

ἐπι-στρέφω turn to; turn round *or* back; *act intr, mid and pass* turn oneself around

ἐπιτήδειος (ᾱ) ον fit, convenient

　　—τὰ ἐπιτήδεια necessaries, provisions

　　—ὁ ἐπιτήδειος relation, friend

ἐπιτηδές for the purpose, purposely; sufficiently; on purpose

ἐπιτήδευμα ατος τό habits

ἐπι-τίθημι put *or* lay upon; grant; add; *act intr and mid* put on oneself *or* for oneself; + *dat* attack, make an attempt upon

ἐπι-τρέπω turn to *or* toward; give over; entrust, put into one's hands; *act intr* turn to; entrust oneself to

ἐπι-χειρέω + *dat* put one's hand to; undertake, attempt, try, venture

ἐπιχώριος ον native, indigenous

ἐπι-ψηλαφάω grope for

ἐπ-οικτείρω have compassion with

ἐπ-οίχομαι go *or* come toward, approach; work at

ἕπομαι ἕψομαι ἑσπόμην + *dat* follow; accompany

ἐπ-οπτεύω look on *or* at; inspect, watch over

ἔπος εος τό word

— **ὡς ἔπος εἰπεῖν** so to speak, almost, practically, virtually

ἑπτά seven

ἑπτακαίδεκα seventeen

ἑπτάστομος ον seven-mouthed

ἐράομαι + *gen* love passionately, fall in love (with); desire, long for

Ἐρατοσθένης ους ὁ Eratosthenes

ἐργάζομαι work, do, accomplish

ἔργον ου τό work, deed, action, enterprise; fact, reality; business

ἐρείπια ων τά ruins, wreckage

ἐρέσσω row

Ἐρέτριᾱ ᾱς ἡ Eretria

ἐρέω I shall say

ἐρῆμος (η) ον solitary, desolate; destitute, empty

Ἑρμῆς οῦ ὁ Hermes

ἔρομαι ask, inquire

ἕρπω, **ἑρπύζω** creep, crawl; go; come

ἔρρω go away; be lost

ἐρυμνός ή όν fortified, protected

ἔρχομαι εἶμι ἦλθον come, go

ἐρῶ *fut from* λέγω

ἔρως ωτος ὁ love; desire

ἐρωτάω ἐρωτήσω *or* ἐρήσομαι ἠρώτησα *or* ἠρόμην ask, request; inquire

ἐρωτικός ή όν of love; prone to love, amorous; sexual

ἐς + *acc* into

ἐσβολή ῆς ἡ attack

ἐσθής ῆτος ἡ dress, clothing

ἐσθίω ἔδομαι ἔφαγον ἠδέσθην eat

ἐσθλός ή όν good; noble; brave, valiant

ἑσπέρᾱ ᾱς ἡ evening; west

ἕστηκα *perf of* ἵστημι I stand

ἑστίᾱ ᾱς ἡ hearth; house, home

ἑστιάω entertain

ἔσω + *gen* inside

ἑταῖρος ου ὁ companion, comrade, friend

Ἐτεοκλῆς έους ὁ Eteocles

ἕτερος ᾱ ον the other, one of two, another

ἐτησίαι ων οἱ periodic winds

ἔτι yet, as yet, still; besides

ἑτοῖμος (η) ον ready, at hand

ἔτος ους τό year

εὖ well, properly, rightly; luckily

εὐ-αγγελίζω bring good news

Εὔβοιᾱ ᾶς ἡ Euboea

εὐδαιμονέω be happy

εὐδαιμονίᾱ ᾶς ἡ happiness, prosperity

εὐδαίμων ον happy; fortunate; prosperous, wealthy

εὐδιάβατος ον easy to be crossed

εὕδω -ευδήσω *imperf* -ηῦδον sleep; fall asleep

εὐ-εργετέομαι receive a kindness

εὐεργέτης ου ὁ benefactor

εὔζωνος ον well-girdled

εὐήθης ες simple, silly

Εὐθύκριτος ου ὁ Euthycritus

εὐθῡ́νω guide; correct; accuse, call to account; examine the
conduct (of an official)

εὐθύς, εὐθύ forthwith, at once; + *gen* straight to *or* toward

εὐκνήμῑς (gen ῑ́δος) well-greaved

εὔκοπος ον easy

εὐκοσμίᾱ ᾶς ἡ good order; decency

εὐλαβέομαι be cautious, circumspect *or* careful

εὔλεκτρος ον fit for marriage, lovely

εὐλογέω give thanks; bless

εὐνή ῆς ἡ bed, couch; marriage bed

εὐπλόκαμος ον with fine locks

εὐπρεπής ές beautiful; decent

εὐπρόσοδος ον accessible; affable

εὑρίσκω εὑρήσω ηὗρον/εὗρον ηὑρέθην find, find out, discover

εὖρος ους τό breadth, width

εὐρύς εῖα ύ broad, wide

εὔτακτος ον well-disciplined, orderly

εὔστοχος ον well-aimed

εὐτυχέω be lucky, meet with success; turn out well

εὐτυχής ές lucky, fortunate, happy; prosperous, successful

εὐφιλής ές well-beloved

Εὐφίλητος ου ὁ Euphiletus

εὐφραίνω cheer, gladden; *mid and pass* be glad *or* cheerful

Εὐφράτης ου ὁ Euphrates

εὐχαριστέω give thanks

εὐχετάομαι pray; boast; assert, profess

εὔχομαι εὔξομαι ηὐξάμην pray (for), boast; assert, profess

εὐώνυμος ον of good name; of the left hand

ἐφ-άπτομαι + *gen* touch

ἐφ-ίημι *act tr* send to, against *or* at; let go; lay upon, entrust; *mid* + *gen* aim at, long for, desire

ἐφ-ίστημι *act tr* set *or* place up on, at *or* near; set up, appoint; set over; check, stop; *act intr and mid* stand on, tread on; approach, be at hand; be set over

ἐφ-οράω look on, observe

ἐφ-ορμέω lie at anchor; blockade

ἐφ-υβρίζω insult; maltreat

ἔχθιστος η ον most hated, most hateful

ἔχθος ους τό, **ἔχθρᾱ** ᾱς ἡ enmity

ἐχθρός ᾱ όν hated, hateful; hating, hostile

　　—**ὁ ἐχθρός** enemy, adversary

ἔχω ἕξω *or* σχήσω ἔσχον have; hold; obtain; be able; + *adv* be, be in a state

ἕως as long as, while; until

Z

ζάθεος ᾱ ον most holy

ζάω βιώσομαι ἐβίων live, be alive

ζειρά ᾶς ἡ long cloak

Ζεύς Διός *or* Ζηνός ὁ Zeus

ζέφυρος ου ὁ west wind

ζηλόω rival; envy, be jealous

ζηλωτός ή όν admired; envied; enviable

ζημίᾱ ᾱς ἡ loss; penalty, punishment

ζημιόω punish

ζητέω seek, seek for

ζωή ῆς ἡ life

ζώω = ζάω live

Η

ἦ truly

ἤ or; than

　　—**ἤ ... ἤ** either ... or

ᾗ where; how, as

ἥβη ης ἡ youth, prime of youth; manhood

ἤγαγον *aor from* ἄγω

ἡγεμονίᾱ ᾱς ἡ leadership, command

ἡγεμών όνος ὁ/ἡ guide, leader

ἡγέομαι think, mean, believe, consider; + *dat* lead the way, go
　　before; be leader

ἤδη now, already

ἠδέ and

ἥδομαι ἡσθήσομαι ἥσθην + *dat* rejoice, be pleased *or* glad, delight
　　in

ἡδύς εῖα ύ sweet, pleasant, lovely, agreeable

ἠέλιος = ἥλιος

ἥκιστα least, not at all

ἥκω have come, be here; be back; have come to, possess; arrive,
　　come to pass, occur

ἠλακάτη ης ἡ distaff, spindle

ἦλθον *aor from* ἔρχομαι

ἡλικίᾱ ᾱς ἡ time of life, age

ἥλιος ου ὁ sun

ἧμαι sit

ἦμαρ ατος τό day

ἡμεῖς we

ἡμέρᾱ ᾱς ἡ day

ἡμέριος ον a day long; short-lived

ἡμέτερος ᾱ ον our

ἥμισυς εια υ half

ἤν = ἐάν

ἤνεγκα, ἤνεγκον *aor from* φέρω

ἤπειρος ου ἡ mainland

ἠπειρώτης ου ὁ inhabitant of the mainland

Ἡρακλῆς έους ὁ Heracles

ἠρόμην *aor from* ἐρωτάω

ἡσσάομαι be defeated *or* beaten

ἥσσων ον less, weaker, inferior; subject

   —**ἧσσον** less

ἡσυχάζω rest, be quiet

ἡσυχίᾱ ᾱς ἡ quiet; a quiet place

ἥσυχος ον quiet

ἤτοι ἦ τοι surely, verily, indeed

ἦτορ τό heart

ἦτρον ου τό belly, abdomen

ἡττ- = ἡσσ-

ἠΰκομος ον lovely-haired

ἠΰτε as, just like, as if

Θ

θάλαμος ου ὁ chamber, bedroom

θάλασσα ης ἡ sea

θαμά often

θαμβέω be astonished *or* amazed (at)

θάμβος ους τό astonishment

θαμίζω come often, frequent

-θαν- *often from* θνήσκω

θάνατος ου ὁ death

θάπτω θάψω ἔθαψα ἐτάφην bury

θαρσέω be bold *or* confident

Θάσος ου ἡ Thasos

θαυμάζω be astonished *or* amazed, wonder; admire; wonder at

θαυμαστός ή όν wonderful

θεάομαι view, look at

θεῖος ᾱ ον divine; holy, sacred; godlike

θέλω = ἐθέλω

Θεμιστοκλῆς έους ὁ Themistocles

θεόδμητος ον god-built

θεοειδής ές godlike

θεόθεν from the gods

θεόμαντις εως ὁ soothsayer

θεός ου ὁ/ἡ god, goddess; deity, divine being

θεράπαινα ης ἡ maid-servant

θεράπων οντος ὁ servant

Θερμοπύλαι ῶν αἱ Thermopylae

θερμός ή όν warm, hot

θέρος ους τό summer

θεσμός οῦ ὁ law, rule; custom

Θεσσαλίᾱ ᾶς ἡ Thessaly

θέσφατος ον announced *or* decreed by god

　　—**τὰ θέσφατα** oracles

θεωρέω look at, see

Θηβαῖος ᾱ ον Theban

θήκη ης ἡ tomb

θήρ θηρός τό wild beast

θηράω hunt; catch

θηρίον ου τό animal, beast

θησαυρός οῦ ὁ treasure house; treasure

Θησεύς έως ὁ Theseus

θητεύω work for hire

θνήσκω θανοῦμαι ἔθανον die, perish; be killed

θνητός ή όν mortal; human

θοός ή όν quick, swift

θορυβέω make a noise *or* uproar; trouble, disturb

Θρᾷξ Θρᾳκός ὁ a Thracian

θρασύς εῖα ύ bold, daring

θραῦμα ατος τό fragment

θρηνέω wail, lament

θρόνος ου ὁ seat, chair; throne

θυγάτηρ τρός ἡ daughter

θυλάκιον ου τό little bag

θῡμός οῦ ὁ soul, life; mind, heart; spirit

θῡμόω make angry; *pass* become angry *or* excited

θύννος ου ὁ tunny fish, tuna

θύρᾱ ᾱς ἡ door

θυρίς ίδος ἡ small door; window

θύρσος ου ὁ thyrsus (wreathed staff of followers of Bacchus)

θυσίᾱ ᾱς ἡ sacrificing; sacrifice

θύω sacrifice; *mid* sacrifice for oneself

θωκέω sit

θώρᾱξ ᾱκος ὁ breastplate

I

ἰαμβεῖον ου τό iambic verse

Ἰάσων ονος ὁ Jason

ἰαχέω, ἰάχω cry aloud, shout

ἰδέ and

ἴδιος ᾱ ον one's own, personal, private; peculiar, strange

　　—**ἰδίᾳ** separately, privately, for oneself

ἰδιώτης ου ὁ private person; private soldier

ἰδού look! there! behold!

ἴδρις ι knowing, skillful, experienced

ἱερεύς έως ὁ priest

ἱερός ᾱ όν holy, sacred

　　—**τὸ ἱερόν** holy place, temple

ἵημι ἥσω ἧκα εἵθην send

Ἰησοῦς ὁ Jesus

Ἰθάκη ης ἡ Ithaca

ἰθύνομαι level, aim

ἱκανός ή όν sufficient, enough

ἱκέτης ου ὁ suppliant, entreating

ἱκνέομαι come, arrive

ἵκω come, arrive

Ἴλιος ου ἡ Troy

ἵμερος ου ὁ longing, yearning; love; charm

ἵνα where; in order that

Ἰνδός οῦ ὁ an Indian

Ἰοκάστη ης ἡ Jocasta

ἰός ου ὁ arrow

ἴος ἴα ἴον one

ἱππάζομαι ride horses

Ἱππαρμόδωρος ου ὁ Hipparmodorus

Ἵππαρχος ου ὁ Hipparchus

ἱππεύς έως ὁ horseman, knight

—οἱ ἱππεῖς the knights (second class of citizen in Attica, required to possess land and a horse)

Ἱππίᾱς ου ὁ Hippias

ἱππιοχαίτης ου shaggy with horse hair

ἵππος ου ὁ horse

ἰσόθεος ον godlike, equal to a god

ἴσος η ον equal

—τὸ ἴσον equal share; equally

ἵστημι *act tr* στήσω ἔστησα ἐστάθην cause to stand; set, place, establish; set up; *act intr aor.* ἔστην *perf. with pres. meaning* ἔστηκα stand, be placed; place oneself

ἱστός οῦ ὁ ship's mast; loom

ἰσχῡρός ά όν strong

ἴσως perhaps, probably; fairly; *with numerals* about

ἴφθῑμος (η) ον strong

ἶφι strongly, stoutly, mightily

ἰχθῦς ύος ὁ fish

Ἰωνίᾱ ᾱς ἡ Ionia

Κ

Κάδμος ου ὁ Cadmus

καθάπερ just as

καθαπτός ή όν fitted out with

καθ-έζομαι sit down

καθ-εύδω καθευδήσω *imperf.* ἐκάθευδον sleep

καθ-ηγέομαι explain, expound

κάθ-ημαι be seated; sit

καθ-ίζω *act tr* make sit down; set down; place; *act intr and mid* sit down

καθ-ίστημι set down, place; constitute, ordain; reduce; *act intr (also mid)* be placed, set down, established *or* appointed; be in a certain condition

καθ-οράω behold, view; perceive

καθ-υβρίζω be insolent; insult

καί and, also, even

   —**καί … καί** both … and

καινός ή όν new

καινόω make new; inaugurate

καίπερ although

καιρός οῦ ὁ right season, opportunity; time

καίτοι and yet

κακός ή όν bad, evil; mean, cowardly

   —**τὸ κακόν** evil, ill, mischief

κακουργέω do evil, act badly; damage; ravage

καλέω καλῶ ἐκάλεσα ἐκλήθην call, call by name; summon; invite

καλός ή όν beautiful, fair, lovely; noble, good; agreeable

Καλυψώ οῦς ἡ Calypso

κάμηλος ου ὁ/ἡ camel

κάμνω καμοῦμαι ἔκαμον work hard; be weary

καπηλεῖον ου τό shop; tavern

καπνός οῦ ὁ smoke

κάρᾱ ᾱτος τό head

καρδίᾱ ᾱς ἡ heart

καρπάλιμος ον swift, quick, hasty

καρτερός ά όν strong, staunch; steadfast; mighty, valiant, courageous, brave; cruel

κασιγνήτη ης ἡ sister

κασίγνητος η ον brotherly, sisterly

κασίγνητος ου ὁ brother

Κάστωρ ορος ὁ Castor

κατά + *acc* over; among, throughout; at; during; in relation to; according to

κατα-βαίνω go *or* come down

κατ-αγγέλλω announce, proclaim

κατ-άγνῡμι break in *or* to pieces, shatter

κατ-άγω lead *or* bring down; *mid* come to land

κατα-δείδω fear greatly

κατα-δύω *act tr* submerge, dip; cause to sink; *act intr and mid* go under water, sink

κατα-θεάομαι look down upon, view

κατα-θνήσκω die

καταθύμιος ᾱ ον being in *or* upon the mind

κατα-καίνω kill

κατα-καίω -καύσω -έκαυσα -εκαύθην burn

κατά-κειμαι lie down

κατακλίνομαι lie down

κατα-κόπτω cut down, slay, kill; tear to pieces

κατα-κτείνω kill

κατα-λαμβάνω seize, take possession of, occupy; catch, overtake, meet

κατα-λέγω relate, tell, explain; list

κατα-λείπω leave behind; forsake, abandon; lose

κατα-λεύω stone to death

κατα-λύω dissolve; destroy, end, abolish, depose, disband

κατα-νεύω *and fut mid* nod in agreement; consent

κατα-νοέω perceive, observe

καταντικρύ just opposite

κατα-ξαίνω tear to pieces; card wool

κατα-παύω stop

κατα-πίνω swallow down

κατα-προδίδωμι betray utterly

κατα-ρέζω stroke, caress

κατ-αρνέομαι deny strongly

κατα-σκάπτω demolish

κατα-σκευάζω prepare, adorn; get ready; *mid* prepare oneself *or* for oneself

κατα-σπουδάζομαι be earnest (about)

κατάστασις εως ἡ state, condition; nature

κατα-στρέφω overturn; *mid* subdue

κατα-τέμνω cut into pieces

κατα-τίθημι place *or* put down

κατα-χώννῡμι cover up, heap up

κατ-είργω hinder, stop

κατ-έχω check, restrain; occupy; possess, keep; take possession of;
   put in at

κατ-ηγορέω + *gen* speak against; accuse, blame, reproach; + *acc*
   assert, state

κάτ-οιδα know exactly

κάτοπτρον ου τό mirror

κάττυμα ατος τό shoe sole

κάτω down, downward; beneath, below; + *gen* below, beneath

καῦμα ατος τό heat

κεῖμαι be laid down, lie

κεῖνος η ο that

κελαινός ή όν dark, gloomy, black

κελεύω exhort, command, order; bid

κέλομαι exhort, command, order; bid

κενός ή όν empty

κέντρον ου τό sting, prick, goad

Κεραμεικός οῦ ὁ Ceramicus (a district in Athens)

κέρας ᾱτος or ως τό horn; wing of an army *or* fleet

κεραυνός οῦ ὁ lightning, thunderbolt

κέρδος ους τό gain, profit, advantage

Κέρκυρα ᾱς ἡ Corcyra

κεύθω hide, conceal

κεφαλή ῆς ἡ head

κήρ κηρός ἡ fate, death

κῆρυξ ῡκος ὁ herald

κηρΰσσω proclaim; announce

κηώδης ες fragrant

Κίλικες ων οἱ the Cilicians

κινδῡνεύω get into danger, run a risk, be in danger

κίνδῡνος ου ὁ danger, risk

κῑνέω move

Κίρκη ης ἡ Circe

κίω go (away)

κλαίω, κλάω κλαύσομαι ἔκλαυσα weep, wail, lament

κλαυσ *likely to be from* κλαίω

κλάω κλάσω ἔκλασα break in pieces

κλείς κλειδός ἡ bar, bolt; key; collar bone

Κλεόμβροτος ου ὁ Cleombrotus

Κλέων ωνος ὁ Cleon

κλέος τό report; glory, good repute, honor

κλέπτω κλέψω ἔκλεψα ἐκλάπην steal

κληρονομέω inherit, gain by inheritance

κλῖμαξ ακος ἡ ladder

κλίνη ης ἡ couch, bed; litter

κλίνω incline, bend; turn; *pass* support oneself against; sink

κλύω hear; listen to

κνήμη ης ἡ shin

κνίζω scratch

κοῖλος η ον hollow

κοινός ή όν common, public

——**τὸ κοινόν** public treasury; community

κοίρανος ου ὁ ruler; lord, master

κοίτη ης ἡ couch, bed; marriage bed

κολάζω punish

κόλπος ου ὁ bosom; fold of a garment; bay; hollow, ship's hold

κόμη ης ἡ the hair

κομίζω take care of, tend; carry away, convey; fetch, bring back; bring to

κομπάζω, κομπέω boast, brag

κόρη ης ἡ girl, maiden; daughter

Κόρινθος ου ἡ Corinth

κόρος ου ὁ satiety, surfeit

κορυβαντιάω be in an ecstatic frenzy (like a Corybant)

κορυθαίολος ον with glancing helmet

κόρυς υθος ἡ helmet

κορύσσω equip (with a helmet); arm, array

κόσμιος ᾱ ον orderly, modest; chaste, decent

κόσμος ου ὁ order, arrangement; decency; world

κούρη ης ἡ girl, maiden; daughter

κοῦφος η ον light

κραίνω, κραιαίνω accomplish, fulfill, bring to pass

κρατερός ά όν = καρτερός

κρατέω be strong *or* mighty, have power; be lord, rule; conquer, subdue, prevail over; obtain by force

κράτιστος η ον strongest; most excellent

κράτος ους τό strength, might, power, force; dominion, rule

κραυγή ῆς ἡ crying, screaming, shout

κρείσσων ον, **κρείττων** ον stronger, better; braver; lord, master

Κρέων οντος ὁ Creon

κρίνω κρινῶ ἔκρινα ἐκρίθην choose; judge, bring to trial, question

κρίσις εως ἡ judgment, sentence; trial, lawsuit

κροκόδειλος ου ὁ crocodile

κρυπτός ή όν hidden, covered; secret

κρύπτω hide, conceal, cover

κρύφα secretly; + *gen* without the knowledge of

κτάομαι κτήσομαι ἐκτησάμην ἐκτήθην gain, get for oneself
   —**κέκτημαι** possess, have

κτείνω κτενῶ ἔκτεινα kill

κτῆμα ατος τό possession, property, goods, treasure

κτυπέω crash, resound

κυκλέω move round and round; turn in a circle

κύκλωμα ατος τό wheel

κυνέω kiss

Κύπρος ου ὁ Cyprus

κυρέω hit *or* light upon; happen

κύριος ᾱ ον having power, ruling
   —**ὁ κύριος** lord, master; ruler, owner; the Lord Christ

Κῦρος ου ὁ Cyrus

κῡρόω make valid, confirm, ratify; decide; accomplish

κύω kiss

κύων κυνός ὁ/ἡ dog, bitch

κῳδάριον ου τό little fleece

κώκῡμα ατος τό shrieking, wailing

κῶλον ου τό limb

κωλύω hinder, prevent
κώνειον ου τό hemlock
κώπη ης ἡ handle of an oar *or* sword; oar

Λ

λαβ *aor stem from* λαμβάνω
λαγχάνω λήξομαι ἔλαχον ἐλήχθην obtain by lot *or* fate
λάθρᾳ secretly, stealthily; without one's knowledge
Λακεδαιμόνιος ᾱ ον Lacedaemonian
Λακεδαίμων ονος ἡ Lacedaemon
Λάκων ωνος ὁ Laconian, Spartan
λαμβάνω λήψομαι ἔλαβον ἐλήφθην take, seize, catch, capture,
    obtain; receive; *mid + gen* keep hold of, grasp
λαμπάς άδος ἡ torch
λαμπρός ά όν bright, shining, brilliant; splendid, magnificent
λάμπω, λάμπομαι shine
λανθάνω λήσω ἔλαθον escape a person's notice, be hidden,
    unnoticed; *mid + gen* forget
λᾱός, οῦ ὁ people
λάσιος ᾱ ον shaggy
λέγω ἐρῶ/λέξω εἶπον/ἔλεξα ἐρρήθην tell, relate, speak, say,
    declare, assert
λείπω λείψω ἔλιπον ἐλείφθην leave, leave remaining *or* behind;
    abandon; *act intr* fail, be lacking; *pass and mid* be left, be left
    behind
λέκτρον ου τό couch, bed; marriage bed; marriage
λέξις εως ἡ speech, mode of speech
λεπιδωτός ή όν scaly, scaled
λέσχη ης ἡ conversation, talk
λευκός ή όν white
λέων οντος ὁ lion
λεώς ώ ὁ people
λήγω cease
λήζω, λήζομαι plunder, despoil, scavenge
ληκύθιον ου τό little oil flask
ληστής οῦ ὁ pirate, robber

Λητώ οῦς ἡ Leto
λίᾱν too much
λίθος ου ὁ stone
λιμήν ένος ὁ harbor, port
λιμναῖος ᾱ ον of the marsh
λιπ *aor stem from* λείπω
λογίζομαι reckon; think
λόγος ου ὁ speech; word; proposal; condition; proportion
λοιδορέομαι abuse, revile; blame; criticize
λοιπός ή όν remaining, surviving, future
λουτρόν οῦ τό bath, bathing place
λούω wash, bathe; *mid* wash oneself
λόφος ου ὁ crest of a helmet; hill
Λῡδίᾱ ᾱς ἡ Lydia
Λύκιος ᾱ ον Lycian
λύκος ου ὁ wolf
λῡπέω give pain to, grieve; *pass* be grieved
λύπη ης ἡ sorrow, distress
λῡπρός ά όν said, painful, wretched
λύω loosen; set free, release; break
λώβη ης ἡ disgrace, shame; ruin
λῷστος η ον the best, dearest

M

μαθητής οῦ ὁ pupil, disciple
Μαισάδης ου ὁ Maesades
μαίνω *aor* ἔμηνα make mad; *pass* be mad, rave, rage, be furious *or* frenzied
μάκαρ αρος (*fem* μάκαιρα) blessed, happy, fortunate; rich
μακάριος (ᾱ) ον happy, my dear . . .
μακραύχην ενος long-necked
μακρός ά όν long; tall; long-lasting; tedious
μάλα much, very much, very
μαλακός ή όν soft, tender; gentle; tender
μάλιστα most, especially, mostly; *with numbers* about
μᾶλλον more, rather

μανθάνω μαθήομαι ἔμαθον learn; ask, inquire; understand
μανίᾱ ᾶς ἡ madness, frenzy
μανιώδης ες mad
μαντείᾱ ᾶς ἡ prophecy, oracle
μάντις εως ὁ/ἡ prophet
μάρναμαι fight
μαρτυρέω be a witness
μαστεύω seek, search for; endeavor; strive
μάταιος (ᾱ) ον idle, foolish, vain
ματεύω seek, search for; endeavor; strive
μάτην in vain; groundlessly
μάχη ης ἡ fight, battle; battlefield
μάχομαι μαχοῦμαι ἐμαχεσάμην fight
μεγαλήτωρ (*gen* ορος) great-hearted
Μέγαρα ων τά Megara
Μεγαρεύς έως ὁ a Megarian
μέγαρον ου τό hall
μέγας μεγάλη μέγα large, great, big
  —**μείζων** ον *comparative*
  —**μέγιστος** η ον *superlative*
μέγεθος ους τό greatness, size; importance
μεθ-άλλομαι leap among
μεθ-ίημι *act tr* let loose; release; *act intr* cease, slacken
μεθ-ίστημι place in another way; remove; *act intr and pass* stand among; withdraw, retire; change one's place
μεθύω be drunk
μείζων ον *comp from* μέγας
μειράκιον ου τό boy, lad, young man
μέλᾱς αινα αν black
μέλει μελήσει ἐμέλησε + *dat* it is a concern to
μέλι ιτος τό honey
μέλιττα ης ἡ bee
μέλλω be about to, be going to, intend; be likely, probably *or* certain; hesitate
μελοποιός οῦ ὁ lyric poet
μέλος ους τό limb; song

μέλω be an object of care, be a care to
  —**μέλει μοι** + *gen* I care for
μέμνημαι *pf pass from* μιμνήσκω
μέμφομαι blame
μέν indeed, rather, certainly
  —**μέν … δέ** on the one hand … but on the other hand
Μενέλεως εω ὁ Menelaus
μέντοι however, nevertheless
μένω μενῶ ἔμεινα stay, stay behind; remain; *tr* await
μέρος ους τό part, portion, share; turn
μεσαιπόλιος ον half-gray, i.e., middle-aged
μεσημβρίᾱ ᾱς ἡ midday; south
μέσος η ον middle, in the middle of
μεστός ή όν full, filled up
μετά + *acc* in quest *or* pursuit of; after; + *gen* among; with, together
  with; + *dat* among, in company with
μετα-βάλλομαι change one's mind
μετα-δίδωμι + *gen* give a share of
μεταίτιος ον responsible
μετα-μέλει μοι + *gen of what is repented of* I repent
μετα-νοέω change one's mind; repent
μετα-πέμπομαι send for; summon
μέτ-ειμι be among, between *or* near
  —**μέτεστι** + *dat of possessor, gen of thing possessed* have a claim to
  or share of
μετ-έχω + *gen* have a share of *or* in; partake (of), join in
μέτριος ᾱ ον moderate
μέτωπον ου τό forehead
μέχρι + *gen* until, as far as
μή not, that not; in order not, lest
μηδαμῶς not at all
μηδέ and not, but not; nor; not even
Μήδεια ᾱς ἡ Medea
μηδείς μηδεμία μηδέν no one, none, not even one; nothing
Μηδικός ή όν Median
μηδισμός οῦ ὁ siding with the Persians, Medism

Μήδοκος ου ὁ Medocus

Μῆδος ου ὁ a Mede

μηκέτι no longer

μήκιστος η ον longest; tallest; greatest

μήν truly, indeed; yet, however

μήν μηνός ὁ month, new moon

μηνύω make known, denounce, betray

μήποτε never; in order that never

μηρίον ου τό, **μηρός** οῦ ὁ thigh bone, thigh

μήτε... μήτε neither... nor

μήτηρ μητρός ἡ mother

μηχανάομαι devise, contrive, prepare

μία *fem* one

μιαιφόνος ον blood-stained; murderous

μιαρός ά όν stained, polluted; wicked

μίμημα ατος τό, **μίμησις** εως ἡ imitation; copy; likeness

μιμνήσκω -μνήσω -έμνησα ἐμνήσθην remind (of), put in mind
   (of); *pass* remember; recall to one's mind

μίν him, her, it; himself

μῑσέω hate

μνήμη ης ἡ memory, remembrance, memorial

μνησ *likely to be from* μιμνήσκω

μνηστήρ ῆρος ὁ wooer, suitor

μοῖρα ᾱς ἡ portion, division; lot, destiny, fate

μοιχεύω commit adultery (with)

μολ *likely to be from* βλώσκω

μόλις with difficulty, hardly

μονογενής ές only-begotten

μόνος η ον alone, only

   —**μόνον, μόνως** only, merely

μόρος ου ὁ fate, destiny; death

μόρσιμος ον destined, appointed by fate

μοῦνος η ον alone, only

μοῦσα ης ἡ Muse

μοχθέω toil, weary oneself, be troubled *or* distressed

μόχθος ου ὁ toil, hardship; labor

Μυτιληναῖος ᾱ ον Mytilenaean
μῡθέομαι speak, say, tell
μῡθολογέω tell tales, myths *or* legends
μῦθος ου ὁ word, speech; news; conversation, talk
μωρίᾱ ᾱς ἡ folly, stupidity

N

ναί yes
ναίω dwell in, inhabit
νᾱός οῦ ὁ temple
ναυᾱγίᾱ ᾱς ἡ shipwreck
ναύαρχος ου ὁ sea captain, admiral
ναύκληρος ου ὁ ship owner, captain
ναυμαχέω fight at sea
ναυμαχίᾱ ᾱς ἡ battle at sea
ναῦς νεώς ἡ ship
ναύτης ου ὁ sailor
ναυτικόν οῦ τό fleet, navy
ναυτίλος ον of a ship, seafaring
νεᾱνίᾱς ου ὁ young man
νεᾶνις ιδος ἡ girl, maiden, young woman
νεᾱνίσκος ου ὁ young man
νεβρός οῦ ὁ/ἡ young deer; fawn
νεῖκος εος τό quarrel, dispute
Νεῖλος ου ὁ Nile
νεκρός ά όν dead; *as noun* dead body, corpse
νέκυς υος ὁ corpse
νέμω νεμῶ ἔνειμα ἐνεμήθην distribute, assign, allot; inhabit;
   (drive to) pasture, pasture one's flocks; *mid* graze on
νέος ᾱ ον young; new; strange, unexpected
   —**νέον** newly, anew; lately, just now
νεοσσός οῦ ὁ young bird or animal; child
νεοσφαγής ές newly killed
νεότης ητος ἡ youth; body of young men
νεύω nod, beckon, bow the head, promise
νέφος ους τό cloud

νεώσοικοι ων οἱ sheds, docks (in which ships might be built, repaired or kept)

νεωτερίζω make changes *or* innovations; use forcible measures, offer violence

νή + *acc* by (a god)!

νημερτής ές unerring, true

νῆσος ου ἡ island

νῑκάω conquer, prevail; be victorious

νίκη ης ἡ victory, conquest

νίν him, her, it

νοέω perceive, notice, see; think

νομεύς έως ὁ herdsman

νομίζω νομιῶ ἐνόμισα ἐνομίσθην think, believe; consider

νόμιμος ον customary; legal, lawful; honest, righteous

　　—τὰ **νόμιμα** custom, usage, law

νόμος ου ὁ custom, usage; law, ordinance, statute

νόος ου ὁ mind, understanding

νοσέω be sick

νόσος ου ἡ sickness, disease

νουθετέω warn, admonish, reprimand

νοῦς οῦ ὁ mind

　　—ἐν **νῷ** **ἔχω** have in mind

νύ = νύν

νύκτωρ by night

νύμφη ης ἡ bride; young wife; nymph

νῦν νῡνί now, just now, at present; then, thereupon, therefore

νυν, νυ now, then; therefore

νύξ νυκτός ἡ night

νωμάω brandish, wield, hold

νῶτον ου τό the back

Ξ

ξανθός ή όν yellow; fair-haired, blonde

ξειν- = ξεν-

ξενίζω receive hospitably; entertain

ξένιον ου τό a guest's gift; *pl* hospitality

ξένος η ον foreign; unacquainted with + *gen*
— **ὁ ξένος** foreigner, stranger; guest-friend
Ξενοφῶν ῶντος ὁ Xenophon
ξεστός ή όν smooth, polished
ξηρός ά όν dry, parched
ξιφήρης ες armed with a sword
ξυμ-/ξυν- = συμ-/συν-

Ο

ὁ ἡ τό the; this
ὅδε ἥδε τόδε this, that
ὁδός οὗ ἡ way, street, road, path; journey
ὀδούς όντος ὁ tooth
ὀδύνη ης ἡ pain, grief
ὀδύρομαι lament
Ὀδυσσεύς έως ὁ Odysseus
ὅθεν from where
ὁθούνεκα because; that
οἱ, οἷ for *or* to him
οἱ μέν ... οἱ δέ some ... others
οἴγνῦμι -οίξω -έῳξα -εῴχθην open
οἶδα εἴσομαι ἤδη know, be knowing
Οἰδίπους ποδος ὁ Oedipus
οἶδμα ατος τό swelling, swell; swollen waves, surge
οἴκαδε homeward, to home
οἰκεῖος ᾱ ον belong to a home, a household *or* a family; of the same
    kin, related; intimate, familiar; one's own; private
οἰκέτης ου ὁ member of the household; servant, slave
οἰκέω inhabit, occupy; settle; dwell, live; manage; *pass* be
    inhabited, situated
οἴκημα ατος τό house, dwelling; room
οἰκίᾱ ᾱς ἡ house
οἴκοθεν from one's house *or* home
οἴκο(θ)ι in the house, at home
οἶκος ου ὁ house, dwelling; household; home
οἰκτείρω, οἰκτίρω pity, bewail

οἶκτος ου ὁ pity

οἶμαι think

οἰμωγή ῆς ἡ lamentation, wailing

οἶνος ου ὁ wine

οἴομαι think

οἶος ᾱ ον alone, only, solitary

οἶος ᾱ ον such as, what kind of

   —**οἶός τέ εἰμι** I am able, I can

   —**οἶόν τέ ἐστι** it is possible

   —**οἶον, οἶα** how, like (as), just as, for instance

ὄϊς ὄϊος ὁ/ἡ sheep

ὀϊστός οῦ ὁ arrow

οἴχομαι be gone, be absent, ruined *or* dead

οἴω, ὀΐω, οἴομαι, οἶμαι suppose, think, believe; intend

ὀκτωκαίδεκα eighteen

Ὀλύμπιος ον Olympian

Ὄλυμπος ου ὁ Mount Olympus

ὄλβιος ᾱ ον happy, blessed; rich, prosperous, valuable

ὀλιγαρχίᾱ ᾱς ἡ oligarchy, government by a few

ὀλίγος η ον few little, small

   —**οἱ ὀλίγοι** the few

ὄλλυμι -ολῶ -ώλεσα destroy, ruin, kill; lose; *mid* perish, die, be ruined

   —**ὄλωλα** *pf* be ruined

ὀλοφύρομαι lament

ὁμαρτέω + *dat* accompany

ὄμβρος ου ὁ rain, shower of rain

Ὅμηρος ου ὁ Homer

ὅμῑλος ου ὁ crowd, throng

ὁμίχλη ης ἡ mist, fog; cloud

ὄμμα ατος τό eye; face

ὄμνῡμι, ὀμνύω ὀμοῦμαι ὤμοσα ὠμόσθην swear

ὁμοῖος ᾱ ον like, similar; the same

ὁμολογέω agree (with)

ὁμονοέω be of one mind

ὁμόνοια ᾱς ἡ unity

ὁμοῦ together

ὅμως nevertheless, yet, all the same

ὄναρ τό dream

ὀνίνημι ὀνήσω ὤνησα ὠνήθην benefit; *mid and pass* have profit, advantage, delight *or* enjoyment

ὄνομα ατος τό name

ὀνομαίνω name

ὄνυξ υχος ὁ nail, talon, claw

ὀξυδερκής ές sharp-sighted

ὀξύς εῖα ύ sharp, keen; piercing

ὀπᾱδός οῦ ὁ/ἡ attendant

ὄπη here

ὀπίσω behind

ὁπλίτης ου ὁ heavy-armed (foot) soldier, hoplite

ὅπλον ου τό *usu pl* tool; ship's tackle; arms, armor; camp

ὁποῖος ᾱ ον of what sort, kind *or* quality

ὁπόσος η ον as many, as many as

ὁπότε, ὁππότε whenever

ὀπώρᾱ ᾱς ἡ autumn

ὅπως how, in what manner; in order to

ὁράω ὄψομαι εἶδον ὤφθην see, look; behold, perceive

ὀργή ῆς ἡ disposition, temper; passion; anger

ὀργίζομαι ὀργιοῦμαι ὠργίσθην become angry

ὀρέγω *and mid* reach, stretch out; *mid and pass* stretch oneself out; reach at *or* to + *gen*

Ὀρέστης ου ὁ Orestes

ὀρθός ή όν straight, upright, erect; right, just; upright; decent

ὁρίζω define, limit, mark out by boundaries

ὅριον ου τό boundary, frontier

ὅρισμα ατος τό boundary, border

ὅρκος ου ὁ oath

ὁρμαίνω, ὁρμάω *act tr* set in quick motion; rouse; consider; ponder; *act intr, mid and pass* set out, proceed; hurry *or* rush on, make an attack

ὁρμίζω bring into harbor; *mid and pass* come to anchor

ὄρνεον ου τό bird

ὄρος ους τό mountain

ὅρος ου ὁ boundary, frontier

ὀρφανός ή όν left orphan; destitute, bereft

ὀρφναῖος ᾱ ον dark, dusky

ὀρχέομαι dance

ὅς ἥ ὅ *rel pron* who, which, that; *demonstrative* he, she, it; *possessive* his, her, one's own

ὁσάκις as many times as, how often

ὅσος η ον as great as, how great, as much, far, long as

ὅσπερ ἥπερ ὅπερ who *or* which indeed

ὄσσε τώ the (two) eyes

ὅστις ἥτις ὅτι whoever, whichever; who, which, that

ὅτε when; since

ὅτι that; because

οὐ, οὐκ, οὐχ, οὐχί not

οὗ where

οὐδαμοῦ nowhere

οὐδαμῶς in no way, not at all

οὐδέ but not; and not; nor; not even

οὐδείς οὐδεμία οὐδέν no one, none, nobody, nothing

οὐδέποτε never

οὐδός οῦ ὁ threshold

οὐκέτι no longer, no more, no further

οὔκουν not therefore? not then? is it not?; not therefore, so not; indeed not

οὐκοῦν therefore, accordingly; so then?

οὖν therefore, accordingly, consequently

οὔνεκα + *gen* on account of

οὔποτε never

οὐπώποτε never yet

οὐρανός οῦ ὁ heaven

οὐρέω urinate

οὖς ὠτός τό ear

οὔτε and not

    —**οὔτε ... οὔτε** neither ... nor

οὔτις no one, nobody

οὗτος αὕτη τοῦτο this, this one

οὑτοσί this here

οὕτω, οὕτως, οὑτωσί thus, in this way *or* manner; so

ὀφείλω ὀφειλήσω ὠφείλησα/ὤφελον owe, be indebted
—**ὤφελον** + *infin* I ought; if only I!

ὄφελος τό profit, advantage; usefulness

ὀφθαλμός οῦ ὁ eye

ὄφρα while; until; in order that

ὀφρῦς ύος ὁ eyebrow

ὀχέω *pass and mid* be carried *or* borne; drive, ride

ὄχλος ου ὁ throng, crowd, the common people, mob

ὄψις εως ἡ sight, appearance

Π

παθ *aor stem of* πάσχω

πάθος ους τό occurrence, accident; suffering

παιγνιά ᾶς ἡ play, sport

παιδαγωγός οῦ ὁ tutor

παιδεύω educate

παιδίον ου τό child

παίζω play

παῖς παιδός ὁ/ἡ child, son, daughter; boy, girl

παίω παίσω ἔπαισα ἐπαίσθην strike, smite; hit

πάλαι of old, formerly, before; just past; a long time ago

παλαιός ά όν old, aged; ancient

παλαίστρᾱ ᾶς ἡ wrestling ground, wrestling school

πάλιν back; again, once more

πάλλω swing, wield, brandish, shake

πάμπολυς πολλη πολυ very much, very great; *pl* very many

παμφαής ές all-shining

παμφανάω shine brightly

πανοῦργος ον villainous, knavish; knave, rogue, villain

πανταχῇ everywhere, in every way

πανταχόθεν from all sides

πανταχοῦ everywhere, in every way

παντοδαπός ή όν of all kinds

παντοῖος ᾱ ον of all kinds, manifold

πάνυ wholly, entirely, altogether; very much

πάομαι acquire

παρά + *acc* along; beside; toward; contrary to, against; + *gen* from beside, from alongside of, from; + *dat* by the side of, beside, near; in the presence of

παρ-αγγέλλω announce; instruct, command

παραγγέλμα ατος τό proclamation, command, instruction

παρα-γίγνομαι + *dat* be present *or* at hand; arrive at; assist, help

παρα-δίδωμι give over, hand over, surrender, consign

παρα-κάθημαι sit beside

παρα-καλέω call to, summon; encourage, excite; invite

παρα-κελεύομαι + *dat* exhort, encourage; advise

παρακοίτης ου ὁ husband, bedfellow

παρα-λαμβάνω receive from another; take possession of; capture, seize; take with one

παρα-λείπω neglect

παραμπ-ίσχω wrap up, cover up

παρα-νομέω break the law

παρασάγγης ου ὁ parasang

παρα-σκευάζω get ready, prepare, equip; *mid* prepare for oneself; prepare oneself, get ready *or* prepared

παρα-σπάω draw aside

παραχρῆμα on the spot, instantly, immediately

πάρεδρος ον sitting beside; assessor, associate

παρειά ᾶς ἡ cheek

παρ-είκει it is allowed *or* practicable

πάρ-ειμι be by, present *or* near; have arrived; be possible
    —**τὰ παρόντα** present circumstances

παρ-έχω provide; show

παρ-ηγορέω exhort, encourage, pacify

παρθένος ου ἡ virgin

παρ-ίστημι place by, beside; *act intr and pass* stand beside; be near, at hand *or* present

Παρνᾱσός οῦ ὁ Mount Parnassus

πάροιθε(ν) before; + *gen* in front of, in the presence of

παρ-οξύνω spur on

παρουσίᾱ ᾱς ἡ presence

πᾶς πᾶσα πᾶν all, whole, entire; every

πάσχω πείσομαι ἔπαθον suffer; experience, be affected by

πατήρ πατρός ὁ father

πάτρᾱ ᾱς ἡ, **πάτρη** fatherland

πάτριος (ᾱ) ον of one's father *or* forefathers; hereditary, customary, native, national

πατρίς ίδος ἡ one's country, fatherland

πατρόθεν from the father's side

πατρῷος ᾱ ον of one's father, hereditary, ancestral

Παυσανίᾱς ου ὁ Pausanias

παύω cause to cease, stop, bring to an end; *pass and mid* leave off, cease

πεδίον ου τό plain

πέδον ου τό ground, soil

πεζῇ on foot

πεζομαχέω fight by hand

πείθω πείσω ἔπεισα ἐπείσθην persuade; bribe; *act intr, mid and pass* πείσομαι ἐπιθόμην + *dat* believe, trust; listen to, obey

πειράω πειράσω ἐπείρασα *mid and pass* try, attempt; experience

Πειραιεύς ῶς ὁ Piraeus

πελάγιος ᾱ ον of *or* on the sea

πέλας near; + *gen* near to

Πελοπόννησος ου ἡ Peloponnese

πελταστής οῦ ὁ light-armed soldier, peltast

πέμπω πέμψω ἔπεμψα ἐπέμφθην send

πένης (gen ητος) poor

πενθέω mourn

πένθος ους τό grief, sorrow; misfortune

πέντε five

πεντεκαίδεκα fifteen

πεντήκοντα fifty

πέπλος ου ὁ garment, robe, long dress

περ at any rate

πέρᾱν on the other side

περάω περάσω ἐπέρασα *intr* go

πέργαμον ου τό, **πέργαμα** ων τά castle, citadel

πέρθω πέρσω ἔπερσα destroy, ravage

περί + *acc* about, around; + *gen* around, about; on account of, for; for the sake of; + *dat* around

περι-άγω lead, drive *or* turn round

περι-αιρέω take off all round; take away; *mid* take away from oneself; strip off; rob

περι-βάλλω throw round, about *or* over; embrace, surround; *mid* throw round oneself, put on

περι-γίγνομαι + *gen* overcome, excel, be superior (to)

περι-έρχομαι go round, walk about

περι-έχω surround

Περικλῆς έους ὁ Pericles

περι-κόπτω cut off, mutilate

περι-λάμπω shine round about

περίλῡπος ον very sorrowful

περιμήκης ες very long *or* high

περι-οράω look around for; overlook; suffer; allow

περι-πτύσσω enfold, enwrap; surround

περι-στέλλω dress; take care of; cover; lay out (a carpet)

περι-στέφω encircle with a crown

περι-τίθημι put *or* place round about; put on; *mid* put round oneself

περι-τυγχάνω + *dat* fall in with, meet by chance, encounter, light upon

Περσικός ή όν Persian

πεσ *likely to be from* πίπτω

πέτομαι πετήσομαι/πτήσομαι ἐπτόμην/ἐπτάμην fly

πέτρᾱ ᾱς ἡ rock

πετρόομαι be stoned

πεύκη ης ἡ pine

πῇ, πῆ which way? where? how? why?

πῃ somewhere; somehow, in some way, in any way

πηγή ῆς ἡ spring

πήγνῡμι πήξω ἔπηξα ἐπάγην *act tr* stick, fix, make firm; *act intr and pass* be fixed, stiff *or* frozen; stick

πηδάω spring, leap, dart

Πηνελόπη ης ἡ Penelope

πῆχυς εως ὁ cubit (distance from the point of the elbow to the end of the little finger)

πιέζω press, squeeze

πικρός ά όν bitter; harsh; hateful

πίνω πίομαι ἔπιον drink

πίπτω πεσοῦμαι ἔπεσον fall, fall down

πιστεύω + *dat* believe, trust, confide *or* put faith in

πιστός ή όν faithful, trusty; trustworthy

πίσυνος ον + *dat* trusting in

πίτνω fall

πίων πῖον (gen πίονος) fat; rich; wealthy

Πλάταια ᾶς ἡ *or pl* Plataea

Πλαταιεύς έως ὁ a Plataean

πλάζω strike; beat back; drive away; mislead; *pass* wander, go astray

πλάτη ης ἡ blade of an oar; oar; ship

πλατύς εῖα ύ flat

πλειστάκις very many times

πλεῖστος η ον most, greatest

πλε(ί)ων ον more, greater

πλεονεκτέω claim more, be greedy

πλέος ον full

πλέω πλεύσομαι ἔπλευσα sail

πλέως ᾱ ων full

πληγή ῆς ἡ blow, stroke; a drubbing

πλῆθος ους τό mass, crowd; the greater part, multitude; great number

πληθύς ύος ἡ crowd, throng

πληθύω be *or* become full

πλήν + *gen* except; besides

πλήρης ες full, filled with

πλησίος ᾱ ον near, close by

— **πλησίον** + *gen or dat* near, close to

πλήσσω πλήξω ἔπληξα ἐπλήγην/ἐπλάγην strike, smite

πλοῖον ου τό ship

πλόκαμος ου ὁ lock of hair

πλοῦς οῦ ὁ voyage

πλούσιος ᾱ ον rich, wealthy

πνεῦμα ατος τό wind; breath; spirit; Holy Spirit

πνέω πνεύσομαι/πνευσοῦμαι ἔπνευσα blow, breathe

ποδάρκης ες swift-footed (of Achilles)

πόθεν from where? how?

πόθι = ποῦ

ποι to somewhere

ποιέω make, do; *mid* make for oneself; hold, reckon, esteem

ποίημα ατος τό poem

ποίησις εως ἡ creating; poetry

ποιητής οῦ ὁ poet

ποιμήν ένος ὁ shepherd

ποίμνη ης ἡ flock, herd

ποίμνιον ου τό flock, herd

ποῖος ᾱ ον of what nature? of what kind?

πολεμέω make war; wage war on

πολεμίζω make war

πολέμιος ᾱ ον warlike, hostile

— **οἱ πολέμιοι** enemy, adversary

πόλεμος ου ὁ war; fight, battle

πολιορκέω besiege, beleaguer; harass, pester

πολιός ά όν gray, white

πόλις εως ἡ city, town; city state

πολίτης ου ὁ citizen; fellow citizen

πολῑτικός οῦ ὁ statesman

πολλάκις many times, often

πολλόν much

πολυμαθής ές knowing much, very learned

πολύμητις (gen ιος) of many counsels, much-devising

Πολυνείκης ους ὁ Polynices

πολύς πολλή πολύ much, many; large, ample

— **πλείων** ον more, more numerous; larger, stronger

— **πλεῖστος** η ον most, very much; widely circulated

— **οἱ πολλοί** the majority, the many, the people

— **πολύ** much

πολύτροπος ον versatile, ingenious; crafty

πομπή ῆς ἡ escort; solemn procession

πονηρός ά όν bad

πόνος ου ὁ toil, hard work, hardship; distress, pain; grief, misery

πόντος ου ὁ sea, open sea

πορεύομαι go, march

πορθέω destroy, waste, plunder

πορίζω furnish, provide, supply

πόρρω further; far off

πόσις ιος or εως ἡ drinking; drink

πόσις εως ὁ husband

ποταμός οῦ ὁ river

ποτε at any time; at some time, ever

πότερος ᾱ ον which of the two?

　　—πότερον . . . ἤ (whether) . . . or

ποτήριον ου τό drinking cup

Ποτίδαια ᾱς ἡ Potidaea

πότνια ᾱς ἡ mistress; revered, noble

ποῦ where?

που anywhere; at any time; I suppose, perhaps

πούς ποδός ὁ foot

πρᾶγμα ατος τό doing, deed; action; fact, occurrence, matter, thing, circumstance; business, task, enterprise; affair; public *or* private affairs, state affairs, public business; issue

πρᾱγματεύομαι execute, accomplish

πρᾶος πρᾱεῖα πρᾶον even-tempered

πρᾱ́σσω πρᾱ́ξω ἔπρᾱξα ἐπρᾱ́χθην achieve, do; *act intr* be in a certain state *or* condition; fare

πρέπω be conspicuous *or* seen; be manifest

　　—πρέπει + *dat* it is fitting for; it suits *or* becomes

πρεσβείᾱ ᾱς ἡ embassy

πρεσβεύω be an ambassador; send ambassadors; honor, revere, worship; *mid* send ambassadors, be an ambassador

πρέσβυς εως ὁ old man, elder

　　—πρεσβύτατος η ον oldest

　　—οἱ πρέσβεις ambassadors

πρεσβῠ́της ου ὁ old man

Πρίαμος ου ὁ Priam

πρίν before; *conj* before

πρό + *gen* before, in front

προ-άγω lead on *or* forward; carry forward, bring on

προ-αιρέομαι choose for oneself

προ-αισθάνομαι perceive before, know beforehand

πρόγονος ον ancestor, forefather

προδότης ου ὁ traitor; runaway

πρό-ειμι go forward

προέξ-ειμι go out before

προ-έρχομαι go forth, on *or* forward, advance

προ-έχω have before; *act intr* be before, be the first

πρόθῡμος ον ready, willing; eager; zealous

προ-ϊάπτω send forth

προ-ῑ́ημι send on *or* forward

προ-ίστημι *act tr* place before *or* in front; *act intr and pass* place oneself before; protect; be at the head (of), manage, govern

προ-καλέω call forth; *mid* challenge

πρόλογος ου ὁ prologue

πρόμαχος ον fighting before *or* in front; foremost fighter

πρόμος ου ὁ leader

προνωπής ές stooping forward

προοίμιον ου τό prelude, preamble

προ-πάσχω suffer before

προ-πέμπω send before

πρός + *acc* toward, to; against; in regard to; in relation to; + *gen* from; on the part of; by (a god)!; *with a pass verb* = ὑπό; + *dat* at, on; in addition to

προσ-αγορεύω address, greet; call by name

προσ-άγω *act tr* bring on; lead on; *act intr* advance, approach

προσάμβασις εως ἡ ascent

προσ-άπτω attach *or* fasten to

προσ-βάλλω throw to *or* upon; *intr* + *dat* attack

προσβολή ῆς ἡ attack, assault

προσ-εικάζω liken

προσ-έρχομαι go *or* come up, to *or* forward; approach; advance

προσέτι besides

προσ-εύχομαι pray

προσ-έχω bring to, direct to; bring to land

προσ-ήκει + *dat* it befits *or* is proper (for)

προσήκων ουσα ον belonging to; related; relation

πρόσθε(ν) + *gen* in front of, before; formerly

προσ-ιππεύω ride up to

προσ-κομίζω carry, convey to

προσ-λεύσσω look at *or* on

προσ-πίπτω + *dat* fall against *or* upon; attack, assault

προσ-πίτνω + *dat* fall upon

προσ-ποιέομαι pretend

πρόσπολος ον serving; servant, attendant

προσ-τρέπω supplicate, beg

προσ-φέρω carry to; offer; *mid and pass* behave oneself

πρόσ-φημι speak to, address

πρόσωπον ου τό face, countenance

προ-τάσσω, προτάττω assign

προ-τείνω stretch out *or* forward; offer

προτεραῖος ᾱ ον of *or* on the day before

πρότερος ᾱ ον earlier; former, previous

　　—**πρότερον** formerly, before, sooner

προ-τῑμωρέω help beforehand; *mid* revenge oneself before, punish
　　before

πρόφασις εως ἡ pretext

πρῶτος η ον first, foremost

　　—**πρῶτα** first

　　—**τὸ πρῶτον** at first

πτερόν οῦ τό feather; wing

πτηνός ή όν winged, on wings

πτολ- = **πολ-**

πτολίεθρον ου τό = **πόλις**

πτόρθος ου ὁ shoot, branch

πτΰω spit (out)

πτωχός ή όν poor; beggar

πυθ *aor stem of* πυνθάνομαι

Πυλάδης ου ὁ Pylades

πύλη ης ἡ gate

πυνθάνομαι πεύσομαι ἐπυθόμην inquire; hear, learn; find out

πῦρ πυρός τό fire; lightning

πύργος ου ὁ tower; fortress, bulwark

πωλέω πωλήσω ἐπώλησα ἐπράθην sell

πωλίον ου τό pony

πωλοδαμνέω break in (young horse)

πώποτε ever yet

πῶς how? in what way *or* manner?

Ρ

ῥά, ῥ' = ἄρα

ῥᾴδιος ᾱ ον easy; ready

ῥαχίζω cut through the spine, cut in two, splice

ῥέγκω snore

ῥεῦμα ατος τό flow, river

ῥήγνῡμι break, break off, rend

ῥῆμα ατος τό word, phrase

ῥήτωρ ορος ὁ orator, public speaker; statesman; politician

ῥίπτω, ῥῑπτέω throw

ῥίς ῥῑνός ἡ nose; *pl* nostrils

ῥώμη ης ἡ strength

Σ

σατραπεύω be a satrap (a Persian governor)

σαυτοῦ ῆς of yourself

σαφής ές clear, plain, manifest

σέβω honor, revere

σεισμός οῦ ὁ earthquake

σείω shake, brandish

σεμνός ή όν august, sacred, solemn, holy; stately; grave

σεύω put in quick motion; *mid and pass* rush, run

σημαίνω σημανῶ ἐσήμηνα ἐσημάνθην signify, indicate; give a sign *or* signal; point out, announce

σημεῖον τό sign

σήμερον today

σθένω be strong *or* mighty; rule, have power; be able

σῑγάω be silent, keep silence; conceal

σῑγή ῆς ἡ silence

σίνομαι hurt

σῑτίον ου τό food, provisions

σῖτος ου ὁ wheat, grain; bread; food

σιωπή ῆς ἡ silence

σκέλος ους τό leg

σκέπτομαι consider

σκηνή ῆς ἡ tent

σκήνωμα ατος τό tent

σκῆψις εως ἡ pretense, excuse, reason

σκιά ᾶς ἡ shadow

σκληρός ά όν hard

σκοπέω look at, about *or* out; consider; examine; pay regard to, heed

σκοταῖος ᾱ ον dark; in the dark

σκοτεινός ή όν dark; in the dark

σκότος ου ὁ *or* εος τό darkness, gloom; night

σκῡτεύς έως ὁ shoemaker, saddler

σός σή σόν your

σοφίᾱ ᾶς ἡ cleverness, skill; wisdom

σοφός ή όν clever; learned; wise

σπάνις εως ἡ need, scarcity

σπαργανόω wrap in swaddling clothes

Σπάρτη ης ἡ Sparta

σπάω σπάσω ἔσπασα ἐσπάσθην draw, pull

σπείρω σπερῶ ἔσπειρα ἐσπάρην sow; *pass* be scattered, be spread abroad

σπένδω σπείσω ἔσπεισα pour out a drink offering; *mid* make a treaty *or* truce, conclude a peace

σπέος σπείους τό cave, grotto

σπήλαιον ου τό cave

σποδιά ᾶς ἡ, **σποδός** οῦ ἡ ashes

σπονδή ῆς ἡ libation; *pl* peace, truce

σπουδή ῆς ἡ haste, speed

στάδιον ου τό stade (606¾ English feet)

σταθμός οῦ ὁ day's march

στέγη ης ἡ covering, roof; house, dwelling

στείχω walk, step, go

στερέω deprive (of something *in gen*); *pass + gen* be deprived (of)

στέρνον ου τό breast; chest

στερρός ά όν stark, harsh

στέφανος ου ὁ crown

στεφανόω crown, wreathe

στῖφος ους τό dense crowd, column of warriors

στόλος ου ὁ expedition; army, armament

στόμα ατος τό mouth

στρατείᾱ ᾱς ἡ expedition, campaign; army

στράτευμα ατος τό army; expedition

στρατεύω serve as a soldier; take the field, march

στρατηγός οῦ ὁ general, leader, commander of an army

στρατιᾱ́ ᾱς ἡ army, force

στρατιώτης ου ὁ soldier

στρατοπεδεύομαι encamp

στρατόπεδον ου τό encampment, camp

στρατός οῦ ὁ army, host; encampment

στρέφω στρέψω ἔστρεψα ἐστράφην twist, turn

σύ σοῦ you

συγγενής ές born with; connected by birth, related; kinsman

συγ-γίγνομαι + *dat* come together; meet; converse with; live with; have sex with

σύγγονος ον brother, sister

συγ-καλέω call together

συγ-χωρέω agree, come to terms with

σῡκοφάντης ου ὁ informer

σῡλάω despoil, pillage, plunder

συλ-λαμβάνω put *or* bring together; seize, arrest

συλ-λέγω collect, gather, call together; *pass* assemble; *mid* collect

σύλλογος ου ὁ gathering, meeting, assembly
συμ-βαίνω come together, meet; agree, make an agreement; happen, fall out
—**συμβαίνει** it happens, it is possible
σύμβασις εως ἡ treaty, agreement
σύμμαχος ου ὁ ally
σύμπᾶς πᾶσα παν all together; the whole
συμ-πέμπω send along with
συμ-πλέω sail together
συμ-ποιέω do along with
συμ-προθῡμέομαι have equal zeal or eagerness
συμ-φέρω contribute; *intr* + *dat* be useful, profitable (for)
συμφορά ᾶς ἡ disaster
σύμφορος ον useful, profitable, favorable; convenient
σύν, ξύν + *dat* with, in company with, together with, in connection with
συν-άγω lead or bring together, collect, assemble; summon
συν-αθροίζω gather together
σύναιμος ον related by blood, kindred
συν-ακολουθέω + *dat* follow along with
συν-αρμόζω fit together, join
συν-δειπνέω + *dat* dine together (with)
συνέπ-ειμι come with
συν-έρχομαι come together
συνήθης ες familiar; customary, habitual
συν-ίστημι place, bring or set together; *act intr and mid* come or stand together; league together
σύνοδος ου ἡ assembly, meeting
σύν-οιδα know together with; be conscious
σύνοικος ον dwelling or living together; companion
συν-τρέχω run together; come together, assemble; rush together
συν-τρίβω rub together; crush, shatter
συνωμότης ου ὁ fellow conspirator
σφαγή ῆς ἡ slaughter; sacrifice; murder
σφάγιον ου τό sacrifice
σφάζω slaughter

σφάλλω σφαλῶ ἔσφηλα ἐσφάλην make fall or stumble; destroy, ruin

σφᾶς them

σφενδονάω sling

σφενδόνη ης ἡ sling; collet of a ring

σφέτερος ᾱ ον their (own)

σφήξ σφηκός ὁ wasp

σφόδρα, σφοδρῶς very much, vehemently

σφῶι both of you

σχεδίᾱ ᾶς ἡ raft

σχεδόν almost

σχῆμα ατος τό form, shape, outward appearance; constitution, nature; manner

σχολάζω be at leisure; linger, delay

σῴζω σώσω ἔσωσα ἐσώθην save, keep safe, preserve, protect

Σωκράτης ους ὁ Socrates

σῶμα ατος τό body

σῶος α ον safe

σῶς σῶν safe and sound; sure

Σώστρατος ου ὁ Sostratus

σωτήρ ῆρος ὁ savior, preserver, deliverer

σωτηρίᾱ ᾶς ἡ safety

σωφρονέω be sensible, discreet or moderate

σωφροσύνη ης ἡ moderation; chastity, decent behavior

T

ταλαίπωρος ον suffering, wretched, miserable

τάλᾱς τάλαινα τάλαν enduring, suffering, wretched; cruel

ταλασιουργέω spin wool

Ταξίλης ου ὁ Taxiles

τάξις εως ἡ line of soldiers

τάρασσω stir up, disturb; agitate

ταραχή ῆς ἡ disorder

ταρβέω be afraid or alarmed

τάσσω, τάττω τάξω ἔταξα ἐτάχθην arrange; draw up in a line or in order of battle; appoint; give instructions

ταῦρος ου ὁ bull

ταύτῃ in this way

τάφος ου ὁ burial; grave

τάχα soon; perhaps

τάχιστος η ον swiftest, quickest, fastest

ταχύς εῖα ύ swift, quick, fast

τε and

— **τε . . . καί** both . . . and

τέγγω wet, moisten

τειχομαχέω attack the walls, besiege; fight by siege

τεῖχος ους τό wall; fortification, castle

τεκ *aor stem from* τίκτω

τέκνον ου τό child

τέκτων ονος ὁ carpenter, joiner, builder

τελευταῖος ᾱ ον last

τελευτάω complete, accomplish, finish; *intr* end, die, be fulfilled

τελευτή ῆς ἡ end, death

τελέω τελῶ ἐτέλεσα ἐτελέσθην end, bring to an end, complete, finish, fulfill; accomplish

τέμνω τεμοῦμαι ἔτεμον ἐτμήθην cut; lay waste

Τένεδος ου ἡ Tenedos

τέρας α(τ)ος τό monster

τέρμων ονος ὁ boundary

τέσσαρες α four

τέταρτος η ον fourth

τετμεῖν *aor infin* arrive at, overtake, find

τετράκις four times

τετράπαλαι long, long ago

τετράπους πουν four-footed

τεύχω make, build; cause, create

τέχνη ης ἡ art, skill, craft, trade

τέως meanwhile

τῇδε here

τηλόθι far away

τηνικαῦτα then, at that time

τίθημι θήσω ἔθηκα ἐτέθην put, place, set; reckon, count

τιθήνη ης ἡ nurse

τίκτω τέξομαι ἔτεκον bring forth, bear; beget

τῑμάω estimate; honor, respect, revere

τῑμή ῆς ἡ honor, esteem; dignity, privilege

τῑμωρέω (and mid) + dat avenge; help, succor; + acc punish

τῑμωρίᾱ ᾶς ἡ vengeance

τίνω τείσω ἔτεισα ἐτείσθην pay; pay a penalty or debt; honor; atone

τίς τί who? which? what?

　　—**τί** why?

τις τι anyone, someone, a certain

τιτθός οῦ ὁ teat, nipple

τιτύσκομαι aim at

τλάω bear, endure

τλῆναι aor inf suffer, endure, bear; dare, risk

τοι let me tell you; certainly; then

τοιγάρ so then, therefore, accordingly; therefore indeed

τοίνυν yet, so then, therefore; further; moreover

τοιόσδε ἅδε όνδε, **τοιοῦτος** αὕτη οὗτο(ν) of such kind or quality, just such

τοκεύς έως ὁ parent; pl parents

τόκος ου ὁ childbirth, birth; child; (of money) interest

τόλμα ης ἡ courage, boldness

τολμάω bear, endure; dare

τολμηρός ά όν enduring, steadfast, bold; daring

τόξον ου τό bow

τόπος ου ὁ place, spot

τόσος η ον, **τοσόσδε** ηδε ονδε, **τοσοῦτος** αὕτη οὗτο(ν) so great, so much; pl so many

τότε then, at that time

τραγῳδίᾱ ᾶς ἡ tragedy

τράπεζα ης ἡ table

τραῦμα ατος τό wound

τρᾱχύς εῖα ύ rough, rugged; harsh

τρεῖς τρία three

τρέπω τρέψω ἔτρεψα ἐτράπην turn, turn round; divert, direct; turn to flight; *mid and pass* turn oneself (to)

τρέφω θρέψω ἔθρεψα ἐτράφην feed, nourish, rear, bring up; *pass* be fed; grow (up); live; be brought up

τρῆμα ατος τό hole

τριάκοντα thirty

τριᾱκόσιοι αι α three hundred

τριήρης ους ἡ trireme, ship with three banks of oars

τρίς three times

τριταῖος ᾱ ον in three days; on the third day

Τροίᾱ ᾱς ἡ Troy

τρόμος ου ὁ a trembling

τρόπος ου ὁ manner, way, fashion

τροφή ῆς ἡ food, nourishment; rearing

τροφός οῦ ὁ nurse

τροχίλος ου ὁ plover

τρυφάω live delicately *or* in luxury; revel

Τρωικός ή όν Trojan

Τρώς Τρωός ὁ a Trojan

τυγχάνω τεύξομαι ἔτυχον hit; gain, get; *intr* happen

τύπτω beat, smite

τυραννεύω + *gen* be a tyrant *or* absolute ruler (over)

τύραννος ου ὁ absolute monarch, sovereign, lord, master; tyrant

τῡρός οῦ ὁ cheese

τυφλός ή όν blind

τύχη ης ἡ chance; fortune

Υ

ὑβρίζω be *or* become uncontrolled *or* insolent; insult, maltreat

ὕβρις εως ἡ insolence; outrage, insult; hubris

ὑγίεια ᾱς ἡ health

ὑγιής ές healthy; unwounded

ὑγρός ά όν wet, moist

ὕδρᾱ ᾱς ἡ water serpent, hydra

ὕδωρ ατος τό water; rain

υἱός οῦ ὁ son

ὕλη ης ἡ wood

ὑμεῖς you (pl)

ὑμέτερος ᾱ ον your

ὑμνέω sing; praise

ὑός = υἱός

ὑπ-ακούω listen to; obey

ὑπεκ-πέμπω send away *or* escort secretly

ὑπέρ + *gen* over; above; for, on behalf, in defense of, for the sake of, because of, by reason of; + *acc* beyond, exceeding

ὑπερ-βαίνω step over; transgress; pass over

ὑπερεπ-αινέω praise exceedingly

ὑπερ-ήδομαι rejoice exceedingly

ὑπερπόντιος ον beyond the sea; across the sea

ὑπερ-τρέχω outrun; surpass; supersede

ὑπερώιον ου τό upper storey, upper room

ὑπήκοος ον obedient, subject

ὑπηρέτης ου ὁ servant; assistant

ὑπ-ισχνέομαι ὑποσχήσομαι ὑπεσχόμην promise

ὕπνος ου ὁ sleep

ὑπό + *gen* by

ὑπόγαιος ον, **ὑπογειος** ον underground, subterranean

ὑποζύγιον ου τό beast of burden

ὑπο-λείπω leave behind

ὑπο-νοέω suspect

ὑπόσχεσις εως ἡ, **ὑποσχεσίη** ης ἡ promise

ὑπο-φθάνω be beforehand, anticipate

ὑποχείριος ον under one's power, subject

ὕπτιος ᾱ ον on one's back

ὗς ὑός ὁ/ἡ pig

ὑστεραῖος ᾱ ον following, later, next

ὕστερος ᾱ ον coming after, following, later

    —**ὕστερον** afterward, later, in future

ὑφίημι send down; lower; slacken

ὑψηλός ή όν high

ὕψι high, on high

ὑψίπυλος ον with high gates
ὕει it is raining

Φ

φαγ *likely to be from* ἐσθίω
φαεινός ή όν shining, beaming
φαίδιμος ον shining; illustrious; famous, glorious
Φαίᾱκες ων οἱ Phaeacians
φαίνω φανῶ ἔφηνα ἐφάνην *act tr* bring to light, show; *pass* appear;
  be conspicuous; be seen
φανερός (ά) όν visible, manifest, conspicuous
φάος ους τό light
φαρέτρᾱ ᾱς ἡ quiver
φάρμακον ου τό drug, medicine; poison
Φαρνάβαζος ου ὁ Pharnabazus
φάσγανον ου τό knife, sword
φάσκω claim, say, assert
φάτνη ης ἡ manger, crib; horse stable
φαῦλος (η) ον bad; slight, trifling; useless, mean, common,
  worthless
φέγγος ους τό light
φείδομαι φείσομαι ἐφείσαμην + *gen* spare
φένω slay, murder
φέρτερος ᾱ ον better, braver, preferable
φέρω οἴσω ἤνεγκα/ἤνεγκον ἠνέχθην bear, carry; suffer; endure;
  bring; produce; *mid* bring with one
  —χαλεπῶς or βαρέως φέρειν bear impatiently, endure with a
  bad grace
φεῦ ah! alas!
φεύγω φεύξομαι ἔφυγον flee, take flight, run away; flee before
  (someone); shun; be banished; be an exile; be accused *or*
  prosecuted
φημί φήσω ἔφησα *imperf* ἔφην say, speak
φθάνω φθήσομαι ἔφθασα/ἔφθην come *or* reach before, be sooner
  or first
φθέγγομαι cry aloud; speak

φθογγή ῆς ἡ voice; speech

φθονέω envy, grudge, bear ill-will

φιλέω love

Φίλιππος ου ὁ Philip

φιλομμειδής ές sweet-smiling, laughter-loving

φίλος η ον loved, beloved, dear; friendly
   —**ὁ φίλος** friend, companion

φιλόσοφος ου ὁ philosopher

φιλοτῑμίᾱ ᾱς ἡ love of honor *or* distinction; honor, distinction

φοβέω φοβήσω ἐφόβησα ἐφόβηθην terrify, put to flight; *mid and*
   pass be frightened; fear; be alarmed *or* afraid

φόβος ου ὁ fear, flight

φοίνιος (ᾱ) ον bloody

φοιτάω go to and fro; roam wildly about; go regularly, frequent

φονεύς έως ὁ/ἡ murderer

φονεύω murder, slay

φόνιος (ᾱ) ον murderous; bloody

φόνος ου ὁ murder, slaughter

φορέω wear

φράζω φράσω ἔφρασα make clear; declare, tell, utter

φρήν φρενός ἡ *usu pl* midriff; breast; soul, mind, heart; sense

φρονέω think, be wise; understand

φρόνιμος ον in one's senses; prudent, sensible, wise

φροντίζω think, consider; give heed to, care about + *gen*

φροντίς ίδος ἡ thought, care; reflection

φροῦδος η ον gone away; gone, departed

φυγάς (gen άδος) fugitive, banished, exile

φυγή ῆς ἡ flight, escape, banishment

φυλακή ῆς ἡ keeping guard; watch, guard; watchfulness

φύλαξ ακος ὁ guard

φυλάσσω φυλάξω ἐφύλαξα ἐφυλάχθην *act intrans* watch; keep
   guard; be on one's guard; *act trans* watch, guard, keep, preserve,
   protect; *mid* shun, avoid

φύξιμος ον able to flee

φῡράω mix up, knead

φῦσα ης ἡ wind (in the stomach)

φύσις εως ἡ nature, inborn quality; disposition

φύω *act tr* φύσω ἔφῦσα produce, beget, bring forth, make to grow;
  act intr and pass φύσομαι ἔφῦν *perf* πέφῦκα grow, spring up, be
  born; be by nature

φωνή ῆς ἡ voice, speech, language

φώς φωτός ὁ man

φῶς φωτός τό light

X

χαίρω χαιρήσω ἐχάρην rejoice, be glad
  —**χαῖρε, χαίρετε** hail! welcome! farewell!

χαλεπός ή όν hard, severe, difficult, dangerous; disagreeable

χαλεπῶς with difficulty; harshly
  —**χαλεπῶς φέρειν** bear impatiently, endure with a bad grace

χάλκεος ᾶ ον, **χαλκοῦς** ῆ οῦν of copper *or* bronze, brazen

χαλκεύς έως ὁ smith, worker in metal

χαλκός οῦ ὁ copper; bronze; brass

χαρά ᾶς ἡ joy, delight, pleasure; darling

χαρίεις εσσα εν graceful, lovely, charming, pleasing

χαρίζομαι show favor *or* kindness

χάρις ιτος ἡ joy; favor; gratitude; thanks
  —**χάριν** + *gen* for the sake of, on account of
  —**χάριν ἔχω** feel gratitude

χαρμονή ῆς ἡ joy, delight

χάσκω gape, yawn; swallow up

χάσμα ατος τό cleft, chasm

χαυλιόδων οντος ὁ with projecting teeth *or* tusks, projecting

χεῖλος εος τό lip

χειμέριος (ᾱ) ον wintry

χειμών ῶνος ὁ winter; frost, cold; storm

χείρ χειρός ἡ hand

χειροτονίᾱ ᾱς ἡ voting (by show of hands), election

χειρόω (*and mid*) master, subdue

χερσαῖος ᾱ ον living on dry land

χέω χέω ἔχεα ἐχύθην pour; pour out, shed

χήν χηνός ὁ/ἡ goose

χθόνιος (ᾱ) ον in, under, of *or* beneath the earth; native, indigenous; of the nether world

χθών χθονός ἡ soil, ground, earth; country

χίλιοι αι α a thousand

χιτών ῶνος ὁ tunic

χιών όνος ἡ snow

χλαμύς ύδος ἡ cloak; military cloak, short cloak

χλωρός ά όν light green, yellow; green, fresh

χοιράς άδος ἡ low *or* sunken (rock)

χολάω be bilious, angry *or* melancholy

χόλος ου ὁ gall, bile; wrath, anger

χορεύω dance in a chorus; dance

χορός οῦ ὁ dance; choral dance; chorus

χράομαι χρήσομαι ἐχρησάμην use; be possessed of, possess; have dealings with; treat, practice

χρέος ους τό debt

χρή *imperf* (ἐ)χρῆν it is necessary, it must, it is right *or* proper; it is fated; there is need

χρῆμα ατος τό thing, matter; business; *pl* goods, money

χρησμολόγος ου ὁ oracle monger

χρησμῳδός όν prophesying, oracle singing

χρηστός ή όν good

χρῑστός ή όν anointed; the Anointed One, Christ

χρόνος ου ὁ time

χρύσεος η ον, **χρῡσοῦς** ῆ οῦν golden

χρῡσός οῦ ὁ gold

χύτρᾱ ᾱς ἡ pot, jug

χώρᾱ ᾱς ἡ locality; district, country, land

χωρέω come, go

χωρίον ου τό country, land, place

χῶρος ου ὁ district, place

Ψ

ψαύω + *gen* touch; affect

ψευδής ές lying, false

ψευδομαρτυρέω bear false witness

ψεύδω ψεύσω ἔψευσα ἐψεύσθην cheat, defraud; *mid* lie, cheat
ψηφίζομαι give one's vote with a pebble; vote for, resolve, decide
ψῑλοί ῶν οἱ light troops (such as archers and slingers, as opposed to
  hoplites)
ψῡχή ῆς ἡ spirit; life; soul, heart
ψῦχος ους τό cold

Ω

ὦ o!
ὧδε thus, so, in this manner
ὠθέω ὤσω ἔωσα ἐώσθην thrust, push; thrust back
ὤλεσα *aor from* ὄλλυμι
ὦμος ου ὁ shoulder
ὠμός ή όν raw; cruel, brutal, savage
ᾠόν ου τό egg
ὥρā ᾱς ἡ season; time of day; hour; moment; right time; beauty
ὡς as, just as (if); that; when, how
ὡς + *acc* to (*used of motion to a person*)
ὡσαύτως in the same manner
ὥστε with the result that, so that
ὠτός *gen of* οὖς
ὠφελέω help, aid, benefit; *pass* be helped, derive profit

About the Authors

JAMES MORWOOD was educated at Peterhouse, Cambridge. He later went on from the post of Head of Classics at Harrow School to take charge of the teaching of the Greek and Latin languages at Oxford University, where he is at present an Emeritus Fellow of Wadham College. He has authored and coauthored many books on classical languages and literature.

STEPHEN ANDERSON was educated at Trinity College, Dublin and St John's College, Cambridge. Since 1980 he has taught at Winchester College, where he was Head of Classics from 1984 to 2008 and is currently Senior Tutor. He is coauthor of a number of classical textbooks widely used in both schools and universities.